The Dynamics
of Folklore

The Dynamics of Folklore

Revised and Expanded Edition

Barre Toelken

Utah State University Press
Logan, Utah
1996

For
William A. "Bert" Wilson, friend and mentor,
whose mantle I inherited, along with
his chair, desk, office, archives,
house, chimney, bookcases, and job

Rolling Home

Utah State University Press
Logan, UT 84322-7800

Typography by WolfPack
    Cover Design by Michelle Sellers

Manufactured in the United States of America

10   9   8   7   6   5   4   3   2

Library of Congress Cataloging-in-Publication Data
Toelken, Barre.
    The dynamics of folklore/Barre Toelken.--Rev. and expanded ed.
        p.   cm.
    Includes bibliographical references and index.
    ISBN 0-87421-203-0
    1. Folklore—Methodology. 2. Folklore—United States. 3. United States—Social life and
customs. I. Title.
GR40.T63   1996
390'.01—dc20   95-50243
                                                                             CIP

Contents

Illustrations

Preface

UP TO THE 1970S, IT WAS COMMON FOR MOST FOLKLORISTS, AND MOST FOLK-lore textbooks, to pay more attention to the items of folklore than to the live processes by and through which folklore is produced. This led at least one folklorist to lament that folklore scholarship tended to "dehumanize" folklore. Briefly put, this book is an attempt to humanize folklore by urging an approach to folklore study that stresses "the folk" and the dynamics of their traditional expressions. In this approach, my thinking is very much indebted to the works of those who have focused on style, performance, context, event, and process, rather than on genre, structure, or text. However, the book does not attempt to do away with generic considerations. My hope is rather that it will constitute a theoretical complement to other works on folklore by provid-ing a balance, or, to use another figure, by suggesting other equally valid ave-nues by which the living performances of tradition may be perceived and studied.

No particular folklore school is espoused or represented here; indeed, the suggestions offered by this book should be palatable to a broad spectrum of the-oretical positions, for in it I try to provide a fair, eclectic combination of the main trends in folklore today, with the focus admittedly on the active, live aspects of folk and their lore.

Students complain, with justification, that literature is often killed in the classroom, that social sciences in the academic setting can cause us nearly to overlook people, that the music in a book of technical analysis is nowhere near as interesting as music falling on the ear from a live source. The same kinds of objections have been made to folklore classes and folklore texts: since it is possi-ble to separate the lore from the "folk" and spend endless hours dissecting and studying the resultant texts, it is indeed possible for folklorists to overlook, or to avoid intentionally, those very dynamic human elements that make the field an exciting one to begin with. But let us remember that the word "text" comes from Latin *textum*, "that which is woven," that is, a fabric, and thus it can stand as a ready metaphor for any human construction.

I hope this book can present some views of cultural "weaving" that have not been particularly characteristic of the academic approach. For one thing, where possible I have followed the lead of the tradition-bearers themselves, using their terms, topics, and perspectives. For another, I have not filtered out the so-called obscene elements that are so characteristic of folklore. In real life, and therefore in folklore, the ingenuous and friendly hospitality of Bess Hockema stands side by side with the brash machismo of "Jigger" Jones, the logger; and next to the shy, home-oriented customs of the Japanese American family there exists the open, exciting gaming and street jive of urban African American youths. Since folklore is not limited to rural environs, minority groups, and past times, I have looked as much as possible to all situations where we may see folklore in performance the way it is normally performed.

In so doing, I have stressed groups with whom I have had considerable acquaintance (loggers, Navajos, Westerners, Japanese Americans, farm families) so I could use anecdotal examples from my own experience to illustrate the main points of the book. For parallel ideas I have referred to the published work of others, but I have not pretended to scrape up extra fieldwork for this book just for rhetorical (or political) balance. For example, I have not done much work in folklore among Mexican Americans; they are certainly one of the most dynamic folk groups in the United States today, but for that very reason I have decided not to "throw them in" for mere color. Their traditions are too important for that. But I have tried to indicate works to which the reader can refer so as not to be limited by the peculiarity of my experiences.

A picture may not be worth a thousand words in folklore, for we always want multiple pictures of any folk performance or event. Nonetheless, an attempt is made in this book to present pictures of some of the dynamic processes that are discussed. The pictures concentrate chiefly on folklore actually being performed or on folk traditions being passed directly from one person to another. In addition, a few pictures are provided only so that items discussed in the various chapters may be scrutinized by the interested reader.

In the task of compiling this book and providing analytical remarks about its contents, I am primarily indebted to the people who so graciously allowed me to use their most cherished customs, beliefs, and performances. "Informants" are identified in the notes to each chapter, but I must give particular thanks to the Yellowman family and my other adopted relatives in southern Utah, the Damon and Howland families in Massachusetts, the Tabler family in Oregon, the Kubota family of Utah and California, and the Wasson-Hockema family in southwestern Oregon for allowing me to talk about them at such great length here.

All whose words are quoted have given their permission either directly to me or to other fieldworkers who recorded the materials. Some people did not want their names mentioned but nonetheless allowed their remarks to be quoted or paraphrased. No one has received payment for materials used here, but neither have the folk expressions become mine or the publisher's by virtue of appearing in this book. Even if it were not for copyright law (which protects the ownership of spoken texts), the various folk "performances" offered here, mere fossils on the printed page, remain among the cultural property and under the personal proprietorship of those who are still telling stories, singing songs, building barns, and playing the dozens in complete (and admirable) disregard for the fortunes of textbooks, the passions of students, and the aspirations of university professors. The appearance of their folklore in these pages does not interrupt the regular traditional process, nor does it diminish the cultural possessions of tradition-bearers. On the other hand, it would certainly impoverish the student of culture if these texts and expressions and events were not available. The flesh, blood, and bones of the live folklore discussed here belong to those who have been the tradition carriers; the commentaries are mine, guided and informed by their remarks.

For assistance in fieldwork details and analysis leading to some of the passages in this book, I am indebted to Ray Scofield, who helped with logger folklore and with the songs sung by Mrs. Clarice Judkins; to George Wasson for his intermediary role with the Wassons and Hockemas; to my wife, Miiko, and to Misa Joo, Seiko Kikuta, and Chiyoe Kubota for guidance in interpreting Japanese American cooking custom and symbolism; to Twilo Scofield for helping provide a full description of the Woddli-Tabler Thanksgiving dinner; to Edwin L. Coleman II, Beverly Robinson, and Patricia Turner for suggestions and interpretations on African American folklore; to Joseph Epes Brown for unfailing wisdom in regard to Native American culture, religion, and worldview; to William A. Wilson for insight into the proprieties of outsider interpretation of Mormon folklore, as well as valuable perspectives on the importance of folklore study generally.

Photographers other than myself are identified in the photo captions, but I must mention here my sincere thanks to the following people for allowing me to use their fine pictures. Suzi Jones let me pore over her extensive photo collection of Northwest traditions; the American Folklife Center generously supplied a number of photographs from the Center's collecting projects; William Tabler, formerly a logger and scaler near Sweet Home, Oregon, loaned me pictures he took of loggers in the woods during the 1940s; the Fife Folklore Archives section of Utah State University's Special Collections Division, under the direction of Barbara Walker, has an immense collection of color slides taken by folklorists Austin Fife, Alta Fife, and William A. Wilson, which were generously put at my disposal. Historical logging photos from glass plates taken in the early 1900s were supplied by the Special Collections Division of the University of Oregon Library.

Professors Louie Attebery of the College of Idaho, George Carey of the University of Massachusetts, Amherst, and Patrick Mullen of Ohio State University were my distant advisors during the writing of the first edition of this book. In addition to perspectives I have gained over the years by following the work of folklorists like Roger D. Abrahams, Richard Bauman, Dan Ben- Amos, Alan Dundes, Henry Glassie, Dell Hymes, Albert Lord, and John Miles Foley (i.e., those who have worked mainly on the performative aspects of folk expression), I have benefitted very much while working on this revision from advice and from ongoing discussions with my immediate colleagues at Utah State University—Steve Siporin, Barbara Walker, Randy Williams, Jay Anderson, Leonard Rosenband, and Clyde Milner II—as well as from more distant colleagues such as Neil V. Rosenberg, Patrick Mullen, Simon Bronner, Bengt af Klintberg, Michiko Iwasaka, David Buchan, Jack Santino, David Hufford, Jan H. Brunvand, Sandy Ives, Wolfgang Mieder, Lynwood Montell, Barbara Kirshenblatt-Gimblett, Barry Ancelet, Carol Edison, Meg Brady, Jim Griffith, Polly Stewart, Roger Welsch, Jo Radner, Bob McCarl, Chip Sullivan, Jerry Parsons, Joe Hickerson, Alan Jabbour, Knut Djupedal, and Ellen Stekert—a formidable array of folklorists, believe me. My continuing dialectic interaction with Elliott Oring has forced me to be more clear and logical in my formulations and my associations with German colleagues like Hermann Bausinger, Hannjost Lixfeld, and Rolf-Wilhelm Brednich have continually encouraged me to take a broader look at European perspectives in the study now referred to there as *Alltagsforschung* (research in the everyday) and *empirische Kulturwissenschaft* (empirical cultural science). The book has been deeply affected by their help and would not be in its current state without their generous advice. Of course I accept the responsibility for the way it now stands, but I cannot overstate the really considerable role these colleagues have played in shaping the final product and giving me reasons to believe it was worth doing.

Utah State University Press has been exceptionally fortunate in having John Alley as editor and Michael Spooner as director, considering the quality they have brought to the press's offerings generally and to the development of a folklore component in particular. When I was trying to decide where to publish this revision of *The Dynamics of Folklore*, it was their skills and commitment that convinced me that USU was the best place to do it. Working with these talented professionals has made it even more clear that I made the right choice.

Introduction

INTO FOLKLORISTICS WITH GUN AND CAMERA

ANYONE LOOKING INTO THE SUBJECT OF FOLKLORE FOR THE FIRST TIME WILL perhaps be surprised to discover that the scholarly discussion of the subject has been taking place for over two hundred years, mostly among people who have approached it from vantage points related to other interests and disciplines: language, religion, literature, anthropology, history, and even nostalgia and something close to ancestor worship. Indeed, the famous story of the blind men describing the elephant provides a valid analogy for the field of folklore: The historian may see in folklore the common person's version of a sequence of grand events already charted; the anthropologist sees the oral expression of social systems, cultural meaning, and sacred relationships; the literary scholar looks for genres of oral literature, the psychologist for universal imprints, the art historian for primitive art, the linguist for folk speech and worldview, and so on. The field of folklore as we know it today has been formed and defined by the very variety of its approaches, excited by the debate (and sometimes the rancor) brought about by inevitable clashes between opposed truths.

The earliest "schools" of folklore were mainly antiquarian; that is, they concerned themselves with the recording and study of customs, ideas, and expressions that were thought to be survivals of ancient cultural systems still existing vestigially in the modern world. Many early scholars were interested in primitive religions and the ancient myths that may have informed their development. Still others were interested in the roots of language and in the study of the relationships between languages in far-flung families. Still others, often country parsons, busied themselves in noting quaint rural observances that might have hearkened back to pre-Christian times. Among the many encouragements to the study of tradition, not the least was the appearance of Darwinian theories in the mid-1800s; if life could be said to have developed from simple to complex forms, then, many argued, culture itself might have evolved in the same way. Folk observances and fragments of early rituals were taken as simple elements from an earlier stratum of civilization, studied because they might reveal to us the building blocks of our own contemporary, complex society. The focus for these studies was primarily on lower classes, peasants, simple folk, "backward" cultures, and "primitives," for it was believed that these kinds of people had avoided or resisted longest the sophisticating influences of so-called advanced culture. Conversely, urban dwellers, immersed in literacy and sophistication, were thought to be immune to folklore or beyond its limitations. From their ranks came those who studied "the folk."

Under these circumstances, it is not surprising that the main arena for early folklore study was the rural environment. In fact, among the German folklorists, the term *Volkskunde* denoted the entire lifestyle of the rural people, and *das Volk*, "the folk," were conceived of as a homogeneous group. The assumption seems to have been that only away from the influence of technology and modern civilization—with their possibilities for education and mobility—could one find those antique remnants of tradition that might reveal to us the early stages of our cultural existence. This basic assumption for the normal habitat of folklore still exists today in many European and South American countries where folklore is understood to be, by definition, the traditions of rural people, who are ethnically and regionally homogeneous. In fact, up until very recently the rural scene has been the basis for most American folklore studies as well, for American culture itself has been defined—in its own terms—by a vanishing frontier, a disappearing pioneer tradition, a fading of the "good old days." Modern America has been thought by many to be totally lacking in folklore, almost in direct proportion to the time that separates Americans from their own rural frontier.

Since early American folklorists saw the rural atmosphere as one that might harbor fading remnants of folklore, they made their way to the Appalachians and other "remote" spots in search of the treasures of olden times. In tune with the feeling of the countryside in which the materials were sought, the accompanying descriptions were markedly bucolic: Folklorists spoke of *reaping* rich *harvests* of lore, *gleaning* last remnants of song, *plowing* narrow *fields* of folklore, tracking elusive genres in the *nooks* and *byways* of the *back country*; one heard about small *eddies* of ethnic groups, *song catching* in the mountains, and, inevitably, the nurturing of a *field* considered *ripe* for the *picking*.

Even though these words are still used, modern folklorists do not limit their attention to the rural, quaint, or "backward" elements of their culture. Rather, they will study and discuss any expressive phenomena—urban or rural—that seem to act like other previously recognized folk traditions. This has led to the development of a field of inquiry with few formal boundaries, one with lots of feel but little definition, one both engaging and frustrating.

The person who wishes to look into this expanding discipline will want to have more detailed guides and maps for the terrain. It will come as neither a surprise nor a satisfaction to find that more than one folklorist has defined the field as being made up of those things that folklorists care to talk about. One will need to know that this field has particular battlegrounds, heroes, and monuments. There was the Ballad War, in which a whole generation of scholars fought over the question of communal origins versus individual composition for the traditional ballad (modern scholars are inclined to view that battle as unfortunate and even needless, yet out of it came a mature field of ballad scholarship that one must master in order to proceed into fruitful areas of new folksong research and speculation). There was the Solar Mythology School of Max Müller and others, which related nearly all mythic phenomena to sun, moon, and stars (the Reverend R. F. Littledale, using Müller's own theories, subsequently proved that Müller himself was a sun god). There was the myth-ritual theory urged by Lord Raglan, among others, which insisted that the heroes of myth and folklore could only have derived from ritual characters and not from historical people. (This view had been under attack for years when Francis Lee Utley finally proved, using Raglan's list of attributes for the hero, that Abraham Lincoln got a perfect score and therefore was a ritual character who had never really lived.) And there have been skirmishes over the widespread view that folklore is simply (1) pagan *detritus,* stuff left over from previous, barbaric times, passed along by ignorant and illiterate peasants who didn't know any better, or (2) degenerated material from once courtly sources. J. G. Frazer felt that folk remnants could tell us what culture was like in earlier days, that the study of today's primitives could show us what we had been like at that stage of development. Others busied themselves to collect bits of folklore before it should degenerate altogether and cease to exist. These views obviously reflect the European-American premise of linear movement of time and history, and they represent thus a cultural attitude toward tradition rather than a critical observation of how tradition really operates.

Perhaps the most subtle battle in modern folklore is the constant attempt of scholars to reform the widespread journalistic use of the words *folklore* and *myth.* In the newspapers, and in the common understanding of many people, the terms have come to mean "misinformation" or "misconception" or "outmoded (and, by implication, naively accepted where believed) ideas." The misunderstanding and misapplication of these terms seem to stem from a modern continuation of that notion referred to previously, that only backward or illiterate people have folklore; where it exists among us, by implication, it represents backward or naive thinking. As subsequent chapters will show, this use of *folklore* to imply intellectual deficit is simply not borne out by the facts: something we call folklore is found in great plenty on all levels of society, and scholars are at some pains to account for its persistence and development.

These wars, the struggles over definition, and the dizzying variety of critical approaches may initially put off the person newly interested in folklore. They need not cause fear, however, if put in a proper perspective. The great wars are over, anyhow, largely because there is now a profession of folklorists who talk to each other (sharply, at times, to be sure) and share perspectives and approaches.

There are universities in which folklore is taught as an advanced undergraduate and graduate discipline, and many of America's leading folklorists are former classmates.

We have not become immune to the well-educated, well-intentioned myopia suffered by Müller and Raglan, however, so it is all to the good that each era of folklore study has continued to have its mavericks, young upstarts who do not accept present boundaries of the field. While one generation of established scholars studies texts and artifacts, a new group arises to call attention to the folk themselves; then others come forward to insist that a focus on context or communication or performance or structure would do better justice to the subject. The Young Turks of one era in turn become the middle-aged professors who teach folklore courses in the university, only to deal with the mavericks in their own classes.

Some leading folklorists have described the current state of the discipline in terms of schools, acknowledging that, in spite of widespread agreement about the field in general, there are distinct and well-structured methods of scrutinizing materials. The full account of these schools given by Richard Dorson in *Folklore and Folklife: An Introduction* is obligatory reading for anyone starting out in folklore. A characterization of these schools by their focus may help show their real differences in critical stance.

The most prominent single approach is that which asks us to look at the *artifacts* of folklore: "the text," the final product of the folk performance, whether it be made of words (a ballad, a tale, a proverb) or of physical materials (a quilt, a barn, a chimney) or of music (a fiddle tune) or of physical movements (a dance, a gesture) or of culture-based thought and behavior (popular belief, custom). As long as we note the broadened use of the term, we may call this the *text orientation* to folklore. Usually, texts are grouped into genres and scrutinized for their content, their structure, and their kinship with other texts. Comparative approaches such as the historical-geographical method (sometimes referred to as the Finnish School, it is as much a critical stance as a methodology) are based on the concept that a study of text or artifact variation can reveal the real contours and principal features of the folk item. The focus is thus on the folk expression as an object of interest, and the processes of its development are inferred from a study of the range of features changed or retained in those variant items considered to be versions of the same item. No doubt one reason for the strength and wide development of this view is that many early folklorists were trained in literature, where the text is usually central. But folklorists today use the word "text" broadly, in its etymological fullness: a woven object, hence a culturally "constructed" expression.

A different stance, one long familiar to anthropologists and now championed by many folklorists, may be called the *ethnological* orientation. Its main focus is the group of people that produces the lore and provides the live cultural matrix within which a text is articulated and understood. Here, the text or artifact is important, of course, but the principal features scrutinized by the scholar are the dynamics of the group: what it is, how it functions, how it perpetuates itself, what its coordinates for reality and logic are, what its systems (subgroups, clans, status levels, moieties, kinship patterns) may be, and how all these functional societal realities are expressed in vernacular formats. While the basic question for the textual approach might be, "What is the item like, and how does *it* function?" the main question for the ethnographic approach might be phrased, "How does a particular culture express itself and its shared values in shared traditional ways?"

Another more recent orientation seizes on *performance* as the primary grouping of phenomena to be studied. Here the individual performer or creator of traditional artifacts is viewed operating in and *for* an audience made up of the group of people whose tastes and responses condition—and occasion—the performance. The primary question here is, "Who is expressing what for whom—and when, how, and why?"

Still another scholarly preference is a leaning toward the explanation of how and why certain kinds of folklore continue to operate in any given instance. This orientation may be termed the *functional* approach. Why do certain elements of folklore come into being? Why do we continue to pass them on? Observing that traditions can hardly exist when they make no sense or fulfill no purpose at all, the functionalists seek to account for folklore's generation and survival by studying particular instances and applications of traditional expression and behavior.

Probably the most prominent approach to folklore in recent years has been *contextual,* addressing details of the immediate surroundings in which folklore takes place and out of which folklore may grow. One of the most basic areas of scrutiny here has been the psychological: the immediate personal, biological, and psychosocial drives and constraints felt by an individual as a tradition is practiced. Drawing especially upon the work of Freud and Jung, folklorists have sought to relate basic mental processes to the kinds of idea sets that foster traditional behavior and expression from culture to culture. Beyond the psychological bearings of the individual, many folklorists explore the immediate physical context in which an artifact or a folk expression is produced: the group of people who may be present, the weather, the occupational situation, or any other setting that may induce or modify traditional behaviors or performances. On still another level, contextualists are interested in geographical factors—how region may exert an influence on the maintenance or development of traditional expressions. Broader yet is the interest in historical context, the ways in which certain periods of humanity's experience may occasion the development or the dismemberment of folk tradition. (Historical and geographical concerns expressed as contextual interests should not be confused with the historical–geographical method mentioned in connection with the first area of focus, in which the artifact itself is the main subject.) Social, political, and economic contexts have become obligatory considerations in current work on the folklore of gender, ethnicity, and occupation, thus extending the reading range of modern folklorists.

Contextual perspectives are demanded of all folklorists today; most of the major practicing scholars can be found centering their interests on any one or several of the areas of focus previously mentioned, but they all take contextual evidence into consideration as a standard obligation. Perhaps it is this recognition of the unavoidable effects of context that sets modern folklore scholarship apart from that of the late 1800s and early 1900s. Certainly, the very best works of folklore criticism are combinations of all these interests; Alan Dundes's and Alessandro Falassi's *La Terra in Piazza* is a prime example of a multi-disciplinary approach to a particular folk tradition, the running of the Palio horserace in Siena, Italy. Joan N. Radner's *Feminist Messages: Coding in Women's Folk Culture* brings the specialties of several scholars together into a rich treatment of gendered meaning in context.

Of other possible areas of focus that have not become very well defined yet, one of the most important is folk *aesthetics,* a concern with the aesthetic ideas of folk performers and their communities. To what extent does the exercise of a culture-centered aesthetic (taste) play a role in the performance of any traditional song or story, the production of a folk play, the construction of a quilt or a barn? Scholars are likely to pay attention to the observable community standards for what a barn or a quilt should look like, but they have been relatively hesitant to take seriously the aesthetic reflections of the performers themselves, especially with regard to the way traditional artists may extend, challenge, or contradict the customary conventions. There are exciting exceptions to this, and they will be discussed further in Chapter 5. A tour de force treatment of folk aesthetic is Henry Glassie's *Turkish Traditional Art Today.*

It is common for newcomers to the subject of folklore to see these varying orientations as pedantic disputes among desperate sects of purists. Why make these distinctions? Do they really matter? Is this not merely academic posing? But in fact these are empty objections. In *any* field one needs to determine what one is studying, and to outline at least in general those approaches to the subject that have been considered fruitful by those who have spent a considerable amount of time trying to understand the materials. One does not study medieval literature without first determining whether the literature in question is in fact medieval; one does not try to discuss poetry without first determining that the items under consideration are poems; one does not presume to discuss classical music without first determining the composer and date; and one may as well not begin talking about folklore unless there is a willingness to help establish what the ingredients of the field are, what the processes seem to be, and what the nature of the discussion should be. It is not purism but utility that leads to the discussion of what folklore is and what the focal areas are through which it may be examined. Liking the subject is only a prelude to talking about it. The old "heart-throb" school of literary criticism is gone (forever, one hopes), and we may similarly wish that the essentially elitist heart-throb school of folklore is gone forever; one does not study folklore simply by adoring the proletariat, or by clutching a guitar and sighing, but by coming to grips with serious and complex matters related to everyday expression and cultural dynamics.

It should be apparent by now that folklore is not a static field of inquiry. Not only are its approaches and methods subject to change as we sharpen our perceptions (as is true in any active inquiry), but the very content of the subject expands as our study shows us new kinships and forms. Other areas, such as medieval literature, have continually developed new approaches, but the materials studied have remained pretty much the same over the years. In folklore, by contrast, where a hundred years ago we were studying mainly tales, songs, and beliefs, we now include barns, quilts, chain letters, proxemics, games, and many other genres. The multiplicity of traditional expressions and the diversity of critical approaches to them make for an extremely exciting field of study; they also inhibit the writing of books on folklore, for one expert's favorite line of reasoning may be of only minimal use in the classroom of another. Yet it does seem to me that all these approaches are, or could be, complementary and that no single one needs to be championed as the only way for which a textbook must provide exclusive maps and charts.

This book is founded on the simple assumption that there must be some element all folklore has in common (or else we could not lump it all together). No doubt an astute student could name several possible unifying characteristics, but I have chosen a particular one: all folklore participates in a distinctive, dynamic process. Constant change, variation within a tradition, whether intentional or inadvertent, is viewed here simply as a central fact of existence for folklore, and rather than presenting it in opposed terms of conscious artistic manipulation vs. forgetfulness, I accept it as a defining feature that grows out of context, performance, attitude, cultural tastes, and the like.

The various leading theories of folklore will be mentioned or implied in the discussion and will be noted in the bibliographical sections at the end of each chapter. The student should turn to these works for sound theoretical accounts of various particular problems in folklore; the present book, on the other hand, will provide examples of the dynamism in folklore, leaving readers free to follow particular theoretical interests on their own. To put it another way, the variety of folklore expressions and the interdisciplinary nature of the folklore field call for a book to discuss and illustrate folklore without defining it so narrowly as to inhibit particular theoretical interests or practical applications.

Accordingly, this book will be highly anecdotal and suggestive, for it aims to provide perspectives and to introduce the dynamics in a broad field. Examples come from my own fieldwork, from collections done by my students, from friends, from fellow folklorists. Some of my examples, such as the urban legend of the girl with a bouffant hairdo who is found to have a nest of black widow spiders in her coiffure, are as dated as the bouffant hairdo itself; others, like the "death car" for sale cheap in a local used car lot, may drift through our experience every couple of years. Both are examples of the continuing viability of folklore *and* its changeability. Readers will be able to augment my examples with their own repertoires of folklore. In any case, the book does not rest on antiquarian interests but on viability. If you haven't heard these urban legends, which ones *have* you heard?

I have wanted to avoid embarrassment for anyone whose folklore, originally delivered in its usual "home" context, is quoted here as vivid example. Some names are thus withheld or changed by request to ensure privacy and to avoid making individuals into objects of scrutiny; this is especially a concern with Native American materials, particularly in those tribes where an individual may be perfectly willing to give his or her own opinion but cannot speak for the entire tribe. In addition, many of our Native American friends have been shocked at the way in which we so glibly throw their names around in our classes: said a young Navajo woman at a recent meeting of scholars interested in working with American Indian narratives, "You people get *paid* to study us and to put our names in your books." Thus, while I have made certain that the materials from Native American backgrounds I have referred to here are acceptable for public scrutiny, I have not always named the specific source.

The reader hitherto unfamiliar with folklore must realize that many of the materials circulating in oral tradition among members of close groups might easily fall into the category of crude or obscene when they are quoted in print. Some scholars even estimate that some 80 percent of orally transmitted material would be thought crude by someone if it were encountered out of context. Because the central interest of folklorists today is to deal with folklore as it actually is, I have made no attempt to expurgate the texts referred to here; instead, I have omitted some materials rather than change their essential nature by "cleaning them up." This is not to champion "obscene" materials per se, but to point out that all folklore is phrased in terms appropriate to—and usually demanded by—the group in which it is performed. Often these particular manners of expression are registered as inappropriate when they are heard by outsiders, when they are presented out of their normal context, when their audience is expanded beyond the usual local group for which and in which the performance makes sense. For these reasons, the reader is urged to go beyond the antiseptic environment of the page, beyond the restrictions of local views on propriety, and take a close look at the real folklore of real people for what it truly is. I hope this book will provide some helpful considerations for that quest.

Before the quest can get under way, of course, we need to have some basic terminology for describing (and recognizing) the features of the folklore we seek to understand. The *genres* (that is, the forms and kinds) of folklore fall into a number of partially overlapping categories. For convenience, the American

Folklife Center in the Library of Congress uses the characterization which appeared in Public Law 94-201 (January 2, 1976) in Congress's own definition of folklore as expressive culture: ". . . a wide range of creative symbolic forms such as custom, belief, technical skill, language, literature, art, architecture, music, play, dance, drama, ritual, pageantry, handicraft." These kinds of expression are of course those which may be found on all levels of any culture; what makes them folklore is that they "are mainly learned orally, by imitation, or in performance, and are generally maintained without benefit of formal instruction or institutional direction." What are some of the particular "forms" under these rather broad headings? Most folklorists divide them up (again, for focus and convenience in discussion) into verbal folklore (that is, expressions people make with words, usually in oral interchange), material folklore (expressions which use physical materials for their media), and customary folklore (expressions which exist through people's actions).

Verbal folklore includes genres like epics, ballads, lyric songs (lullabies, love songs), myths (stories of sacred or universal import which people, cultures, religions, and nations believe in), legends (stories of local import which people believe actually happened but they learned about from someone else), memorates (culturally based first-person accounts and interpretations of striking incidents), folktales and jokes (fictional stories which embody cultural values), proverbs, riddles, rhymes, chants, charms, insults, retorts, taunts, teases, toasts, tongue twisters, greeting and leave-taking formulas, names and naming, autograph-book verses, limericks, and epitaphs, to name only a few of the most common.

Material folklore includes vernacular houses and barns (designed and made by those who use them rather than by trained architects), fence types, homemade tools, toys, tombstones, foods, costumes, stitchery, embroidery, tatting, braiding, whittling, woven items, quilts, decorations (Christmas trees, birthday party decor), and culturally based musical instruments and rhythm makers—insofar as they are learned by example within an ongoing tradition shared by people with something in common.

Customary folklore includes shared popular beliefs that are not transmitted by formal systems of science or religion ("superstitions"), vernacular medical practices, dances, instrumental music, gestures, pranks, games, traditional work "canons," celebrations (festivals, birthday/wedding/anniversary/funeral/holiday/religious observances not required by law or theology).

Obviously, the *custom* of celebrating a birthday usually involves the *material* expressions embodied in the cake, the presents, and the decorations, and the *verbal* singing of "Happy Birthday." Verbal expressions like proverbs and riddles often emerge at customary gatherings like weddings and funerals, where material items like certain foods and traditional clothing will also be part of the normal scene. Thus, while we may list these genres and categories separately (as we might also list parts of the human body separately in an anatomy class), we will normally expect to find all these forms actually functioning together interactively in customary frames of realization which involve many different kinds of expression at once, as we shall see more fully in the following chapter.

BIBLIOGRAPHICAL NOTES

The bibliographical supplements to the chapters in this book are meant to be selective, suggestive, and conversational, not exhaustive. The works cited are in many instances the sources or instigations for concepts advanced in the book; others are exemplary or typical of parallel or even contrasting ideas. Some will be repeated because of their application to different chapters. Most references to articles in periodicals are to work that has appeared since 1960, although there will be numerous exceptions to this rule where certain articles on particular subjects are too germane to omit.

I assume that the interested reader, and especially the student of folklore, will become acquainted with some of the standard works in the field, chief among them the following: Stith Thompson, ed., *Motif-Index of Folk Literature* (Bloomington: Indiana University Press, 1955-1958), for the basic compendium of recurrent units in orally transmitted folklore; Antti Aarne and Stith Thompson, eds., *The Types of the Folktale,* 2nd rev., *Folklore Fellows Communications,* no. 184 (1961), for the standard listing of recurrent narrative clusters in tale form; Maria Leach, ed., *Funk & Wagnalls Standard Dictionary of Folklore, Mythology, and Legend* (New York: Funk & Wagnalls, 1949), for a somewhat dated but encyclopedic view of folklore and its ingredients written by numerous folklorists of the day; Jan Harold Brunvand, *The Study of American Folklore: An Introduction,* 3rd rev. ed. (New York: Norton, 1986), for clear and brief delineations of the generic categories in folklore; Alan Dundes, ed., *The Study of Folklore* (Englewood Cliffs, N.J.: Prentice-Hall, 1965), for an anthology of important essays on folklore by a wide variety of scholars; and Richard M. Dorson, ed., *Folklore and Folklife: An Introduction* (Chicago: University of Chicago Press, 1972), for a modern invited symposium of professional folklorists on principal areas of interest to the serious student.

While this book will cite primarily the leading professional folklore journals, the reader, along with other serious folklorists, should make it a matter of obligation to follow up particular interests in other reputable anthropologically oriented publications as well as to check the smaller but important regional folklore journals and professional journals in geography, psychology, literature, linguistics, dialects, natural history, and history. Each of these latter fields, of course, has its own professional interests and demands, and it is well to remember that scholars in these areas do not always use the word (or the concept) *folklore* in the way professional folklorists might prefer. Thus, while the student should not hesitate to look into the recent journals and the contemporary standard texts of these fields for specific considerations on approach, theory, analytical models, and vocabulary, a good previous foundation in current folklore theory will be necessary to prevent disorientation and indigestion. Wherever possible, this book will call attention to some of the more helpful nonfolkloristic resources, and it will attempt to flag the topics on which specialists in the various fields may differ in their understanding (the concept of folk art, which will come up numerous times herein, is an example).

The term "folklore" was coined by a gentleman-antiquarian, William J. Thoms, one of the many well-read Victorian hobbyists interested in what were then called popular antiquities. Suggesting to readers of *The Anthenaeum* in 1846 that "a good Saxon compound, Folk-lore,—*the Lore of the People. . .*" would be a proper way of describing "the manners, customs, observances, superstitions, ballads, proverbs, etc., of olden time. . .," Thoms consciously created the umbrella term for a field of study which engaged some of the foremost writers and scholars of his day. Thoms's letter is reprinted in Alan Dundes, *The Study of Folklore* (Englewood Cliffs, N.J.: Prentice-Hall, 1965), 4–6.

Richard M. Dorson, in *The British Folklorists: A History* (Chicago: University of Chicago Press, 1968) and in *Peasant Customs and Savage Myths: Selections from the British Folklorists,* 2 vols. (Chicago: University of Chicago Press, 1968) provides the most complete, and certainly the most readable, account of the exciting developments among English scholars during the emergence of the field we now call folklore. Much of the theoretical orientation of modern British and American folklore scholarship has its origins in the arguments and discussions recorded in these books. For a comparison between the Anglo-American orientation in folklore and that found commonly in Latin America, see Américo Paredes, "Concepts about Folklore in Latin America and the United States," *Journal of the Folklore Institute* 6 (1969): 2–38; also, note that since its inception *JFI* (subsequently renamed *JFR—Journal of Folklore Research*) has provided a continuing account of folklore concepts and work in progress in a variety of countries.

Historical: Among Dorson's many works that deal with history and folklore, a good, brief sample would be "The Debate over the Trustworthiness of Oral Traditional History," in *Volksüberlieferung: Festschrift für Kurt Ranke zur Vollendung des 60. Lebensjahres,* ed. Fritz Harkort, Karel C. Peeters, and Robert Wildhaber (Göttingen: O. Schwartz, 1968), 19-35. A more recent book-length treatment of the intersection of history and folklore is Edward D. Ives, *George Magoon and the Down East Game War: History, Folklore, and the Law* (Urbana and Chicago: University of Illinois Press, 1988). Social historians routinely use folklore in their works; for a brilliant example, see Robert Darnton, *The Great Cat Massacre* (New York: Random House, 1984).

Anthropological: An organic view of all connotative literature as folklore is given in an anthropological frame by Munro S. Edmonson in *Lore: An Introduction to the Science of Folklore and Literature* (New York: Holt, Rinehart, and Winston, 1971); while very provocative, it pays little heed to the oral/nonoral distinction so basic to much of modern folklore theory. Three studies which approach folklore from an anthropological perspective are William R. Bascom, "Folklore and Anthropology," *Journal of American Folklore* 66 (1953): 283–90; William R. Bascom, "Four Functions of Folklore," *Journal of American Folklore* 67 (1954): 333–49; and Elliott Oring, "Three Functions of Folklore," *Journal of American Folklore* 89 (1976): 67–80. An incisive survey of developments in the field of folklore since 1972 (when Richard Bauman and others articulated a shift from textual interest to concerns for process and performance) is J. E. Limon and M. J. Young, "Frontiers, Settlements, and Development in Folklore Studies, 1972–1985," *Annual Review of Anthropology* 15 (1986): 437–60.

Literary: Probably the classic work is Stith Thompson, *The Folktale* (1946; reprint ed., Berkeley: University of California Press, 1977); in it, the tale is discussed as a distinct literary genre that has been shaped by the processes of traditional transmission. Many regions of the country are so well characterized by their folk literature that published collections are now included in literary studies. For an exceptionally well-conceived example, see Suzi Jones and Jarold Ramsey, eds., *The Stories We Tell: An Anthology of Oregon Folk Literature* (Corvallis: Oregon State University Press, 1994 [volume 5 of a six-volume series on Oregon literature]). For a discussion of how legends may be seen as folk literary dramatizations of cultural abstractions, see Michiko Iwasaka and Barre Toelken, *Ghosts and the Japanese: Cultural Experience in Japanese Death Legends* (Logan: Utah State University Press, 1995).

Psychological: Both Freud and Jung were extremely interested in folklore and mythology, although their theories have been beaten "to airy thinness" by their avid students. Freud believed that dreams are the less-developed materials of folklore, jokes, proverbs, and myths (see, among many others, Sigmund Freud, *The Interpretation of Dreams*, trans. A. M. O. Richards [New York: International Universities Press, 1958] and *Jokes and Their Relation to the Unconscious*, trans. James Strachey [London: Routledge and Paul, 1960]). Jung felt that the recurrent patternings in myth and folklore indicated an inherited fund of potential images shared by human beings generally, although he was more disposed than his disciples to the idea that local manifestations of these images might vary considerably. A helpful article is Carlos C. Drake, "Jungian Psychology and Its Uses in Folklore," *Journal of American* Folklore 82 (1969): 122-31. Joseph Campbell, once almost exclusively a Jungian, eventually combined Jung's theories with the resources of anthropology, archaeology, history, botany, and literature in his impressive four-volume work *The Masks of God: Primitive Mythology, Oriental Mythology, Occidental Mythology, and Creative Mythology* (New York: Viking Press, 1959-1968); although the examples he cites are partial to his particular viewpoint, the work, especially volume 1, is interesting reading. Among present-day folklorists, probably Alan Dundes and Elliott Oring are the most consistent in their employment of psychological perspectives (mainly Freudian). Several of Dundes's most influential essays are republished in his *Interpreting Folklore* (Bloomington: Indiana University Press, 1980); some of Oring's work is brought together in *Jokes and Their Relations* (Lexington: University Press of Kentucky, 1992). An overview of the relationships between psychology and folklore as propounded by an early disciple of Freud can be found in Ernest Jones, "Psychoanalysis and Folklore," *Jubilee Congress of the Folklore Society: Papers and Transactions* (London: Folklore Society, 1930): 220–37, reprinted in Dundes's *The Study of Folklore*, 88–102.

Artistic and Art-Historical: This is one of the unfortunate areas wherein trained experts in art and museology differ markedly from experts in folklore on the subject of folk art. For the former, folk art is usually seen as naive or untrained art, or as whatever is left over after one has exhausted the fine arts. Primitive art—that is, art produced by nontechnological peoples—is often given serious notice, as in Paul S. Wingert, *Primitive Art, Its Traditions and Styles* (New York: Oxford University Press, 1962) and in Ralph Linton, "Primitive Art," *Kenyon Review* 3 (1941): 34-51, reprinted in *Every Man His Way: Readings in Cultural Anthropology,* ed. Alan Dundes (Englewood Cliffs, N.J.: Prentice-Hall, 1968): 352-64. But folk art that lies outside the primitive category, while taken seriously by folklorists, is often stereotyped as "quaint and folksy" by art historians. Munro Thomas, in *Evolution in the Arts* (Cleveland: Cleveland Museum of Art, 1932): 361-462, gives it fair but minuscule mention, while one of the standard art history textbooks, H. W. Janson's *History of Art: A Survey of Major Visual Arts from the Dawn of History to the Present Day* (Englewood Cliffs, N.J.: Prentice-Hall, 1962)—in spite of its omniscient-sounding title—overlooks folk arts altogether. One of the most informative pieces on folk art is the chapter so titled by Henry Glassie in Dorson, *Folklore and Folklife*, 253-80. Subsequently, Glassie produced what must be the fullest study of a single nation's folk art, *Turkish Traditional Art Today* (Bloomington: Indiana University Press, 1993); it is a model of definition, sensitive description, and cultural understanding. Steve Siporin's *American Folk Masters: The National Heritage Fellows* (New York: Harry N. Abrams, 1992) celebrates the wide variety of folk artists recognized by the National Endowment of the Arts as the United States' equivalents to Japan's Living National Treasures during the first ten years of the National Heritage Fellowship Awards program. In *Exploring Folk Art: Twenty Years of Thought on Craft, Work, and Aesthetics* (Ann Arbor: UMI Research Press, 1987), Michael Owen Jones brings together his wide-ranging and provocative insights on a subject which has been his lifelong specialty.

Language and Linguistics: Of those whose work has aligned language study with the processes of tradition, the most prominent have been anthropologists seeking to understand better the relationship between culture and meaning. Dell H. Hymes, "The Contribution of Folklore to Sociolinguistic Research," *Journal of American Folklore* 84 (1971): 42-50, as well as Dell H. Hymes, ed., *Language in Culture and Society: A Reader in Linguistics and Anthropology* (New York: Harper & Row, 1964) are samples of work by a dedicated and continually developing scholar in the field. One should review, as well, the work of Benjamin Lee Whorf, for example, his *Language, Thought, and Reality* (Cambridge, Mass.: MIT Press, 1956); Harry Hoijer, ed., *Language in Culture* (Chicago: University of Chicago Press, 1954); John J. Gumperz and Dell H. Hymes, eds., *The Ethnography of Communication*, American Anthropological Association Special Publications, vol. 66 (Menasha, Wis.: American Anthropological Association, 1964); and, for a broader modern look at the whole live process of language, Peter Farb, *Word Play: What Happens When People Talk* (1974; reprint ed., New York: Bantam, 1975). One of the most exciting developments in recent folklore-and-language studies has involved a re-examination of women's language in its vernacular contexts. Among the most interesting are Deborah Cameron, *Feminism and Linguistic Theory* (London: Macmillan, 1985); Jennifer Coates and Deborah Cameron, eds., *Women in Their Speech Communities: New Perspectives on Language and Sex* (London: Longman, 1988); Joan Newlon Radner, ed., *Feminist Messages: Coding in Women's Folk Culture* (Urbana: University of Illinois Press, 1993).

The antiquarians are often glibly dismissed for not knowing as much as we do today (may the charity of later generations be more generous when it comes to the scrutiny of present-day truths), but they and their works make some of the most fascinating reading in all folklore. The newcomer to folklore must be warned that an entry into John Brand's *Observations on Popular Antiquities: Chiefly Illustrating the Origin of Our Vulgar Customs, Ceremonies, and Superstitions*, 2 vols., arr. and rev. Henry Ellis (London: R. C. and J. Rivington, 1813) is an overwhelming and fascinating detour from which readers seldom recover. Brand and other students of antique times were erudite and serious scholars, mostly, and were often the masters of several languages. They were among the central thinkers of their day, and they overlooked little in their searches through notebooks, country customs, and church and town records to find elements of thought and action that had flourished before the coming of Christianity. Brand lamented the way in which the Puritans and their successors had tried to obliterate the older customs (obviously his use of *vulgar* means "of the common people" and does not include the modern inference that *common* means "lowly"). Other representative antiquarians, often identifiable by the titles of their works, were Sabine Baring-Gould, *Curious Myths of the Middle Ages* (London: Rivingtons, 1866), among numerous works on songs and fairy tales; Henry Bourne, *Antiquitates Vulgares* (Newcastle: J. White, 1725); Allen Cunningham, *Songs: Chiefly in the Rural Language of Scotland* (London: Smith and Davy, 1813) and *Traditional Tales of the English and Scottish Peasantry* (London: Taylor and Hessey, 1822); Francis Grose, *The Antiquities of England and Wales*, 6 vols. (London: S. Hooper, 1773-1787); Alfred Nutt, *Celtic and Mediaeval Romance* (London: D. Nutt, 1899); Thomas Percy, *Reliques of Ancient English Poetry*, 3 vols. (London: J. Dodsley, 1765); Walter Scott, *The Border Antiquities of England and Scotland*, 2 vols. (London: Longman, Hurst, Rees, Orme, and Browne, 1814-1817); Thomas F. Thiselton-Dyer, *British Popular Customs* (London: G. Bells and Sons, 1871); William J. Thoms, *Anecdotes and Traditions* (London: Printed for the Camden Society by J. B. Nichols and Son, 1839); Edward B. Tylor, *Primitive Culture*, 2 vols. (London: J. Murray, 1871). Dorson gives a very full and fair account of them in *The British Folklorists*, mentioned earlier; more recently, Francis A. De Caro has related the antiquaries to our whole conception of how the field of folkloristics has developed in "Concepts of the Past in Folkloristics," *Western Folklore* 35 (1976): 3-22.

No doubt the best-known German scholars of the early period were Wilhelm Mannhardt, whose *Germanische Mythen* (Berlin: F. Schneider, 1858) became the resource for many subsequent conjectural studies on the origins of medieval European symbols, and Jakob and Wilhelm Grimm, whose collection of *Kinder-und Hausmärchen*, 2 vols. (Berlin: Realschulbuchhandlung, 1812-1815), undertaken in part due to their interest in the processes of language features, has been basic to all subsequent studies of European tales (and has made the name Grimm a household word throughout much of the world). Subsequently Johannes Bolte and George Polivka, in their monumental *Anmerkungen zu den Kinder-und Hausmärchen der Brüder Grimm*, 5 vols. (Leipzig: Dieterich'sche Verlagsbuchhandlung, 1913-1932), provided linguistic and cultural notes and explanations for the Grimms' collection, which made the materials even richer and more useful for folkloristic examination.

Alexander Haggerty Krappe, *The Science of Folklore* (1930; reprint ed., New York: Norton, 1964) shows the influence of the European scholarly-antiquarian stance at the turn of the century. Krappe, an American, was sure that folklore was essentially rural and antique, and it followed that progressive America would not provide much for the scholar. Statements such as, "In every modern country the rural populations are still addicted to beliefs and practices long since given up by the bulk of the city people" (p. xvii) and "In the city proper, as is well known, the typical proletarian is the most traditionless creature imaginable" (p. xviii) give a typical picture of the state of mind of the well-educated scholar interested in folklore before the professional folklore explosion of the 1950s and 1960s. Even lately, some folklorists have felt the need to explain the importance of folklore in terms of what it could teach us about "high culture;" see, for example, Francis Lee Utley, "Oral Genres as Bridge to Written Literature," in *Genre* 2 (1969): 91-103, reprinted in *Folklore Genres*, ed. Dan Ben-Amos (Austin: University of Texas Press, 1976); the paper is of solid pedagogical value, for often students can see their own relationships to literature through comparison with traditions they already take part in. On the other hand, most folklorists today feel that folklore need not be rationalized as a field whose primary function is to acquaint us more fully with elite culture.

The ballad wars cannot be quickly summed up, for they range from petty differences to substantial and creative scholarly arguments. The best single account is still D. K. Wilgus, *Anglo-American Folksong Scholarship since 1898* (New Brunswick, N.J.: Rutgers University Press, 1959), esp. chs. 1, 2. One should also consult Sigurd Bernhard Hustvedt, *Ballad Books and Ballad Men* (Cambridge, Mass.: Harvard University Press, 1930)—an unfortunate title, since one of the principal belligerents of the fray was Louise Pound, with her *Poetic Origins and the Ballad* (New York: Macmillan, 1921); Francis B. Gummere, another combatant, wrote *The Beginnings of Poetry* (New York: Macmillan, 1901), *The Popular Ballad* (Boston: Houghton Mifflin, 1907), and *Democracy and Poetry* (Boston: Houghton Mifflin, 1911); George Lyman Kittredge, a student of Francis James Child (the first principal American ballad anthologist and scholar) wrote an essay, "The Popular Ballad," in *Atlantic Monthly* 101 (1908): 276 ff., and collaborated with Helen Child Sargent in the introduction to a one-volume abridgment of Child's great work, *The English and Scottish Popular Ballads* (Boston: Houghton Mifflin, 1882-1898). Although the flaming commitment to ballad studies characteristic of the old war seems to have waned, there are continuing attempts to assess and study this particular form of folk expression. Of several obligatory works, students should certainly consult Tristram P. Coffin, *The British Traditional Ballad in North America*, rev. ed. Roger deV. Renwick (Austin: University of Texas Press, 1977); David Buchan, *The Ballad and the Folk* (London: Routledge & Kegan Paul, 1972); Albert Friedman, *The Viking Book of Folk Ballads of the English Speaking World* (New York: Viking, 1956); Patricia Conroy, ed., *Ballads and Ballad Research* (Seattle: University of Washington Press, 1978); Joseph Harris, ed., *The Ballad and Oral Literature* (Cambridge: Harvard University Press, 1991); M. J. C. Hodgart, *The Ballads* (New York: Hutchinson's University Library, 1950); D. K. Wilgus and Barre Toelken, *The Ballad and the Scholars: Approaches to Ballad Study* (Los Angeles: William Andrews Clark Memorial Library, 1986).

Some of Max Müller's theories are put forward in *Chips from a German Workshop*, 4 vols. (London: Longmans, Green, 1867-1875); *Natural Religion: The Gifford Lectures Delivered before the University of Glasgow in 1888* (London: Longmans, Green, 1889); *Anthropological Religion* (London: Longmans, Green, 1892); and *Contributions to the Science of Mythology*, 2 vols. (London: Longmans, Green, 1887)—among many others. Reverend Littledale's refutation appeared in "The Oxford Solar Myth: A Contribution to Comparative Mythology," in *Echoes from Kottabos*, ed. R. Y. Tyrell and Sir Edward Sullivan (London: E. Grant Richards, 1906), 279-90. Richard Dorson gives a full account of the controversy in "The Eclipse of Solar Mythology," *Journal of American Folklore* 68 (1955): 393-416, reprinted in Dundes, *The Study of Folklore*, 57-83.

Raglan's statement on the hero is found in its fullest form in *The Hero: A Study in Tradition, Myth, and Drama* (London: Methuen, 1936). Utley's witty and embarrassingly thorough rejoinder is *Lincoln Wasn't There, or, Lord Raglan's Hero*, College English Association Chapbook (Washington, D.C.: College English Association, 1965). James G. Frazer, *The Golden Bough*, 3rd ed., 12 vols. (London: Macmillan, 1907-1915) is both a delight and a frustration; while the examples in it and the theories suggested are illuminating and thought-provoking, the instances of folk custom outside Europe are often derived from the accounts of missionaries and other well-meaning but myopic tourists who had no professional training in how to observe people of other cultures with impartiality or clarity of vision. See Theodor H. Gaster's enviable abridgment of the work that gives modern evaluations of Frazer's theory and method: *The New Golden Bough* (New York: Criterion Books, 1959). George Laurence Gomme, in *Ethnology in Folklore* (London: K. Paul, Trench, Trubner, 1892), argued against the simple notion that folklore was made up of survivals from particular levels of human existence that could tell us, like tree rings do today, what things were like when our culture was at a particular stage. Gomme argued that much folklore in England was pre-Aryan and had been retained and maintained precisely because of the pressure from newly arrived, intrusive, but stable "higher" civilizations. In this, he anticipated the modern notion that folklore is partly a function of internal group dynamics, of "esoteric" response, not to be easily explained only as leftovers from the past. The idea that folklore is always breaking down is discussed by Alan Dundes in "The Devolutionary Premise in Folklore Theory," *Journal of the Folklore Institute* 6 (1969): 5-19; that it has had such a central role in folkloristics is challenged by Elliott Oring in "The Devolutionary Premise: A Definitional Delusion?" *Western Folklore* 34 (1975): 36-44, and by William A. Wilson in "The Evolutionary Premise in Folklore and the 'Finnish Method,'" *Western Folklore* 35 (1976): 241-49.

The standard single work on the "Finnish Method" is Kaarle Krohn, *Die folkloristische Arbeitsmethode* (Cambridge, Mass.: Harvard University Press, 1926), trans. Roger Welsch as *Folklore Methodology* (Austin: University of Texas Press, 1971). Typical examples of full attempts to study the variations in a particular folklore item are Paul G. Brewster, "Some Notes on the Guessing Game, How Many Horns Has the Buck?" *Bealoideas: Journal of the Folklore of Ireland Society* 12 (1942): 40-78, reprinted in Dundes, *The Study of Folklore*, 338-68; Bertrand H. Bronson, *The Traditional Tunes of the Child Ballads*, 4 vols. (Princeton, N.J.: Princeton University Press, 1959-1972); Henry Glassie, "The Types of the Southern Mountain Cabin," in Brunvand, *The Study of American Folklore*, 529–62; Holger 0. Nygard, *The Ballad of "Heer Halewijn," Its Forms and Variations in Western Europe: A Study of the History and Nature of a Ballad Tradition*, Folklore Fellows Communications, no. 169 (Helsinki, 1958); Stith Thompson, "The Star Husband Tale," *Studia Septentrionalia* 4 (1953): 93-163, reprinted in Dundes, *The Study of Folklore*, 414-74. In his presidential address to the American Folklore Society, D. K. Wilgus made a special plea for the centrality of textual concern; see "'The Text Is the Thing,'" *Journal of American Folklore* 86 (1973): 241-52.

The ethnological approach is used by far too many scholars to allow for a fair representation here. The following put forth the premise that traditional items in a culture cannot be studied except with direct reference to the cultural context from which they spring: Ruth Benedict, *Patterns of Culture* (Boston: Houghton Mifflin, 1934) and Bronislaw Malinowski, *Argonauts of the Western Pacific* (New York: E. P. Dutton, 1922) are classic. More recent studies by Clifford Geertz, such as "Ethos, World View and the Analysis of Sacred Symbols," *The Antioch Review* 17 (1957): 421-37, his *The Religion of Java* (Glencoe, Ill.: Free Press, 1960) and *The Interpretation of Cultures* (New York: Basic Books, 1973) show the continuing application of this culturally holistic approach. For a collection of essays by various specialists of this orientation, see Alan Dundes, ed., *Every Man His Way: Readings in Cultural Anthropology* (Englewood Cliffs, N.J.: Prentice-Hall, 1968).

Many folklorists focus on performance and performance styles. For some solid perspectives see Roger D. Abrahams, *Deep Down in the Jungle: Negro Narrative Folklore from the Streets of Philadelphia*, rev. ed. (Chicago: Aldine, 1970), and its companion,

Positively Black (Englewood Cliffs, N.J.: Prentice-Hall, 1970), in which African American toasts and dozens are discussed as performances (rather than as "texts") and in which the whole dynamic of urban Black life, including economics and politics, is seen in terms of performance modes. For a more general theory on the subject, consult Richard Bauman, *Verbal Art As Performance* (Prospect Heights, Ill.: Waveland Press, 1984), which contains not only Bauman's earlier essay from the *Journal of American Folklore*, but several supplementary pieces by other specialists in the study of performance. The relationships between live performance and eventual appearance of a "text" in printed form are discussed by Elizabeth C. Fine in *The Folklore Text: From Performance to Print* (Bloomington: Indiana University Press, 1984). Critical issues in the discussion of performance meanings are taken up by Dennis Tedlock in *The Spoken Word and the Work of Interpretation* (Philadelphia: University of Pennsylvania Press, 1983); Tedlock illustrates many of these issues in his presentation of Native American narrative performances in *Finding the Center: Narrative Poetry of the Zuni Indians* (New York: Dial Press, 1972; repr. University of Nebraska Press, 1978). The interactive, reflexive dynamics of verbal performance are brilliantly discussed by John Miles Foley in *Immanent Art: From Structure to Meaning in Traditional Oral Epic* (Bloomington: Indiana University Press, 1991). Michael Owen Jones makes it clear in *The Hand Made Object and Its Maker* (Berkeley: University of California Press, 1975) that the idea of performance is not to be limited to songs and stories, but must be extended to cover all kinds of expressive activities—including the production of material items—performed for others.

As it will become clear from the rest of this book, context is one of the most important single considerations in folklore study today. Two clear statements on this are obligatory reading: Alan Dundes, "Texture, Text, and Context," *Southern Folklore Quarterly* 28 (1964): 251-65 and Dan Ben-Amos, "Toward a Definition of Folklore in Context," *Journal of American Folklore* 84 (1971): 5-15, reprinted in *Toward New Perspectives in Folklore*, ed. Américo Paredes and Richard Bauman (Austin: University of Texas Press, 1972), 3-15. Kay Cothran discusses the effect of immediate personal context (male narrator, female interviewer, wife of narrator sitting nearby) on anecdotal performance in "Talking Trash in the Okefenokee Swamp Rim, Georgia," *Journal of American Folklore* 87 (1974): 340-56. For an excellent discussion of the effects of region on people and their folklore, see Suzi Jones, "Regionalization: A Rhetorical Strategy," *Journal of the Folklore Institute* 13 (1976): 105-20. The dynamic relations among nature, geography, setting, and culture are brilliantly discussed by Yi Fu Tuan in *Topophilia* (Englewood Cliffs, N.J.: Prentice-Hall, 1974; repr. with new preface, New York: Columbia University Press, 1990). The historical context of folklore is of course the foundation of Richard Dorson's standard, *American Folklore* (Chicago: University of Chicago Press, 1959). The early chapters of Lewis Mumford, *The City in History: Its Origins, Its Transformations, and Its Prospects* (New York: Harcourt, Brace, and World, 1961) delineate a combination of geographical, historical, mythic, and folkloric forces that interplayed as a context for the earliest villages and towns; see esp. pp. 5-35.

Aesthetics in folklore will be taken up more fully in Chapter 5. For a central statement on the subject, see Michael Owen Jones, "The Concept of 'Aesthetic' in the Traditional Arts," *Western Folklore* 30 (1971): 77-104.

Although "obscenity" is only one aspect of response to folklore out of its usual habitat, it is a matter the student should try to settle accounts with early. The *Journal of*

American Folklore dedicated an entire issue to the subject (vol. 75, no. 297 [July-September 1962]). One might also consult G. Legman, *No Laughing Matter: Rationale of the Dirty Joke,* 2nd series (New York: Breaking Point, 1975); and Vance Randolph, *Pissing in the Snow and Other Ozark Folktales,* ed. Rayna Green and Frank Hoffman (Urbana, Ill.: University of Illinois Press, 1976).

The basic standards for contemporary folklore research and study are set forth in the following works (books especially focused on fieldwork will be cited later): Jan H. Brunvand, *The Study of American Folklore: An Introduction,* 3rd ed. (New York: W. W. Norton, 1986); Richard M. Dorson, ed., *Handbook of American Folklore* (Bloomington: Indiana University Press, 1983); Robert A. Georges and Michael Owen Jones, *Folkloristics: An Introduction* (Bloomington: Indiana University Press, 1995); Elliott Oring, ed., *Folk Groups and Folklore Genres* (Logan: Utah State University Press, 1986). An excellent overview of the folklore field in America is provided by Simon J. Bronner, *American Folklore Studies: An Intellectual History* (Lawrence: University Press of Kansas, 1986). German folklorists since World War II have developed an equally exciting field, often using the term *empirische Kulturwissenschaft,* "empirical cultural science," as a gloss for folklore study. See Hermann Bausinger, *Volkskunde von der Altertumsforschung zur Kulturanalyse* (Tübingen: Tübinger Vereinigung für Volkskunde, 1979) and his *Formen der "Volkspoesie"* (Berlin: Erich Schmidt Verlag, 1968); Günter Wiegelmann, Matthias Zender, and Gerhard Heilfurth, *Volkskunde: Eine Einführung* (Berlin: Erich Schmidt Verlag, 1977); H. Bausinger, U. Jeggle, G. Korff, and M. Scharfe, *Grundzüge der Volkskunde* (Darmstadt: Wissenschaftliche Buchgesellschaft, 1978); Rolf W. Brednich, *Grundriss der Volkskunde* (Berlin: Dietrich Reimer Verlag, 1988; rev. ed. 1994).

For an ongoing measure of "what's going on" in folklore, the student should be especially attentive to special publications which usually bring together, by invitation, the most active and best known scholars in the field and in related areas of interest. Special topical issues of the *Journal of American Folklore, Western Folklore,* and *Journal of Folklore Research* have addressed gender, personal narrative, new directions in folklore, generic definitions, and single genres (like the ballad). Another source of insight into the current directions of the field will always be the "Festschrift," the celebratory book of collected essays written by colleagues in honor of a senior scholar who has had a profound impact on others in the profession. Three excellent examples are Linda Dégh, Henry Glassie, and Felix J. Oinas, eds., *Folklore Today: A Festschrift for Richard M. Dorson* (Bloomington: Indiana University, 1976), which contains key essays by forty-four of the best-known international folklore scholars; Simon J. Bronner, ed., *Creativity and Tradition in Folklore: New Directions* (Logan: Utah State University Press, 1992), published in honor of W. F. H. Nicolaisen by inviting scholars from the fields in which Nicolaisen himself worked to offer their current thinking; and Roger D. Abrahams, ed., *Fields of Folklore: Essays in Honor of Kenneth S. Goldstein* (Bloomington, Ind.: Trickster Press, 1995), which includes nineteen essays by Goldstein's colleagues and former students. Virtually every year a new folklore festschrift appears; they are all worth special attention.

Folklore is not a single topic or a single discipline; rather, its essence lies in a strong valuation of vernacular expressions of all sorts, an interdisciplinary strategy for studying them, and a humanistic respect for the people who perform them.

Chapter 1

THE FOLKLORE PROCESS

FOLKLORE COMES EARLY AND STAYS LATE IN THE LIVES OF ALL OF US. IN SPITE OF the combined forces of technology, science, television, religion, urbanization, and creeping literacy, we prefer our closest cultural associations as the basis for learning about life's normalities and transmitting important observations and expressions. From the childhood rhythms of "Patty Cake" to the joy of humorous graces ("Good bread, good meat, good God, let's eat") to the imagined sophistication of drinking games ("Cardinal Puff," "Fuzz-Buzz"); from courtship protocol to showers to wedding customs (like wearing a wedding ring) to birth cigars; from birthday spanks and presents to tree house clubs to stag and hen parties; from the Tooth Fairy to the Birthday Girl to Santa Claus; from African American dozens to Native American "forty-nine" songs to *curanderismo;* from Valentine's candy to Easter eggs to firecrackers to pumpkins to turkey to fruitcake to Tom-and-Jerries; from riddles to barroom jokes to epitaphs, funeral customs, and placing flowers on a grave; from wart cures to waiting twenty minutes for a full professor; from vanishing hitchhikers, exploding poodles and overcooked clients in tanning salons to miraculous carburetors (kept off the market by the auto industry) and death cars for sale (cheap); from the pink and blue of the nursery through the white of the wedding to the black of the funeral, we continue to wend our traditional way through life. To the surprise of those who thought (and perhaps hoped) that folklore was a part of the disappearing rural scene, city children turn out to have more children's folklore than rural children do. The offspring of educated parents often are found to be more avid carriers of popular belief ("superstition") than others. Folklore is not dying out, nor is it to be found only in the backwoods or among illiterates. One ballad may go out of oral existence over here, but a hundred ethnic jokes spring up over there.

THE EDUCATIVE MATRIX

Clearly, folklore is alive and well. It constitutes a basic and important educative and expressive setting in which individuals learn how to see, act, respond, and

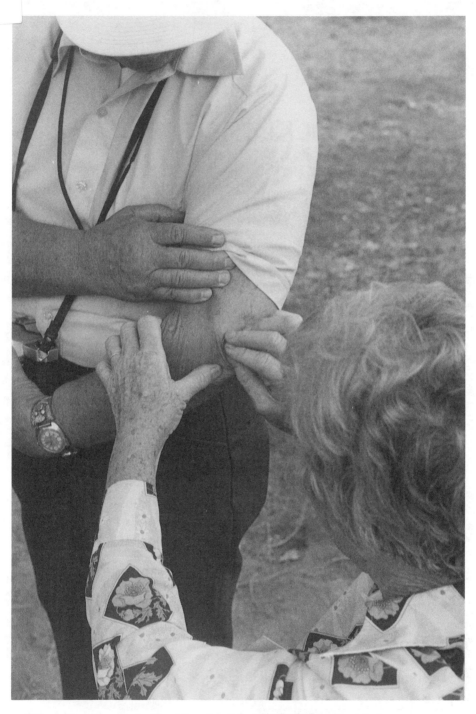

Wart charmer Onie Ruesch of southern Utah rubs a nickel on a wart, then gives the coin to the patient, thus "buying the wart." The patient keeps the nickel in his pocket until the wart is gone.

Paulmina Nick New, member of an Italian community in the mining town of Price, Utah, provides Italian customary foods (here garlic bread) to family and visitors. Photo by Steve Siporin.

Hunting for Easter eggs is not required by religion or state ordinance but is enjoyed by many families as a springtime custom for children. Here, four-year-old Mallory Gibson of Tooele, Utah, happily signals a find. Photo by Randy Williams.

express themselves by the empirical observation of close human interactions and expressions in their immediate society (that is, the family, occupational or religious group, ethnic or regional community). Folklore structures the world-view through which a person is educated into the language and logic systems of these close societies. It provides ready formulas for the expression of cultural norms in ways useful and pleasurable to us and to any group with which we share close and informal expressive interactions.

Folk Language

Very early in life, long before we have come under the well-intentioned influence of professional teachers, we have learned the basic structure and meaning of an entire language. Past this point we refine it and add to its vocabulary. Before we are four years old, using rules we know mostly by inference, we create new sentences we have never before heard, continually guided by the recognition and responses of those around us whose very speech we have used as the pattern for our own learning. If we say something they do not understand, we try again or in another way. If we say something they like very much we are likely to keep it "on file" for further pleasurable use (we sometimes retain baby talk when encouraged by the laughter of our doting parents). We do not need language instruction, and except in those settings where the passing of grammar quizzes has become an important activity, we do not require any further training in the grammar we already know how to use. Language is a traditional frame for learning, a basis for human interaction, a form of practical or pleasurable expression, and a way of structuring and placing meaning on the myriad experiences coming at us from our world. Yet languages are not all alike: Japanese, Navajo, and English differ not only in grammar and vocabulary, but in the ways they envision—and thus describe—the world. A language not only communicates; it articulates a worldview.

In addition to spoken language, we use gesture, facial expression, body position, tone of voice, proximity to others, and a large and complex vocabulary of options that tell us not only what to say on certain occasions but when not to say anything, or when it is necessary to change the "dialect" to something more appropriate (such as when Great Aunt Martha enters the room while we are telling a travelling salesman joke). As we mature, we are taught several more formal or technical languages as the need arises. In addition to the gestures we have picked up by observation (for example, shrugging the shoulders in some cultures means "I don't know"), we also must learn a number of arbitrary and formal gestures (such as those we must know if we are to become ballet dancers, baseball umpires, opera singers, traffic police officers, basketball referees, or teachers of sign language to the deaf). The informal gestures learned from those close around us are always open to continual modification according to their use and context at a particular moment, but the more formal gestures are less open to change, for they are parts of a language "dialect" used in dealing with outsiders. We use different words and gestures in a joke than in a graduation speech; we speak to friends in slang, but write for strangers in standard English. Deaf people who communicate by signing also have a vivid vocabulary of gestural slang learned from each other, not from instruction books.

Folk Learning and Logic

In Western cultures children usually learn music harmony the same way they learn their early language: they pick it up. They come to know how to harmonize even though they cannot articulate the technical rules in musicians' terms. Some never learn and are encouraged to keep quiet. But how does someone learn to harmonize? And why do we learn? And why is it pleasant for us to harmonize with others when they are singing? After all, many cultures do not use harmony at all. These questions cause us to become conscious of what people learn in a close society, how they come to learn it, why, and from whom. The study of folklore leads us to recognize that there may be an assumption about one kind of harmony in one culture, another kind in another culture, and none at all in still another. In fact, all forms of culture-based expression are likely to vary from one human communicative network to another, yet within each system there is an internal consistency, a logic. Most people growing up in a given culture will learn to harmonize, so to speak, on all levels of human interaction, and they will not require an anthropology text or a music teacher in order to do so. What is appropriate and normal in the local tradition at the moment will determine the nature of the folk expression, and since the expression is thus culturally meaningful, we can say that *doing it* is a kind of performance for a discerning, close audience. And most of us have mastered the logic of it—what "works" and what doesn't—by the age of seven.

Learning Styles and Clusters

In many cultures telling jokes is a prominent kind of vernacular expression. We will return to it in another chapter, because joke telling represents a culturally important medium of learning and expression. At this point it is enough to use joke telling simply as a means of discovering some bases of our own expertise in folklore, our dynamic application of cultural logic. Anyone who has listened to jokes and has later told them knows that, generally speaking, we need to hear a joke only once in order to "have" it. We do not memorize the joke verbatim, nor do we take lecture notes on it. In fact, if someone tells the joke as if it has been memorized word for word, the audience will not like it. When we tell a joke, we are reshaping and recomposing clusters of ideas that we have heard expressed in a similar context at another time, but we are arranging them according to an understood—though unarticulated—cultural logic.

A learning process has taken place, and it is now followed by an expressive event, a performance, but only if we judge the context to be right. If the setting is appropriate and the joke performance is well executed, the joke teller will notice the pleasure of his companions, reinforcing his own pleasure in telling the joke. At this point, the joke telling has become another educative experience, and the joke has solidified itself into a cluster of potential ingredients in the mind of the teller; but no matter how many times the same person tells the same joke, it will seldom, if ever, be performed exactly the same way twice, for a dynamic process (dependent on context, mood, intonation, and reason for telling) is now in motion as that first event is continually reshaped, rephrased, and re-experienced in the mind and actions of the performer. Moreover, the performer will try to work within that set of expectations shared by the audience of the joke. All of these factors work simultaneously as a joke (or any other kind of folklore) is being heard, appreciated, learned, and, later, performed in another analogous setting.

But this process is far more subtle than it initially seems because a joke almost never openly articulates what it is that is funny. That is, the joke is a loaded reference to assumptions and concerns shared by the teller and the audience. In order for a joke to "work" logically, this reference has to be understood by everyone in terms of its appropriateness (often ironic) to the way in which the joke is phrased (its punch line, its vocabulary, its innuendo). Thus, the "meaning" of a joke is almost never in the text, but resides in what the performance can touch off among those who are present. And some people just never get it, which may be a barometric reading on their abilities to be fully competent in their own culture or language. Three examples may suffice at this point to illustrate the way in which jokes trigger off shared associations which are not overtly stated in the "text":

1. "The Dream"

I collected this story in December of 1966 from Matthew Yellowman, who was then about twelve years old. His father had been telling Coyote stories, which can be told only in winter (in Navajo terms: between the first killing frost and the first thunderstorm). During a pause in the narration, his son volunteered this joke. An accurate phrase-by-phrase translation of the text as it was told at that time (transcribed from the tape recording) reads as follows:

> Long ago, they say,
> A man (on the side over there) said,
> "Which of you had a dream last night?" he said.
> Another said, "I didn't; I don't know."
> "I had a dream last night," another one said;
> "Last night I dreamed I was sitting on four bird eggs,
> and three of them weren't mine;
> only one was mine," he said.

In order to discover the meaning of this brief narrative, we need to ask at least two questions which do not arise directly from the text, but which derive from our observation of the performance: a) why did the Navajos laugh (that is, what is there about this dramatized conversation that has the capacity to invoke or provoke laughter)? and b) why—even with an immediate translation—do non-Navajos not find the narrative funny?

If the humor is based on absurdity (say, the clear oddity of a person sitting on eggs), then we would imagine the absurdity to be equally visible to all intelligent human beings. We could then conclude our speculation by observing that absurdity is apparently not registered alike by all cultures, just as, for example, slipping on a banana peel, which is thought of as a very funny accident in American comics, might be seen by another culture as a serious warning from God. According to this approach, Navajos think dreaming of sitting on eggs is funny while the rest of us do not. But this "explanation" abandons us right where we began—with a vivid realization that cultures are different. And as a discussion of humor it is virtually worthless, for it leaves important questions unanswered while avoiding the problem of meaning altogether.

For purposes of our discussion, it would be interesting to find some equivalencies, some ideas (not topics, per se) which are in some way emotionally parallel to what happens in a Euro-American joke. And there is such a parallel: talking about dreams in the company of strangers is—for the Navajo—something like discussing racial differences or sexuality in the company of strangers is for Whites. That is, the subject is one of those areas of belief and cultural value which are "under stress," so to speak—controlled by taboo and anxiety. Normally, Navajos would not talk about their dreams in the company of strangers since most memorable dreams are associated with "nightmares," or "Alpträume," and are thus inescapably connected with beliefs about *yenaald-looshi*, the "skinwalkers" who represent witchcraft in the Navajo belief system. Discussing them with strangers (who might actually be skinwalkers) would produce considerable anxiety.

Recognizing this allows us now to ask a number of questions which might not have been initially possible: Why did Matthew Yellowman suddenly volunteer a joke on such a "loaded" subject? How was this subject appropriate to the general conversation? In what way(s) did it help to articulate something which was not being articulated in other ways? And what is there about the narrative as Matthew told it that makes it funny rather than outrageous?

As far as the text itself is concerned, we are in position to react to the narrative more intelligently, for we know that the opening line brings up a topic of anxiety for the Navajos. The first response, from an anonymous character, is that he does not remember his dream, or at least declines to talk about it—and from the normal Navajo viewpoint this would be a proper answer to the leading question. The last respondent remembers his dream and—contrary to everyday custom—is willing to reveal it to others; instead of sharing the anticipated nightmare, however, he tantalizes everyone's anxiety by giving an account of a dream image just loaded with natural contradictions:

a) a human is apparently shown doing something only a bird can do;
b) a heavy object is shown doing something only a light object can do;
c) a male is shown doing something only a female should do.

In the Navajo language, some of these absurdities are richer than one can translate. For example, Navajos are matriarchal, matrilineal, and matrilocal; women are central to the culture, and they own the children outright. Thus, a male providing the female role of nurturing is a reversal of nature. Additionally, birds and people fall into two distinct categories in Navajo ("those who cry out" and "those who articulate"), and the crossover here between the two—combined with implied differences in size, weight, and gender—provides an image so impossible that it would be either terrifying or funny. There is also the possibility that the dreamer might be suggesting that he has had to raise four children, only one of whom was his own (but since Navajo children belong to their mothers and trace their descent through their mothers, the discrepancy here would be in a man's concern over a question which is none of his business).

Without another modifying element, all of the above discrepancies have the capacity to suggest disharmony, imbalance in nature, and therefore mental and physical sickness (for Navajos, health is the central concern of religious ritual, and health is seen as based primarily on natural harmony and balance). So indeed, all of the absurdities mentioned above are not necessarily funny for Navajos; indeed, the potential is for anxiety—a "stress" introduced into culturally charged values.

But there is another level of meaning which is more important than this, one which clearly converts all these potentially dangerous images of humorous relief. The "key" to the joke lies in a grammatical usage that cannot be easily translated into English, unfortunately. In this joke, the last scene is described in a past tense which includes another past tense of completion. And the word used for "bird eggs" (usually *tsídiibi yeezhii*) is *tsídiiyazhi* (literally, "young birds," thus referring to the eggs actually in the process of hatching). The last scene would have to be translated something like this:

> "Last night I dreamed I had been hatching four birds, and three of them turned out not to have been mine; only one had been mine," he said.

In this fuller, though more awkward translation, the Navajo understanding is that the action has been completed, the birds have hatched and already left the nest. The fact that the dreamer has recognized one of the resultant birds as his own offspring can have only one meaning, and it is humorously ironic: he has actually dreamed that he himself was a bird. The audience realizes this but he does not; he tells the dream as *if* it is made up of discrepancies, but we see that there are no discrepancies. The audience laughs in part because it knows something the dreamer does not; he thinks it was remarkable to dream about sitting on eggs, and we say to ourselves, "Of course you did; you dreamed you were a bird."

There are two other culturally related elements of humor in the performance of this joke. One of them is that, while Navajos usually avoid talking about dreams, there are scattered occasions when someone might say to friends, in jest, "What have you all been dreaming?" as if to say, "What are you all thinking about?" This is done for fun or to create conversations; but since the discussion of dreams is considered potentially dangerous, the only acceptable or proper response to such an invitation is to relate (or create) a funny narrative—otherwise the result would be threatening because of the Navajo belief that speaking about something brings it into reality. So the text we have been discussing fits into a narrow and precarious kind of Navajo oral tradition, and the narrative—when we perceive its humorous function—dramatizes the appropriate resolution by converting a cluster of potentially bothersome natural discrepancies into the harmless irony of a dreamer who foolishly misunderstands his own dream.

But such joking conversations in real life are normally initiated among and by adults, for older people have a better sense of what can be properly said or appropriately avoided. The present performance was given by a Navajo teenager, as if somehow the rules of decorum had been reversed or were being tested. Rather than this being in itself objectionable, however, it fits into another kind of Navajo humor: "grandmother jokes." When a grandmother holds up a grandchild, she will often speak "for" the child by changing her voice to a higher range and saying things that are far too sophisticated for the child actually to have thought. This action of placing a younger person into the framework and logic of an older person is seen as funny.

So, we can describe our joke performance as a story in which a youthful narrator inserted himself into an adult frame in order to articulate dramatic enactment of a situation where

a) the audience (adults) might know more than the speaker (a child);
b) the subject matter (questions about Coyote stories) might be dangerous if not resolved;
c) potentialities of health vs. witchcraft (the unmentioned but understood level of Coyote stories) were involved;
d) the audience nonetheless could resolve these matters harmoniously (by acknowledging that an apparently dangerous subject was in fact not dangerous).

In my estimation, the joke came out as a direct dramatic equation of the situation then in progress: we three non-Navajo scholars had come specifically to record and ask questions about the Coyote stories, which for the Navajo are far more complex than the mere entertainment of youngsters on winter evenings. Our questions brought up the implied possibility that we knew more than the narrator. Like the first speaker in the joke, we had asked them to discuss a potentially threatening subject in the company of strangers. Moreover, we were *dissecting* the motifs which for the Navajos function as dramatic enactments of integration and moral behavior. And we were asking about one level of meaning when there were other far more important levels which were being unmentioned and unexamined—levels which even a Navajo teenager knew about.

2. "Das Bier"

I heard this joke in Tübingen, Germany, in 1984, before the walls separating East and West Germany fell. It was the custom in both East and West to tell jokes articulating the absurdly delicate situation of individuals in conflict with the Communist system.

> A: Kennst Du den Unterschied zwischen Deinem Bier und dem Honecker?
> B: Nein, kenn' ich nicht.
> A: Das Bier ist flüssig; Honecker ist überflüssig.
>
> B: Kennst Du den Unterschied zwischen Deinem Bier und Dir?
> A: Nein.
> B: Das Bier bleibt; Du kommst mit!
>
> (A: Do you know the difference between your beer and Honecker?
> B: No, I don't know.
> A: The beer is fluid; Honecker is superfluous.
>
> B: Do you know the difference between your beer and you?
> A: No.
> B: The beer stays here; you're coming with me!)

The listener must not only know that Honecker was the leader of East Germany (this is clearly a joke which is rapidly retreating into oblivion) but also why someone might get into trouble with secret police for suggesting that Honecker is (or was) superfluous. The joke does not *say* anything about police, nor does it say that a person drinking beer with another person needs to be careful about what he says. But without the political and social setting suggested by the first part of the joke, the second part means virtually nothing.

I discussed this joke with some Navajo friends. Their first question was "dii haat'ish it'e *Honecker*?" (What is a "Honecker?"). I explained that he was a politician, and that some people felt he was superfluous. "I think all politicians are superfluous," said one of my friends, "so this is a really hard question then, because how is anyone supposed to tell one politician from another?" Another Navajo then asked, "Why is this Honecker fellow like beer, anyway? Is it because he makes the people drunk so he can get elected?"

Another wanted to know why I thought the second man was a policeman. I answered that the second man takes the first man away, leaving the beer behind, and the phrase "Du kommst mit," something like "you're coming with me" in English, sounds like the statement of a policeman. "But of course the two men go away from the bar together," he answered, "no one would go away with a bottle of beer and leave his friend there!" "Besides," said another, "the guy can't be a policeman, because German policemen [*beshbich'aa'i silao,* literally, "steel-hat soldiers"] always ask people for *naaltsoos* [paper, meaning papers/identification], and this one didn't even want paper." The first one then said, "I know what this story is about: two friends are out drinking beer, and they get so drunk that they can't even tell the difference between a politician and a bottle of beer, and so they decide to get out of there."

Overlooking their insistence that the joke suggested cooperation rather than competition or conflict between the two speakers, I pointed out that there was a nice pun in the German words flüssig/überflüssig, and that even in the English fluid/superfluous there was a reverberation of humor. They pondered the idea that German and English were related languages, "like Navajo and Apache," as one of them rightly pointed out. "Well, that explains why the joke isn't very funny, perhaps," said one of them.

3. "The Travelling Salesman"

This joke was told by folklorist Roger Welsch to a group of friends who had been telling stories and anecdotes about life on the Great Plains. It sounded at first like another account of distance and sudden storms, which had been the main topics in the conversation.

A salesman was driving his horse and buggy along there by Bolus in the 1920s and he saw one of those black storms coming up on the horizon, and it was getting on toward night, so he didn't know if he'd find some place to get shelter for the night or anything. But way down the road he saw just the glimmer of a light, and it turned out to be coming from a real small sod house—the kind a lot of people were still living in in the 20s. So he stopped and knocked to ask if he could spend the night and get out of the storm. Well, the old farmer came out and talked to him for a while, but he said, "Well, we don't have any room: there's just me and my wife, and there's only one bed, so there's no room. But why don't you come in," he says, "and have something to eat anyway, and maybe we'll figure something out." So the salesman went in, and they told him to sit down at the table and help himself. All there was, though, was a big bowl or tub of cottage cheese that the guy's wife had been making up above the stove on a shelf. Halfway through the meal, the wife took the bowl off the table and put it back on the shelf. Well, by this time they were pretty well acquainted, so the farmer says, "We'll just

work something out here. My wife will sleep next to the wall, I'll sleep in
the middle, and you can sleep on the outside. It'll be crowded, but that's
a big storm coming up, and we can't let you spend the night outside."
So they put the guy's horse into the stall with the farmer's, and they
went to bed. Later on in the night that storm struck, and they could
hear the horses getting freaked out and kicking at each other, so the
farmer got up, got dressed, and went out to get things straightened out.
And as soon as he was out the door, the woman reached over with her
foot, you know, and nudged this guy's leg, and said, "Okay, young man,
now's your chance." So he got up and ate the rest of the cottage cheese.

Most American readers of this joke will not feel the need for the lengthy
explanation of the sort required for the Navajo dream, nor do they require any
instruction on German politics. They already know what a travelling salesman
joke is, and probably what they will find humorous about this one is that the
expected sexual contact between the salesman and the wife does not come
about. Old-timers who grew up in the Great Plains during the Depression may
recall that for many people a bite of food was of far greater interest than sex,
and their laughter may be thus conditioned by another set of shared attitudes.
But these responses would not be possible unless the audience—at least a substantial part of it—had already learned the features utilized by the narration
which touch off a constellation of culturally processed fears and concerns: the
fear of storms, the intrusion of a stranger, the possibility of extramarital sex, the
scarcity of food, the familiar framework of the travelling salesman joke formula.
The fact that the story is widely told in the West as a joke featuring a young
teamster staying overnight with a farm couple and their daughter is an index to
a more general cultural fascination with the intrusion of a male stranger into a
nuclear family, coupled with hunger, shortage of food, and perhaps stupidity or
naiveté. When the older couple go out to separate the horses and the young
daughter tells the young man "Now's your chance," he gets up and finishes off
the turnip greens.

The means by which this kind of learning takes place is a process called
folklore; it is how we learn what a house is and how to find our way around in
one (as well as how to tell a house from a home). It teaches us about time and
its coordinates, and it allows us to learn and to become continually saturated
with a total worldview made up of those various networks of human interaction
in which we participate. As we shall see, the process seems to begin with our
capacity to register something that might be called cultural metaphor, a shared
awareness that a word or phrase has meanings that go beyond apparent manifest
of lexical content. This talent must be learned, though it is seldom picked up
through overt instruction. And some people are better at it than others.

Folklore functions in part as an informal, vernacular system for learning the
daily logic and worldview of the people around us. What we learn is more in

the way of style and performance than specific content. We may say that folklore itself is characterized by (1) certain cultural rules that determine strongly what gets articulated and how and when, and (2) by a looseness, an informality, an inclination toward rephrasing and change, that will eventually result in an individuation on the surface of all articulations *(variants,* as they are called by folklorists). How does such a complex of rules and freedoms operate? How are their forms to be studied? Where to begin and how to define such a vast spectrum of human expression, complete with its cultural matrix?

DESCRIBING FOLKLORE

Since the time of the Grimm brothers in Germany, scholars have sought out vernacular artists, studying their language, tales, customs, and beliefs, first in fear that the traditional world was disappearing (or becoming moribund), and more recently in the belief that only through a study of folklife can we ever understand the nature of human cultural history and expression. Some have concentrated on those particular genres (forms) of folklore listed in the introduction, while others have concerned themselves with certain categories of genres (for example, oral lore to the exclusion of material objects or vice versa). Others of a more anthropological orientation have centered their attention on traditional groupings of people (ethnic, regional, religious, occupational) and have concentrated on how folklore codifies and articulates the dynamics of the group itself. More recently, scholars have studied the interactive expressions of any group of related people: computer users, gays and lesbians, gangs, and lawyers, to name only a few.

Nonetheless, in spite of more than one hundred years of intensive study in Europe and America, folklorists have produced neither a satisfactory definition for that body of materials on which they fondly spend their scholarly lives nor an acceptable, consistent set of critical terms with which to discuss it. Certainly, one reason is the almost startling variety and superficial dissimilarity of the materials themselves, ranging as they do from barns to ballads. The study of this vast array of cultural expression needs to be interdisciplinary in nature, and this has resulted in the amalgamation of a field that carries a sense of diffuseness, one that sometimes encourages scholars in other fields to disbelieve that folklorists know what they are doing or that they are doing anything at all. Another lamentable result is a lack of precision in scholarly conversation as folklorists attempt the theoretical study and discussion of a constantly evolving field.

The Term Folklore

Still another problem, which seems at first more complicated than it really is, is that most folklorists today do not even feel that the word *folklore* itself adequately identifies or defines the area they are talking about. For one thing, they voice sincere doubts that there is any such static group as might be implied by *the folk.* Indeed, the closely associated German term, *das Volk,* means something like a genetically similar group, like the way *ethnic group* is used in English. But we know very well that most people in the world belong to several close groups, each based on different kinds of interactions, learning processes, and expressions. We are recognizing now, at least, that the idea of a single folk unit as the defining feature of the human context in which an individual grows up must probably be rejected.

Further, the word *lore,* even though it does indicate something about learning or knowledge, does not cover the wide range of communicative expression and experience and performance that has become the focus of the professional folklorist. It suggests that vernacular traditions are learned, not practiced; actually they are both known *and* done. William Thoms, who made up the term *folklore* in the nineteenth century, and many of those who first became involved in the study of what were then called *popular antiquities,* were not trained as professionals in this field nor could they have anticipated the development of their elite hobby into a demanding academic discipline. As a result, subsequent folklorists have had to create their own conceptions of a field of inquiry along the way, often using terms (and biases) drawn from their own academic specialties. Nonetheless, the word *folklore* is in widespread use and seems to be here to stay. And most scholars have at least some notion of the kind of thing they are talking about, even though its precise outlines and definitions are not easy to produce.

Actually, *folklore* is a word very much like *culture;* it represents a tremendous spectrum of human knowledge and expression that can be studied in a number of ways and for a number of reasons. Its primary characteristic is that its ingredients seem to come directly from dynamic interactions among human beings in vernacular performance contexts rather than through the more rigid channels and fossilized structures of technical instruction or bureaucratized education, or through the relatively stable channels of the formally taught classical traditions.

Naming of Parts

In the introductory comments to his anthology *The Study of Folklore,* Alan Dundes suggests it is inadvisable even to try to define *folklore.* Instead, he gives an inclusive list of items and genres that have been studied by folklorists over the years: in this view, folklore is as folklorists do. Each folklorist, of course, specializes in only a few topics on any comprehensive list, but in spite of the varying interests and definitions urged by different folklorists, there should be in fact an area of general agreement among them from which a unified description of folklore dynamics may grow. It should be as applicable to string figures as to ballads, to barns as to oral epics.

Because a number of folk genres are simply not oral in nature, oral transmission can never be definitive for folklore. As well, an insistence on a certain kind of content is unworkable because of the great disparity between the genres, some of which—hand gestures, for example—may be said to be entirely lacking in content or to be entirely content, depending on one's viewpoint.

The simple list of traditional items (taken from those areas we have been interested in because they seem traditional) is also inadequate for definition, for if it remains open-ended, it will remain non-definitive. If it is a closed list, it will represent only a parochial prescription and will be almost irrelevant for anyone who may want to expand or contract the list. Moreover, a list based on genre overlooks the fact known to any field researcher that folk expressions seldom occur in one genre at a time (the ballad text is related to its tune; the written graffito may have been learned in conversation; the carved "witching" stick or dowsing rod owes as much to popular belief as to the whittler's craft). We are obviously talking about a multidimensional set of occurrences and contexts. Single genre designations, while they may help us to think more clearly about the ingredients and forms of the folklore field, also help us to overlook the dynamics we seek to understand. Thus, for purposes of discussion, the "dangers" in the open-ended list are probably more acceptable for us to put up with as we scrutinize a field characterized by variety and dynamism.

Let us then assume that folklorists may be said to have some generally informed, if not precisely charted, notion that vernacular traditions exist, and that expressions made by an individual under the influences of culture-oriented traditions will share some characteristics that will argue for grouping them in a common field. Implicit in the study of folklore today, moreover, is the understanding that we may add to our list as the field becomes more clearly defined and as new cultural expressions are better understood. As with other disciplines (such as history, literature, music, mathematics), the term *folklore* will no doubt continue to be used in reference both to the content of the field (the material we collect and study) and to the discipline itself.

Variety and Variation

What element or elements do the ballad and string figure have in common? On what grounds may one place *barn* and *folksong* on the same list? What similarities exist between a quilt and an oral epic? How may we speak of latrinalia and folk dance as being in the same academic area? There may be in fact several elements shared by some of these items, but there is only one that works in them all. It has nothing to do directly with content or with genre, with method of transmission, with the definition of the group, or with level of literacy. The similarity lies in a common process. All these items have the common quality that—as long as they continue to exist in their natural habitats—they are in continual and dynamic variation through space and time.

Since variety is not in any way limited to folklore, since all things in a culture change through time, how are the items on our list to be differentiated from other entities that vary: Shall we include automobiles, clothing fashions, telephones? For several reasons, no. The items and events of folklore are recurrent forms of local, dynamic human expression—artifacts and performances created one at a time under particular circumstances. A quilt or a barn, as practical as its use may be, extends far beyond its mere thingness or its function. It is designed or phrased in such a way as to express and reflect the personal *and* cultural values in design and workmanship out of which the artisan works, and it is these designs and values, not the quilt or barn itself, that may be said to be dynamic, and thus to be folklore. Moreover, the traditional artifact is not usually produced with the sharply varying demands of a vast, paying, consumer market in mind. Traditional expressions, whether they be lingual, musical, gestural, or physical, reflect the notions of the performers in relation both to their own peculiar talents and aesthetics and to the tastes of the local network of people for whom they perform—the group whose members are familiar with their art: those from whom they have learned through traditional exchange.

This should not be construed as excluding folk crafts, in which certain technical demands are made on the artists for which they must be trained by their mentors. Any chair must have enough legs to stand, and any pot must be able to hold something. Different materials and aims require particular handling by the potter or weaver or carver, and these are usually transmitted to them by someone else so that they will not spend their early careers creating attractive blunders. We are, then, distinguishing between traditional ideas about "pot-ness," say, and those technical devices through which the pot itself is produced.

To put it another way, the barn, pot, ballad, or tale as we find it in vernacular performance is a particular rendering of a pre-existing idea, produced at a particularly appropriate time. The prototypes of barn-, pot-, ballad-, and tale-ness that circulate among members of a group are based more on cultural attitudes than on technology. In these terms, our critical job is to present and study the processes of folklore that exist through time in a group of people by a comparative study of the items produced from the cultural premises of that group.

Thus, while certain technical competences often must come into play, the production of any traditional item is not chiefly related to professional training or to the external demands of technical or economic necessity. Of course some crafts become popular, and the artisan may make money. Some artisans are able to support themselves through their crafts. But their work has primarily local and cultural origins, and most often this is precisely why outsiders seek to buy it.

The process of folklore may be said in this sense to be local, communal, and informal. This does not argue that formal people have no folklore, or that folklore is not shared among members of a highly trained profession. Rather, it suggests that even in the most formal groupings of any society, active traditions are passed not as a part of the formal training but as units of meaning interchanged commonly enough with other familiar people that a recognizable clustering of premises, formulas, and styles is built up and transmitted out of which the informal performer acts. Formal opera singing itself is not regarded as a part

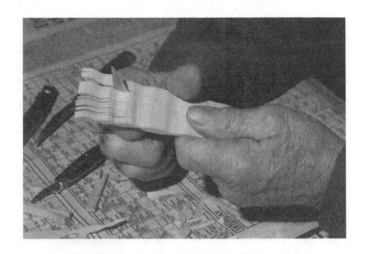

Vernon Shaffer of Malad, Idaho, a consummate carver and whittler, splits a piece of fine-grained softwood for a fan. Photos copyright © 1984 by Jan Boles.

Vernon Shaffer displays some of his handiwork in whittled fans. Photo copyright © 1984 by Jan Boles.

of folklore, for example, but opera singers may possess and transmit jokes, tales, beliefs, and customs ("break a leg") informally that particularly reflect the traditional values, beliefs, and attitudes of opera singers.

Similarly, nuclear physics *per se* would not ordinarily come under the scrutiny of folklorists, but there are numerous traditions passed among scientists (for example, legends of German rockets not lifting off properly until urinated upon); such traditions are clearly not connected so much to the formal or technical aspects of physics and rocketry as they are to the shared experiences and anxieties of simply being a scientist. Generally speaking, the performers of traditional expressions do so because they want to or must, and usually their audience is made up of participating members of the same group in which the dynamic exchange of traditions through the years has formed the matrix out of which the performer operates.

For these reasons we may characterize or describe the materials of folklore as culturally constructed communicative traditions informally exchanged in dynamic variation through space and time. *Tradition* is a compendium of those pre-existing culture-specific materials, assumptions, and options that bear upon the performer more heavily than do his or her own personal tastes and talents. We recognize in the use of *tradition* that such matters as content and style have been, for the most part, passed on by the culture, but not invented by the performer. *Dynamic* recognizes, on the other hand, that in the processing of these ideas in performance, the artist's own unique talents of inventiveness *within* the tradition are highly valued and are expected to operate strongly. Time and space dimensions remind us that the resulting variations may spread geographically with great rapidity (as jokes do) as well as down through time (good luck beliefs). Folklore is made up of informal expressions passed around long enough to have become recurrent in form and content, but changeable in performance.

MODE AND MOVEMENT IN FOLKLORE

Our focus here is on the mode of transmission rather than on the medium. The critical factor is not whether an item is found in oral circulation or in print (or on a record), but whether it does or does not exhibit dynamic, substantive variation. Of course, the plain fact is that the informal, vernacular mode among humans is chiefly oral and gestural (we talk and gesture to each other more often than we build barns, for example). Folklorists are generally agreed that these everyday expressions tend to become viable over a period of time or across a geographical area mostly among people who share some basis for everyday communal contacts, some factor in common that makes it possible, or rewarding or meaningful, for them to exchange vernacular materials in a culturally significant way. Such human clusters have been called *folk groups* by many folklorists, but we should bear in mind that the grouping envisioned here is not static (as that term might imply) but is as dynamic as the materials it produces,

for most people belong to several such groupings, and some (such as occupational) are subject to constant change.

It is particularly to the element of dynamic variation through space and
time that this book directs its attention, for these coefficients provide a subject
area on which virtually all folklorists are in agreement, and for that reason it
offers an acceptable set of premises that can be serviceable to our understanding
of folklore without the necessity of abandoning critical interest in the continuing debates on structure, texture, function, and meaning.

Indeed, few folklorists would deny that folklore scholarship is based
almost entirely on the study of variation. Nearly every scholar mentions the
matter of variant study as basic to the critical examination of the materials.
Weak folklore studies are often the hasty output of writers who have failed to
take into consideration a fair or representative sampling of variants. The most
heavily used critical tools in folklore, the type and motif indexes, are founded
on the proposition that in folklore no single item can be called *the* tale or song
or barn. It is axiomatic that we need more than one instance of a tale or motif
or ballad or popular belief even to know whether in fact we are dealing with an
expression shaped by tradition. If fifty texts of one ballad were unearthed that
were all alike in every detail, most folklorists would argue that they were not
traditional because their identical phrasing would be an indication they had
been duplicated on paper and thus could not be individual transcriptions of
live performances. Structural and comparative studies are predicated entirely
on the observation that certain units are continually recombined within the
frame of a genre or type, and that an examination of patterns thus produced
leads to valuable insights into the genres themselves and into the processes by
which they are developed.

Not only do folklorists examine a maximum number of variants before
making critical approaches to a particular item or genre, but many folklorists
see the process of variation itself as the very essence of their material. In the lingual, musical, and kinesic traditions the item is the performance, and the performance is nearly always a particular variation of a hypothetical prototype (one
suspects Plato might have made a good folklorist).

In his study of traditional ballads, David Buchan declares that the story in a
ballad is "a conceptual entity whose essence may be readily and accurately con-
veyed by different word groups." William R. Bascom, speaking of all forms of
folklore, puts it this way, "Change occurs each time new variations are introduced and again these innovations are subject to acceptance or rejection. As this
process continues, each new invention is adapted gradually to the needs of the
society and to the pre-existing culture patterns, which may themselves be mod-
ified somewhat to conform to the new invention."

One photograph of a Pennsylvania Dutch hex sign, one plowshare supporting a mailbox, one tale, one quilt, one ballad, one graffito can never be enough
to establish the existence of a tradition. On the other hand, one hundred items

alike in every detail establishes nothing but the fact of duplication. Variation in the particular appearance of one item is probably the most reliable hallmark of live folklore available to the student. It is not based on the belief that folklore is more "pure" than anything else, but on the observation that folklore is produced and maintained in a distinctive way.

The Twin Laws

Variation, on the other hand, is not a random or a radical process. Balancing the dynamism of change in performance is the essentially conservative force of tradition itself. The weight of the familiar past continually exerts its subtle pressures on the bearers of these materials in at least two ways: The performers remember or adhere to some notions of the basic type (for example, in the use of their own language, or in the singing of a ballad like "Barbara Allen," in which a woman forsakes a man and the man dies), and they are sensitive to the reactions of the audience, most of whom speak the same language or subscribe to certain expectations about the ballad (or the quilt, barn, tale) in content, style, and occasion. These considerations will limit in varying degrees the freedom for variation felt by the performers. They may institute change, either consciously or inadvertently, but they will do so chiefly within the framework of the familiar, acceptable, and culturally logical.

These two forces, or qualities—the one dynamic, the other conservative—are the twin coefficients of the particularized variation that finally does take place again and again in each traditional event—through space (geographical or human) and through time (moments or years). For simple reference, we may refer to these two forces descriptively as the twin laws of folklore process: conservatism and dynamism will probably be the two most prominent characteristics in our perception of (and discussion of) any item tentatively classified as folklore. We will want to know what features of content and style have been carried through from earlier sources (conservatism). And we will need to know the extent to which the bearers of the materials, or the context in which they operate, have worked upon these materials in such a way as to change them (dynamism).

Conservatism refers to all those processes, forces, and attitudes that result in the *retaining* of certain information, beliefs, styles, customs, and the like, and the attempted passing of those materials, essentially intact, through time and space in all the channels of vernacular expression. Traditional matters related to religious belief, cultural mores, and culture-specific worldviews seem much less open to change than, say, the styles and attitudes relating to jokes. Myths (stories that relate or embody sacred or cosmic occurrences) are expressed in terms of a "time before time began," or in "collapsed time" or "distilled time," and are supported by a whole range of religious belief that conduces to a sense of ultimate truth. Although it can be easily demonstrated that myths do in fact change through time, the attempt on the part of the believer is to transmit them intact. They are not to be tampered with or rearranged, and often a special priesthood provides direct protective and conservative custody. Stylistic variation is suppressed or discouraged, for truth is not believed amenable to artistic manipulation. Even in some secular traditional forms, certain singers and storytellers sometimes do memorize their texts, or try to. The conservative dimension promotes retention and discourages change.

Dynamism, at the other extreme, comprises all those elements that function to alter features, contents, meanings, styles, performance, and usage as a particular traditional event takes place repeatedly through space and time. Matters of taste, context, art, playfulness, change of function or meaning, forgetfulness, translation (language or dialect), shift of audience, age or gender of performer (and many more), all encourage continual change in the particular utterance or production or performance of traditional items, even when the bearer of the tradition tries to avoid it. The reasons for this will become clearer in later chapters. Here it is perhaps sufficient to note that when a singer says she is singing a ballad exactly as her father sang it, she may refer to her fidelity to plot and symbol, not her attempt to produce an exact replication of a memorized text. In this sense, a person may indeed repeat a joke "exactly" without using the same words.

In general, oral tradition itself is more lively and variable than written tradition: we are not surprised to find that orally transmitted jokes are more dynamic in form, style, and content than those myths that have been written down for a considerable period of time. In the same way, written language and spelling rules tend to inhibit the natural changes that take place in the evolution of spoken language, and in some cases, as with English, spelling may lag conservatively two or three hundred years behind actual pronunciation.

The Spectrum of Dynamism

We must then envision a kind of model in which conservatism on one end, and dynamism on the other, exert an influence on the particular realization of vernacular expression. All traditional materials will fit somewhere on this model, some closer to one end than to the other. Myths, whose function in most cultures is to provide dramatic experiential models of protected truths and laws which would otherwise be very abstract, are most likely to be closer to the conservative end of our scale. Jokes and other kinds of orally transmitted materials, whose function is largely fictional and pleasurable, are likely to be closer to the dynamic end.

The most typical relationship shown by these laws might be expressed algebraically: C/D, indicating that the conservative feature being passed along is subject to modification by dynamic processes (ballads and barns and folktales are in this category). C/C might represent materials on one extreme end of the scale, in which both the item being transmitted as well as its performance or enunciation are under rigid control (such as might be noticed with some mythic or ritual materials). D/C would represent materials, such as jokes, that are almost entirely open to variations of style and form, but in which the main point is maintained by the force of conservatism, for example, in the necessary retention of a punch line. D/D would represent the hypothetical condition in which entirely dynamic materials are passed along in entirely dynamic ways. This latter category is probably impossible to chart clearly in folklore because under these conditions there is less chance for material to be retained long enough to be passed on, collected, and studied. Gossip, insofar as it may be considered a genre, or a precursor to legend, might be an example here, as would punning and punning traditions.

Conservative			*Dynamic*
C/C	C/D	D/C	D/D
children's verse	ballads	jokes	puns
obscene songs	barns	legends	rumors
myths	folktales		gossip
proverbs			wordplay

(handwritten annotations: next to C/C "Stable, doesn't change a lot."; next to myths "Cosmology explain"; next to proverbs "truth.")

It is obvious that generic categories cannot be placed separately on this spectrum with any certainty because in each individual item or event or performance, depending on local circumstances in the total context of the utterance itself, conservatism or dynamism might play the more powerful or influential role.

We can assume, however, that certain features of some genres tend to encourage conservatism while other features encourage dynamism. Any folksong or poem that depends for much of its effect on rhyme or rhythm will tend to change more slowly than such freer prose narratives as the joke or memorate. Within a tale or a song, certain striking phrases or recurrent, formulaic conventions are likely to be retained ("There was this travelling salesman" or "lily-white hand") while other features of the same text may be quite open to continual change. A proverb, whose sense of cultural truth is very compact and in which the style and rhythm often become part of the meaning, changes very slowly through time, if at all ("A stitch in time saves nine"). In fact, one favorite form of parody is to take a well-known proverb and change its meaning by overt manipulation ("Virtue is its own reward; but then, so is vice"). While one can make parodies of proverbs, one is not free to change the proverb itself substantially in meaning or tone: One may not say, for example, "A stitch in time saves seven," or "A stitch in time may prevent the necessity for even more work later," or "An airplane in time saves nine." That we do not feel entirely free to change the item by whim as it passes through our minds and lips is our reference point to the force of conservatism.

Obscene songs, many of which are entirely dependent for their effect on the clever use of obscene words, seem less open to change than other kinds of folksongs in which the words are not as centrally important as the "emotional core." In a typical joke, the punch line may be remembered exactly and passed on conservatively through considerable time and space while the "setup" may be reworded or reperformed in very different ways. Children's songs and rhymes, dependent on a kind of ritualism in rhythm and word magic, seem less open to change than other kinds of children's folklore. The following verse, for example, has been collected in nearly (but not exactly) identical texts in widely separated parts of the United States and Canada and in England:

Quick, quick	*Listen! Listen.*
The cat's been sick.	*The Cat is pissin.*
Where? Where?	*Where? Where?*
Under the chair.	*Under the chair.*
Hasten, hasten,	*Run! Run!*
Fetch the basin.	*Get the gun.*
Kate, Kate,	*Too late, she'll*
You're far too late,	*soon be done.*
The rug is in a dreadful state.	

These two examples illustrate—perhaps inelegantly—both the conservative retention of phrases, words, and sounds, and the dynamic invention of variation. Clearly, our study of folklore process can hardly get us beyond superficial beginnings unless we are willing to deal with the multiple aspects of variation and the way they exhibit themselves within ongoing cultural expectations.

We can probably say, then, that expressive productions which remain traditional do so because by retaining their variability, they have remained responsive to vital themes of traditional exchange among participants in a close cultural set (they exhibit both conservatism and dynamism). We know that many of our urban legends (the cement-filled car, for one) have moved continually in and out of print, and we know that many of our most popular ballads have had as widespread a life on the page as in the mouth. Thus it would seem that, especially in our lettered society, appearance in print may become a part of the ongoing process. It may or may not represent the fossilization that usually indicates nontraditional status (where dynamism of performance is lost and conservatism is maintained by duplication through technology).

Folklore is traditional (whether oral or material or gestural or musical) only when it is actually used or performed in its indigenous set of live contexts. A ballad collected in the Ozarks and sung by a professor to a class in folklore may be said to be a traditional item which *was*—in its usual performance—a folksong. A Slavic dance taught by a returned exchange student may be a traditional item which was—when danced in its regular habitat under traditional conditions—a folk dance. These intentional performances for outsiders (often for intellectual curiosity or amusement) are not in any way fake; but they *are* different, no matter how faithful to the original the intentional performer tries to be. In fact, in the very attempt to reproduce someone else's tradition "exactly as it was," one most likely ensures that it has become a living fossil. This is no more lamentable than recognizing that any fossil is no longer a dynamic part of the process of life, but the distinction does need to be made. Nothing in this prevents the Ozark singers or the Slavic villagers from continuing the traditions of singing or dancing in their own contexts as long as they please. And nothing can prevent them from changing or even dropping certain songs and dances from the traditional repertoire when they please—even if it outrages the intellectual bystander who feels they should never "lose" their heritage. Life goes on, and so does folklore.

Just as the law of gravity does not itself cause an apple to fall from the tree, the twin laws do not obligate the bearers of tradition to perform in narrowly defined ways. Rather, by reference to them the study of complex and shifting vernacular interrelationships can be made more graspable, allowing us to narrow our discussion to some clearly functional minimal properties of folklore. These simply are described in terms of generalized laws concerning the "behavior" of our material, but they really are based on the behavior of people in their expression of everyday codes.

CULTURAL SELECTION AND CHANGE

Not all changes will strike the auditors or the performer as good. In terms of survival through time, however, we can assume that substantive mistakes will either be corrected or rationalized by subsequent performers or that a given traditional item will become so confused that it will cease to be viable. Of course, we are speaking in ideal terms of the good singer, dancer, midwife, raconteur. There will always be, in an informal setting, a number of people who remember parts of various traditions. These people seldom consider themselves proficient at the tradition even when they are active bearers ("I can't tell a joke right; ask Charlie to tell it"). Thus perhaps a garbled or confused item will not necessarily be corrected or discarded immediately, but generally people will not waste their time on the recitation or practice of traditions that mean nothing at all or have no function. Most people, and especially the competent bearers of tradition, want very much to express themselves and their lore in a communicative, satisfying way.

We can assume, then, that folklore lives through a generally selective process that ensures, as time goes on, that traditions will maintain their viability or change so that they can or die off. If a former magical incantation has become now a nonsense refrain in a ballad, all we can say is that apparently the line has remained viable because it was usable as a refrain. We need not lament on that account the decline of magic or the stupidity of ballad singers. Some students of history, even scholars of oral history, see variation as almost synonymous with error or degeneration. Actually, it is a matter of hypernaiveté for any student of tradition to expect exact duplication in tradition, or to make value judgments on that basis, especially where people seldom think in terms of a fixed text. Moreover, because traditions survive by being continually reperformed and rerationalized for "fit," we can say that the very existence of a vernacular song, story, quilt, or custom is in itself proof that the expression has continued to be of importance to those who have transmitted it to their close associates. If it has lasted, it must "ring true" in one way or another to the people who have used it, and therefore to ignore it or to devalue it because it is "only" vernacular, or because its variations preclude its use as "data," is to overlook the fact that the item *is* data: it is a distillation and ongoing realization of cultural values which are really operative, or else the item would not have become or remained current. The continual reshaping and transmission of culturally based expression is of extreme importance to us precisely because it is dynamic and not under the control of formal watchdogs: It represents in a rich way the ongoing voice of everyday people, and it reflects and embodies the values by which they choose their foods, their mates, their emotional issues, their political and social definitions—in short, the process is the vernacular basis for their history and literature in a more fundamental way than even the most acute listings of famous names, dates, and data can ever describe.

The Medium Is Not the Message

Because most informal expressions among human beings have been embodied in lingual, musical, and kinesic modes (since these are most direct, and the average person is easily capable of reproducing them), it is likely that the study of folklore will always be heaviest in these areas. However, this situation should not obscure the fact that the same kind of informality, expressiveness, and traditional dynamism may also occur when some visual or material mode is used that represents the same level of communication in the same cultural context of traditional exchange. While the written word is often a solidifier, a freezer of dynamism, it may sometimes be a vehicle for tradition when—as with chain letters, graffiti, and ballad garlands—the conditions of informality, community exchange and taste, and anonymous tradition are present. When latrine poems exhibit centrally some of the same dynamic characteristics that we find in ballads, it would surely be poor scholarship to ignore them only because they are not sung or to reject them only because we feel that visible letters constitute a contaminant. The process, not the medium or the content, is central to our investigation.

It seems nonsense, then, to suggest, as some have, that folklore can exist only in a literate culture and in contradistinction to it, based on the argument that without written language one cannot speak of the category of oral expression.

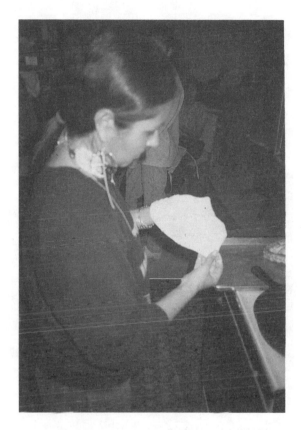

Dah díníilghaazh (here being made by Vanessa Brown in a friend's kitchen) is a standard accompaniment to the diet of urban Navajos (as well as other Native American peoples, who call it "fry-bread"), and is served at parties, cook-outs, and powwows as a kind of native "soul food."

Elisabeth and Hermann Koessner and their daughter Anneliese Erlbacher pause along a mountain trail to yodel in three-part harmony across mountain meadows above Goldegg-Weng, Austria. Formerly a dairying family who used yodels to call in the cows for milking, the Koessners and their extended family now yodel for musical pleasure and to maintain an important dimension of their shared culture.

Oral expression came first, after all; it is written literature, its extension, that has developed into something else. Folklorists deal with a particular and well-established species of learning and expression which uses culture-based interactive codes and formulas. It occurs with or without literacy. If there is no literacy, perhaps most of what happens in a culture might be included in the study of folklore. If there is literacy in a culture, it may very well take part in the dynamic interchange (as with the heavy use of printed broadside ballads in America). Print, for example, in newspaper squibs, in urban legends that appear in "Dear Abby," in items appearing in broadside or popular publications, may take part in the dynamism of folklore as well as in its conservation.

Moreover, since the perimeters of the folk group will change with the focus of the investigation (since most people belong to several close groups), the matter of literacy hardly ever aligns directly with the lore being studied. For example, as citizens, most loggers in Oregon are quite literate, yet as loggers their folklore is primarily oral and will very likely stay that way. Since in such cases the condition of literacy is really peripheral (if not entirely irrelevant) to the discussion, we might say that folklore is often *aliterate*.

Conscious removals of traditional media from their original cultural matrices are familiar to us in all areas of folklore: the revival of folksongs on page and platter by professional entertainers, the mass production of folk toys, the publication of jokes in literate rather than in oral style, the sale of prefabricated log cabins and of corncob pipes made in Japan. What distinguishes these articles primarily is lack of traditional variation; the process has shifted from dynamism to popular reproduction. As a corollary, those people involved in the process are no longer traditional craftspersons as such. They are instead producers and receivers who operate separately, who communicate and express not for each other but for outsiders (although, as occupational coworkers, they may share other kinds of folklore).

The Evolutionary Model

Because of this ongoing change in folklore, it is illuminating to view a traditional item or event as if it were an animal in the evolutionary process. Just as there is no single cat that can be called *the* cat and no single dog that can be called *the* dog, there is no "Barbara Allen" that can be called *the,* or *the original,* ballad. In fact, when we say *cat,* we are really referring to a theoretical prototype, a biological mean that we conceptualize for our own convenience as constituting the most commonly recurrent elements to be found in the widest range of cats. And even if some cats and dogs look very much alike, we will find in the final analysis that the prototype in each case is clear enough for us to make a distinction between dog-ness and cat-ness, or, even within dog-ness, between collie-ness and poodle-ness. Similarly, when we speak of "Barbara Allen," we are referring to our conception of a cluster of characteristics that seem to be connected with a particular narrative song (among other narrative songs), a cluster that gives us enough of a prototype for recognition so that we will not easily confuse it with others.

The Biology of Folklore

In folklore, as in the biological world, variation from a hypothetical norm is universal. No two individuals are exactly alike in every detail no matter how closely related. Variation affects every sort of characteristic, structural or functional, and occurs at every stage of life, in animal and plant life as in tradition. Members of any biological human family or ethnic group participate in the family appearance, but no one is more authentically a member of the family than any other. Indeed, in the biological sciences the very concept of species is based on our perception of the mean of the most frequently recurring characteristics, taking account of all variations from smallest to largest, and described by the scholar without value judgments. This is also what folklorists have done in the best of their work. Moreover, where both geneticists and folklorists once stressed the importance of similarity in family traits, they now generally recognize that the very variety and richness of traits may allow for survival of the type.

In addition, the factors of traditional inheritance versus local adaptation, the possibility for individual items to lose their dynamism (to die) and exist only in recorded (fossilized) form, the occasional chance for a wide variation (mutation) to occur that will in turn die out or propagate a new line of dynamism, and geographical mobility, to mention only a few, all seem analogous to common considerations in the study of evolution and ecology.

These comparisons are of course only for clarification and suggest that the folklorist, like the biologist, must take a multidimensional view of the subject. Folklore and life processes are not the same, because folklore grows out of more conscious aesthetic manipulations than do biological functions, thus biological terms cannot be applied glibly to traditional expressions. The point is simply that in both the animal and traditional spheres the variations occurring constantly through space and time are far more diverse and complex and normal than the word *variation* indicates, and that in both fields meaningful investigation must take such complexities into consideration. One can often speak of these complexities more accurately using terms developed by the scientific fields that have had experience dealing with the nature of variation without value judgment.

Folklore is ever-changing, always developing, on the move. The folklorist must keep pace, in fieldwork, in theory, in vocabulary, in order to understand fully and discuss accurately this dynamic area of human communication. Whoever approaches folklore for the first time might keep in mind, at least tentatively, the major premise of this book: certain items and ideas have become folklore because they have entered into a common, dynamic process that affects their very nature and function. The artifacts and the genres may be many, but a similar process has molded them all. The most rewarding focus of further folklore study will be precisely on the process that binds all these various expressions together into a single field of discussion.

We do well to bear in mind the words of old man Black Elk as he explained a certain feature of the Lakota Sun Dance to Joseph Epes Brown. The sun dancer is pierced above both breasts and is attached to the center cottonwood tree by what appear to be two rawhide thongs. Black Elk stressed, however, that it is really one thong looped around the center pole, a symbol of unity within seeming diversity. "It is only the ignorant man," he said, "who sees the many where there is only the one." In the study of folklore, we look at many manifestations of everyday human expression, but their shaping is all done by a single force: the interactive dynamics of living culture. As folklorist Wolfgang Mieder has phrased it, "Folklore at its best addresses both tradition and innovation and shows how constancy and change are interlinked in the dynamic process of civilization."

BIBLIOGRAPHICAL NOTES

The maintenance of older traditions in a modern, sometimes urban, environment, as well as the development of traditions distinctive to modern situations, are two processes now well recognized by folklorists and anthropologists. Américo Paredes and Ellen J. Stekert, eds., *The Urban Experience and Folk Tradition* (Austin: University of Texas Press, 1971), provide a symposium of scholars who have worked with old and new folklore in the city; Ari Kiev, *Curanderismo: Mexican-American Folk Psychiatry* (New York: Free Press, 1968), examines an older form of folk medicine that has continually reaffirmed its validity in modern times among members of a culture group who live in both rural and urban areas; Abrahams's *Deep Down in the Jungle* concerns the vital, ongoing oral tradition of young Black men in an inner-city setting; Iona and Peter Opie, *The Lore and Language of Schoolchildren* (Oxford: Clarendon Press, 1959) and Mary Knapp and Herbert Knapp, *One Potato, Two Potato: The Secret Education of American Children* (New York: Norton, 1976) and Simon J. Bronner, ed., *American Children's Folklore* (Little Rock, Ark.: August House, 1988) deal with oral materials that have been maintained by children, mainly of urban backgrounds, in some cases for over three hundred years—and with keen modern oral parodies of the most up-to-date sort—demonstrating a combined propensity to conserve and an inclination to create; Robert S. McCarl's "Smokejumper Initiation: Ritualized Communication in a Modern Occupation," *Journal of American Folklore* 89 (1976): 49-66, shows the retention of ancient ritual techniques in a modern, practical setting, while James P. Leary, "Fists and Foul Mouths: Fights and Fight Stories in Contemporary Rural Bars," *Journal of American Folklore* 89 (1976): 27-39, discusses how daily activity of the most common sort develops traditional modes and structures that are reflected in both narrative and human action; James P. Spradley and David W. McCurdy, *The Cultural Experience: Ethnography in a Complex Society* (Chicago: Science Research Associates, 1972), examine a number of common human groupings in the urban environment, showing their customary systems of organization and expression.

Although the data on which it is based are now somewhat antiquated, my essay on college folklore, "The Folklore of Academe," an appendix in Jan Harold Brunvand, *The Study of American Folklore,* gives some idea of the vitality of oral and customary tradition in an environment whose sophistication many would have thought hostile to folklore. Brunvand's chapter on superstition (pp. 300-27) mentions several university-level experiments with urban and well-educated people. As well, several works by Jan H. Brunvand testify to the range and tenacity of urban lore: *The Vanishing Hitchhiker: American Urban Legends and Their Meanings* (1981), *The Choking Doberman* (1984), *The Mexican Pet* (1986), *Curses, Broiled Again* (1989), and *The Baby Train and Other Lusty Urban Legends* (1993), all published by Norton. Gary Allen Fine, in his *Manufacturing Tales: Sex and Money in Contemporary Legends* (Knoxville: University of Tennessee Press, 1992), argues that the contemporary legend has replaced the ballad and the *Märchen* as the narrative genre of choice in the twentieth century. Several scholars have pointed out the liveliness of office traditions, especially with regard to workers' use of copying machines to transmit traditional attitudes and expressions shared by people working in bureaucratic settings. Among the most prominent are Alan Dundes and Carl R. Pagter, *Work Hard and You Shall Be Rewarded: Urban Folklore from the Paperwork Empire* (Bloomington: Indiana University Press, 1978) and Dundes and Pagter's *When You're up to Your Ass in Alligators: More Urban Folklore from the Paperwork Empire* (Detroit: Wayne State University Press, 1987). Alan Dundes demonstrated the continuity of national stereotypes in folklore from ancient times to modern in his controversial but extremely insightful *Life Is Like a Chicken Coop Ladder: A Portrait of German Culture through Folklore* (New York: Columbia University Press, 1984).

The details of language acquisition and the extent of the relationship between worldview and language are still very much under discussion. It is my feeling, based on work with the Navajo and Sioux languages, that language and worldview are inextricably bound, although I do not accept the notion of Whorf that language imprisons us in a single (or simple) ideational set. Here we should recall Whorf's basic work in *Language, Thought, and Reality,* as well as Edward T. Hall's practical application and extension of it in *The Silent Language* (Garden City, N.Y.: Doubleday, 1959) and *The Hidden Dimension* (Garden City, N.Y.: Doubleday, 1966). In the latter book, Hall discusses the traditional uses of space and proxemics in various cultures, touching in part on the corresponding changes in language. Peter Farb takes up a number of Whorf's ideas in fascinating detail in *Word Play;* see especially Chapter 8, "Man at the Mercy of Language," and for language as a setting that educates us, see Chapter 1, "The Ecology of Language." A better understanding of the pervasiveness of early traditional worldview training can be gained from Erik H. Erikson, *Childhood and Society,* 2nd ed. (New York: Norton, 1963). James F. Hamill argues that while all humans are equipped with a logical system, each linguistic and cultural situation creates a particular constellation which is learned and internalized generally by the age of seven: *Ethno-Logic: The Anthropology of Human Reasoning* (Urbana: University of Illinois Press, 1990), 105. A valuable set of essays on communication seen in its cultural setting is provided in Alfred Smith, ed., *Communication and Culture: Readings in the Codes of Human Interaction* (New York: Holt, Rinehart, and Winston, 1966), especially Chapter 5, "Signals: Verbal and Nonverbal," Chapter 10, "Code and Culture," and Chapter 13, "Intercultural

Communication." Ray L. Birdwhistell examines unspoken gestural body language in *Kinesics and Context: Essays on Body Motion and Communication* (Philadelphia: University of Pennsylvania Press, 1970). Alan Dundes shows how fully our daily metaphors, proverbs, slogans, and sayings reflect a rather consistent general worldview in "Thinking Ahead: A Folkloristic Reflection on the Future Orientation in American Worldview," *Anthropological Quarterly* 42 (1969): 53-72, and in "Folk Ideas As Units of World View," in *Toward New Perspectives in Folklore,* ed. Américo Paredes and Richard Bauman (Austin: University of Texas Press, 1972), 93-103. Some interesting observations on metaphors as expressions of cultural worldview in English are provided by George Lakoff and Mark Johnson in *Metaphors We Live By* (Chicago: University of Chicago Press, 1980). For the relationship between Navajo language, worldview, and culture, see Gary Witherspoon, *Language and Art in the Navajo Universe* (Ann Arbor: University of Michigan Press, 1977), and Rik Pinxten, Ingrid van Dooren, and Frank Harvey, *Anthropology of Space: Explorations into the Natural Philosophy and Semantics of the Navajo* (Philadelphia: University of Pennsylvania Press, 1983). Other perspectives on language and learning are being developed, and one of the most important is the concept of gendered codes. See Joan Newlon Radner, ed., *Feminist Messages: Coding in Women's Folk Culture* (Urbana: University of Illinois Press, 1993).

Elliott Oring maintains that in any culture, the perception of jokes requires the development of a sense for "appropriate incongruity," obviously not a simple process, especially when we realize that different cultures joke about different kinds of incongruity. See Oring's *Jokes and Their Relations* (Lexington: University Press of Kentucky, 1992), especially Chapters 1 and 11. Another version of the travelling salesman/cottage cheese joke can be found in "A Traditional Storyteller in Changing Contexts," by Patrick B. Mullen, in *"And Other Neighborly Names": Social Process and Cultural Image in Texas Folklore,* ed. Richard Bauman and Roger D. Abrahams (Austin: University of Texas Press, 1981), 266-79. In it, narrator Ed Bell focuses on a young wagon driver who is more interested in food than in sex, but phrases it in essentially the same plot outline—a good illustration not only of the dynamism of the story, but of Ed Bell's awareness of varying contexts.

John Wilson Foster, "The Plight of Current Folklore Theory," *Southern Folklore Quarterly* 32 (1968): 237-48, suggests that the lack of unanimity among folklore scholars arises because they have concentrated on approaches that have seemed very different while the materials they have studied, seemingly chaotic, "share a common mode of existence governed by their tendency to persist and their tendency to transform. Each instance of folkloristic expression, in fact, is a product of the twin forces of conservation and dynamics" (247). I am indebted to Professor Foster for the lengthy discussions that led both to his article and to the basic theoretical position of this book.

William J. Thoms, writing under the pseudonym Ambrose Merton, sought to provide a solid English term for what had been called antiquities. His suggestion of *folklore* caught on rapidly, and was in wide use among writers within a few years. The original letter appeared in *The Athenaeum,* no. 982 (August 22, 1846): 862-63. Alan Dundes, in *The Study of Folklore,* discusses "What is Folklore?" on pp. 1-3. Although he declines to define folklore, he provides a succinct picture of the field of inquiry today.

We will find in many cases that the production of traditional objects for the consumption of outsiders may in time become influenced by the particular kinds of traditional items the outsider most wants to buy, such as has happened with Navajo rugs. The tradition thus becomes skewed toward exoteric ideas about what the tradition should be like. But, as Kate Peck Kent demonstrates in "Pueblo and Navajo Weaving Traditions and the Western World," in *Ethnic and Tourist Arts: Cultural Expressions from the Fourth World*, ed. Nelson H. H. Graburn (Berkeley: University of California Press, 1976), 85-101, a native tradition may still preside over the process, conception, and mode of presentation, as well as remain associated through custom and popular belief. Graburn's book gives similar examples from Eskimo, Haida, Laguna, Seri, Cuna, Shipibo, Ainu, Sepik, Benin, Lega, and other peoples.

Eleanor Long's fine monograph *"The Maid" and "The Hangman": Myth and Tradition in a Popular Ballad*, University of California Folklore Studies, no. 21 (Berkeley: University of California Press, 1971), was able to show by a close study of many variants that the speaker in the ballad called by Child "The Maid Freed from the Gallows" (Child #95), assumed by ballad scholars to be a woman, was generally thought by traditional ballad singers to be a man. At first this might seem to be a petty detail, but it causes a complete revision in our concept of what the ballad is about and how it achieves its dramatic impact; it also shows what we miss if we consult only a few variants that may not be representative of the *type*. At the other extreme, William H. Desmonde's article "Jack and the Beanstalk," *American Imago* 8 (1951): 287-88, reprinted in Dundes, *The Study of Folklore*, 108-9, based on only one version of the story—and a literary one at that—shows us nothing. For other examples of the amassing of variants for profitable explorations, see Jan Harold Brunvand, "The Folktale Origin of *The Taming of the Shrew*," *Shakespeare Quarterly* 17 (1966): 345-59; Bronson's *Traditional Tunes of the Child Ballads;* Nygard's *The Ballad of "Heer Halewijn,"* and Hector Lee's *The Three Nephites: The Substance and Significance of the Legend in Folklore*, University of New Mexico Publications in Language and Literature, no. 2 (Albuquerque: University of New Mexico Press, 1949).

David Buchan, *The Ballad and the Folk* (London: Routledge & Kegan Paul, 1972) is one of the most highly regarded books on the subject to have been written in recent years. See pp. 158 and 163 especially for the idea of a ballad as a concept with variable wording. Bascom's statement on continual change in folklore comes from his essay, "Folklore and Anthropology," *Journal of American Folklore* 46 (1953): 283-90. My first exposition of the "Twin Laws" was in an article composed jointly with John Wilson Foster, "A Descriptive Nomenclature for the Study of Folklore: Part 1, The Process of Tradition [Toelken]; Part 2, The Evolutionary Model [Foster]," *Western Folklore* 28 (1969): 91-111.

I am indebted to Ed Cray for bringing the high level of conservatism in children's lore and in obscene songs to my attention when I was obstinately fixed on seeing only the dynamic element in folklore. The term *emotional core* was put forward by Tristram P. Coffin in reference to that basic central idea of a ballad whose text is otherwise in flux. The full argument can be found in "Mary Hamilton and the Anglo-American Ballad as an Art Form," *Journal of American Folklore* 70 (1957): 208-14, reprinted in *The Critics and the Ballad*, ed. MacEdward Leach and Tristram P. Coffin (Carbondale: Southern Illinois University Press, 1961), 245-56; Coffin's comments on emotional core begin on p. 246 of the latter. I think the term can safely be applied to the performer's awareness of the traditionally important prototype in *any* performance of folklore.

Later in this study I will suggest that a more serviceable term than *emotional core* would be *ideational core*, since a shared idea (not always an emotion) is central to any folk expression. The "cat's been sick" jingle probably grows out of a shared idea among young people that it is fun to perform socially crude imagery in a social setting (cf. "greasy, grimy gopher guts. . . and me without a spoon!"). The "quick, quick" version I collected from my own children, who insisted on reciting it during meals at home; the "Listen! Listen" version was collected from Rodney Genge in Anchor Point, Newfoundland, by Neil V. Rosenberg. Although the wording is quite different, the two are clearly versions of the same idea—which seems to have less to do with cats' metabolism than with "gross" expression. In rumor (at the highly variable end of our dynamic spectrum), the idea of someone's behavior within certain unexpected or incongruous contexts takes center position, which may be why rumors are passed along as content-rich performances without the need for memorable images or the retention of forumulaic phrasing. See Patricia A. Turner, *I Heard It on the Grapevine: Rumor in African American Culture* (Berkeley: University of California Press, 1993). Near the other end of the dynamic scale, proverbs convey culturally shared ideas using extremely consistent phrases, formulas, and images—suggesting that sometimes the content and the wording are thought to go hand in hand. See Wolfgang Mieder and Alan Dundes, eds., *The Wisdom of Many: Essays on the Proverb* (New York: Garland, 1982), plus anything else by Wolfgang Mieder.

For some very pointed discussion of ballads going in and out of popular print, see Vivian de Sola Pinto and Allan E. Rodway, *The Common Muse* (New York: Philosophical Library, 1957), especially the introduction, pp. 1-29. Urban legends are very susceptible to movement in and out of print. Among many others, see Louie Attebery's account of the cement-filled Cadillac story, "It Was a De Soto," *Journal of American Folklore* 83 (1970): 452-57. See also Florence H. Ridley, "A Tale Told Too Often," *Western Folklore* 26 (1967): 153-56, which concerns the recurrent story of the castrated boy, to be discussed herein in a later chapter.

Jan Vansina, *Oral History: A Study in Historical Methodology*, trans. H. M. Wright (Chicago: Aldine, 1965), sees variation as almost synonymous with error and degeneration, but he bases his remarks on the oral traditions of a very formal African system in which accuracy and fact are high priorities. It seems to me that, even when content accuracy is a chief consideration, exact duplication of wording is relatively rare in orally transmitted materials. For a more moderate view of the matter, see Richard M. Dorson, "Oral Tradition and Written History: The Case for the United States," *Journal of the Folklore Institute* 1 (1964): 220-34. Ed Cray has given a solid account of the role of printed versions in the development of traditional ballads in America in "'Barbara Allen': Cheap Print and Reprint," in *Folklore International: Essays in Traditional Literature, Belief, and Custom in Honor of Wayland Debs Hand*, ed. D. K. Wilgus (Hatboro, Pa.: Folklore Associates, 1967), 41-50.

The application of biological terms to folklore is not new: C. W. von Sydow, a Swedish folklorist, had proposed the term *oicotype* in 1945 to refer to the process of local adaptation in an item of tradition. His essay, translated and published in *Selected Papers on Folklore*, ed. Laurits Bødker (Copenhagen: Rosenkilde and Bagger, 1948), is reprinted in Dundes, *The Study of Folklore*, 219-42. For other suggested terms (usable only as analogies to traditional processes, not as definitions or measurements), see "Descriptive Nomenclature," mentioned earlier, Part 2.

Black Elk's striking account of the Sun Dance is given in Joseph Epes Brown, *The Sacred Pipe* (1953; reprint ed., Baltimore: Penguin Books, 1971); pp. 94-95 give his warning on faulty seeing. Wolfgang Mieder's characterization of folklore as a reflection of civilization's dynamics appears in the introduction to *Tradition and Innovation in Folk Literature* (Hanover, N.H.: University Press of New England, 1987), xii.

Chapter 2

DYNAMICS OF
THE FOLK GROUP

DYNAMICS MAY BE VIEWED SIMPLY, FOR OUR PURPOSES, AS THE FORCES BEHIND the active traditional moments that occur between and among people. What motivates *customary* (i.e., not biological) human interactions? How do they start? When do they cease? How are they received and responded to? Human life is obviously affected by dynamics of many kinds. Of interest to the folklorist and anthropologist are those culturally meaningful dynamics that are known most fully and participated in most actively by members of such groupings as ethnic, regional, occupational, clan, gender, and family clusters.

THE LIVE CONTEXT

Every examination of folklore, every approach to the study of folklore, must take into consideration the multiple and complex interactions that occur among members of a close group whenever a traditional performance of any kind takes place, from a single slang term in its live everyday context to a whole fiesta in its live everyday context. For example, when someone tells a joke, it is almost never done on the spur of the moment, nor is it told in a vacuum, alone to the picture on the wall. There will be a group of people, often closely related by occupation or family ties, who have for various reasons developed a particular shared mood. Something reminds someone of an anecdote and the person tells it, feeling the group will appreciate the application. This will remind someone else of a joke heard at the office, and that in turn will remind another person in the group of some related joke. The kind of jokes, the vocabulary used, the topics, the volume of voices, the length of time devoted to the session, and the protocol of alternating jokes from one teller to another will be determined by unspoken but recognizable attitudes shared or developed by the group. These in turn may be affected by the weather, the time of year, recent historical events (an election, a disaster, a famous trial) or a feeling the group may share about those who are unlike themselves (summer folks, Aggies, Newfies, Texans). All these elements will have something to do with the particular "joke texts" which achieve articulation on a particular occasion; consequently, no text can be fully understood without considerable reference to the dynamics of its context, the total live situation, in which it came forth.

What makes the study of context more complex than it may initially seem is that several kinds of simultaneous surroundings may affect the interactions among the members of a folk group: a particular place (geographic region, a certain room in the house), a particular time (of day, month, year), a certain group of people present, an esoteric language being used, an intensely shared culture or tradition, a particular activity taking place, and so on. The jokes and stories told by an exclusively female group while quilting may thus be quite different from the jokes told by some of the same women when at a grange supper or rodeo breakfast, or baby shower. In some Native American tribal settings, some stories are told only when a whole family has gathered and only at certain times of the year, while travelling salesman stories are more often told by European American men outside their families when "the boys" are gathered together at any time of year.

It should be clear, then, that the word *context* may not fully suggest the varying dynamic environments of folklore, especially those provided by the participants themselves, the folk group. Since most people are members of more than one such group, and since people do not always do the same things when they come together, it becomes necessary for the student of folklore to make (or to have available) close observations of that particular group in which a traditional performance takes place, preferably focusing on the dynamics, whatever they may be, of the performance itself.

In doing so, however, it is well to remember the Heisenberg principle, the fact recognized by scientists that the very presence of an observer is bound to have some effect on the phenomenon under scrutiny. In folklore fieldwork, this may produce negative results when the observer impedes the process under study, confusing results when the process takes place only because the observer is present, or positive results when the observer is able—as an outsider—to ask about things or observe matters that would be difficult or impossible for an insider to deal with.

The Folk Group: Environment for Esoteric Dynamics

Chapter 1 suggested that a folk group can be described as any group of people who share informal vernacular contacts that become the basis for expressive, culture-based communications. In addition to these observations, we would expect to find that the group will have maintained itself through its dynamics for a considerable time and that the expressive communications have thus become the educative matrix in which children of the group—or newcomers to it—are brought up.

"A considerable time" defies a pat definition; how much time is considerable? We want to be able to exclude ephemeral informal groups who share dynamic personal experiences (on a hayride, a picnic at the beach) that have not been extensive enough to have produced a traditional system of communication directly related to identity of the group. On the other hand, some of the examples that follow will indicate that antiquity is not a necessity, either.

One of the key features of a folk group will always be the extent to which its own dynamics continue to inform and educate its members and define the group. Because the members share so much information and attitude, folk groups are what Edward T. Hall would call *high context groups*: for them, meaning and action are more directly related to context than to the simple denotations of words themselves. In some cultures, people share a tremendous amount of context with everyone; the Navajos and the Japanese, for example, are high context groups whose members all see themselves as parts of a single community that "knows." Nonetheless, even these large high context cultures are observed to have smaller localized folk groups based on village affiliation, family, clan membership, occupation, and so forth.

In America, Hall would say that on the whole the larger society is *low context*, preferring to get meaning from information, data, and the formal content of language itself. However, we know that within the larger culture there are many folk groups that do provide high context dynamic systems for their members. What are these high context groups like? What is it that their members share? How do the people relate to each other and to the traditions passed along in such a group? In what ways do the traditions bear upon the lives of the members when they are in the group and when they are elsewhere? These are only a few of the questions to be asked about the folk group and its dynamics.

Probably the smallest group that can be called a folk group is the *dyad*, two people who participate in an ongoing relationship which is so close that each partner provides an immediate reflexive counterpart to the other: life partners, close friends, dorm mates, occupational or military "buddies," to name only a few, express their relationship with words, phrases, gestures, insults, and facial expressions which they share more intensely with each other than with anyone else. Elliott Oring has argued that folk dyads (that is, couples with ongoing close contacts—not simply any two people who happen to share proximity for a while) use an expressive traditional system which (a) tests their shared sensitivity to an immediate experience, (b) symbolizes their intimacy in a shared code that signals their awareness of each other's attitudes, and (c) recalls past experiences in which they jointly participated. These systems of mutual reference are *traditional* in that they are recurrent in the dyad's expressive repertoire, consistent in meaning without the necessity of internal explanation, and referential to previous patterns of behavior central to the couple's sense of itself. These are, indeed, the basic qualities of any folk group.

Folk group is therefore not a static label to be applied simply where people are observed to be loggers, quilters, Ozarkers, or Russian Old Believers; rather, the term should indicate a dynamic system of human interchange where the members of any group interrelate on a high context level of attitude, reference, connotation, sense of meaning, and customary behavior, precisely as members, and to be members, of that group. And the group persists not because it has a certain number of bodies, but because its members continue to use their shared vernacular system of reference.

Loggers, for example, are not a folk group simply because they are all engaged in a rural industry; we notice by observation that there is a way of being a logger that each person learns from the others. In terms of the formal designation, or denotation, one may be called a logger by cutting trees for a living. But one becomes a logger on the folk group level only by participating in the dynamics of loggerdom, being absorbed by the live context, being taken in as "one of the boys" often after a long period of insults, teasing, pranks, and customary tests. Loggers themselves see their group as an esoteric system with its own attitudes and rules. Without acknowledging the power and wisdom of the group a person can hardly expect to join the ranks as a full participant; for one thing, such a person would be a hazard to others in the woods, for he does not have time to learn all the hard rules of survival and cooperation by experience. He must go with the group, for his benefit and theirs. At the same time, there is a certain sense of personal independence called for in logger custom that elevates the value of the individual and encourages him not to knuckle under to the group. If we look for both of these ingredients expressed in logger folklore, we shall not be disappointed.

Esoteric Recognition of Dynamics

One way to get a sense of the group's own concept of itself is to ask its members what they recognize as important tokens of membership. In the case of loggers: How do you recognize another logger on the street? What kinds of words are used by loggers among themselves? What kinds of songs and stories do you tell? What do you do to greenhorns? What are the important things to watch for on a logging crew? And so forth.

Some aspects of logger folklore are regional. Anyone from the eastern part of America will probably wonder why the word *lumberjack* is not used here instead of *logger,* for example. The reader from the Northwest will have seen "lumberjack" mostly in print, and it will seem elitist. Ask a Pacific Northwest woodsman, and you might hear that "'lumberjack' is what city folks call a logger" or "a lumberjack is a guy who stacks lumber in a mill; they're all pantywaists—don't call *me* one of them" or "a lumberjack is a guy who steals wood."

On the other hand, some logger terms and customs are nationwide, *stagged britches* (pants cut off with a knife at the cuff and left ragged so they rip easily and the logger will not be tripped by brush snags getting caught in the material) being one of the most common both in customary dress and terminology. Thus there are both local and universal aspects to logger lore and to the loggers' concept of the group's dynamics. The best approach might be to focus on a particular area and see what the loggers in that setting think about their own traditional characteristics, remembering that scholarly descriptive words like *folklore, traditional, customary,* and so on are not likely to be in the everyday vocabulary of those interviewed.

In the Pacific Northwest one often hears that a logger can be recognized by "his tin hat, hickory shirt, tin pants, and cork boots." This is obviously a high context statement, for the hat is not really of tin but is the usual workman's hard hat; the shirt's appellation is based on a trademark; the pants are made of heavy canvas or rubber (to ward off the water in the soggy Northwest forests); and the boots are not of cork but are caulked (pronounced "corked") and fitted with sharp hobnails for increased stability and traction in the woods. Beyond this, one may note that most loggers feel they are above wearing tin pants, and thus the description is meant to be confusing to the outsider, both through content, which may not be totally true, and by word play on *tin, hickory,* and *cork.* The fact remains that a typical logger in the Northwest wears calf-length laced boots with a high heel, stagged black pants (cut about eight to ten inches above the ground), a gray-striped workshirt, red Logger's World suspenders, and a hard hat. Only the last is a requirement brought in recently by law; the rest of the uniform constitutes a folk costume by means of which loggers belong and recognize each other. Yet obviously anyone could dress up in such an outfit and—at least momentarily—*look* like a logger.

More active and dynamic than costume in the workings of a folk group are the kinds of verbal interaction that take place among and between members. But a researcher would certainly be in the way trying to collect logger folklore on the job; and if one tried to do it by joining a crew, the recollections would have to be written down later, after the work was done. In an attempt to sidestep this problem for the purposes of illustration here, I asked several loggers to share with me the topics, words, and stories they felt were closest to their notion of what loggers are and how they relate to each other. The following is a partial inventory, based on a list of "favorite logger topics" given to me by logger Bill Hamilton: hard work, humor, independence, boasts, pranks, names, camp life, sex, and customs. First, so the subsequent stories and descriptions can be better understood, here is a brief glossary of common terms used by loggers in the Northwest woods.

Esoteric Vocabulary

apple-knocker a part-time logger.

barber chair a tree that starts to split and fall before the cut is finished; it breaks off high, kicks out, and sometimes kills.

bucker a sawyer whose principal job is to cut up fallen trees into standard-sized logs.

bull (adj.) main, principal; usually refers to the most important item or person among several, as in bull-block, bull-cook, bull-buck. Sometimes used in a noun phrase like bull-of-the-woods, usually a reference to the toughest man in the vicinity, sometimes to a woods boss. According to Bill Hamilton, "There is no such thing as a bull-hooker, bull-faller, or bull-climber; each one of these is unique, and one is not more important than another."

chaser a man who kicks chokers off logs being drawn in from where they have been bucked; his job is to detach the logs from the line at the cold deck (the stack from which logs are then reloaded onto logging trucks for the trip to the mill).

choker a heavy cable that acts as an adjustable clamp or noose with which logs are pulled up from the hillside to the central area of a logging operation by means of high lead rigging, a system of cables, blocks, and pulleys powered by a "donkey" (a powerful engine).

choker hole a nonexistent "tool" to aid in getting the choker cable under a large log; the new man on a crew will be sent for a bale of choker holes.

choker-setter the worker who places the cable around the log so it can be pulled in to the cold deck. This job is seen as the basic unit of the actual logging team and constitutes generally the first rung of the logger's hierarchy in the woods. It is also considered one of the most dangerous jobs because logs often roll or pitch end-for-end when the slack is taken up on the main cable.

climber sometimes called a high-climber; the man who climbs a tree and cuts the top off so the tree can be used as a central spar pole for a high lead logging operation. This kind of logging is done today primarily with a mobile mechanical spar pole, so the climber is increasingly a rarity in the woods. Since a tree can split when its top comes off, the climber was considered to have one of the most hazardous jobs, and the employment often attracted those who needed to demonstrate their bravery. A common custom of climbers was to climb on top of the still-swaying spar pole and, either standing or sitting, roll a cigarette and smoke it with studied nonchalance.

Coos Bay splice a splice in a steel cable apparently made by someone more accustomed to splicing rope (Coos Bay is a prominent fishing and seaport town on the Oregon Coast); hence, derogatory.

corks heavy logger boots with sharp hobnails; although spelled *caulked* boots, both the boots and the nails are referred to as corks.

crummy the crew van or truck that carries loggers back and forth to their jobs, probably so named after the earlier crew car on logging railroads. "Where'd that term came from? That ought to be obvious; everybody's got a lip full of snoose, boots full of mud, and britches full of splinters." Often the crummy is hosed out at the end of its homeward run by a junior man on the crew.

A "climber," or "topper," waves to fellow loggers from the top of a freshly cut spar pole.

faller the mainstay of a logging crew, the man who actually cuts the trees down.

gut hammer in a logging camp, the dinner bell or triangle.

gypo (adj.) most often used in connection with the word *outfit* to mean a small, private, independent logging company, often run by a single family or small group of friends.

haulback the smaller cable used to haul the main line back out to the woods where the choker-setters are working.

haywire a small-gauge wire used to set up and extend the first lines of a high lead operation. Since the main cables are too heavy to be dragged around the entire perimeter of the operation, the haywire is used first, and then by means of it the main cables are drawn around and tightened.

haywire outfit any logging operation that uses lighter-gauge cable than the job demands; therefore used in a derogatory sense to indicate a company so parsimonious that it is willing to endanger the lives of its men.

hooker, also *hook tender* the boss of a given logging operation. The name is based on an obsolete item of logging paraphernalia; nowadays no hook is used, but often the greenhorn is sent to "get the hook for the boss."

knot bummer a man whose job is to knock the limbs and any large protruding knots from the logs, usually with an ax.

Mormon silk baling wire (based on the Mormons' high reputation for farming).

misery whip a two-man cross-cut saw; also known as the *Swedish fiddle.*

nosebag usually a lunch box, but applied to any container used for bringing food into the woods. Named after a horse's feed nosebag in recognition of the hard work done by a logger in the woods.

piss-fir Willie someone accustomed to small trees; a "wimp," an incompetent person.

prune picker a farmer, hence someone unused to hard logger work (many of the inland valleys of the Northwest contain extensive fruit orchards).

show the general area where a particular company is engaged in logging; the logging show may be made up of several *sides,* although a clear distinction between these two terms is not always made.

side a particular area where logging is going on; a logging company may have several sides operating at the same time.

skidroad a roadbed made up of logs placed side by side crosswise to the direction of traffic over which logs were hauled in earlier times into the mills over swampy or spongy terrain. In logging towns, various service businesses grew up along the skidroad, and it became known as the low district of town. Many western loggers feel that Easterners have mistakenly derived the term *skid row* from *skidroad* by an effete parallel to such terms as *millionaire's row.*

slickshod wearing boots without corks, therefore being in the woods without proper traction, a danger to oneself and, potentially, to others.

A modern logger working in the woods with chainsaw and hard hat. Photo by Suzi Jones.

A logger in the 1930s (probably a foreman, judging by his sweater and cap) shows how big the tree was by lying on the freshly cut stump. The board under him prevents him from sticking to the abundant pitch.

snoose in the Northwest woods, a moist snuff, especially Copenhagen, for dipping (carrying a small pinch usually behind the lower lip) while working in the woods, since smoking is often prohibited, especially during dry season.

springboard a board inserted in a small cut in the side of a tree. Early Northwest fallers stood on it while falling a tree; it kept them above the brush and allowed them to cut above pockets of pitch often encountered low on big trees.

whistle punk often the youngest man on the crew, who relayed the signals of the choker-setters to the man running the donkey engine, which supplies power to pull the logs into the cold deck.

widow maker a heavy broken branch so caught in the other branches of a tree that it may be dislodged by a wind or by the tree being cut, thus providing an unseen hazard for the loggers below.

Hard Work

Part of a logger's sense of his occupation becomes evident in his grudging pride for the excessively hard work demanded of him. Sometimes this comes out in jokes that refer to other occupations as easy or uninteresting because the labor is not so difficult, and sometimes it comes out in the high praise of those who have been able to work as loggers without complaint. In the former category, often it is the farmer, the sailor, or the mill worker who is singled out for ridicule; in the latter, it is often the Swede who emerges as the epitome of the long-suffering, hard-working logger. Sometimes, in a wry, humorous inversion, it is the logger himself who is described as being so simple and stupid as to labor hard and long at an occupation that can only lose him money or his life. In one narrative common in the Northwest, an unemployed logger gets a temporary job on a nearby farm. He milks the cows, plows the fields, milks the cows again, feeds the stock, plows in the late evening until it is too dark to see. The next morning he is up at 4:00 A.M. and comes to the breakfast table with all his gear packed, ready to leave. The farmer says to him, "I thought you were looking for steady work." "I was," he says, "but there's about four hours at night I don't get nothing done but sleep around here."

Two Swedes, fallers, come to work for a local company and cut trees quietly and diligently in the woods for ten years. Another man is hired at that time who follows behind them, bucking the trees up into logs for six years. One day the bucker quits. One old Swede says to the other, "When that young feller came, I knew he wouldn't stay."

Although the Swedes are often dealt with satirically in logger stories and yarns, the image of the much-admired hard worker comes through solidly. As well, stories are told extolling the ability of Swedes to drink more, lift more weight, and dip more snoose than others on their crews. One old logger told me with a straight face that in the old days, when any unidentified man on the crew was killed during the day, the first step in finding his identity was to pull

Standing on springboards to provide a level work platform above the brush on steep ground, two loggers in the 1920s begin falling a Douglas fir. Note the kerosene bottles (for cutting the pitch buildup on the saw-blade) below saw to the left and above to the right and the two double-bitted axes with which the fallers will make an undercut (indicated by the area stripped of bark) that will bring the tree down.

his lower lip out; if there was a hole the size of a quarter burned inside it (from a life of snoose use), the conclusion was that he was a Swede. The story is told that during the Depression an old Swede was working with a gypo outfit, setting chokers. The crew hadn't been paid for three months and everyone was complaining all day long as they worked. Finally, during lunch, the Swede took issue with his fellow workers: "What are you guys complaining for? I know there ain't no money, but we sure got a gude yob."

It is said by loggers that a wealthy man once went into the streets of Portland, Oregon, to see if he could find a likely recipient for some charitable assistance. He stopped people randomly on the street, asking them what they would do if he were to give them a million dollars. He stopped one young man who said, "Wow, if I had a million dollars, I'd buy myself a big house, some fancy cars, and I'd be able to get married and live in high style." This didn't satisfy the charitable intentions of the millionaire, so he looked further, and asked a second man, who responded, "Well, if I had a million dollars, I'd invest it in a chain of cheap, fast-food stores, and I'd make even more than a million dollars in profit right off." The wealthy man thought this was on the selfish side, and he looked further, stopping a logger to ask the same question. "What would I do with a million dollars? Well, I guess I'd just keep on logging till it was all gone." Ranchers in Utah tell the same story with appropriate revisions.

Humor in a Dangerous Setting

In many dangerous occupations humor provides, at least in part, a means of mitigating the daily fears and anxieties that beset the people who share the same concerns but who are hesitant to articulate their fears. Often loggers will describe a terribly dangerous job with hilarity; in the midst of terrible pressure and anxiety, when a job has been done in spite of insurmountable difficulties or odds, they will speak of themselves with hyperbolic modesty; on other occasions when anxiety threatens, they will break the tension with an unconscionable string of braggart's lies. In the examples that follow, one sees the delicacy of a "macho" humor that stretches a thin protective membrane over an abyss of fear and concern.

The lead horse on a horse logging crew gets spooked and begins prancing and kicking in thick brush, sending men and clods of dirt flying in all directions and endangering the lives of the driver and helper, who are trying to attach the drawbar to a chain around a precariously lodged log. After fighting the horse, slapping with the reins, yelling at the top of his lungs, and narrowly escaping being kicked several times, the "skinner" drops the reins, goes limp, turns to his companions, and says, in the mildest of voices, "I do believe this horse used to be in show business, don't you?"

There's this one old bucker, working out on the end of this big log stuck way out over the canyon. He gets way out near the end of this log and starts his cut, but he loses his balance, and falls way down into the canyon. Well, those boys was really concerned about him and they watched for a long time and finally they see him come crawling up through the brush. He dusts himself off, and just climbs back up on the log and says, "Lucky I was catty on my feet, or I mighta killed myself."

Well you know how them old toppers are—when they've been on the job for a few years they get started thinking that pretty soon their number is going to be up. They think maybe it's the next tree that'll split and kill them off. Lots of those guys get to be alcoholics and have to be taken off the job because they start getting careless. One thing and another, you know, and pretty soon, sure enough, they just get killed on the job. There was this one old topper we had working with us one time, and he was getting pretty old, but as toppers go, you know, he must have been feeling really old, 'cause he had been at it a long time. Well, we tried to get it out of him, how old he was, and finally he says, "Well, boys, you remember when Jesus walked on the water?" he says, "Well, I was right behind him on a spruce top."

When I was a choker-setter, we used to use up a pair of work gloves pretty quick. You have to have pretty heavy work gloves on to keep from getting all them metal jaggers from the cable into your hand. Well, just about the time you'd get one pair of gloves broke in, if you left them sitting around someplace, somebody would come along and run off with them. So we got in this big argument among a bunch of us choker-setters about who it was was stealing our gloves. And one day we were arguing about it while we were eating lunch and one old faller came walking by and says to us, "I don't know what you guys are moaning about; I've wore out more cork boots than all of you have gloves."

One time I was working on this side, and one of the fallers just got started into his cut with his power saw really wound up, and he stepped up on some brush, some loose brush near the tree where he was trying to make a stand, and he tripped and fell in toward the saw. Couple of us ran up to see if he was okay, and we yelled at him, "Did you hurt yourself?" But he came back, "No—I fell, but luckily it was toward my work."

Once we had this big old log snagged up there and the old hooker was down trying to help us fight that hang-up out of there, and we just couldn't get the log out any which way. While we was standing around, finally, a woodpecker come along and lit right on the log. The hooker says, "Well, go ahead and eat it up, I can't do anything with it."

Boy, we finally just had to leave that log in there; that country was so steep it'd wear the hairs off the bottom of a chipmunk's tail.

Walkaway: The Independent Logger

Complementary to the logger's close group interaction in a dangerous occupation is his insistence on independence. This is manifested in logger stories and custom, especially in the days of the logging camp, by the ease with which a worker might quit his job and go on down the road to another logging show. In the early 1900s, loggers often went more by their nicknames than by their legal names, sometimes in order to stay clear of the law. Some of the common nicknames are listed later in this chapter, but one particular character who shows up time and time again in logger legend is a man known only as Walkaway. According to the usual story, someone named Walkaway comes into camp, asks for a job, and is usually put to work driving a team or doing some kind of labor in conjunction with the younger crew members. Eventually, curiosity gets the best of a young man, and he begins pestering Walkaway about his real name. Walkaway refuses to talk about it. The young man then insists on knowing how he got the name Walkaway, at which point Walkaway hands him the reins to the team and walks into the woods. An hour or so later, when the foreman checks to see why the load hasn't come in yet, he finds the young man standing on the skidroad with the team and a load of logs. "Where's Walkaway?" the foreman demands. "I don't know," the young man replies. "I just asked him how he got his name, and he walked off into woods." "My God, he's done it again!"

> There was lots of guys who used to work in the logging shows up in Alaska who used to have a kind of calendar they used so they'd know when to move on: They'd keep this beer bottle next to their bed, see, and fill it up with cigarette butts, and when it got full, then they'd just move out. I heard there was this one guy called Down-the-Road Dugan; he kept a pair of corks in two different crummies so that no matter which one went down off the side first he could go with it. He was famous for walking off the job, and once he seen one of the fallers heading down the road to get his nosebag, you know, at lunchtime, and Dugan thought the guy was quitting the job and yelled, "Wait up, I'll go along with ya." Then he found out the guy was just going to lunch, but the foreman had already heard him and he yells down the road, "That's okay, Dugan, just keep on a-goin'!" And there was these old guys from the old days that would sit around at night and just brag about how much wandering around they'd done. There was this one old guy we had, and every once in a while he'd throw his head back and say, "Oh, I've dangled afar with a big stick and a small bundle." And there was this other old guy who'd get mad and fed up with the

job after a couple of weeks, but he wouldn't be able to quit, you know, because he needed the dough, see, so he'd just yell out every time when he fell into the sack at night, "Oh God, come down in the shape of a wild goose, and carry me off to hell!" There was another old-timer I knew, and if you just went up and asked him, "What state are you from?" he'd get all huffy and make believe he was mad, and he'd say, "I'm from all forty-seven and I'll be from this one if you'll just turn me loose until sundown."

There was this faller working in Washington some years ago and he gets this idea in his mind to quit early, see, so he just comes in from the woods and the foreman docks him five dollars for not bringing in his ax and springboard. Well, about eight years after that he comes back to the same camp as a hooker. Well, he works there for a while, then finally he gets fed up and decides to quit again, so this time he hauls in all the lines and the blocks from the woods, all the tree blocks, you know, guylines and all the gear, and loads all this gear and everything, even the donkey sled, on the flatcar and here he comes pulling into camp with the whole crew and gear riding the car. The boss threw a fit about it because they just got that one side set up, but the hooker says to him, says, "Last time I come through this camp I got docked five dollars for not bringing in my tools, so I don't want to lose anything when I quit this time."

Pranks: Inducting the Greenhorn

Pranks, often aimed at the new man on the crew, are among the most commonly encountered interactions in the woods. If one of the crew is newly married, some men will be willing to lose a considerable amount of pay during the day to gather all the insects they can cram into his lunch bucket after the noon break so that when he takes it home and his wife opens it, the house will swarm with grasshoppers, bees, spiders, and butterflies. Someone with mechanical ability on the crew will spend his spare time running a hot line from the electrical system of the crummy to the seat that will be occupied by the new man on the crew. The greenhorn will be sent to find a cable stretcher, a left-handed wrench, a sky hook, spark plugs for a diesel tractor, or a bundle of choker holes, all of which don't exist; on the other hand, he may be sent to find any number of obscene-sounding objects that actually do exist (a bucket of ape shit or a bull prick), although he may assume from the term that they do not. In the one case, he will get in trouble with the foreman or hooker for wasting his time on a fool's errand, and in the other he will be in trouble for not bringing back the needed implement. Since anyone is fair game for a prank, loggers learn to be very wary of each other, especially during the brief lull toward the end of lunchtime, when it is common for friends and colleagues to set fire to the fringed pants of a dozing crew member, hide his gloves, or place unmentionable substances in his hat. Of course the pranks played upon the newcomer are a means of incorporating him into the camaraderie of the logger society or forcing him out; they are not expected to engender fights, although it is assumed that the butt of any prank will properly become incensed. Perhaps the most delicious pranks of all are those that can be played on senior members of the crew, who should know better than to be caught. It is their prerogative to catch and thrash anyone associated with such a prank.

One typical trick played on newcomers to a logging crew in the Northwest is the axmanship test. The older men on the crew will gather around a stump and start a noisy argument about who can strike the ax a certain number of times in the same cut. The new man on the crew is asked, when he comes up to investigate, whether he thinks he can strike three or four ax blows into the same crack. He of course is interested in demonstrating his accuracy and usually agrees to try. Then he is told that the rules of the game require that he be blindfolded. It is too late for him to back out now, so he agrees to try his accuracy without being able to see. After the blindfold is put on, he is placed in front of the stump and given an ax; he brings the ax down sharply on the stump to whistles of amazement and general congratulations from the crew. Then he is told to do it a second time, and the comments of the crew make it clear that he must have hit the same spot with blind accuracy. When he raises his ax for the third blow, however, his gloves or his lunch box will be placed on the stump to be neatly dissected by his own unerring blow. People who cannot take pranks of this sort are sometimes ostracized, but perhaps more often they leave the crew for better pastures. What remains is a group whose members continually reaffirm their total dependence on each other by being able to joke and play pranks that would certainly be considered insulting, outrageous, and disastrous if applied to someone outside the group.

> We had this one trick we used to play on guys in the logging camp. We had these showers outside the bunkhouse, and everybody had to use them to get cleaned up before going into town for a good Saturday night, you know. The problem is that these showers had the taps for hot and cold water outside the stall, so a guy had to turn the water on and get it adjusted the way he liked it, and then climb in and take your shower. What we used to do was hide around the corner and wait until some guy got in and started lathering up in the shower and then we'd barricade him in there, turn off the hot water, and turn the cold water on full. Used to just leave him there to find his own way out, while the rest of us would go on down to town.

> Up in Washington when they used to ride to work on the logging trains, sometimes it would be a long while before you'd get into the side, so you would just doze for most of the trip until you got up to

work. Well, if you were riding in on a rainy morning, everybody would have slickers on, sort of like ponchos, see? Well, when some green man would start nodding off pretty well, the guys would nail down his slicker to the bed of the car, then pour kerosene down the back of it and light it on fire. Soon as the guy started getting warm, he'd wake up and see that his coat was on fire. But when he tried to jump up, see, his coat wouldn't move, because it's all nailed down. So the only way out was to rip off all the snaps, and by this time the guy was usually moving so fast he'd jump right off the train. Then of course he'd have to walk to work in the rain.

You know a steam donkey [engine] had a hose coming out of the boiler so it could be used for cleaning off the engine. Sometimes the guy around the landing would put mud in that hose and blow a load of it at some passing logger. One chaser loaded it up one day and let it go at the old wood buck who was carrying wood to fire up the donkey. A rock about the size of a marble hit the old wood buck right between the eyes. He dropped that wood and chased that chaser about four miles back to camp, then thrashed him so solid he couldn't work for two days.

Names and Expressions: Folk Poetry in the Woods

Although many loggers may feel themselves immune to or disinterested in the kind of poetry encountered in a school setting, nevertheless vivid expression confers a high status upon the user within the loggers' folk group. One seldom describes a person or a job without colorful and hyperbolic language. The following examples are only a few of the poetic expressions one might hear in the woods. Indeed, they are among the paler examples available.

Well, the problem with him is, he's a push-a-pen; he only works from the ears up. When I went in to see him about my problem, and I told him everything that I thought he ought to know, why, his heart swelled up just as big as a raisin.... Anyway, he's so dumb he couldn't feed guts to a Hudson Bay hound. I don't know why I expected anything out of him, because you could see right away he was dumb. His wife was the ugliest woman I ever saw—she was so buck-toothed she could eat apple pie out of a jug.

Well, I won't say I'm very smart, but I've been able to stay on my feet and alive in the woods for many a year. Probably I got some good advice early on, because when I left home Daddy said, "Don't walk under any boxcars or haul-backs if they are moving." But I know some guys who are really dumb in the woods, and I suppose they won't be around long unless they get into the management and save their lives that way. We got one guy in our company who's so dumb he don't know if he was punched or bored. He don't even know if Christ was crucified or killed with a marlin spike.

Two loggers, comparing the severity of work in steep country: "Why, down in the Rogue country, you know, that country is as steep as a cow's face." "That's nothing, I was working up in Alaska, one place, the side we had to work on for three months was as steep as the back of God's head."

Of course we had lots of good names for people back then. The boss, you know, was sometimes the Commander, or Nuts of the Outfit, or My Strength and Redeemer, of course not to his face. Some of the guys even had names for Jesus Christ, like Nazareth Blacky or Jerusalem Slim, and I remember a lot of the old-timers had nicknames like Pasco Slim, Ashland Ole; there was a couple of foremen called Roughhouse Pete and Panicky Bill. We had one climber called Billy the Monk, and there was rigging men like Brooklyn Joe, and of course Down-the-Road Dugan; and everybody knew about characters like Walkaway. And there was this one character everybody knew as Three-Day Jake—he never worked more than three days at any one location, but he just kept circulating from one camp to another. They always gave him some kind of job around the kitchen so they wouldn't have to keep training somebody.

Now there's one thing that I do know, and that is, the best logger is a cross between a gorilla and a mountain goat. Now you think about that.

Did I ever hear of anybody named "Down-the-Road Dugan"? What do you mean? *I'm* Down-the-Road Dugan!

Responses to Life in Camp

Logging camps are an increasing rarity in all parts of the country, but they remain a very strong feature of logger folklore, especially when older loggers reminisce about "the days when logging was tough" to their friends at lunch or over drinks on weekends. Somehow the logging camp has remained an essential icon of logger lore long after it has ceased to be a functional part of the actual logger setting. Probably because it was a time when men were gathered together for mutual living experiences over a considerable period of time while the occupation mushroomed, the camp functions in the folklore as a kind of symbol for the fraternity. However, it is not fashionable to be pleasantly nostalgic about the camps, for they were notorious in their inhospitality to human life: There were often vermin in the beds, outrageous smells in the bunkhouse, unpalatable (sometimes unrecognizable) food in the kitchen, and—the bane of masculine fantasy—there was always a dearth of women. The stories about camp life, then, feature the privations that once functioned, along with the hazards of the job, to weld loggers into a close society.

I worked one time in a camp where nobody knew what was happenin'; as far as I was concerned, that camp was a home for the old and a school for the young. They didn't know nothin' there, and I wasn't in any position to teach them. All they knew how to do was eat, and they ate so fast that no matter how close you came to the head of the chow line, there'd always be somebody coming out belching.

That was what they called a "fast camp"; they only had two signals—go ahead, and stop. There was three meals in that camp: cornmeal, oatmeal, and miss-a-meal.

Well, in a lot of these old camps, you know, they had this custom where guys would take turns doing the cooking. Of course, some camps had regular cooks in there, if there was a lot of guys and the company could afford to bring somebody in to do nothing but cook. But in some of the smaller camps, and on them gypo crews, why, the guys would just take turns doing the cooking. And sometimes they got this bargain going where each guy would cook until somebody complained about it, and then the guy that did the complaining would have to be the next cook. In a situation like that, see, nobody's any better a cook than anybody else, so if one guy's going along okay, everybody would just go along with that, no matter how bad it was, because usually nobody wanted to get stuck with all that kitchen work.

So there was this one guy who got cookin' in the camp for quite a while. Nobody liked the stuff he put on the table, but anyway they got used to it and they didn't complain, so he got stuck with it for quite a while. So he got real sick of that kitchen, and he got to looking for ways to make somebody complain about the food he set out. Well, he tried everything he could think of—put Tabasco into the dessert, put salt in the coffee, burned the meat, and did whatever he could to make somebody complain, but they wouldn't have no part of it. So he got real frustrated about it, and when he was out in the woods one day trying to hunt up some fresh camp meat, some "side-hill salmon," you know, he come on to this big pile of fresh moose pellets. A real stack of mountain muffins, you know? So he says to himself, "By God, them guys would complain if I fed 'em that for supper." So he scoops all these pellets up into his knapsack and hauls them off to the cook shack and he whups up this tremendous supper before the guys get there and trims it off with this big fine pie made out of them moose pellets. Well, that night all them guys came in, sat down, and gritted their teeth and waited for the garbage. But then they got this big meal which was better than anything they ever had while he had been cookin'. And then to top it off, he brought out that big pie and laid it on the middle of the table and told them guys to dig in. So of course they did and they laid into that pie like it was going out of style. Course, they all starts gagging, spitting, and turning green, and one guy keeled over right off the bench, and just before he passed out he yelled, "My God! Moose turd pie!—*Good,* though!"

Sex

Although loggers seem to agree that sex is one of the favorite topics of conversation and joking among loggers, they are extremely hesitant about expressing their thoughts on the matter outside the confines of the esoteric group. One elderly logger, for example, was willing to allow his repertoire of songs to be recorded and placed in an archive only with the stipulation that it would never be played for a woman under twenty-one, because he was afraid some of his own grandchildren might discover his relationship to songs he had carefully sheltered them from during his life. While sex is a common topic among many loggers, it is a considerable impropriety to talk about it in mixed company or in print. Typically, loggers will adopt a polite, almost hyper-literary style when talking about sex, or else they will attempt to avoid the subject altogether when talking with outsiders. Said one logger to me, "Sex? I leave it alone. Why, some women will get pregnant if their husband goes by the bedpost on a motorcycle with his coveralls on." Another logger recalls how delicately an African American hook tender he had known revealed the nature of his ethnic background: "Well, you know I'm really an Indian. My grandma was ice-fishing and a Black man come out there on the ice to see what she was doing. Well, she had moccasins on, and he had corks, and my old man was the result of their conversation."

It would be interesting to speculate on the motivations behind logger diffidence on the matter of sex when they are speaking to people outside their own group. No doubt the subject can be approached fruitfully from a psychological perspective as well as from the sociological observation that many loggers also are members of a larger cultural group with northern European, perhaps Puritan, backgrounds that still urge a conservative attitude on the propriety of such topics in mixed company. For loggers, there is an intensification of the distinction made between propriety on the job and propriety in town because many operations and items in the woods are referred to by sexual and anatomical names and because, while the men are trading stories and jokes among themselves, sex is a very prominent topic. The completely different dialect used when loggers come home is, for our purposes at least, indicative of their own awareness of an internal dynamic system shared without question by loggers, a system of expression so special and vivid as to require innocent outsiders to be shielded from it. It also demonstrates an awareness that context controls style and meaning.

Of course, in recent times women have been entering many "traditionally" male occupations, and they have found, generally, that they are held to the same rules of conduct and vocabulary. That is, a woman must become a logger in loggers' terms in order to be accepted. A woman I know got a job in the woods in the 1970s. Her letter to me shows the obligation she felt to make it in the woods, her sensitivity to the importance of logger lore, and her awareness of how her gender had an effect upon her relationship to the crew:

> I have now spent six months with loggers. It was tough, but of course they are my kind of people, and in retrospect, I can see I loved it. I took copious notes, although they seemed superficial, juvenile. For example, I noted in January that the hairs in my nose froze every day, and I was literally constipated by fear (they drive like madmen). Loggers don't use Saran Wrap on their sandwiches—they use wax paper so they can grill them in the warming fires. I took a bad fall while scaling one day in snow and ice—slipped in a clear cut of piss fir and fell 30 feet. One of the fallers, Shitty Pants by name, called out to me, and the energy to yell, the strength required for me to yell back, "I'm FINE!" was beyond belief, as I was hurt so bad. Once I realized the ribs weren't broken, and got the blood stopped, I buried myself in the branches and cried. I quit taking a bath after work because I was so offended by the ring around the tub. I ruined one pair of suspenders from peeing on them. The men like to say SHIT and get it over with. Some of them need for me to say SHIT, too. Sometimes I say PISSED, because I'm so conscious of SHIT. Today a few FUCKS flew around the crew bus, and everyone watched me very closely....
>
> From a folklore point, the work is fascinating. I'm avidly collecting hand signals. I tend to spend a lot of time with the old-timers, and as always, they love to talk to an interested woman. There are some decided advantages to my sex. One of my favorite stories is told by an old faller, who describes being chased by a bull, across a large meadow, without a tree in sight. He ran and ran, and could see the bull was gaining on him. His fear grew, and no matter how fast he ran, the bull got closer until he could finally feel hot breath behind him. With his last bit of strength, the faller scrambled up a tree. At this point I cried, "But you said there were no trees !" "Well, there had to be!" he roared.

Popular Belief and Custom

Much of this folklore implies that loggers participate in a chiefly male, occupationally oriented group only. Especially the exclusiveness of sexual topics in their folklore might indicate that they share very little of their own ideas and worldview with their family or other members of their community. But the folklorist must look at the total context in which a logger lives to determine the extent to which the logger also participates in a somewhat larger folk grouping, that of a community of individuals related to the logging industry. Loggers' picnics, loggers' carnivals (in which loggers—and sometimes their wives—participate in competitive games based on occupational skills), various kinds of social fraternities that include entire families and towns, public reciting of logger poetry at county fairs, should be taken as evidence that the loggers' sense of themselves is not limited strictly to the inner circle of the occupation itself. If the folklorist interviews the wives and families of loggers, a larger and richer picture of logger folklore dynamics will emerge. For example, many women who raised their families in the logging towns of the Northwest during the 1920s recall the very tight and cheerful community support for almost any individual in trouble, any family in crisis, any young couple at their wedding. Mrs. Vintie Holt recalled that when a marriage occurred in an Oregon logging community in the 1920s, the people of the town would usually circle the newlyweds' house, everyone holding hands, and serenade them far into the night. On some occasions, of course, a shivaree was held: friends, both male and female, would descend on the newlyweds' home, abduct them both, and place them in a wheelbarrow and parade them through the camp to the accompaniment of singing and laughter. Thus, even though the newlywed husband might expect mean pranks to be played on him in the woods by his male colleagues, the community as a whole played a friendly, supportive role. The loggers in the community, of course, took part in both sides of these activities. It would be unfair to draw even the barest delineations of logger folk dynamics without taking the specific and larger dimensions of life in logging communities into consideration.

Out in the woods among the loggers, of course, there were the usual popular beliefs about bad luck, forebodings of disaster, means of avoiding accident and misfortune, and the like. Loggers had a widespread belief that if a man couldn't sleep at night, or if he awoke with cold hands or cold feet, it meant he would have an accident at work. If a logger had one of these presentiments, it would be common for him not to go to work the next day and everyone would understand. If a wife knew of her husband's hunch, she would encourage him to stay home from work on such a day. Thus, the belief had two sides—the aspect experienced by the worker in the woods, and the response recognized and encouraged by the members of his immediate community at home.

A related popular belief among loggers in the Northwest is that accidents, especially deadly accidents, are most likely to occur during the last few days—and most likely on the very last day—of a man's employment. This kind of belief, experienced by the men in the woods, caused a considerable amount of anxiety during a man's last days of employment; apprehension under these circumstances was recognized by other loggers not as a sign of fear, but as a functional, normal aspect of finishing a dangerous life in the woods. Obviously there is a comment here on the assumptions made by loggers on the probabilities of a man being able to survive his employment in the woods. The community side of this belief is reflected in the custom among many logging foremen of firing a man before his appointed termination day and paying him up through the day he would normally have quit. This allows a man to forgo the apprehension and the psychological danger of the last day at work. Vintie Holt pointed out to a folklore field worker that her husband had had cold hands and sleepless nights two days before he was killed—on what was to have been his last day of work in the woods. It is certainly not far-fetched to suggest that any anxiety generated by these beliefs may actually contribute to enough malaise during the last days on the job virtually to ensure that a person might make a fatal mistake during a delicate maneuver. Be that as it may, the logger, in male company—perhaps over a drink—would characteristically pass it off as a macabre joke: "Did I ever hear of getting killed on the last day of work? Well, I guess if you got killed, it would be your last day of work, wouldn't it? [Laughs.] Anyhow, you know, no matter whether you're injured or killed, they leave you there by the cold deck and take you in with the last load of the day, so you won't lose out on the day's pay. And no matter what, a day's pay is a day's pay."

In these examples of logger folklore, the actual dynamics are not spelled out. Rather, they are to be inferred from the topics, styles, language, and attitudes expressed in the lore itself. The examples follow the lines suggested by loggers themselves, grouped together by topic rather than genre, and with a considerable overlap in intent and meaning. It is only proper that this should be so, for real dynamics operate in the interactions among people, not as categories invented by the observer. Even so, the dynamic system suggested in these examples needs to be augmented by the reader through further reading and field research; the dynamics themselves will change somewhat according to the age of the loggers one interviews, the particular kind of trees they cut, the part of the country, the methods of logging used, and so on. What is given here, then, is only a start: a clear indication that loggers as a group do conceive of themselves as a group, and largely through the live folklore they share with each other within the immediate circumstances of their job.

Folklorist Robert S. McCarl discovered that smokejumpers in the woods of Idaho held and expressed many of the same values as those he found among urban firefighters in Washington, D.C., but that their differences in environment and techniques also accounted for many variations. As well, he showed that, like workers in all hazardous occupations, the firefighters played serious pranks on newcomers to ensure that only the most stalwart would stay on the job—since lives depended on a deep level of trust. Moreover, like members of virtually all occupations—urban or rural—firefighters and loggers recognize a traditional *canon* of work technique which vividly shows who "knows the ropes" and who doesn't. Occupational folklore can be quite specific, or it can be shared among similar occupations; in the same way, the folklore of any single folk group does not exist exclusively of other traditional practices with which any given individual may be familiar by virtue of "membership" in a number of close groups.

Loggers and firefighters may also belong to other close folk groups whose contexts will act similarly upon members under other unique situations shared. For one, a specific logger will no doubt participate in family folklore; he may also share ethnic folklore, if he is, say, of Swedish descent and still participates in Swedish traditions; he might also be a Mormon, and on that basis share with other Mormons such expressions as J. Golden Kimball stories, Nephite legends, esoteric stories of marvels, providences, revelations, and the like; if he is a life-long resident of Oregon, he may furthermore share in the regional suspicion of people from out of state (especially from California) and may use a whole battery of regionalisms—such as *webfoot* to denote someone who lives in the rainy part of the state west of the Cascade Mountains. And, of course, like my former student, the logger might be a woman and share close associations and values with other women. In the 1980s and 1990s, Oregonians in the area where logging forms a large part of the economy have rallied together to fight what they consider outside interference by environmentalists trying to protect animals or plants which—in the view of the logging community—are of lesser value than the trees or the loggers. One sees recipes for Spotted Owl quiche and T-shirts (some of them home-made) advertising big red and white cans of Cream of Spotted Owl Soup. Each of these groupings provides a relatively high context situation in which group members recognize each other and talk to each other by using that special cultural dialect that binds them together. Folk groups may be exclusive, but they are not mutually exclusive.

THE MULTIPLICITY OF TRADITION

The probability that most people belong to more than one folk group is a consideration that remains central in the study of folklore dynamics; it requires us to recognize that a given person may have a wide repertoire of potential traditional dynamic interactions, each of which is set in motion by certain particular live contexts. The logger folk group as perceived and participated in by the loggers themselves is primarily male and occupational in its live setting. The insider recognizes and performs for other insiders a certain variety of appropriate jokes, gestures, pranks, and speech customs. It is these live, traditional interactions and not the cutting of trees per se that defines the logger as a member of a folk group.

We watch for the same kind of issues when we look at other folk groups suggested by factors other than occupational. In other words, we will want to recognize that it is not theology that makes a Mormon a member of a folk group, it is the dynamic traditional interactions a Mormon shares with other members of the same faith (customs, proverbs, jokes, slang terms), factors distinctive to a sense of "us." Similarly, in the case of ethnic groups, the question of whether the group is a folk group will rest not on surnames or skin color or genetics but on the existence of a network of dynamic traditional interactions. An African American who does not participate in any Black traditional systems is not a functioning member of any Black folk group. Anglo Americans who *do* participate fully (language, custom, dance, food, etc.) in an American Indian tribe may be said to be members of that folk group—whether or not their grandmothers were Cherokee princesses—while someone who is genetically 100 percent Native American may not be a member of a tribal folk group if he or she does not participate in its folk customs. Thus we look at the nature of the dynamic interaction, not at superficial details. How is a person said to be a member of a Serbian American folk group: by having a Serbian name and learning to dance the *kolo* in college or by participating fully in the ongoing vernacular traditions of an American Serbian community? Obviously, the latter.

Just as obviously, because one chooses to join some groups but is born into others, participating in these ethnic traditions is not in the same dimension as participating in the loggers' occupation. Where can we look, then, to find in the ethnic group the dynamic equivalent of occupational lore? What is it that they "do" together that is traditionally distinctive enough to provide a basic recognition of an "us"?

Dynamics of Ethnicity

One of the best areas of ethnic focus is traditional food lore, partly because people change their inherited tastes in food very slowly, partly because when people eat at home, they are with a close group whose members share a high family or ethnic context. Especially in the case of immigrant groups—who are well known for their tendency to maintain traditions which may have changed or disappeared in the original home country—family meals and meals shared with other immigrants become celebrations of ethnicity, practically sacramental assertions of a continuation of an "us." Watch the ethnic foods that come forth at a Scandinavian or a Greek wedding, at a Portuguese fishing celebration on a saint's day, at a Japanese funeral, at a New England Thanksgiving. Ask what recipes are passed along family or ethnic lines. What foods do you connect with your ancestry? Why? And when? It is no accident that many multicultural communities have found the local cookbook one of the only satisfactory ways to describe and celebrate the reality of local culture variation. For example, as a Bicentennial project the Butte Silver-Bow Bicentennial Commission in Montana issued *Butte's Heritage Cookbook,* a rich compilation of ethnic recipes along with stories about their national origins and about the people who brought them to Butte, a mining town of incredibly varied cultural backgrounds.

I have suggested that one of the best ways to detect and experience folk group dynamics is to observe how and why the members of a given group recognize each other. What cues tell insiders they are dealing with other insiders as insiders? What cues tell outsiders they are operating in a different set of assumptions than their own? If we take folk foods as a point of focus, how can we be sure that we are dealing with real traditional dynamics as compared to commercial interests or the perfunctory enjoyment of ethnic foods by multicultural hobbyists? After all, not everyone who eats *chow yuk* is Chinese; not everyone who eats matzoh-ball soup is Jewish; not everyone who eats *teriyaki* chicken is Japanese. The dynamics tell us the difference, for it is not so much that you are *what* you eat, but you may be partly defined by *how* you eat, and *why*, and *when*.

Esoteric Eating: Japanese Americans

One possible start is to observe a picnic where most participants are members of the same ethnic group. What do they do and what do they bring that one might not see if the occasion were a mixed group where others' tastes are central? At first, one might notice the usual hot dogs, hamburgers, and soft drinks; then, as focus improves, one might be puzzled by some unknown substances: What are those things wrapped up in grape leaves? What holds those balls of rice together? Those things look like chicken, but they're dark brown. What's that yellow stuff the old-timers are drinking? And after the questions comes the tasting, which in the case of ethnic foods is far more complicated than the chemical action of food on the taste buds. If one suggests eating raw fish to a group made up of Japanese Americans and European Americans, half the room will smile and the other half will look sick. What accounts for this?

I once watched an artist trying to explain to an audience of teachers what he felt art should "do" to the viewer. His effort was received with polite boredom until he brought out a fresh lemon, cut it, and began sucking one half with considerable relish. The audience's immediate response was to pucker, squint, grimace, and shudder—obviously because they recognized the taste, and the visual stimulation of seeing someone else having the experience was enough to cause them to have it, or at least to have a vicarious but real response to it. Ethnic foods—their appearance, smell, and taste, as well as their customary construction and deployment—create a similar response of recognition, and in addition to personal tastes there is the further dimension of the experience of belonging to a close group with whose members one has shared and enjoyed the same responses many times before. This experience is strong evidence of the continued vitality of folk dynamics.

Ingredients and Terminology

What might we find at an ethnic picnic that triggers such cultural reflexes in the insider but inspires only questions in the outsider? A close look at the typical foods taken to a Japanese American picnic will indicate the extent to which occasional recreational foods may lead us to more interesting observations on the relations between food and folk dynamics. The most distinctive items at a Japanese American picnic fall into a few particular categories: *gohan* (cooked rice; uncooked short-grained rice is called *okome)*, otsukemono* (pickled vegetables), *sushi* (various finger-foods made with rice seasoned with vinegar), and *teriyaki* (various meats baked, barbecued, or broiled in soy sauce). Of these, *gohan* is easily the most important, not only because many of the picnic foods are made with cooked short-grained rice, but because it is usually served with all other foods as well. Its important position in Japanese foodlore is apparent in the use of the word *gohan* to mean food in general; if someone calls "Gohan!" it is the equivalent of the American "Soup's on!" At a picnic, the rice is seldom eaten in a bowl; rather, it is made into round or triangular balls, usually with a salted item in the center (such as *umeboshi,* a pickled plum).

Sushi uses *gohan* as its primary ingredient, but it stands in Japanese American folk tradition as a separate category because of the distinctive way in which the rice is mixed with other items. One of the most popular forms of *sushi* is *norimaki. Nori* is a kind of paper made from dried sea algae; vinegar-soaked rice is laid out across the sheet in a small mound, other colored ingredients are added (usually in uneven numbers), and the whole item is rolled into a cylinder about one and one half or two inches in diameter. The roll is cut into cross sections about one inch thick, which are then stacked on a plate. Looking at the cross section of *norimaki,* one sees first the dark green "seaweed" sheet on the outside, then a white circular rice filling in the middle of which are usually three or five colored ingredients. Another kind of *sushi* features a small, hand-sized pocket of fried bean curd *(age)* into which the rice has been packed. Since this kind of *sushi* was offered to the fox deity (Kitsune) in Japan for prosperity in business, some older Issei still refer to it as *kitsunezushi;* usually in America the term is *agezushi.* Balls made of this specially cooked rice are referred to as *nigirizushi,* from the verb *nigiri,* "to grasp." Still another kind, which features other chopped-up items mixed in with the rice, is referred to as *chirashizushi (sushi* made of mixed separate items).

An extensive use of meat in Japan is fairly recent due to the early Buddhist influence, which recommended against using animal substances in human food. Japanese Americans, however, seem to have adopted the American propensity for meat-eating, but in their own traditional way they have maintained distinctive Japanese methodologies for producing the appropriate taste. One of these is the process called *yaki,* literally "roasting, baking, broiling." If vegetables and meat are slowly stir-cooked together in a large heated pan, the term used is *sukiyaki;* because this dish requires elaborate preparation and careful cooking, it is seldom taken on picnics, but it is commonly used in the home when special guests visit. Pieces of any meat may be chopped into sizes easily handled with chopsticks or the fingers and cooked separately in a thick mixture

Sushi is made of vinegared rice in combination with various colored ingredients. *Makizushi* is rolled in a paper called *nori* that is made from a sea algae; the preparation involves a process that is taught within families by literal hands-on experience. Here, four generations of a Japanese American family make *sushi* together for New Year's 1996, coached by their mother, grandmother, and great-grandmother, Chiyoe Kubota.

During New Year's 1996, great-granddaughter Sachiye Lubahn helps her "Baba" evaporate the sweet rice vinegar from the *sushi* rice with a fan that has been used by the family since the 1930s.

A sheet of *nori* is toasted lightly over a stove burner before being rolled into *sushi*.

Vinegared rice with colored strips of ingredients, which will appear in the center of the roll, are placed on a sheet of *nori* and rolled up with a bamboo placemat.

The density of the roll (hence its capacity to hold together) is controlled by the consistency of tension during rolling. The "feel" of it is passed on manually by Miiko Toelken to daughter Chiyo in 1977.

The same concern with proper technique is shown by her great-grandmother's attention to Sachiye Lubahn's work in 1996.

Usually, *makizushi* rolls are cut so that the central ingredients (usually 3, 5, or 7 in number, except when prepared for funerals, when four colors are used) form a colorful core; but special molds are now used which can produce a flower or some other design.

of soy sauce, sugar, and other flavorings; this process is known as *teriyaki* and is a typical way of fixing meats for picnics.

Of extreme interest and importance to the folklorist is that Japanese Americans of the second and third generations, most of whom consider themselves far more American than Japanese, seldom use the Japanese language as a means of communication. Of course, some second-generation people who grew up speaking Japanese at home use it when talking to their parents, but for the most part, the Japanese language is not in everyday use among members of the Japanese American folk group. Nonetheless, almost all members of this group, regardless of generation, recognize and use all the Japanese words for folk foods, as well as for items and implements used in their preparation, and they are aware of distinct cultural attitudes concerning their arrangement and seasonal use.

For example, Japanese Americans use the honorific prefix o- for many of the foods, some even attaching the form to *gohan,* unaware that *go-* is already an honorific. *O-gohan,* while technically nonstandard Japanese, reveals an ongoing concern for propriety in traditional foods. Another similar element is the use of traditional Japanese phrases before and after eating, usually spoken with head bowed quickly, palms together: *itadakimasu,* indicating the intention of accepting food, and *gochisosama,* a compliment to the cook and a gesture of respect for food generally. This is another key indication that for this group of people foods are indeed a cultural link as well as a method of survival.

The foods one might find at a Japanese American picnic are also used centrally at all occasions of import to the community: weddings, funerals, holidays *(Obon, Hanamatsuri,* New Year's) and at any celebration or special event where visitors or dignitaries may be present. Thus we may say that the very presence of these foods indicates that a dynamic folk interaction is taking place. Of course, an insider (a Japanese American) would note further the qualities of the foods and the traditional aspects of their preparation and appearance. Just as the loggers' recognition of each other is based not simply on recognizing the clothes but how they are worn, the Japanese American recognition of folk food in a live, dynamic context is not based exclusively on the foods themselves but on how they are done (that is, whether it is obvious they were produced properly and appropriately by traditional standards). Asked what she considers really distinctive about Japanese American traditional food, a Nisei grandmother from Ogden, Utah, Mrs. Chiyoe Kubota, answered that the most important elements would be (1) the foods and ingredients themselves, (2) the flavor, (3) the arrangement, (4) *tsukurikata,* "how the food is made," and (5) *kirikata,* "how the food is cut." The matter of flavor is distinctive, of course, because of the various spices and materials used, many of which are indeed imported from Japan even today: *shoyu* (soy sauce), *ajinomoto* (monosodium glutamate), *shoga* (ginger), *mirin* (sweet cooking sake), *sake* (fortified rice wine), *miso* (fermented bean paste, either white or red). Not only do these distinctive seasonings provide particular flavors not found in other ethnic foods, but their precise applications to different kinds of foods can be learned only by lengthy practice and association with traditional cooks who have themselves learned the process usually in their own families. Thus Mrs. Kubota can say that the taste, methods, and arrangements are distinctive aspects of Japanese American folk foods; she does mention that the recognition of ingredients is basic, but she insists that their preparation and especially their looks are the keys to the recognition of ethnic dynamics.

Still other foods should be mentioned here as distinctively used by Japanese Americans in traditional foodways. There is a widespread use of Japanese green tea *(ocha)*, a preference for short-grained rice (partly because it is more glutinous and sticks together better than long-grained rice, which may be puzzling to those European Americans who have been led to believe that rice should be dry and flaky). Japanese Americans enjoy *umani* (vegetables seasoned and cooked together in a stew), *sashimi* (sliced raw fish, usually sea bass or tuna, served with hot mustard or horseradish), octopus—either raw or cooked, squid—either raw or cooked, *manju* (a sweet bean paste bun), *yokan* (hardened sweet bean paste or jelly made into solid rectangles, or sliced and eaten with tea), *tofu* (soy bean curd, often cut up into small squares and used as an ingredient in everything from soup to *sukiyaki*), and *omochi* (a rather dense rice cake made from pounded, cooked sweet rice).

Food and Community

Omochi is certainly one of the more interesting folk foods from the standpoint of the esoteric scholar, for it is made of a special kind of rice and is produced in a communal manner. A large mortar *(usu)* made of stone, wood, or concrete is filled with steamed sweet rice, which is then pounded with large wooden hammers *(kine)*. Two or sometimes three people take turns hammering the rice with these large mallets, timing their actions to the rhythms of a song sung by all present. At a certain beat in each measure, a woman reaches into the mortar and moves the glob of rice so it will not stick. Each movement must be timed carefully or the woman's hands would easily be crushed by the mallets; she wets her hands on one beat, reaches in and moves the rice on another, and each person wielding a wooden hammer strikes on a certain beat. People in the community take turns at all these jobs, although usually the most knowledgeable and agile woman is allowed to retain the job of turning the rice. Some communities have begun to use a *mochi*-machine more recently, but the communal, celebratory element is still retained even so. When the *omochi* has been sufficiently pounded to a consistent rubbery pulp, it is formed into small, flat rice cakes ranging from about four inches in diameter down to two inches. These cakes are sold to be given away to friends and relatives at New Year's time; they are placed in a small stack on the family altar or in front of pictures of the family ancestors, and one small *mochi* cake is put into the bottom of each bowl of the special soup *(ozoni)* eaten on New Year's morning.

Dense, glutinous rice cakes eaten by Japanese and Japanese Americans at New Year are produced traditionally by pounding steamed sweet rice with wooden mallets called *kine* in a mortar called an *usu*. Here, *nisei* internees at the Topaz (Utah) Relocation Center make *mochi* during their incarceration during World War II. *Mochi* cakes are placed on the family altar, offered up in local Buddhist churches, used during the New Year season as snacks (with soy sauce), and appear at the bottom of the *ozoni*, a fish-based soup served early on New Year's Day. Photo courtesy of the Utah State Historical Society.

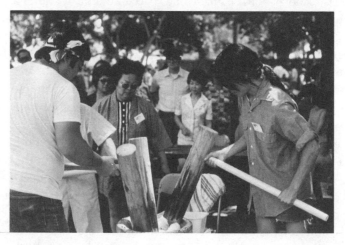

Although *mochi* is normally made indoors during the winter just before the New Year, Japanese Americans participating in the Smithsonian's Festival of American Folklife on the national Mall in Washington, D. C., in July, 1975, were willing to demonstrate their ongoing custom out of season before interested strangers. Photo by Miiko Toelken.

The basic "tools" for making *sushi* are the *shamoji* (wooden rice paddle), *handai* (cedarwood bucket), and *sudare* (bamboo placemat for rolling).

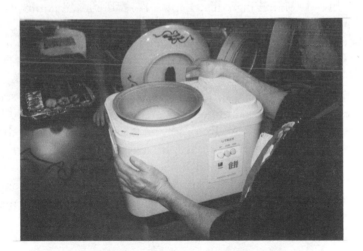

Modern Japanese and their *nisei* and *sansei* relatives in the United States make *mochi* at home using an oscillating machine; but even though the hammers and the rhythmic singing have been replaced by technology, the customary use of *mochi* has been extended and strengthened because more people can accomplish it.

In this kind of custom, the dynamics of the folk group can be seen vividly. Not only does the sweet rice function as a means of feeding the community on a larger level, but it is used symbolically to feed the spirits of the family's ancestors. In addition, it is the occasion for a communal gathering, and it is the larger symbol of the community's own recognition of its long-term kinship with rice and all the seasonal and religious observances connected with it.

A number of cooking implements have retained their Japanese names in America. Commonly known are such terms as *shamoji,* a wooden spatula for serving rice; *hashi,* chopsticks; *sudare,* a bamboo mat used for rolling the *norimaki; suribachi,* a grooved ceramic mortar for grinding sesame seeds and the like; *handai,* a round wooden tray with a three- or four-inch vertical edge used for mixing and seasoning *gohan* for *sushi.*

Custom and Number

Foodlore of course entails much more than simply the culinary techniques of presenting familiar ethnic tastes. Custom and cultural aesthetics also play a large role in how foods are produced. In the case of Japanese Americans, one very strong cultural element brought from Japan dictates that in arrangements of things such as flowers and foods, any individual but related components should be presented in uneven numbers, typically, three, five, and seven. In the case of *norimaki,* the seasoned rice that is rolled up in a sheet of dried sea algae with several colored ingredients at the core, the usual family variety has three colored segments, while festive occasions call for five and very special occasions (like weddings) require seven. The colors themselves originally had particular meanings, but the one that remains in Japanese American folklore is red, which connotes prosperity and good luck. The red ingredient in *norimaki* is usually made with shredded shrimp dyed red. When such food is served at a funeral, however, four central ingredients are used because the word for four, *shi,* sounds exactly like the word for death, *shi* (although, of course, their characters are quite different). The use of four central ingredients in *norimaki* is considered appropriate, therefore, at funerals, while it is considered inappropriate and perhaps even insulting or shocking at another time: one would never serve *norimaki* with four central colored ingredients at a picnic or at a wedding.

The number four, in fact, is avoided whenever there is a reference to such human matters as birthdays or anniversaries; many Japanese Americans, following the older Japanese tradition, either downplay or omit fourth birthdays, fourth anniversaries, and fortieth birthdays. Similarly, in counting the generations of Japanese Americans, one would normally use the regular Japanese words *ichi* (one), *ni* (two), *san* (three), *shi* (four), but the very fact one is counting human generations requires a shift from *shi* to *yon,* an alternative word for four taken from another numerical system. Thus the first generation, the immigrants from Japan, are called *issei* (literally, "first people" or "first generation"), the second generation *nisei,* the third generation *sansei,* and the fourth, *yonsei.* The customary attitudes toward the number four are thus reflected not only in the production of Japanese folk foods, but throughout the culture generally. This further demonstrates the deep connection between foods and other world-view aspects of an entire culture. In Japan, while hotels usually omit the fourth floor and people avoid giving gifts or packaging items in fours, the "rule" banning four ingredients in sushi is relaxing. But it is kept alive in the United States probably because it represents ethnic meaning.

A Year of Food

Another example of dynamic vitality in Japanese American food folklore is the existence of a traditional food calendar, which allows us to see the importance of the traditional foods not only in and of themselves, as just described, but as they fit into the larger customary observances during the year. This is a common phenomenon in all cultures, of course; for example, most Americans find it at least familiar to think of turkey in connection with Thanksgiving. Turkey may be eaten at any other time, but turkey with all the trimmings is by tradition more appropriate for some families on Thanksgiving Day than any other food. There are great differences among American subcultures as to what foods are appropriate on which holidays; even the concept of the kinds of foods appropriate at certain times of the day will vary considerably. For some rural New Englanders, for example, apple pie is a common breakfast food while for most other Americans it is a dessert. For many southerners, it's not breakfast if it doesn't include grits. In the case of the Japanese American food calendar, we will expect to find particular foods associated with certain holidays, and we will not be surprised to find a substantially different attitude toward the foods that are eaten at certain times of day within those holidays.

One of the best examples of this is the New Year's Day custom of eating *ozoni* soup with one's family the very first thing in the morning. This soup is made of a fish stock and contains some green vegetables (such as Chinese cabbage or spinach), *kamaboko* (a fish cake, sliced), and at the bottom a soft, dense, rubbery cake of *mochi.* For those European Americans who spend New Year's Eve drinking heavily, this would be a very strange if not dubious treat for New Year's morning. For the Japanese American, however, it sets the stage within the close family group for an entire day of eating traditional foods, many of which feature fish—indicative of fertility—and the color red, which is appropriate to ideas of good fortune associated by the Japanese with the New Year. An inventory of the entire day's activities will appear in Chapter 4, but here we should note that New Year's Day for Japanese Americans is a kaleidoscope of those same traditional foods that they might find in use sporadically throughout the year. It is as if New Year's Day is a conscious celebration of ethnicity through food, of shared traditionality through the dynamics of group members sitting down to eat continuously for the entire day as they visit from house to house. This conscious use of traditional foods as a means of maintaining and strengthening cultural interactions among members of a folk group certainly indicates not only the group's vitality, but the position of food traditions in the study of its folklore.

Dynamics and Identity

As we would no doubt find in the case of most immigrant groups in America, there must be a number of reasons for maintaining food customs, but the case of the Japanese Americans in particular illustrates a set of dynamics that seems to reach beyond mere sociological observations about group identity. In fact, we might have expected the extinction of many of these food customs because of the very scarcity of several of the ingredients, especially during the Second World War, when relationships with Japan were fractured. Moreover, the Japanese Americans, especially in the second and third generations, have been extremely eager to prove themselves Americans without substantial foreign attachments. Many of the foods discussed here are so exotic as to call attention to themselves as foreign, a possible negative factor for those Japanese Americans who wished to become clearly Americanized. What can account, then, for the maintenance of strong Japanese food customs among people who themselves sought to strengthen their American identity? Why didn't they give it all up and adopt the generalized American food system? Surely the dynamics of folklore give us one of the best answers for these questions.

For one thing, it is important to note that in Japanese custom the family, not the individual, is the basic unit of society. The earliest creation myths are founded upon family relationships, the early feudal governments of Japan were based on family systems, and, indeed, in Japan today the family is still often seen as a microcosm of the country, of corporations, and of the universe.

The most central single family custom is sitting down to eat together. The concept of the family as the central unit of stability and normality has led to a very strong set of traditions within which each Japanese learns what is right and what is wrong both as an individual and as a member of a culture. Eating traditional foods together with other Japanese people is one very powerful way of reaffirming one's position within the total family system. No wonder, then, that among the very earliest Japanese immigrants to America were farmers who immediately set about growing Japanese vegetables and producing Japanese condiments for the other Japanese in America.

Apparently these earliest immigrants stuck together very tightly as a community, and most of them, at least by their own admission, were planning to make money and eventually return with it to Japan. Of course, as time went on, many decided to settle in the United States and get married; many of these people sent for brides from Japan so that, as nuclear families began to be established on the West Coast, the parent, or *issei,* generation was pretty solidly Japanese in its orientation and food customs.

As the *nisei* generation came along, in accordance with Japanese family custom, the children spent a good deal of time at home, usually speaking Japanese with their parents and speaking English only in school. And even now, in the third and fourth generations, it is customary for Japanese Americans to live rather close to their *issei* parents and grandparents. Thus they maintain a close family system in which the sharing of traditional foods is one of the few strong ties between the immigrant generation and the present Americans of Japanese descent. Further, not many generations have passed in this immigrant group when compared to the generations of European groups who settled the eastern seacoast two and three hundred years ago. Even in those older groups ethnic foods are still culturally functional, and we would expect them to be even more so in the case of more recent immigration, especially among people with such strong and continuing family ties.

For many Japanese Americans, Buddhism has further encouraged the generations to live together rather than separately and has stressed filial piety as the basic means of maintaining stability and security in the world. This has strengthened still further the tendency of the younger generation to follow the older ways, and in a culture where traditional cooking is so central to cultural recognition, we would expect this force to have had a considerable impact on maintaining food traditions as well.

Certainly, as Marvin Opler and others have pointed out, there must have been an intensification of Japanese folklore during the internment years of the Second World War, when most Japanese American citizens and their resident alien parents were placed in civilian concentration camps, mostly in the American West. Opler studied the conditions in the Tule Lake internment center and concluded that Japanese folklore had experienced a strong revival because of the tensions and anxieties of internment; after the war, he contended, Japanese Americans went their own way and dropped a good many, if not most, of these strongly Japanese traditions. But we should note that the Tule Lake camp was the one camp where Japanese nationals were segregated for their return to their home country, as well as where Japanese Americans who openly favored the Japanese cause in the war were sent. Under these circumstances, we might expect nationalistic Japanese tradition to have run strong.

But the case is even more complicated, for what Opler and others unwittingly encountered is that we knew little of Japanese American folklore before the Second World War, largely because the Japanese and Japanese Americans reserved most of their folk traditions for use at home and at special celebrations, hence they were not easily or multiformly observed by non-Japanese. During the camp experience, however, they were under heavy observation, for the government hired teams of anthropological and sociological investigators to record the reactions of people to internment. During these years, the Japanese Americans probably had as many anthropologists following them around as had the Indians. After the war, when interest in the Japanese Americans as objects of scrutiny waned, their use of folklore returned to the family setting and to those customary celebrations like *obon* where they now reside as solidly as they did before.

Folk Dance and Community

A late summer visitor to Salt Lake City or Ogden, Utah, hoping to find some remnants of the Mormon pioneer culture—or at least a few cowboys buying supplies—will instead see a major downtown intersection blocked off and full of Asian people dressed in kimonos and dancing around a colorfully decorated gazebo. It is the Japanese American community celebrating the ancient holiday of *Obon*, during which the spirits of departed ancestors are symbolically entertained with dances, songs, foods, and prayers of celebration.

The origins of *Obon* are lost in the mists of history, but the celebration is said to be based on the *Ura-Bon-Sutra*, which recounts the legend of Moku-ren, a Buddhist monk who wanted to rescue his mother from the Hunger Devil. Buddha inspired him to ask all the local monks to make generous offerings of food so her spirit's pain would be lightened for seven generations. By the early seventh century A.D., the *Ura-Bon* celebration had been noted in Japan, and by the eighth century the festival had become a regular courtly holiday among Japanese Buddhists.

The event also reflects an older Japanese belief that the spirits of dead ancestors come home each year to visit their families. In early times, on the first evening of the festival, fires were lit in people's yards and on nearby hills to guide the souls on their way back home. The next evening a neighborhood dance (*odori*) was performed, using tunes and dance steps drawn from community tradition. On the third day of the festival the families sent their spirit relatives back to "the other side" by lighting the way with roadside torches, or with small lanterns which floated down the river or outward on the ocean tide.

Many scholars believe that the practice carries on a pre-Buddhist custom of venerating ancestors and demonstrating the reciprocal nurturing that is central to the interaction of generations. In Japan and elsewhere today, celebrations of *Obon* certainly focus on the idea of responsibility to departed parents, the "debt which can never be repaid." But what does this ancient festival have to do with American citizens of Japanese ancestry living far away and several generations distant from Japan? And how did it find its way to Utah and many other areas of the western United States? Why does it thrive in "Mormon country?"

A typical *Obon* celebration in the western United States looks much like its counterpart in Japan, with some elements foregrounded, intensified, and maintained even more conservatively than in Japan. For example, in Japan, it is usually the older members of the community who wear kimonos; other participants—neighbors and passersby—wear simple street clothes. In the United States, most of the women dancers and many of the men wear kimonos, though not always in a way that would pass for standard in Japan.

In both countries the dancing takes place around a small pavilion called a *yagura*, from which strings of colored lanterns (supplied by Japanese soy sauce or airline companies) run out to nearby moorings. The *yagura* is decorated with crepe paper and colored banners (the good luck colors, red and white, are often augmented with blue in the U.S.); it contains a sound system, which supplies the music, and a medium-sized *taiko* drum, on which the local Buddhist reverend (or sometimes a visitor from Japan) will beat out a vigorous rhythm.

In Japan, it is customary for live musicians to sit and play on the *yagura*, but in the United States, recorded music is used, partly because there are not as many players of the old instruments (especially the *samisen*), but mostly because the village and neighborhood musicians in Japan play their own local songs; in the United States, the people have come from many parts of Japan, and it is not considered proper to leave anyone's locality out of the festivities of *Obon*. Thus, Japanese Americans are acquainted with the dance tunes and steps from all over Japan, but their distant cousins in Japan usually dance to a more limited local repertoire. The dancing goes counter-clockwise in a circle and is usually led—in the United States—by a group of people who have been practicing the dance for some months. As a dance proceeds, others in the community join in, and by the time the song is over, the area may be crowded with several concentric circles of dancers.

Taiko drumming has become more and more popular among young Japanese Americans over the past few years, and *Obon* celebrations in the West now routinely feature several "breaks" in the dancing to allow for *taiko* teams to put on a demonstration. The drummers are mostly *sansei* and *yonsei*—the same generations who now often take up the formal study of Japanese when they attend university. The growth of interest in *taiko* is one of several indications that the conservation of older customs includes a dynamic element of involvement, selection, and intensification of expressive forms that carry strong ethnic meaning.

The food which is sold in booths surrounding the *Obon* arena (or nearby in the foyer of the Buddhist church) is distinctly Japanese, but is also designed to be palatable to a broad range of onlookers. The focus is on rice, teriyaki chicken, noodles, and sushi, and not on the raw fish, eel, or octopus which are thought to be too exotic for the tastes of the general public. Clearly, although the food is distinctly Japanese, it is intentionally geared to the recognized tastes of the larger interethnic community—a concern that does not arise in Japan. Moreover, most of the food is made either in *nisei* homes or in the kitchen of the Buddhist church, and is sold to make money for church projects. Thus, the very presence of the food attests to the ongoing food-preparation traditions that characterize the ethnic dimensions of Japanese American home and church life as well.

To many Americans, all this gorgeous color, rhythm, gaiety, and tasty food may seem inappropriate as a way of celebrating dead ancestors, but a brief look

Japanese Americans and their families come together during the summer *Obon* festival to memorialize departed relatives and to nurture the symbols of their ethnic identity through dance, dress, and food styles from their Japanese heritage. Here are Obon dancers at the Ogden, Utah, Buddhist Temple.

Young women at the Ogden, Utah, Buddhist Temple share their inherited culture through the *Obon* dance.

Obon dancing allows this *nisei* grandmother and her granddaughter at the Portland, Oregon, Buddhist Temple to share their culture across generations and with other ethnic Japanese, living and dead, the world over.

Taiko drummers in Ogden, Utah, demonstrate their command of ancient Japanese drumming during an evening pause in the *Obon* dancing. The carefully choreographed group drumming is used by a number of Japanese American communities in the United States as a unifying cultural expression for young people.

at Japanese folk custom provides a useful perspective. The most distinctly "Japanese" aspects of *Obon* are its focus on deceased people (early classical Buddhism sees death as normal and focuses more on enlightenment than on the survival of single personalities after death) and its assumption that family ties persist beyond the grave. As a person dies, his or her spirit moves from *konoyo* (this world here) to *anoyo* (the world over there, yonder), the realm where the dead reside. "Over there," a person's spirit remains closely involved with the events going on at home. If the proper memorials and celebrations are observed by the living family, the spirit slowly evolves into a local deity, called a *sorei* or *kami*, and responds to the petitions of the living by exercising concern for their fortunes: enhancing the catch of fishermen, assuring the fertility of crops, easing childbirth, and influencing the financial stability of the whole family. In other words, the obligations and debts which are thought to exist between generations of a Japanese family are not interrupted by death, but are rather intensified by it.

In Japan, one index of this obligation is seen in the complex sequence of funeral memorials: A typical funeral is followed by another memorial funeral on the seventh day afterward, and then—depending on the local custom—the fourteenth, twenty-first, twenty-eighth, thirty-fifth, forty-second, and forty-ninth days; then, again, on the first year, seventh, fourteenth, twenty-first, twenty-eighth, and in some families, the fiftieth and one hundredth years. In a large family, this can mean that substantial amounts of time and money are expended on memorials. Folklorist Michiko Iwasaka confirms, "We Japanese spend most of our lives dealing with death." Japanese Buddhists in the United States have shortened these observances somewhat, for example by holding the seventh-day memorial on the afternoon of the original funeral, and by observing the seventh- and fourteenth-year rituals only rather than the fully articulated calendar described here.

Many Japanese and Japanese American customs in daily life are also dictated by death traditions, although many people are unaware of it. For example, most Japanese hotels do not have a fourth floor, and usually people do not give gifts or buy items in groups of four. Chopsticks are never stuck upright in a bowl of rice (this is only done with the rice placed beside the body at a funeral); food is not passed from one set of chopsticks to another (because bone fragments are removed from the crematorium in this manner); beds are never arranged with their heads to the north (only the body at a funeral is laid out in this manner); and people do not wear shoes inside a house (only a corpse wears shoes indoors).

In Japan, *Obon* brings thousands back to their hometowns and neighborhoods for evening dancing in the streets and daytime reunions with family. Indeed, many Japanese who have moved to larger cities for jobs seem to feel that *Obon* is only to be celebrated back home, where the *kami* of the family are situated, and many businesses close to accommodate the workers' and owners' desire to go home. The *Obon* season overloads the Japanese train and bus systems beyond their famed capacity.

In the mainland United States, *Obon* consists mostly of afternoon and evening dancing on a Saturday or Sunday, often in a city center or in the parking lot of a Buddhist church. In Utah, the Japanese American communities in Salt Lake City, Ogden, and Honeyville work out a calendar months in advance so that their events do not conflict and everyone can attend one another's *Obon*. In Hawaii, *Obon* lasts several days in some areas, and the arena often includes the stalls of souvenir and food vendors.

Shinto is the official religion of the Imperial Household of Japan, and it is characterized by formal rituals performed by priests; Buddhism, although it also has formal rituals, is characterized in Japanese practice by folk customs, foods, and dances that surround the ritual event. In Japan, most people are married by a *Shinto* ritual and buried in a Buddhist ceremony, and festivals occurring throughout the year may be oriented to either of these systems (sometimes to both). But in America, the Japanese American communities have retained mainly their connection with Buddhism, partly, it seems, because it represents the everyday, vernacular customs of ordinary people and because the festivals allow for an ethnic expression not based on theology and dogma.

In America, where religious affiliation is one's own business, everyone can feel free to participate in the *Obon-odori*, whether or not they attend the religious services that accompany the event in the nearby Buddhist church. Because of its pre-Buddhist origins and stress on family ties, *Obon* functions as an essentially vernacular event, driven by the ethnic identity and the family affinities of its participants and not by a formal religious structure. Even so, the most active dancers are usually members of the local Buddhist community. Some Japanese Americans of other faiths, including Mormons, join in the dancing and also form the audience of enthusiastic onlookers (and eaters) surrounding the dance circle. The festival feels particularly "at home" in Mormon country because Mormons, too, express a great interest in family, ancestors, and the idea of family connections between the living and the dead.

Of course, *Obon* dances are also held across the United States wherever Japanese Americans have settled (including Seabrook, New Jersey, where former internees from the Arkansas relocation camps were invited to move after World War II), indicating that celebration of ethnic and family ties, not geographical placement, forms the core of the festival. The famous Japanese folklorist Yanagita Kunio (often referred to as the founder of Japanese folklore study) insisted that festivals like *Obon* are important precisely because they are physical, dramatic ways of engaging people in forming live symbols of their culture, no matter how abstract the ideas might seem. In the very act of celebrating (and celebrating with) ancestors, he said, people are keeping their culture alive and dynamic.

We can see in the particular elements of *Obon* still other subtle reasons for the festival's enduring cultural meaning. In addition to emphases like family and community identity, which are considered positive virtues in America and might have aided acculturation, other features proclaim the distinct differences in Japanese attitudes and worldview. The kimono is a good example, for its design (both in pattern and in color) proclaims it to be a different idea about clothing: it says, "This is Japanese." In addition, it restricts movement and thus limits the way a person can walk or dance, which is in stark contrast to American assumptions about personal freedom. Donning a kimono forces the wearer to look different from other Americans and to move in ways that subordinate the individual to Japanese norms. Because women's kimonos are more restrictive than men's (men's legs can be visible in public, which means they can dance more energetically), the traditional Japanese attitudes governing gendered behavior in public are preserved more clearly here than in everyday kinds of Japanese American expression.

Similarly, the music and the dance are patently different from American styles, and they require the dancers to learn the particular dance steps that go with a given tune. Indeed, people practice every year so the *Obon* dances will be done "right" and in unison—this in a country where popular dances feature steps which allow innovation and personal expression. The focus in these dances is not on the American individual, not on the similarities between cultures which might make it easier to fit in, but rather on the Japanese concepts of teamwork, practice toward perfection, group orientation, and the engagement with culturally meaningful patterns that relate a single person to the group's identity. Rather than being viewed as factors inhibiting acculturation, these are seen by most Japanese Americans as cultural elements that have sustained them in a diverse society. The *taiko* drumming, which has become so popular, illustrates the same set of considerations: it is distinctly different from other forms of American music, and it gains much of its impact from the choreographed teamwork of the drummers, whose rhythms represent their culture and its norms in the medium of complex percussive sounds. The foods served at *Obon* are not hamburgers and hot dogs, but sushi and teriyaki chicken: different without being too different and distinctively, identifiably Japanese. In a setting where "fitting in" has allegedly been a paramount consideration for Japanese immigrants, food—like the examples noted here—provides a way of re-experiencing difference, distinctiveness, survival of one's kind.

This festival is not a romanticized vestige of a vanishing past, not an equivalent of the Ghost Dance—which sought to reverse the cultural and religious erosion experienced by Native Americans—but a dramatization of a culture's survival and achievement in a diverse society. Japanese American family folklore continues to be, sometimes along with Buddhism, the central dynamic feature of Japanese American cultural awareness. I hope it is evident from these few examples that this is not simply because "Japanese women so love to cook and dance," but because methods of food preparation and consumption in a family setting and ethnic dancing in a community context are powerful expressions of participation in the group's dynamics.

Dynamics of Family Folklore

Immediate Family

In some cultures (like those of northern Europe, the United States, and Canada), the individual, not the family, is considered the basic, indivisible unit of society. Nonetheless, family folklore may be said to be the first and basic dynamic traditional system encountered by most people the world over. In the family setting, as observed in Chapter 1, we learn our language, dialect, and elemental worldview all from hearing and observing others' speech and action. It is in this setting that we learn to participate in certain traditional roles. And it is within these growing dynamic interactions that we develop a strong sense of an "us." As we grow older, we are made aware of still larger implications and meanings for the family "us": For instance, we can distinguish between our own immediate family (with its dinner table customs, baby teeth disposal practices, family words) and that larger group of cousins, uncles, and grandmothers, who gather at family reunions or in smaller groups at Christmas or Seder. This larger family may also have customs, and they may or may not coincide with those of the smaller family. For example, Christmas in my own family meant opening one small gift on Christmas Eve, then waiting until my parents were up Christmas morning to open the rest. No particular custom dictated the order or frequency of opening presents. Christmas dinner required no blessing beforehand, but the meal itself was festive, with the special extra items usually reserved for Sunday dinners.

Horizontal Family

Christmas with my larger family, however, had other contours. Dinner was central and came before the opening of gifts. The preparation was done entirely by the women, who filled the kitchen of whichever house (we children never knew the mechanism for this delicate choice) while "the menfolk"—including the young boys—gathered in another room where jokes were told, cigars were smoked, and an occasional drink was shared. Dinner always began with a blessing, given impromptu by one of the youngest present at the request of the aunt or grandmother who had presided over the preparations. Of course the youngsters had all been coached by uncles to substitute a parody (like "Good bread, good meat. Good God, let's eat!"); sometimes, to everyone's amazement, a child would actually give the parody, receive an appropriate scowl from a mother, and begin again.

Presents were passed out one at a time by one of the children, who was designated "Santa" for the purpose. The entire room watched as the person opened the gift. Other nostalgic details could be added here, but you will be able to supply better ones from your own personal experience with your immediate family "us" and your extended family "us."

Vertical Family

Beyond this larger frame, still another family eventually emerges: the family tree "us"—the vertical family as we recognize its existence in time, often through family scrapbooks, genealogies, diaries, and the anecdotes of grandparents. This still larger family enters into the traditional dynamics chiefly through inherited items and family custom. We see it in comments like, "Oh, our family has *always* done it this way." On our Christmas tree were several "really old" decorations handed down from my great-grandmother's time. On one bed was an old, crazy friendship quilt, with pieces of fabric from dresses and ties still recognizable to the old-timers in the family. There were areas and farms still called by the names of family members long dead.

There were annual visits to relatives we knew only from their gravestones and from what we took to be their sentiments, expressed in rhymes or aphorisms we assumed they or their closest kin had made up themselves:

> *Man goeth to his long home.*
>
> *Peace to thy dust,*
> *dear friend farewell.*
>
> *Remember me as you pass by,*
> *For as you are so once was I.*
> *As I am now you soon must be.*
> *Prepare for Death and follow me.*
>
> *Boast not thyself of tomorrow*
> [on a grave of three small children]
>
> *The grave is near the cradle seen*
> *And swift the moments pass between*
>   [girl, age 3]
>
> *Parents and Friends adieu:*
> *Here in this Earth I wait for you.*
>
> *I have come to my grave in a full age*
> *as a shock of corn fully ripe.*
>   [woman, age 87]
>
> *My time was short. What age are you?*
>   [boy, age 7]

These engraved messages mean something different to members of the family than they do to outsiders. They seem to represent serious communicative relationships with our family tree; on the other hand, we are quite conscious that other families' tombstones can be appreciated for other reasons. In Knights's Corner Cemetery, near Pelham, Massachusetts, we often stopped just to read the gravestone of a man allegedly poisoned by his wife. Since it did not concern our family, we considered it humorous:

Warren Gibbs
died by arsenic poison
Mar. 23, 1860
AE. 36 yrs. 5 mos.
23 dys.

Think my friends when this you see
How my wife hath dealt by me
She in some oysters did prepare
Some poison for my lot and share
Then of the same I did partake
And nature yielded to its fate
Before she my wife became
Mary Felton was her name

Erected by his Brother
WM. GIBBS

This tombstone was a continuing and vital part of Gibbs and Felton lore, for the families had been feuding for years. The murder charge was never proven, but the stone remains to proclaim the Gibbs version of the story. It has been toppled, defaced, and stolen numerous times, and it is now said to be protected by the curse of William Gibbs. Here an inanimate object continues to maintain an important role—perhaps a central one—in the dynamics of family history and tradition. For them it was serious; for us it was funny.

In Norwegian, the three recognizable dynamic sets for the family are called *familie, slekt,* and *aett,* an indication that the distinctions are important enough to the Norwegians to warrant particularizing terms. The *familie* is the familiar, immediate, so-called nuclear grouping at home. The *slekt is* a particular generation of related people: a family reunion would bring the *slekt* together. *Aett* refers mainly to one's lineage, descent, the "vertical" family line through time. Other cultures have still more distinctions: the Navajo clan is made up of one's mother's relatives, while the Japanese clan is based on one's father's relatives and on regional origin.

The Ethnic Family

The next larger dynamic unit along these lines would seem to be a nation or a people, the ethnic group in which the various family sets operate. When a Jewish

Folk tradition, not law or religious commandment, dictates how different cultures mark the resting places of their dead. In Monticello, Utah, many gravemarkers depict the nearby Blue Mountain with its famous horse head (a natural formation of trees, rocks, and meadows). In addition, many Mormon families include the names of the family's children, living and deceased.

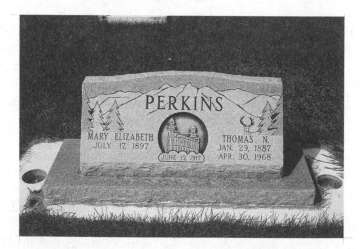

Mormon gravestones often show the temple where the couple was married; this one also indicates that the couple enjoyed the mountains and forests of northern Utah, that the husband was a hunter, and that the wife is not yet deceased, but anticipates being buried next to her husband.

Many graves in Astoria, Oregon, show what kind of boat the deceased used for fishing. Mr. Severson fished the Columbia River with a gillnetter, while Mr. Koppen trolled for salmon on the high seas. As well, intimate messages for loved ones or ethnic thanks addressed to the whole community provide a kind of dialectic between the living and the dead.

The "weeping lady" gravemarker in
Logan, Utah, is said by many to shed real
tears on Halloween, or at the full moon,
or on the anniversary of her children's
deaths—prompting nighttime visits by
those who wish to witness the phenomenon (or scare a friend.)

Irish families in Butte, Montana, often mark their graves with Celtic crosses, while the gravestones of Serbian goldminers in Sutter Creek, California, show their heritage by language and by use of the Cyrillic alphabet.

ОВЂЕ ПОЧИВА
МАРИЈА П.
ВАСИЉЕВИЋ.
Р.1894.У.1932.
ОВАЈ СПОМЕНИК
ПОДИЖЕ ЊЕЗИН
СУПРУГ ПЕТАР
СА ЂЕЦОМ
ВЈЕЧНАЈОЈ
ПАМЈАТ И
ПОКОЈ ДУШИ

Graveyards in Japan hold the cremated remains of entire families and are decorated mostly with statues of Buddha or Bodhisattvas rather than portraits of the deceased.

The grave of a young English visitor to Freiburg im Breisgau (southwestern Germany), well over a hundred years old, is virtually never without an anonymous gift of flowers in her arms—obviously a local custom which has been maintained by people who have no connection with the young woman beyond shared empathy for someone who died and was buried far from home.

family sits down to a Seder, they know that other Jews are also doing it the world over. On the other hand, for many other Americans, the sense of nation is a political, not a cultural, matter, and there may be little congruency between what happens on the national level and what happens in the family. In countries like Japan there is a powerful congruency among traditional dynamic systems, where the family and its lore are the core of national cultural existence. In Austria, on Christmas Eve, when one family prepares its traditional Christmas supper and then gathers about the tree (after Christkindl has erected it secretly and rung a silver bell), the participants have the substantial awareness that almost everyone in the entire country is doing exactly the same thing. This kind of cultural congruency between the dynamics of family and nation is understandably difficult to part with, and when an Austrian or Japanese family emigrates to another place, the immediate family level of this dynamic system will be the only cultural support left. It would be a wonder, under these circumstances, if family folklore among many immigrants did not become more intense than it was in the home country.

We have ample proofs from sociologists, of course, that all families do not act exactly alike, and we are now aware that the very term *family* must be defined according to the way a family actually takes shape within varying ethnic and economic situations. For many urban African Americans, family can include a dynamic, extended system of biologically unrelated "brothers" and "sisters" in the street, and it can also mean a mother and those of her children living at home. We now recognize the common existence of single-parent families, group living, adopted families, and same-gender parenting, all of which of course provide different contexts and occasions for family traditions to arise and be passed on. For these reasons, the word *family* is only an initial indicator of some particular set of dynamic interactions based primarily on kinship. The "us" referred to in any particular instance must be defined by those aspects of kinship that determine what relationships in fact exist and what performances will properly express them. Our awareness that we function in such sets as *familie, slekt,* and *aett,* even when we do not necessarily use separate words for them in English, should indicate to us that these are cultural groupings of traditional dynamics and not just convenient categories for the scholar.

BIBLIOGRAPHICAL NOTES

The folk group, regardless of its size or basis of organization, is the primary live context for any folk performance. For more specific discussions of group dynamics, the ways groups are known to pass on information, their tendency to persist through time as well as to change dynamically, and their importance as the matrix for traditional expressions, one should consult the following important works. Homer Barnett, in his *Innovation: The Basis of Cultural Change* (New York: McGraw-Hill, 1953) addresses a number of larger issues in cultural dynamism that also apply to our understanding of the dynamics of the close groups in which folklore is performed. Erving Goffman's *Interaction Ritual*

(New York: Doubleday, 1967) and *Frame Analysis: An Essay on the Organization of Experience* (New York: Harper & Row, 1974) are only two of his works on group dynamics; see his bibliographies for other important references in this area. *The Sociology of Small Groups* (Englewood Cliffs, N.J.: Prentice-Hall, 1967) by Theodore M. Mills has some interesting observations that may be applied to folk groups by adding the dimension of cultural tradition to his "levels of group process" (pp. 57-59); since not all folk groups can be classified easily as small, however, Mills's findings will not apply in all instances of folklore study. A standard in the discussion of social organization is Robert Bierstedt's *The Social Order*, 3rd ed. (New York: McGraw-Hill, 1970), esp. pp. 272–328 and 359–408.

The role of the folk group in continually reshaping the original performances of a creative individual was stressed heavily at the beginning of the twentieth century by Phillips Barry, a passionate scholar of the traditional ballad. His "Folk-Music in America," *Journal of American Folklore* 22 (1909): 76; "Native American Balladry in America," *Journal of American Folklore* 22 (1909): 365; "Communal Re-Creation," *Bulletin of the Folk-Song Society of the North-East* 5 (1933): 4-6, all support his concept of "communal re-creation," in which he held that songs originally composed by one artist were continually recreated by the community. Probably today's folklorists would feel that the entire community is not actively involved in such a process, for not all people in the community are singers and not all singers perform the same repertoires. At the same time, the idea is an attractive one if we extend it to account for all continual reperformances and reshapings of folk expression by any members of a folk group.

Earlier studies of folk groups assumed—intentionally or not—that all members of a particular group would be more or less equal in their recognition and use of esoteric expressions. We now know that within each folk group there may be meaningful subdivisions based on such factors as age or gender. Thus, in a family which traditionally eats certain foods or sings certain songs, the children may understand and use the traditions and beliefs differently from the adults, and the women may use different codes than the men, although all participants are active members of the family subculture. This makes the concept of a discrete folk group very problematic; most members of any group will have had to master a complex of interactive but sometimes mutually exclusive codes in order to cope successfully with the wide range of ever-changing social contexts. See, for example, Polly Stewart's essay "Wishful Willful Wily Women: Verbal Strategies for Female Success in the Child Ballads," in *Feminist Messages: Coding in Women's Folk Culture*, ed. Radner (Urbana: University of Illinois Press, 1993), 54–73, as well as all the other excellent essays in this collection. Stewart argues convincingly that women singers and audiences of the English-Scottish ballads may use the same apparent texts for quite distinctively different gendered meanings. See also Jay Mechling, "Children's Folklore," in *Folk Groups and Folklore Genres*, ed. Elliott Oring (Logan: Utah State University Press, 1986), 91–120; Charles W. Sullivan III, a leading scholar of children's folklore, has covered these issues in "Johnny Says His ABCs," *Western Folklore* 46 (1987): 36–41; "Children's Songs and Poems," in *Children's Folklore: A Source Book*, ed. Brian Sutton-Smith, Jay Mechling, et al. (New York: Garland, 1995); and "Narrative Expectations: The Folklore Connection," *Children's Literature Association Quarterly* 15 (1990): 52–55.

Folk dyads are treated by Elliott Oring in "Dyadic Traditions," *Jokes and Their Relations* (Lexington: University Press of Kentucky, 1992), 135–44; see also Regina

Bendix, "Marmot, Memet, and Marmoset: Further Research on the Folklore of Dyads," *Western Folklore* 46 (1987): 171–91. The discussion of this important "minimal set" for folklore was initiated by Oring in an exploratory piece, "Dyadic Traditions," *Journal of Folklore Research* 21 (1984): 19–28.

Most folklorists today deal with live context as a matter of course. Probably the two most important articles addressed directly to the importance of this consideration are Alan Dundes, "Texture, Text, and Context," *Southern Folklore Quarterly* 28 (1964): 251-65, and Dan Ben-Amos, "Toward a Definition of Folklore in Context," *Journal of American Folklore* 84 (1971): 3-15 (also in *Toward New Perspectives in Folklore,* ed. Américo Paredes and Richard Bauman [Austin: University of Texas Press, 1971]). Ben-Amos suggests that folklore as a live process "can be considered a sphere of interaction in its own right" (p. 15). Some suggestions for analytical considerations of live context are provided by Roger D. Abrahams in "Folklore in Culture: Notes toward an Analytic Method," *Texas Studies in Language and Literature* 5 (1963): 98-110.

The basic statement on the function of in-group folklore is by William Hugh Jansen in "The Esoteric-Exoteric Factor," *Fabula: Journal of Folktale Studies* 2 (1959): 205-11 (reprinted in Dundes, *The Study of Folklore,* 43-51). More detailed explorations into the kinds of tension and misunderstanding that regularly occur between members of various in-groups are to be found in Edward T. Hall, *The Silent Language* (Garden City, N.Y.: Doubleday, 1959), *The Hidden Dimension* (Garden City, N.Y.: Doubleday, 1966), and *Beyond Culture* (Garden City, N.Y.: Doubleday, 1977). Although these books are written for the general reader, they are treasuries of illustrations for the esoteric/exoteric factor. Hall, the originator of the term *proxemics,* discusses high and low context groups in the last-named work.

In most occupational groups that experience hazard on the job, the survival of the individual is closely allied to the survival and success of the entire group. At sea or in the woods, a new man on the crew needs to know far more than he can learn rationally on the job. Inducting the greenhorn is thus more than a spare-time exercise in fun and games. See the remarks of Horace Beck in "Sea Lore," *Northwest Folklore* 2 (1967): 1-13, as well as Robert S. McCarl Jr., "Smokejumper Initiation: Ritualized Communication in a Modern Occupation," *Journal of American Folklore* 89 (1976): 49-66. McCarl's work on the folklore of urban firefighters, based on more than a year's fieldwork, is published in *The District of Columbia Fire Fighters' Project: A Case Study in Occupational Folklife,* Smithsonian Folklife Studies, no. 4 (Washington, D.C.: Smithsonian Institution Press, 1985). For several other approaches to occupational lore, see Robert H. Byington, ed., *Working Americans: Contemporary Approaches to Occupational Folklife,* Smithsonian Folklife Studies, no. 3 (Washington, D.C.: Smithsonian Institution Press, 1978); and *By Land and by Sea,* ed. Roger D. Abrahams, Kenneth S. Goldstein, and Wayland Hand (Hatboro, Pa.: Legacy Books, 1985). Most of the study in this area of folklore has focused on prototypical male occupations, and most of the researchers have been male folklorists and ethnographers, which indicates that gender must play as important a role as occupational frames in the construction of group meaning and in the process of documentation and analysis.

A more extensive glossary of loggers' terms, especially those used on the West Coast, can be found in Walter F. McCulloch, *Woods Words: A Comprehensive Dictionary of Logger's Terms* (Portland: Oregon Historical Society, 1963), although McCulloch, formerly dean of the Forestry School at Oregon State University, deferred to the tastes of the general public enough to leave out many of the more vivid examples. Another list is given by Wilbur A. Davis in "Logger and Splinter-Picker Talk," *Western Folklore* 9 (1950): 111–23. An Oregon version of the Walkaway story, with some brief remarks on its background, is given by Rod Collins in an article of the same name in *Northwest Folklore* 2 (1967): 18. Folklorist Jens Lund has succeeded in bringing loggers' poetry and contemporary song to the attention of a wider audience of scholars; with the production of such tapes as *Northwest Logger Poetry* (Olympia: Washington State Folklife Council, 1985) and through logger poetry gatherings, Lund has shown how loggers, like cowboys, have developed a tradition of poetic recitation not suspected by people outside their occupational contexts. See also Hal Cannon, ed., *Cowboy Poetry: A Gathering* (Salt Lake City: Peregrine Smith Books, 1985).

I would like to thank the following people for sharing the logging stories and comments I have used in this chapter: Bill Hamilton, Ernie Sanford, Joseph Hannon, Greg Hamilton, John Urquhart, Vintie Holt, Leo Bishop, Ray Scofield, Tom McBride, and George Wasson. Because some of the stories were collected in the woods, without the benefit of a tape recorder, I have retold them here in a somewhat literary style to set them off from the verbatim texts transcribed in the loggers' own words. Most of the narratives were recorded in local taverns and in loggers' homes.

It is abundantly clear that there are almost unlimited bases for calling a group a folk group: religious affinity, regional identity, occupational definition, age, gender, ethnic awareness, and so on. For a few revealing discussions of these matters, one might consult Bruce E. Nickerson, "Is There a Folk in the Factory?" *Journal of American Folklore* 87 (1974): 133–39; William A. Wilson, "The Paradox of Mormon Folklore," *Brigham Young University Studies* 17 (1976): 40-58; Suzi Jones, *Oregon Folklore* (Eugene: University of Oregon, 1977). Joan Radner argues that women's cultures are based on gendered and situational contexts on the cultural, community, and individual levels as they are "constructed through the social relations of particular communities"; thus, while women may constitute a folk group in a given social context, there is no universal women's worldview. Each women's folk group, taken separately, will have its own set of expressive systems, which may include a code which protects the users from the dangers of expressing themselves openly. It seems to me that this concept can be applied to other folk groups as well, and particularly to those which derive all or part of their identity by an enforced opposition or deviation from a related but dominating group (children vs. adults, minority vs. majority group, etc.). See Radner's insightful essay, "Strategies of Coding in Women's Cultures," in *Feminist Messages: Coding in Women's Folk Culture*, 1–29.

As David Hackett Fischer points out in *Albion's Seed: Four British Folkways in America* (New York and Oxford: Oxford University Press, 1989), 8–9, all cultures include a number of identifying genres which they take with them when they migrate to a new area. Of these, one of the most central and long-lasting is food lore, according to Oring, who points out that ethnic food traditions survive in lively usage after other cultural elements have changed or died out. See Oring, "Ethnic Groups and Ethnic Folklore," in *Folk Groups and Folklore Genres*, 23–44. In this connection, a fine exposition can be found in Linda Keller Brown and Kay Mussell, eds., *Ethnic and Regional Foodways in the United States: Performance of Group Identity* (Knoxville: University of Tennessee Press, 1984).

I am indebted to several Japanese and Japanese American acquaintances for their perspectives on ethnic aspects of their foods. Particularly helpful have been Chiyoe Kubota and Asako Marumoto of Ogden, Utah; Mary Joo of Caldwell, Idaho; Ayako Kawai of Nampa, Idaho; Seiko Kikuta of San Jose, California; Yachi Shiotani of San Diego, California; Donna Misao Joo and Yoko McLain of Eugene, Oregon; Nancy Nakata of Portland, Oregon; Harumi Taniguchi and Itsuko Asada of Seabrook, New Jersey; Tomiko Shibaoka of Tokyo and Shingo Kawaguchi of Shimizu, Japan; and Miiko Kubota Toelken, my wife.

Important discussions of Japanese culture in America are to be found in John De Francis, *Things Japanese in Hawaii* (Honolulu: University of Hawaii Press, 1973); Fumi Kawamoto, "Folk Beliefs among Japanese in the Los Angeles Area," *Western Folklore* 21 (1962): 13-26 (esp. pp. 23-24, "Food Superstition," in which, among other things, there is listed a belief in the avoidance of three slices of anything on the grounds that the Japanese term for it, *mikiri*, means "to cut one's flesh"). Harry H. L. Kitano, *Japanese Americans* (Englewood Cliffs, N.J.: Prentice-Hall, 1969) mentions a widespread consciousness among Japanese that the attraction of cultural pluralism is precisely that a foreigner can keep some cultural elements and discard others (pp. 144-45). Marvin K. Opler, in "Japanese Folk Beliefs and Practices, Tule Lake, California," *Journal of American Folklore* 63 (1950): 385-97, discusses what he considered to be a revival of older Japanese custom in the so-called relocation camps in which Japanese Americans were interned during the Second World War; Rosalie H. Wax, in *Doing Fieldwork: Warnings and Advice* (Chicago: University of Chicago Press, 1971), discusses the Japanese at Tule Lake and her anthropological work among them on pp. 59-174. See also Barre Toelken, "Cultural Maintenance and Ethnic Intensification in Two Japanese-American World War II Internment Camps," *Oriens Extremus* 33 (1990): 5-23, for a discussion of the ways folklore was utilized in stabilizing ethnic identity among a people under stress. Descriptions and discussions of ongoing Japanese traditions in America are also given in Nancy Araki and Jane Horii, *Matsuri: Festival! Japanese American Celebrations and Activities* (Union City, Calif.: Heian International, 1985). Some of the many ways folklore articulates the shared values and concerns of close groups are detailed by Robert Darnton in *The Great Cat Massacre and Other Episodes in French Cultural History* (New York: Random House, 1984).

Joseph Campbell, in *The Masks of God: Oriental Mythology* (New York: Viking, 1962), discusses the Japanese concept of the mythic past as based solidly on the model of family relations (pp. 465-74). Especially interesting are his summary and comments on the *Kojiki,* one of the principal mythic texts of ancient Japan, in which it is made clear that in Japanese thought there are concentric areas of concern in what he calls the religious "cults": there is first a concentration on the domestic center, then the community, then the generalized craft or occupational scene, then the national scene. Each of these is seen as congruent with the rest; hence, anything that threatens one of these threatens the stability of the others. See also Richard M. Dorson, ed., *Studies in Japanese Folklore,* Indiana University Folklore Series, no. 17 (Bloomington: Indiana University Press, 1963), for a number of interesting studies of Japanese traditions, many of which may be traced further into the American context, as we will discuss in Chapter 4.

In studies of graveyards and epitaphs, researchers have noted a continuing relationship between elements of cultures and the specifics of cemetery structure and meaning. In "Social Commentary from the Cemetery," *Natural History* 86, no. 6 (June-July 1877), Edwin S. Dethlefsen and Kenneth Jensen observe, "The community cemetery is an entity of the past. As families have lost their geographic cohesiveness, modern gravestones have lost much of their individuality." *Over Their Dead Bodies: Yankee Epitaphs in History,* by Thomas C. Mann and Janet Greene (Brattleboro, Vt.: Stephen Greene, 1962), is not a complete or particularly scholarly book, but it is full of excellent examples of the traditional contents of New England gravestones when it was still fashionable to provide extensive commentary on the stone. The Gibbs gravestone in Knights's Corner graveyard, near Pelham, Massachusetts, was written up in the *Springfield Union* as "Pelham Epitaph Carries Feud Beyond Grave," by Neil L. Perry, Wednesday, August 20, 1969, p. 23; such articles are often extremely valuable sources of folklore. Feature articles such as this one, column fillers, articles on local elderly people, and the like must not be overlooked for the perspectives and leads they can supply the folklorist interested in relating folk ideas and performances to the live society. For a sampling of what modern scholars are doing with grave markers, see Richard E. Meyer, ed., *Cemeteries and Gravemarkers: Voices of American Culture* (Ann Arbor: UMI Research Press, 1989; repr. Logan: Utah State University Press, 1992).

For bringing the terms *familie, slekt,* and *aett* to my attention, I am much indebted to Norwegian folklorist Knut Djupedal. Some interesting perspectives on the dynamics of the family can be gained from William J. Goode, *The Family* (Englewood Cliffs, N.J.: Prentice-Hall, 1964). But since the nature and make-up of families in America change rapidly, it would be wise to keep abreast of the dynamics if we want to understand the resultant folklore—which of course is directly related to the contemporary shared culture. Two excellent studies are Stephanie Coontz, *The Way We Never Were: American Families and the Nostalgia Trap* (New York: Basic Books, 1993) and Judith Stacey, *Brave New Families: Stories of Domestic Upheaval in Late Twentieth Century America* (New York: Basic Books, 1991). A particularly interesting program sponsored in 1976-1977 by the Smithsonian took folklorists Amy Kotkin and Steve Zeitlin to selected cities around the United States, where they gave presentations and displays of family folklore to interested parties and solicited their oral histories in return. See Steven J. Zeitlin, Amy J. Kotkin, and Holly Cutting Baker, eds., *A Celebration of American Family Folklore: Tales and Traditions from the Smithsonian Collection* (New York: Pantheon Books, 1982).

Because interest in our own ethnicity has become more acceptable since the demise of the melting pot concept, and because scholarly investigation of ethnic groups has concurrently been freed of the specter of racism (once based, I suppose, on the vague feeling that if we paid attention to someone's ethnic background it could only be in scorn), we can now find many more treatments of ethnic folklore than would have been possible thirty years ago. For a work concerning a people with a solid sense of their own ethnic identity, one might consult Asen Balikci, *The Netsilik Eskimo* (New York: Natural History Press, 1970); especially helpful is Rosan A. Jordan, "Ethnic Identity and the Lore of the Supernatural," *Journal of American Folklore* 88 (1975): 370-82. *Western Folklore* 36, no. 1 (January 1977) presents an entire special issue on ethnicity in folklore edited by Larry Danielson; see especially Yvonne Lockwood, "The Sauna: An Expression of Finnish-American Identity," pp. 71-83, and Stephen Stern, "Ethnic Folklore and the Folklore of Ethnic Identity," pp. 7-32. A more recent work, with essays on a number of ethnic groups (Cornish, German, Italian, Chinese, African American, Hispanic, Gypsy, Iranian, Native American, Jewish, Swedish, and Latino), is Stephen Stern and John Allan Cicala, eds., *Creative Ethnicity: Symbols and Strategies of Contemporary Ethnic Life* (Logan: Utah State University Press, 1991).

Ever since the 1860s, the citizens of Mendon, Utah, many of whose ancestors came as Mormon converts and settlers from England and Wales, have celebrated May Day with a Maypole dance. Photo by William A. Wilson.

Chapter 3

THE FOLK PERFORMANCE

IT IS DIFFICULT, IF NOT IMPOSSIBLE, TO DESCRIBE THE DYNAMICS OF FOLKLORE without referring to traditional events or performances, vernacular expressions articulated among members of a high context group. Just as the dynamics discussed in Chapter 2 are only hypothetical if nothing happens, so a traditional performance or event tells us little if it does not occur in a traditional framework. For this reason, John Miles Foley calls performance "the enabling event" in which the referents supplied by tradition are brought to life by the skilled articulations of speakers, singers, builders, weavers, and other vernacular artists. This chapter focuses on performance as a central aspect of dynamics by showing some details of traditional expressive interaction.

PERFORMANCE IN PLACE

The following anecdote of a Navajo storytelling event concentrates on the people and how they did what they did, their ideas concerning what happened, their reasons, how they got into the event, and how the whole interaction was seen by three non-Navajo visitors. A later chapter focuses on the inventory of ingredients for such events, but obviously, in reality, events as dynamic performances and people as dynamic participants cannot be separated.

Context

Background: three folklorists (Barre Toelken, Jan Harold Brunvand, John Wilson Foster) have arrived at a Navajo home after a long drive. Toelken is already known to the family; the other two are interested observers.

Setting: a small frame house in a desert town in southern Utah, just north of the Navajo reservation. The inhabitants of the house are Navajo and have moved off the reservation because of hard times. The children go to public school but their parents try to keep home life traditional. Everyone speaks Navajo at home; the parents speak only a few words of English.

Time: about 9:30 P.M. in late December. There is snow on the ground, and it is very cold. This is the time of year when Coyote stories can (and should) be told. And this is the only season when string figures can be made.

Situation: the father, Yellowman, sits in a chair, dozing; small children are playing on the floor. The mother weaves on a vertical loom at the far side of the room. The folklorists sit quietly, talking occasionally in low tones. In White American terms, nothing is happening, although in Navajo custom this is a common way of enjoying someone's company. One hour passes in this manner. The teen-age children of the family come in suddenly, accompanied by a Mormon missionary, who wakes up the father to remind him that the children should be in church this coming Sunday. He notices the White visitors: "You fellows with the Bureau of Indian Affairs?" "No, just friends, visiting." There is a puzzled look from the missionary; he departs. The teenagers say hello and sit down quietly; the father returns to a half-doze. After about fifteen minutes he says sleepily, in Navajo, "Perhaps these visitors are Mormons, too?" "No," I reply, "this one is from back East originally; he likes to study old stories, as I do. This other one is from Ireland."

This translates in Navajo as "He comes from beyond the ocean," and Helen Yellowman turns suddenly from her loom, grins, and holding her hands as if using a machine gun, makes a whispered t-t-t-t sound. "What does she mean?" asks Foster. "She thinks you're from Vietnam; that's also called 'beyond the ocean.'" Foster replies, "Tell her Vietnam is a vicarage tea party compared to Northern Ireland." The translation suffers and the macabre humor is missed. There is some puzzlement, but general cheer ensues because the visitors are not Mormons. "Now let's have some coffee," Yellowman says.

The Performance

Everyone converges on the kitchen. While coffee is being prepared, Brunvand asks for a piece of string; he has a game he wants to show the children, and he pretends not to know the Navajos' great interest in string games. He makes a simple cat's cradle and shows it to a nearby child of about ten. "Could you do that?" The boy asks him innocently to do it again, slowly. Then, with mock care and deliberation, the boy reproduces the same figure perfectly, holds it up briefly, and then starts quickly on a more complicated one. He asks Brunvand with a grin, "Can you do that one?" Brunvand acts stumped. The boy produces another and another. The string passes to others in the family, and in rapid succession we see a Navajo rug, a bolt of lightning, two coyotes racing away from each other, a bat, and a worm that crawls over and under two parallel strings.

"Where did you learn those designs?" we ask. The children confer with their father for a while, then one answers, "I don't know. I guess it's all from Spider Woman. They say if you fall into Spider Woman's den she won't let you out unless you can do all these. And then if you do these in the summer you won't get out at all anyway."

Patsy Bedonie shows how to make the string figure for *dilyéhé*, the Pleiades, the constellation used by Navajo singers ("medicine men") as an indication of when dawn will occur during all-night healing ceremonies.

Patsy Bedonie of Hoskanini Mesa on the Navajo Reservation demonstrates a string figure of a worm crawling over branches.

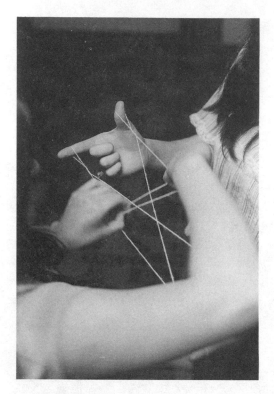

Teenagers Chiyo Toelken and Patsy Bedonie do a series of string games (Cat's Cradle) figures in which each person must take the string off the other's fingers by making a new pattern.

"Why is that?"

"Well, we're only supposed to do it in the winter when the spiders are hibernating, because it's really their kind of custom to do things with string." During this conversation, the mother has gone back to weaving momentarily, and the other children are still doing string figures.

"Spider Woman taught us all these designs as a way of helping us think. You learn to think when you make these. And she taught us about weaving, too," a teen-age daughter puts in.

"If you can think well," the first boy adds, "you won't get into trouble or get lost. Anyway, that's what our father says."

Toelken: "But Spider Woman didn't teach *you* these things, right? Where did *you* learn them?"

"Well, we probably picked them up from each other and from our father, but they were already around, you know. All the people know about them. Spider Woman taught us."

Yellowman speaks now for the first time and, taking the string, makes a tight design. "Do you know what that is?" he asks us. We do not. He shows his children and they all respond: "So̱' Tso" (literally, "Big Star," Venus). He nods with satisfaction and makes another figure; he holds it up to us, and we shake our heads. He holds it up to the children, and they respond, "Dilyéhé." Since I have never heard the term I ask one of the children to translate it; everyone looks blank. "That's the only word there is for it." Suddenly, in an attempt to explain, Yellowman motions us all outside. There, shivering in the night wind, we watch him carefully hold the string figure above his head and point beyond it with pursed lips to the Pleiades.

Back inside, he helps cover our embarrassment at not knowing our astronomy by making string figure caricatures of those present: a face with vague glasses to represent Brunvand, another with a loop hanging down for Foster's beard, another with a piece of string trailing down to suggest the power cord on Toelken's tape recorder.

Finally, the father puts the string down and says seriously, "It's too easy to become sick, because there are always things happening to confuse our minds. We need to have ways of thinking, of keeping things stable, healthy, beautiful (hózhó). We try for a long life, but lots of things can happen to us. So we keep our thinking in order by these figures and we keep our lives in order with the stories. We have to relate our lives to the stars and the sun, the animals, and to all of nature or else we will go crazy, or get sick."

Now there is a silence of about ten minutes, but no one moves away from the table. There is an air of expectancy. The mother comes in and pours more coffee for everyone. We start the tape recorder. The father clears his throat and begins speaking slowly. The following transcript presents his delivery, one phrase at a time, and his audience's response.

*Ma'i [Coyote] was walking
along over by Kayenta, up
   by those cliffs.*

children exchange quick
glances, smiling broadly

*He was hunting for something to
   eat but he wasn't having
   any luck.*
*He got very hungry, going
   along there,
   And his stomach was making
   noises.*

one girl giggles, quietly
(Navajos generally do not
complain about hunger.)
smiles, heavy expelling of
breath
[pause: four seconds]

He couldn't take it.
*He was almost crying, he was
   so hungry.*

   ⁓

*Ma'i was going along and he
   met Golízhí [Skunk].*

narrator smiles; audience
smiles (Golízhí, literally
"one with the stinking urine,"
is often the butt of Ma'i's
attempts to manipulate
others.)

*He said, "Come along with me
   and we'll hunt together.*
*Maybe we'll find some prairie
   dogs and cook them up."*
*"I'm not a hunter,"
   Golízhí said to him.*
*"I won't be any help. The prairie
   dogs will smell me and run
   into their houses.*
You should get someone else."

   ⁓

[pause: three seconds]

"There isn't anyone else around."
Ma'i was starting to get angry.
*He was so hungry he could eat
   a skunk, if he could find
   some way not to get
   urinated on.*

laughter (Ma'i is too anxious
to get food; anger should be
avoided.)

*"Come along anyway. We'll
   find something."*
Ma'i asked him that four times,

(Ma'i is trying hard to get a
recognizably poor hunting
companion. Four requests
usually create an obligation
to respond.)

So Golízhí went along with him.

   ⁓

smiles, expelling of air
[pause: four seconds]

*They went along together but
   they didn't find anything
   to eat.*

It was getting dark.
And Ma'i was so hungry.
  that he could hardly walk.

  ⏜

laughter, including
narrator
[pause: four seconds]
(Shiłna'ash, literally "one
who travels with me," is a
term used for close friends
and relatives.)
[pause: two seconds]

"Let's stop and make camp here,
  Shiłna'ash," Ma'i said.
"We'll build a fire and play
  some games."

  ⏜

"I don't know about that; I
  don't know any games,"
  Golízhí said.

  ⏜

[pause: two seconds]
(In another story Ma'i lost
his eyes by begging the birds
to remove them and carry them
into the sky.)
one boy looks up at the
ceiling; others giggle;
narrator smiles
[pause: two seconds]

"Well, I'll teach you a game I
  learned from the birds.
We'll take our eyes out and
  throw them in the air.
Then we'll catch them in our
  eyesockets," Ma'i said.

  ⏜

"I don't know that game."

  ⏜

[pause: two seconds]

"It's a good game," Ma'i said.
"You can see for a long distance
  when your eyes are up there.

  ⏜

everyone laughs
[pause: two seconds]

"I don't know how to play it;
  You go first."

  ⏜

[pause: four seconds]

Ma'i pulled out his eyes and
  threw them up in the air.
He said, "Come back to my
  sockets!
Come back to my sockets!
Come back to my sockets!
Come back to my sockets!"
Ma'i said.

  ⏜

They came back to his sockets.

  ⏜

[pause: two seconds]
expelling of air; smiles
[pause: two seconds]

Then he did it again, and he
  threw them higher.

"Come back to my sockets!
Come back to my sockets!
Come back to my sockets!
Come back to my sockets!

And they came back to his
sockets.

He did it again.
He threw them way up.
He could see all around the
countryside while they
were up there.
He said, "Come back to my
sockets!
Come back to my sockets!
Come back to my sockets!
Come back to my sockets!"
Ma'i said.

They came down and got caught
around the branches of a
tree.

Everything got dark for him.
He couldn't see.
He groped around all over and
finally found the tree.
It was an old tree with pitchballs
all over it.
He could feel them with his hands.
He pulled two of them off and
put them in his eye sockets.

He couldn't see very well
with those eyes.
So he got too close to the fire.
All that pitch melted down into
the corners of his eyes.

That's how coyotes got all
that brown stuff in the
corners of their eyes.

much giggling (Ma'i is
carrying his example to
excess.)
[pause: two seconds]

[pause: four seconds]
narrator slows down, sounds
nasal and almost tired (Ma'i
has "committed himself" to
the usual fourfold pattern,
ignoring Golízhí, totally
carried away by his own
pleasure.)

[pause: two seconds]

extended laughter, lasting
seven seconds

narrator laughs so hard that
these lines are distorted

laughter
[pause: two seconds]

laughter
[pause: two seconds]

That's what they say.	[pause: five seconds] audience looking at floor, general smiling, expelling of air
Now let's hear that back.	[pause: ten seconds] narrator looks at visitors for the first time and acknowledges the tape recorder

Informant's Commentary

After a replaying of the tape, general conversation ensues, and we ask if he knows the other story where Coyote does the same things with the exception of the ending: "That's how coyotes got those yellow [amber] eyes." I ask which is the final story: do coyotes have pitchballs for eyes, as in that other story, or has the pitch melted, as in the one just told? And in either case, how can coyotes see?

Yellowman answers, "Coyotes can see. Everyone knows that. Just watch them. Why do you ask?"

"Do you believe these stories?" we ask.

"Of course. That other one is where Ma'i learned something from the birds. Birds are *supposed* to see up in the air."

"Then do you believe a person can see with pitchballs for eyes?"

"No. This is Ma'i. He can do anything he wants. But anyway the story isn't about eyes, it's about what Ma'i is doing. He cries about being hungry, he chooses a poor hunter for a partner, then he calls Golízhí *shiłna'ash* even though he might eat him. Maybe he shouldn't see those things. It's not right to fool around with our bodies that way. It can make you sick. That's how eye diseases came about. That's the important thing. That's what the story is about. If my children hear these stories they'll grow up to be good people. They won't play around with their bodies and they won't try to see things they shouldn't. You people are teachers, but I think there's a lot you don't know."

One day Ma'i was walking along out in a place called "Where-the-Wood-Floats-Out."	(Yellowman starts another performance)

Content and Meaning

A careful observer will notice several important aspects of this performance. First and most evident is that the various observed events were very much affected by the presence of outsiders (though not caused by us). How can we be sure that what we saw was in fact traditional if we recognize that it was enhanced or focused by our presence? What would have happened had we not been there? Here is a puzzle in the same category as the tree falling in the forest where no one can hear it (does it make a noise?)—with a major exception: assuming our informants are not kidding us, we have their word that these things happen, in the winter anyway. Indeed, from the testimony of Yellowman, these performances are not only appropriate, they are almost obligatory. Thus, while the particular event may have been sparked by a certain set of circumstances that included our visit, we are justified in believing that some other set of esoteric conditions would have brought about a similar performance at another time.

But our presence apparently did relate to another important aspect of this performance: the content. Take a closer look at the sequence listed above, and note that from the very first the traditional behavior throughout is related to the presence of guests:

1. A period of friendly silence occurs while the guests and hosts enjoy each other's proximity.
2. An interruption brings the family's new religious orientation to the attention of visitors, followed by a careful ascertaining of the visitors' religion so that they would not be offended by being offered coffee—a Navajo staple but a stimulant discouraged by Mormons.
3. Coffee is offered, and the visitors can now be brought even closer to a Navajo traditional family setting—one in which winter tales may normally occur.
4. String figures are begun innocently but end in the pointed demonstration that the visitors, for all their interest, are ignorant about important ways of seeing, of avoiding confusion, getting lost, and sickness.
5. A Coyote story is told that dramatizes the foolish and competitive ways we may mistreat our bodies in the selfish pursuit of personal goals (which continues the topic of health and seeing brought up in the string figures, continues the thread of outsiders' ignorance, and probably refers to our eagerness to obtain coyote stories, trying to see things that are beyond us).
6. A recognition of the tape recorder is made and an overt expression of concern is voiced on the subject of teachers not knowing what is important, not seeing well enough to get what they need.
7. The next story, the beginning of which is noted above, is the one Yellowman told every time I visited him to collect stories. It features Ma'i and Golízhí in a tale of selfishness and frustration—a signal, I now believe, that my desire to collect all the Coyote stories was too compulsive and would end in disappointment.

One need not read very deeply to see the delicate irony of this performance situation, in which a father uses traditional modes of expression to show his children how much they know in comparison to their potential teachers. Yet the subject is handled gently and covertly, showing respect and warmth for the guests while giving a tremendous boost of morale to the children.

Another important and obvious aspect of that rather full Navajo evening is the fact that for the Navajos it was a *high context* event and not a series of separated genres, as a Euro-American scholar might set them down. By the scholar, the genres or forms of folklore might be listed as follows: greeting customs, weaving, foodways, games, folk astronomy, storytelling, folk philosophy. While the Navajo would certainly recognize these differences in behavior, it is likely that they would see no situational reason to separate them out; rather, they all fall into a more important category: those things performed between the first killing frost and the first thunderstorm—that is, in winter, as winter is defined by nature. The category foremost in the Navajo concern, then, is not "what genres of traditions people practice," but "what traditional practices articulate our relations to nature."

We can appreciate easily how much of the evening was based on the shared context of Navajo life, categories, and custom. The family literally flooded into the kitchen for coffee, obviously knowing what was to come. They already knew the string figures, and the star constellations and animals they represent (some Navajos still navigate at night by patterns so learned and they recall stories of ancestors who escaped from enemies by this means). They had already heard so many Coyote stories that they knew what was coming in this one, what Coyote's weaknesses are, and how those weaknesses represent ludicrous behavior or foolish attitudes for the Navajo (thus they knew when and why to laugh). They knew that what their mother was doing on her loom was directly related to what they were doing in their string games. And they knew, further, that all these matters related to rituals and dances that also are unavoidably a part of the winter season. In this context, the whole evening was a performance constellation. Some of these ideas, fortunately, came forth in conversation, but in many regards we visitors were only seeing the surface. We were registering primarily the generic elements which could be observed by any congenial outsider.

There are enough studies of separated folklore genres to make us aware that we sometimes amputate rather than dissect when we study traditional events. We become painfully aware of it when, as with a complex culture like that of the Navajo, a hundred years of anthropological and folkloristic study seem to have brought us very little closer to understanding. We need to guard against similar fragmentations when we study our own folklore or that of groups more closely related to us. Basically, we can say that a clear delineation of genre or structure of a folk item is only one small part of understanding a folk performance. Without the whole live context and the comments of the performers, it is unlikely that we will ever get very close to understanding—or even seeing—the dynamics that underlie the traditional process.

But beyond our readiness to look deeper than genre distinctions, we need also to recognize that there are various levels of seeing traditional articulations,

Cooking outdoors for the participants in
a *kinaaldá*, the girls' maturation ceremony, Mrs. Billie makes *dah
díníilghaazh* (lit. "it bubbles up and stays
there," a deep-fried version of *nánees-
kaadí*) near Shonto, Arizona, 1990.
Photo by Lore Erf.

In the early morning darkness, Yazzie Johnson makes *nánees-kaadí* in her hogan near Blanding, Utah, in 1955. The only light comes from the smoke hole above and the fire in the center of the one-room round dwelling. Baked over the open fire or in a dry frying pan, *náneeskaadí* (lit. "it was patted") has been the staple food of Navajos for several generations.

Náneeskaadí was eaten three meals a day, along with coffee and canned fruit by Yellowman's family in Montezuma Creek Canyon, Utah, when the author lived with them in the 1950s. Helen Yellowman and her daughters Joanne and Helen have a red herbal sunburn preventive on their faces.

and these are dependent on what the audience (or researcher) knows in relation to what the performer knows. For convenience, Japanese folklorist Yanagita Kunio (1875–1962) told his students to anticipate three different levels of scrutiny in their fieldwork: The first, and most basic, is composed of that which the observer can see empirically (a festival takes place, a song is sung, a kite is made, a custom is practiced); the second level is based on what we can hear (we listen to the shouting of marchers in the festival parade, we hear and understand the words and notes of the song, we listen to the kitemakers' explanation of his good luck design, we hear the proverb or dialect phrase that accompanies the custom); the third, and most delicate to deal with empirically, arises from our participation—and even belief—in the performance (we take part in the singing, shout in the festival parade, sing the lullaby to our own children, and make or fly the kite and believe in the efficacy of its design; we ourselves observe the custom and feel its validity). This last level is more or less related to what has been termed the "participant-observer" role which remains somewhat controversial as a research method in western anthropology (in which objective observation is supposed to be unburdened by personal involvement): how can the researcher retain a fair, analytical distance if she or he actually participates and believes in the traditional custom? Yanagita had a practical answer to this: there *is* no way to be totally disengaged or unbiased, especially when dealing with one's own culture. Rather, he required his students to consider their relationships and responses to the tradition under scrutiny as parts of their analytical approach. In the following examples, we will notice that one or more of Yanagita's three levels will be evident in the way a folk performance is viewed and interpreted.

TINA'S PROVERB

Context and Performance

I attended a party one evening at the home of a senior professor who had recently remarried. His new wife, Tina, a well-educated and elegant person fluent in several languages, was busy producing hors d'oeuvres in the tiny kitchen while he played the witty host to a group of his colleagues. However, Kester soon became afraid Tina would never be able to leave the kitchen, so he stepped through the doorway to offer his help. All at once we saw him propelled back into our midst accompanied by a sharply spoken Polish phrase from the kitchen.

"What did she say?" we asked. "I don't know, but whatever it was, she really meant it." He was cheerful but visibly puzzled. Naturally, when later in the party Tina joined us in an obviously good mood, we pressed her for an explanation of her magical phrase, for we had never witnessed our colleague—himself a forceful and charismatic person—so deftly put in his place. "No, no, I could never tell you," she said. "It's a very crude Polish proverb I heard my mother use occasionally. I could never repeat it to you in English. It's too crude. I'm sorry—it just slipped out before I could think, because of the circumstances, and I didn't even realize I was saying it." Several of us pursued the question off and on during the evening, but to no avail. It was not until the waning moments of the party, when only a few close friends remained, that the proverb finally came forth: "Well, essentially it says, 'A husband in the kitchen is like a boil in the anus.'"

Meaning

Here the performance of the proverb and the final perception of its meaning by the audience were separated by about three hours, which would not have been the case, presumably, had we been Poles in Poland. Clearly, however, the performance itself was of great importance to the performer, who needed a culturally sanctioned way to eject an alien from a context that was culturally hers. Though in legal terms they both owned the kitchen, Tina's cultural background had trained her to have control there. She did not want to reject her husband's help or to suggest anything personal about his culinary talents (if so, she could have said, "Out of the kitchen, you incompetent oaf!"). Indeed, Kester was a rather good cook and used the kitchen, solo, on many occasions. Here, the dilemma was a cultural one (how to entertain guests properly after a marriage), and it was solved—at least for the performer—in a culturally generated manner: "The way we Poles see it, a man gets in the way," a rather dull paraphrase of an exciting moment, after all.

Style and Occasion

Stylistic and physical dimensions of the performance were equally interesting and important. Sudden response, sharp vocal tones, loud volume, and physical action (shoving) made a certain amount of the message clear long before the words themselves were translated. The proverb "text," then, was only part of a larger set; shall we not call it a *proverbial performance?* This is another instance of the necessity for contextual observations. Proverbs seldom, if ever, occur at random. People usually do not just sit around "telling proverbs" (even in that case, there would be a context). Nor do we walk up to a stranger and say, "Hi there; did you know that a bird in the hand is worth two in the bush?" Proverbs normally come forth in response to a situation in which a person feels called upon to offer culturally appropriate advice to another person (in Europe and America, usually a friend or a relative).

Another aspect of performance may be seen in the meaning and the poetic style of the proverb itself. While the actual performer has chief control over the dynamics and the stylistic devices mentioned above (volume, action, and so on), the structure and wording of the proverb are the conservative features and are really the extended performance styles of the culture itself. We ask here not only, "How did Tina say the proverb in a certain context?" but, "How have the Poles phrased an attitude about a man's place in the kitchen?" While there are many ways to approach this question, perhaps the literary method allows the quickest route. The simile suggests some kind of equation between "a husband in the kitchen" and "a boil in the anus": x is like y. The nature of the equation comes from the imagery of the boil applied as a value judgment to the man. One easily thinks of such a boil as, perhaps first, objectionable; then, in no particular order: out of place, undesirable, potentially dangerous, dirty, painful; then, by extension: something that objectionably gets in the way of important, obligatory work, something that cannot be ignored, something that must be gotten rid of at all costs before one can get the job done.

Interpretation

Admittedly, these are *assumptions* about the value judgments suggested by the boil image. They are founded on the idea that such a boil would be seen as unpleasant by Poles and that the negative attitudes cited help us to understand the proverb's meaning. If ethnographic evidence were to show that posterior boils were highly prized in Poland as good luck omens, we would be forced to reinterpret the performance above, perhaps seeing the performer as one who remembered the proverbial text but had forgotten its real meaning so that she had misapplied it. In this case, the dynamic part of the performance would emerge as the most important and effective (for the husband was in fact ejected from the kitchen), and the conservative aspect—the continuity of culture-based attitude—would be seen as eroded. Since such ethnographic evidence is not likely to appear on this subject, the possibility of misinterpretation is hypothetical, but nevertheless the performance and its live context are only the beginning of a full study of folkloric meaning. In any case, it is clear that the three-second performance was far more forceful, meaningful, and persuasive than all this intellectual discussion. The impact of a folk performance like this lies mainly in its capacity to distill all these features into one articulate event that makes a difference. John H. McDowell calls this "*performative efficacy*, the capacity to make and remake the world through speech."

In Yanagita's terms, we all *saw* Tina's performance on level 1, *heard* it on level 2 (although it required translation before level 2 could come into focus), but probably none of us present *believe* the proverb and I doubt if any of us would ever use it under similar circumstances. Indeed, the very fact that I find the anecdote striking enough to mention and discuss here is a sign that for me level 3 represents an oddity worth looking at. At the same time, I am unlikely to explain to members of my own family that "a stitch in time saves nine" means that repair work done in a timely manner will save a person more work later on when things break down altogether because of inadequate maintenance, for they would look at me as if I had just announced that daylight is caused by the sun. In fact, it may be that our awareness of level 3 discrepancies between our own cultural norms and those we seek to study is precisely what interests us in much of folklore and motivates us to account for it. Yet, to understand folklore most fully, as Yanagita insisted, and as William A. Wilson has more recently urged, we need to accord level 3 in our own culture the same intense and serious scrutiny we give to the traditions of others—despite what Brian Sutton-Smith has called the "triviality barrier," the hesitation to look at our own everyday customs as significant because they seem too, well, everyday.

There are proverbs of all sorts, offering what might at first appear to be conflicting advice ("Look before you leap!" "He who hesitates is lost."). Arguing that proverbs thus advise expediency rather misses the point: it is always the situation that brings up the context for the advice which seems to be needed, and situations in life differ considerably, as we know. We might advise one person here to leap and another person there to hesitate. But since the proverb allows phrasing the advice in a culturally recognized form, it comes out not as our own personal opinion (which might be considered arrogant or intrusive anyway) but as a cultural norm, with all the authority, antiquity, and stability of that category.

The performance and perception of proverbs allow both speaker and audience to exercise culturally comfortable philosophies and to demonstrate in so doing their own hold on tradition, their membership in the group. So important is this function of proverbs in Nigeria that some tribal courts are more likely to rule favorably for the person who knows and uses proverbs most correctly in addition to other evidence brought forward in a case. Here, the performance of traditional philosophy and the recognition of its stabilizing influence in the culture are more important in and of themselves than the relatively superficial question of who stole a chicken, or who is in the kitchen.

AUDIENCE

Speaking of verbal folklore, William Hugh Jansen insists that performance implies not only a speaker but an audience (the same concept, of course, is implicit in Roger D. Abrahams's work on rhetoric in folklore): "The speaker, or the reciter of a bit of folklore steps outside himself as an individual and assumes a pose toward his audience, however small, that differs from his everyday . . . relationship to that same audience." The matter of pose, of self-conscious movement into another role, varies considerably according to the genre of folklore and particular contextual settings—especially as we try to apply the idea to nonverbal folklore. But even in the verbal category we know that some sea songs were sung routinely as a way of timing and pacing the actions of men during daily work aboard ship, while other songs were sung chiefly ashore—perhaps in dockside taverns and pubs—where someone would step forward and consciously sing a lead part. Applied to material culture, we observe that a Japanese woman cooking traditional daily food for her family is not setting the pose for her audience which might be inevitable if she were producing traditional food for a Japanese wedding. These variations in self-consciousness and pose must be held in mind as we discuss the following general situations.

Here we want to understand the importance of an audience as the responsive part of a folk performance. As William Wilson says of the function of audience in Mormon folklore, "If the story is to live, [the storytellers] cannot, in the telling of it, depart too far from the value center of the audience whose approval they seek." I think Wilson's term *value center* is a good one, for it represents a "critical mass" of cultural concern and attitude shared by enough people that it can be transmitted through time as a philosophical constellation. It is the human counterpart to Coffin's term *emotional core* in ballads, that central clustering of action and image that characterizes the main *idea* of the ballad. I suggest the term *ideational core* for the same quality in all items being performed (since emotion may not always be the defining feature). There is a something being done, performed, by someone who has done it before, for an audience of people who already know it. Their reason for doing and experiencing the performance time and time again is of course that—beyond the pleasure of entertainment—such familiar performances help to reinforce and maintain the central ideas of the group (their value centers), help to induct newcomers (children, greenhorns) into the group, help to re-experience important emotions, and help to define outsiders and strangers.

An accurate perception of a traditional performer-audience relationship must rest on each instance of expression taken separately. For example, a traditional singer might sing an old sailing song for a group of fellow seamen who already know the song, though perhaps each might sing it in a somewhat different way. The same singer might sing the song at a festival for people who have never heard it or who know it only from records. Or it might be sung for other family members at home. In each case, even though there is an audience, the dynamics of aesthetic and cultural interaction will be different. If there are suggestive or obscene verses, the singer would be more likely to use them in the first instance, leave them out in the second, and perhaps use some of the least suggestive in the third, all because of the singer's perception of the audience in each case. On the other hand, the performer can get away with greater modifications in length or phrasing for the second, comparatively unknowing audience than with the first or third.

Formative Influences

In one New England family where sea songs are sung around the Thanksgiving dinner table, there are family hesitancies about some verses that would be totally ridiculous aboard ship. The chorus of the old song "Rolling Home," sung as a memorial to family members who did not come home from the sea, can have a metaphorical, almost religious, feeling:

Rolling home, rolling home,
rolling home across the sea,
rolling home to old New England,
rolling home, dear land, to thee.

On shipboard the anticipation of getting home and the nostalgia of leaving behind the girls of the port can be re-experienced in the verses:

Good-bye you fair Hawaiian ladies,
we must bid you all adieu—
we'll recall those pleasant hours
that we often spent with you.

We will leave you our best wishes
as we leave your rocky shore—
we are sailing home for Rockport;
you won't see us anymore.

But those verses, sung at the Thanksgiving dinner table, tend to reduce the chances of the chorus having the religious connotation of "rolling home" to heaven; they are likely to give aunts and grandmothers indigestion by reminding them of the human weaknesses of their male ancestors (who would have considered them strengths). The singers need to know this if they want to avoid causing family indignation at a festive, semi-religious occasion. Such a consideration on board ship, however, would seem laughable and overscrupulous.

Among seafarers, moreover, the singer may easily substitute "Mexican," "Australian," "Japanese," or any other seaport nationality for "Hawaiian," while among family singers (not seated at the Thanksgiving dinner table) the allowable substitutions are set by those ports and nations actually known to have been visited by ancestor sailors. Thus, particular words within the song may be changed or maintained because of the audience present at a given performance. When "Rolling Home" was sung by a member of that family in a film about the Oregon coast, the words "rolling home to misty Oregon" were substituted for "rolling home to old New England"; a single older member of the family watched the film to that point and then stalked out angrily because he considered the change totally unacceptable (although he accepted other typical changes mentioned above). If the performance had been live, this one member of the larger audience would have constituted a negative traditional audience, which very likely would have impeded the singer's willingness to make that particular change (or at least to repeat it in the same company).

In their study of northern Athabascan languages, Ron and Suzanne Scollon discovered a Chipewyan Athabascan verb which is used to mean three separate but obviously parallel actions: a dog picking a bone clean, a woman picking berries, and someone listening carefully and understanding what someone else is saying. Maybe "gleaning" is the closest English equivalent, and it well represents the engagement, the work, the "subsistence economy" of human interaction (as the Scollons put it) which typifies the role of a traditional audience.

Central Audience

The central audience of a folk performance can be defined as any person or persons present who know and hear the tradition well enough to exert an influence on the nature of the performance. This audience includes the performer and may indeed be limited to the performer on some occasions. *insiders*

Bystander Audience

There may be other audiences as well—for example, bystanders, aficionados, tourists, paying customers—and they may in fact be most enthusiastic about those aspects of performance style that match their own stereotypical expectations. These people may also affect the nature of the performance, but the influence may lie along the lines of their own taste. So, for example, when a traditional singer is asked to perform a few songs for a local public school, pieces may be chosen according to what the singer feels local folks ought to know and enjoy; if the audience is a group of college professors, the singer is more likely to sing the kinds of songs most easily shared with intellectual outsiders. At the Hachiman Mikoshi festival in Tokyo, the bearers of Shinto shrines get drenched with water along the parade route as a part of the fertility imagery. The onlookers and policemen get wet, too, but they can leave or move and they do not have to carry a shrine from dawn to dusk yelling "wasshoi! wasshoi!" *sensitive*

Outsider Audience

In some cases, a traditional artist's perception of audience variation is so strong that he or she will not perform for outsiders at all. I tried to collect songs from an old Utahn who had been a central figure at all weddings and celebrations in the Uintah Basin. His response to me was a deep chuckle, and then, "Aw, I'm no singer; you don't want to hear those old songs I sing." And he stayed cheerfully adamant about it for a full day. A woman in Oregon sang innumerable "heart songs" from the turn of the century, but steadfastly refused to sing the old mountain songs she knew from her grandfather: "Oh, you college folks don't really know how crude and rough those mountain songs are. No, you don't want to hear *them*." These are not only expressions of modesty or embarrassment; they are acknowledgments of an inappropriate or "foreign" audience.

Cultural Audience *Santa Claus* *oneness*

In addition to these highly varied audiences for folk performances, there is an implied cultural audience that either approves or disapproves of the tradition itself. Consider the old man who told me, about a kind of basket he had learned *present in spirit* to make when young, "Oh, no, I don't do it much anymore; nobody cares about it. Nobody will learn it. What's the use, anyhow? Nobody cares about this kind of thing anymore." Compare that with the quilter who said, "My quilts are on my family's beds all over this country [meaning locale]; people like my quilts, and when I give one away it's like knowing a part of me is being appreciated by someone, even if I die." Our awareness of this larger implied audience helps us see how nonentertainment folklore may be approached, for we can observe that people are not always performing for a physically present audience.

Some Audiences Considered

This is an important subject for us, for singing, the telling of a story in its traditional context, and the speaking of a proverb in an appropriate situation are all easily understood as performances, because they seem very much like the self-conscious performances we see and hear on stage, screen, radio, and television. Viewing other kinds of folk expressions as performances may be a bit more complicated; we need to ask what sort of performance can be said to take place when someone is quilting? What does a dowser perform, and for whom? When a Ukrainian American cymbaly (hammered dulcimer) player plays for a Ukrainian wedding reception, it is easy to see who is performing and for whom; but for whom did the dulcimer *maker* perform when crafting the instrument, working alone for many nights? And in all cases, since we are trying to see simultaneously the dynamism and the conservatism in a folk expression, to what extent did the tastes and demands of these presumed audiences modify or encourage certain elements of the performance or occasion the whole performance itself?

Quilts

For most quilters, the central audience, the one that may impose the greatest influence on the performance, is made up of other quilters. Their practiced eyes not only see the final quilt and its colorful design but notice the piecework, the sewing articulation and fineness of stitch, as well as the finesse of the quilting, that process of attaching the backing and filling to the more prominent top pattern. From this observation we should recognize the existence of a dynamic folk group called *quilters,* made up of performers and audiences, which exists as a viable entity in addition to its members belonging to other folk groups as well. And this audience need not be present when the quilt is actually constructed (though in the form of a quilting circle or "bee," it may be present from start to finish).

There are other important audiences for the quilter. The family, who do of course pick up at least some of the ways of judging a quilt, may also apply some of the beliefs about quilt meaning and usage. For example, in some families it is considered good luck for a newly married couple to receive a Double Wedding Ring quilt; in other families it is felt inauspicious to give a married couple the

Wandering Foot quilt, for the subtle influence of its design might cause the husband (not the wife!) to "wander." Mormon couples often receive a "Temple quilt" as a wedding present, with the outline of the temple where they were married stitched in the center of the quilt. Many believe that these quilts are not to be placed on the bed, but rather to be put carefully away and brought out only on special occasions—such as a wedding anniversary. Others believe that the quilt should be on the bed to remind them of the temple's role in their ongoing family life. Since these beliefs are not shared by all quilters and their audiences, they seem to be related as much to family or religious folklore as to quilting per se.

The buying public, which may range from "outsider" tourists looking for something folksy to take home from the Ozarks to "bystander" art experts buying quilts for a museum show, also exerts an influence on the quilter, but it is less immediate in time and less considerate of insider lore. Very possibly, these broad categories could be subdivided, for isn't the art specialist—well schooled in folk art—more discerning and demanding than the tourist? Only a specific instance would tell us. However we demarcate the varying levels of audience participation in the aesthetics or structure of the final traditional performance, we will probably always notice two general kinds of audiences: insiders and outsiders.

Hammered Dulcimers

Although he was not a musician, John Palanuk of Springfield, Oregon, was a maker of Ukrainian-style hammered dulcimers. He did not play them, and until recently no one in his immediate family did either. Who was his audience then? Whose tastes and demands did he satisfy by producing these traditional instruments? For whom was he performing when he built an instrument? First of all, unlike some craftspeople, he did not make dulcimers to sell to strangers, so the "tourist art" category does not fit his case at all. Rather, he made dulcimers because the local Ukrainians use them on festive occasions; they are needed by the people he identified with, and there was no one else to make them. Palanuk himself was not brought up making traditional instruments; he had been a farmer and a mechanic and was considered very talented with his hands. In the same shop where he fixed his lawnmower he occasionally built a dulcimer, making all the parts, wooden and metal, out of pieces he had saved. If he had learned to make dulcimers from other traditional instrumentmakers, we could have said that he was a part of his own central audience, judging his "performance" by reference to an inherited system of culture-based knowledge of wood resonance, color, design, and so on.

Instead, however, John Palanuk had figured out how to make dulcimers just by being around them all his life. The design, the sound, the usage, were all dictated for him by the way dulcimers have always looked in the various Ukrainian communities of which he was a member. For example, he carefully included an extra small hole on each instrument "because you have to put

Ukrainian American John Palanuk of Springfield, Oregon, adjusts the strings (made of salmon-trolling wire) on one of his many hammered dulcimers.

Lulabell Seegmiller provides rhythm on the tines of a pitchfork for the Haywire Band—consisting of two or three guitars, two or three harmonicas, and a pitchfork—of Springdale, Utah, which for years provided entertainment and dance music for isolated communities in southern Utah.

In a typical folklore tableau scene, Franklin George and Melvin Wine exchange tunes and fingering technique at the West Virginia State Folk Festival at Glenville. Photo by Carl Fleischhauer, courtesy of the American Folklife Center, Library of Congress.

money into the instrument to pay the boy who plays it." But the internal structure, the composition of such things as bridges and tuning devices, he had to learn by himself using good mechanical sense and woodworking talents. In the case of John Palanuk, we can suggest that the Ukrainian community as a whole was his audience for the performance of dulcimer-making, while in terms of general mechanical traditions (making do with pre-existing pieces of metal, using steel salmon fishing line for string) Palanuk (and other shop workers) are potentially the central audience. These simultaneous audiences are discernible because we can see at least these two sets of interactions helping to dictate and channel what Palanuk did when he made a dulcimer.

In the Ukrainian community, of course, are people who play the dulcimer. Viewed from the instrumentmaker's standpoint, these are bystanders; they belong to the larger community but are not themselves engaged in making dulcimers. They are part of the community audience for Palanuk. They need not be present while he works. From the standpoint of musical tradition, however, these dulcimer players—who come forth at weddings and baptisms to play in small bands (usually hammered dulcimer, accordion, drums, and violin)—are "inside" performers, while John Palanuk was a part of their audience as a "bystander" who knew the songs and dances but did not play the instruments. None of these components operates very well without the others; John Palanuk and his community are a typical example of the interdependence, the symbiotic relationship, that sustains tradition in a dynamic community.

Tall Tales

The same two kinds of audiences (insiders and outsiders) can be seen in other kinds of folk performances as well. Take the telling of tall tales: some people—Len Henry, Hathaway Jones, B. F. ("Huckleberry") Finn, to name three prominent Munchausens of the Northwest—told tall stories, or "windies," as a regular habit. Their immediate central audiences were those other raconteurs with whom they swapped stories and the usual group of local admirers—"the boys down at the store"—who knew the stories but did not consider themselves to be "characters" enough to tell them. Other observers may be local but not so knowledgeable, such as the youngster down the street who still hasn't figured out which are the true stories but knows that something funny is going on (partly at his or her expense), or strangers who have no way at all of knowing what is going on. The central and bystander audiences may listen to a tall tale with quiet amusement and nodding of heads, laughing openly, as if at a joke. The stranger, irked at being told a falsehood and having no basis on which to share the joke with the others, may respond, "Aw, I don't believe such a thing," or may just leave in a huff.

I saw an exasperated eastern tourist in a desert town in southern Utah trying to interest a service station mechanic in fixing his overheated car. "Does it always get this hot around here?" he demanded. The mechanic responded, with a straight face, "Well, when it *really* gets hot in these parts the farmers start feeding cracked ice to their chickens to keep 'em from laying hard-boiled eggs." Another attendant added, "Couple of years ago we had a power outage and the ice machines broke down and every cafe in town had specials on boiled eggs for three weeks." The tourist didn't laugh, but two teenagers leaning against the wall did, and had to turn away. "Wait till summertime sets in, you'll see some *real* heat," the first mechanic said. The tourist had no time to wait, and drew the conversation back to the car, which was eventually attended to. This is a good example of two insiders performing for themselves and to two (bystander and outsider) audiences at once. Probably without the stranger the performance would not have occurred, so we cannot dismiss the outsider as unimportant in the total event. The understanding and style used by the two mechanics as tall-tale performers and the responses of the two locals were of different sorts, both more knowledgeable than that of the tourist, yet different in quality from each other. Moreover, the outsider believed he was being lied to, but the insiders and bystanders knew it was the absolute truth being expressed in clever hyperbole.

Riddles

The same kinds of levels occur in a traditional rendering of a European or American riddle: there is the performer who remembers the riddles, their phrasing, and their answers. There is perhaps the central audience of others who also know the riddles and their answers. These are insiders, and they can—and do—correct each other's phrasing or solutions. The local bystanders in riddling, as with tall tales, are often the neophytes of the family or community; they have heard the riddles but do not know them very well. As they learn them, of course, they become—as riddlers—insiders. The strangers are those who do not know the riddles or who, because of different backgrounds, have no way of perceiving the key metaphor or image that gives the riddle its core meaning. Insiders eventually learn the riddles by heart so that for them performance and reception involve a pleasant and poetic word game the knowledge of which provides a constant demonstration of membership in the group and its traditions. Strangers, even intelligent ones who know other riddles, are often at a loss to answer correctly or to begin figuring out even a plausible answer. Alan Jabbour gives an account of a riddling session that occurred when he and others were recording the traditions of the Hammons family in West Virginia. Several riddles had been recited, some of which Jabbour had recognized; then Burl Hammons said, "And what is that one about . . .

> *Crooked as a rainbow and teeth like a cat,*
> *You can guess all night but you can't guess that."*
> *His sister, Maggie, said, "Yes, yes—*
> *As crooked as a rainbow and has teeth like a cat,*
> *You can guess all night but you can't guess that."*

Jabbour tried to figure it out and asked help from a friend; then Maggie, in slight exasperation, repeated it again. At the phrase "you can't guess that," Jabbour responded, "I think you're right," immediately followed by Maggie saying, "Well, now, that's a greenbrier." "What? A green . . . " "Yes sir, that's a greenbrier."

It is not hard to imagine that a young person growing up in a tightly knit community would learn riddles such as these—as well as a lot of other traditional expressions—and become a full-fledged insider as soon as possible. The term *local bystander* thus represents a potentially ephemeral position, depending on the tradition being discussed. A Ukrainian in a Ukrainian community might never learn to play the dulcimer, and in that area she would remain a local bystander to the tradition; but she might have learned hundreds of riddles before she was twenty years old and thus would have become, in another traditional setting, an insider and thus part of the central audience. Jabbour suggests in his notes to the Hammons family record that all traditions were learned by the Hammonses as they participated first as a family audience for their father and other relatives (who instructed by giving "model" performances, not by overt teaching) and then by becoming performers themselves, following their own personal predilections for instrumental music, singing, or story-telling. This is the typical folk learning situation.

Pranks

Outside the family audience context, we may refer for another parallel set of audiences to the loggers' or cowboys' initiation of the greenhorn, the hazing of the newcomer. Again there are the insiders who perform, the strangers who know little or nothing, and the local bystanders, the new workers, who—by means of the pranks—become insiders. Each of these audiences is essential: The very fact that the stranger knows nothing about the process helps to strengthen the esoteric sense of heightened participation in a special group. And the victim, to cease being a victim, must try to move as quickly from the outside audience category to the inside audience, there to become a performer to other fresh audiences. Maritime rituals for crossing the equator for the first time remain some of the lengthiest and most complex of these performances.

Dowsing

Dowsing is a way of detecting water, oil, or minerals by the use of a divining rod—often a forked twig cut from a live tree, but sometimes a steel rod, crowbar, welding rod, wire, spring, or chain. The process is nearly always passed on by personal example and oral tradition by one considered adept at it to someone who "has the feel for it" but has not yet learned a technique. There is a sense of exclusiveness about dowsing because, in the words of one dowser, "you either have it or you don't. When I found out I could find water, I was really surprised, but you know, a lot of people can't do it, even if you put them right

Water dowser Eldon McArthur gives instruction in water witching to spectators at the Southern Utah Folklife Festival in Zion National Park, 1977.

Folklorist William A. Wilson, who does not believe in water witching, finds out under Eldon McArthur's tutelage that he can do it anyway.

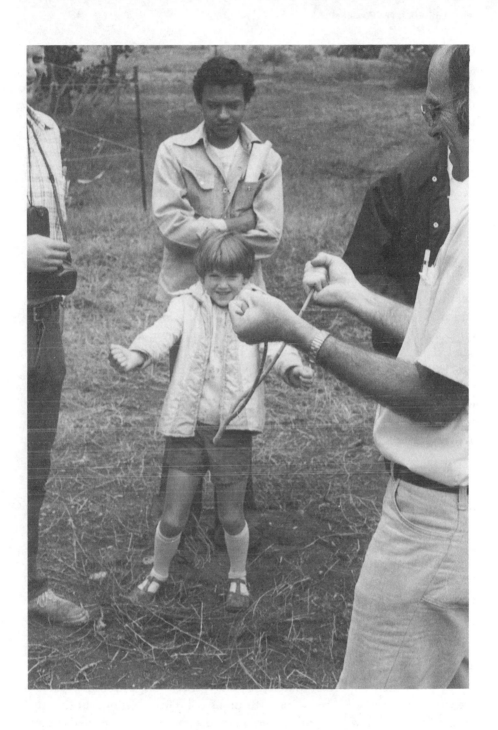

over a vein." Dowsers, or "water witches," therefore have for their most central audience the community of dowsers. They can discuss the process knowledgeably and can correct each other. The local bystanders in the audience believe in dowsing and want to have it done but do not know how to do it. In fact, some people have it done even though they do not believe in it. One Utah rancher told me, "It's a lot of foolishness. I don't believe in it at all. But I wouldn't for my life drill a well without it was witched first." The outsiders are entirely skeptical and have nothing to do with dowsing functionally—although they might be willing to drive to Danville, Vermont, and witness the annual convention of dowsers, just for curiosity's sake.

Signing

Deaf people who have learned how to sign their communications spend a good deal of time signing with others who share the experience of impaired hearing. Their sign language is, basically, as formal as any standard language, and it is formally taught. But among users of sign language there has developed a folk speech, perhaps more properly a folk sign, a kind of visual/gestural slang. Insiders know and use it. Local bystanders (who can hear, but because of their job or their relation to someone deaf have learned formal signing) see it but often do not catch the meaning. Strangers, who know and use no signs more complicated than shrugging for "I don't know," are unaware that there is such a folk communication, even though they may actually witness it happening.

The Audience as Folk Group

Members of religious groups may also experience these levels of performance and audience when they share the oral traditions that have grown out of their common experiences. The Amish have their German proverbs and planting customs; Catholics trade stories of adventures in parochial school (unwittingly repeating stories and motifs heard around the country); Jews tell stories of Elijah coming in disguise to someone's Seder and jokes about Jewish mothers and chicken soup; Mormons tell Three Nephite legends and J. Golden Kimball stories. In each instance, the central audience is made up of insiders who share enough experience and attitude so that connotation runs high (Hall's high context situation), and the value center, as Wilson calls it, is recognized by most if not all participants.

It is extremely important to note that this works in one direction but not in the other. That is, we can say that Mormons tell Three Nephite stories, that most Mormons know what those stories are, that most Mormons derive more live meaning from them than do total outsiders (who are inclined to scoff at the veracity of the legends). But we may not say that every Mormon tells them or believes them. In other words, our recognition of an inside, central audience is not the equivalent of a stereotype and it does not suggest that all members are alike in any way. It does suggest that one group of people may be more likely than another group to perform certain traditions.

Similarly, the toasts, rhymed narratives recited by many Black men, are not known to all African Americans. Like the dozens (continually escalating formularized insults exchanged by men), they feature language that does not match the demands of polite society. Women, especially older women, and men who wish to be more refined or religious are less inclined to learn the toasts and may in fact never put themselves in a context where they may be heard. Nonetheless, we are still justified in saying that present research indicates we are more likely to find the toasts recited by African Americans than by anyone else. And for those Blacks who do share them we can see that the dynamic interaction between performer and audience is closely related to other cohesive factors in the group and is parallel in style to other kinds of performance (chiefly, in this instance, seen in the antiphonal, or call-and-response, relation between performer and audience). In such a case, we expect African Americans, as central and bystander audiences, to get a deeper meaning and a fuller experience out of a toast than outsiders might—even though Black mothers might well be shocked if they heard their own sons reciting one.

William Wilson provides an excellent example of the kind of connotative knowledge shared by an inside, central audience: Mormons listening to J. Golden Kimball stories. Kimball was a leader in the Church of Jesus Christ of Latter-day Saints (commonly called Mormon), but he had been a rancher and a cattle driver, and he had a vivid vocabulary as well as a quick wit and puckish sense of humor. He loved to puncture those whose pomposity got the better of them. The church authorities were so worried about his potential for swearing in public that on one occasion the president of the church, Heber J. Grant, wrote out a speech for Kimball to deliver at the annual conference, which was being broadcast live from Temple Square in Salt Lake City. Before the hushed crowd, Kimball squinted at the speech Grant had handed him and then screeched over the microphone in his well-known high voice, "Good hell, Hebe, I can't read a damn word of this!"

The outsider listening to this—as no doubt many did over the radio— would certainly see the unexpected humor of a crusty old man swearing in church, and on the radio at that. The local bystanders—perhaps, say, non-Mormons who nonetheless had heard some J. Golden Kimball stories before— would fit the incident into a still larger picture of the beloved, feisty, but now untrusted old man giving some superior his just desserts. But the insiders, the Mormons (those present on the occasion and those who still today form the central audience for the Kimball stories), catch a sharper and more ironic humor from the daring deed performed by their favorite trickster figure. In the words of Wilson, "The real laughter is evoked by the word 'Hebe.' Prophet, seer, and revelator—yes. But never Hebe. Therein lies the sacrilege." Wilson goes so far as to suggest that the Kimball stories are not really about Kimball but about Mormons, for they embody all those tensions that inevitably arise when people's own normal inclinations are subordinated to authority.

It is this sense of a "we" that unifies the folk audience, and it is exactly that which allows us to speak of such an entity as a folk group. But the folk group is not a stereotype: it is a community of audiences in which vernacular performances take place and have meaning on several levels. The folklorist watches for those expressions—like the African American dozens or the J. Golden Kimball stories—that are seen in the informal performance repertoires of any close group, but recognizes in so doing that some performances will come through more clearly than others, depending on whether the researcher is an outsider to the tradition (which may limit the perception to Yanagita's level 1), or a knowledgeable bystander (Yanagita's levels 1 and 2), or a part of the central audience (Yanagita's level 3). Folklorists who operate on level 3 are rare unless they focus on the traditions of their own immediate culture. In any case, folklorists always try to develop the capacity to deal fairly with level 2—through study, fieldwork, language acquisition, and research—so that they will be able to glean the most from culturally rich performances while avoiding lopsided or superficial analyses of their functions and meanings for their normal audiences.

BIBLIOGRAPHICAL NOTES

John Miles Foley, an untiring scholar of oral tradition, has focused primarily on the emergent, active moments in which epics and other orally formed and transmitted expressions reach articulation in performance. See his "Word-Power, Performance, and Tradition," *Journal of American Folklore* 105 (1992): 175–301, esp. 278.

The Coyote story performance is given line by line (as closely as my translation permits) from the tape. The recorder was turned on just at the outset of the narrative by permission gained during our conversation upon arrival. The text and the comments try to convey the pacing and style of the performance as well as the responses of the audience. Although I have not been able to correlate volume and tone with the performance as it is represented here in print, the mode of my presentation is obviously much indebted to Dennis Tedlock's impressive *Finding the Center* (New York: Dial, 1972). Explanatory cultural footnotes are in parentheses; timing details in narration are in brackets; the actions of audience and narrator are noted in italics; distinct pauses of more than a second are shown by a tilde (~) in the text. See also Tedlock, "On the Translation of Style in Oral Narrative," in *Toward New Perspectives in Folklore,* ed. Américo Paredes and Richard Bauman (Austin: University of Texas Press, 1971), 114-33. This essay, plus several other seminal pieces, are included in Tedlock's *The Spoken Word and the Work of Interpretation* (Philadelphia: University of Pennsylvania Press, 1983); his work consistently treats performance as a non-separable dimension of audience interaction within culturally constructed events.

The story which begins on p. 125 is discussed more fully in my essays, "The 'Pretty Languages' of Yellowman: Genre, Mode, and Texture in Navajo Coyote Narratives," *Genre* 2 (1969): 211-35; reprinted in *Folklore Genres,* ed. Dan Ben-Amos (Austin: University of Texas Press, 1976), 145-70; "Poetic Retranslation and the 'Pretty Languages' of Yellowman," with Tacheeni Scott, in *Traditional Literatures of the American Indian,* ed. Karl Kroeber (Lincoln: University of Nebraska Press, 1981), 65–116; "Life and Death in the Navajo Coyote Tales," in *Recovering the Word: Essays on Native American Literature,* ed. Arnold Krupat and Brian Swann (Berkeley: University of California Press, 1987), 388–401; "'Ma'ii Joldlooshi la Eeyá The Several Lives of a Navajo Coyote," *The World and I* (April 1990): 651–60; "Fieldwork Enlightenment," *Parabola: The Magazine of Myth and Tradition* 20 (Summer 1995): 28–35.

Lee Haring discusses critical aspects in the presence of an outside observer during a traditional performance in "Performing for the Interviewer: A Study of the Structure of Context," *Southern Folklore Quarterly* 36 (1972): 383-98. He suggests that the performance is valid even if the interviewer is a total stranger, because even then the outsider has become a part of the human context and fills a certain social role, often, as in the instance described in this chapter, providing the central reason for at least part of the traditional performance itself. Jansen's remark is found on pp. 112-13 in his "Classifying Performance in the Study of Verbal Folklore," in *Studies in Folklore,* ed. W. Edson Richmond, Indiana University Folklore Series, no. 9 (Bloomington: Indiana University Press, 1957), 110-18. Roger D. Abrahams sees the folk performance as having an essentially rhetorical nature, in the classical sense of that word. See "Introductory Remarks to a Rhetorical Theory of Folklore," *Journal of American Folklore* 81 (1968): 143-58.

William A. Wilson uses the term *value center* on p. 46 of an extremely provocative essay, written from an insider's point of view, "The Paradox of Mormon Folklore," *Brigham Young University Studies* 17 (1976): 40–58. Tristram P. Coffin proposed the term *emotional core* in "Mary Hamilton and the Anglo-American Ballad as an Art Form," *Journal of American Folklore* 70 (1957): 208-14; reprinted in *The Critics and the Ballad,* ed. MacEdward Leach and Tristram P. Coffin (Carbondale: Southern Illinois University Press, 1961), 245-56; the term itself is discussed on pp. 246-47. The works of Yanagita Kunio are not widely translated into English, though they are found in nearly every library—public and private—in Japan. Basic are *About Our Ancestors* (Tokyo: Monbusho, 1970; rpt. New York: Greenwood Press, 1988); Ronald A. Morse, *Yanagita Kunio and the Folklore Movement: The Search for Japan's National Character and Distinctiveness* (New York: Garland, 1990); and J. Victor Koschmann, Oiwa Keibo, and Yamashita Shinji, eds., *International Perspectives on Yanagita Kunio and Japanese Folklore Studies,* Cornell University East Asia Papers, no. 37 (Ithaca, N.Y.: Cornell University, 1985). Yanagita's insistence that folklorists should begin by making an account of the performances in their own cultures before delving into others is seconded by William A. Wilson in "Documenting Folklore," in *Folk Groups and Folklore Genres,* ed. Elliott Oring (Logan: Utah State University Press, 1986), 225–54.

The "triviality barrier" was first discussed by Brian Sutton-Smith in "The Psychology of Childlore: The Triviality Barrier," *Western Folklore* 29 (1970): 1–8; the concept has been used by many since that time, among them Jay Mechling in "Children's Folklore," *Folk Groups and Folklore Genres,* ed. Elliott Oring (Logan: Utah State University Press, 1986), 91–120.

Especially interesting because of its consideration of performance in direct relationship to context, audience, and event, is Richard Bauman, *Story, Performance, and Event: Contextual Studies of Oral Narrative,* Cambridge Studies in Oral and Literate Culture, no. 10 (Cambridge: Cambridge University Press, 1986), esp. pp. 102–5 for comments on audience. See, as well, Elizabeth C. Fine, *The Folklore Text from Performance to Print*

(Bloomington: Indiana University Press, 1984); and John Miles Foley, *Immanent Art: From Structure to Meaning in Traditional Oral Epic* (Bloomington: Indiana University Press, 1991), which sees audience context as an active aspect of performance, and not simply as a social setting. John McDowell's comment on *performative efficacy* is in "Folklore as Commemorative Discourse," *Journal of American Folklore* 105 (1992): 403–23. I am indebted to Ron and Suzanne Scollon for sharing with me their insights on northwest Athabascan verbs during their intensive fieldwork in Alaska and western Canada.

Tall tales abound throughout Europe and America: one thinks most easily of the "Baron Münchhausen" stories as well as of the regional hyperbolic tales found in virtually every rural part of America. One of the best regional collections is Vance Randolph, *We Always Lie to Strangers: Tall Tales from the Ozarks* (New York: Columbia University Press, 1951). Representing a rich Northwest tall-tale tradition are Susan Mullin, "Oregon's Huckleberry Finn: A Munchausen Enters Tradition," *Northwest Folklore* 2, no. 1 (Summer 1967): 19-25; and Jan Harold Brunvand, "Len Henry: North Idaho Munchausen," *Northwest Folklore* 1, no. 1 (Summer 1965): 11-19. In *Tall Tales from Rogue River: The Yarns of Hathaway Jones* (Bloomington: Indiana University Press, 1974), Stephen Dow Beckham provides a book-length collection of fancy lies by and about a real local character who carried mail along the primitive Rogue River around the turn of the century. Hathaway Jones had a harelip and a cleft palate, and stories about him that still circulate in oral tradition feature this peculiarity of speech in the punch lines. Concerned with tall tales in the Midwest is Roger Welsch, *Shingling the Fog and Other Plains Lies: Tall Tales of the Great Plains* (Chicago: Swallow Press, 1972). The far Midwest is treated by Erik Wahlgren in "Scandinavian Folklore and Folk Culture in the Trans-Mississippi West," *Northwest Folklore* 3, no. 1 (Summer 1969): 1-16. An extremely helpful essay on the nature of tall tales is Gustav Henningsen's "The Art of Perpendicular Lying—Concerning a Commercial Collecting of Norwegian Sailors' Tall Tales," *Journal of the Folklore Institute* 2 (1965): 180-219.

A great number of works have been issued on riddles and riddling. Standard is Archer Taylor, *English Riddles from Oral Tradition* (Berkeley: University of California Press, 1951). Brunvand has an interesting chapter on riddling in *The Study of American Folklore* and adds a useful basic bibliography. The *Journal of American Folklore* 89 (1976) included a special issue (no. 352) on riddles and riddling, edited by Elli Kongas Maranda. On the dynamics of riddling, Lee Haring insists, in "On Knowing the Answer," *Journal of American Folklore* 87 (1974): 197-207, that in the case of African riddles there may be several possible answers, the particular one being brought forward by the context at hand. His argument is answered by Lyndon Harries in "Semantic Fit in Riddles," *Journal of American Folklore* 89 (1976): 319-25. The riddles from the Hammons family are found on pp. 31-32 in Alan Jabbour and Carl Fleischhauer, eds., *The Hammons Family: A Study of a West Virginia Family's Traditions* (Washington, D.C.: Library of Congress, 1973). This combination of two long-play records and an extensively researched booklet, issued by the Archive of Folk Song in the Library of Congress, has established itself as a standard for the recorded presentation of family songs and traditions. See also F.A. de Caro, "Riddles and Proverbs," in *Folk Groups and Folklore Genres*, 175–97.

For a critical discussion of proverbs in their live setting, see E. Ojo Arewa and Alan Dundes, "Proverbs and the Ethnography of Speaking Folklore," *American Anthropologist* 66 (1964): 70-85. Another engaging article is "The Role of Proverbs in a Nigerian Judicial System," by John C. Messenger Jr., in *Southwestern Journal of Anthropology* 15 (1959): 64-73; reprinted in Alan Dundes's *Study of Folklore*, 299–307. In the case of

Nigerian proverbs in tribal court proceedings, it is clear that the person who knows the most appropriate proverbs is usually the one who wins the case. In this high context group, the most traditional person is the one retained and encouraged by the society. More recently, African folklorist Kwesi Yankah has demonstrated that the cultural complications in Messenger's observed courtroom events were far beyond the outsider's ability to register. Using parallel materials from legal traditions in Ghana, Yankah shows how keenly the proverb performances, the audience responses, the assumptions of the legal system, and even family and social alliances are intertwined in the presentation and understanding of judicial evidence. See his "Proverb Rhetoric and African Judicial Processes: The Untold Story," *Journal of American Folklore* 99 (1986): 280–303. In the case of Tina's proverb, the complications are a bit different: while the proverb, spoken in Polish, must represent one of her principal links to her cultural sense of propriety, it nonetheless casts her into the stereotypical American role of being where a woman belongs (in the kitchen), even though politically and personally Tina would not have accepted the sense of limitation in that scene. In this sense, immigrant proverbs may function to highlight discrepancies and unresolved cultural assumptions even as they may provide an echo of a supportive ethnic past.

Stories of the Three Nephites are most easily found in Austin and Alta Fife, *Saints of Sage and Saddle* (Bloomington: Indiana University Press, 1956) and Hector Lee, *The Three Nephites: The Substance and Significance of the Legend in Folklore* (Albuquerque: University of New Mexico Press, 1949).

For an extensive discussion of dowsing (water-witching), see Evon A. Vogt and Ray Hyman, *Water Witching U.S.A.* (Chicago: University of Chicago Press, 1958). A widely used book on signing, *A Basic Course in Manual Communication*, ed. Terrence J. O'Rourke (Silver Spring, Md.: National Association of the Deaf, 1973), gives extensive diagrams for signs, even the most complicated, that have become standard, but it addresses no attention to the subject of slang or folk signing.

Roger D. Abrahams has stressed for some years now the central element of performance in much of Black folklore; especially important are his two related books *Deep Down in the Jungle: Negro Narrative Folklore from the Streets of Philadelphia* (1963, 1970) and *Positively Black* (1970), both cited fully in the introduction. William Wilson's comment on the J. Golden Kimball stories is on p. 55 of "The Paradox of Mormon Folklore." A tremendously interesting compendium of J. Golden stories is provided by Thomas E. Cheney, *The Golden Legacy: A Folk History of J. Golden Kimball* (Salt Lake City: Peregrine Smith, 1974).

A few more *important* studies of performance in folklore are listed here, but remember that these are only a scattered few. Melville Jacobs was one of the very first folklorists to insist on the essentially dramatic nature of oral performances. His works stressed the idea that a narrator, reciting stories to the people around him, was in effect creating a mental drama for them, one in which visible furniture was not necessary but where descriptions and culturally important references could eventually crowd the "stage" with meaningful personages and symbols. His works are of basic importance to our considerations here: *The Content and Style of an Oral Literature* (New York: Wenner-Gren Foundation, 1959) and *The People Are Coming Soon* (Seattle: University of Washington Press, 1960).

Beyond Jacobs, see the following: Roger D. Abrahams, "A Performance-Centered Approach to Gossip," *Man* 5 (1970): 290–301; Richard Bauman, "Towards a Behavioral Theory of Folklore," *Journal of American Folklore* 82 (1969): 167-70, which insists that folklore is not made up of things or materials but is constituted in a "communica-tive process"; Bauman, "Verbal Art as Performance," *American Anthropologist* 77 (1975): 290-311 [reprinted with revisions and supplementary commentaries by other scholars (Prospect Heights, Ill.: Waveland Press, 1984)]; Kay L. Cothran, "Talking Trash in the Okefenokee Swamp Rim, Georgia," *Journal of American Folklore* 87 (1974): 340-56; Henry Glassie, *Pattern in the Material Folk Culture of the Eastern United States* (Philadel-phia: University of Pennsylvania Press, 1968), for material aspects of performance; John J. Gumperz and Dell Hymes, eds., The *Ethnography of Communication* (Washington, D.C.: American Anthropological Association, 1964); Dell Hymes, "Breakthrough into Performance," in *Folklore: Performance and Communication,* ed. Dan Ben-Amos and Kenneth S. Goldstein (The Hague: Mouton, 1975), 11-74; Hymes, "Discovering Oral Performance and Measured Verse in American Indian Narrative," *New Literary History* 8 (1976-77): 431-57; Heda Jason, "A Multidimensional Approach to Oral Literature," *Current Anthropology* 10 (1969): 413-20 (which focuses on models relating to narratives as items. See Roger D. Abrahams's comments on performance in his rejoinder, *Current Anthropology* 12 [1971]: 391). James H. Jones, "Commonplace and Memorization in the Oral Tradition of the English and Scottish Popular Ballads," *Journal of American Folklore* 74 (1961): 97-112, tries to apply the Parry-Lord oral-formulaic theory of com-position in performance to the English ballads; Albert Friedman (pp. 113-14 in the same issue) argues stoutly against certain faults in the reasoning of Jones's article, but the basic point remains valid and has not been adequately pursued since. Charles W. Joyner, "A Model for the Analysis of Folklore Performance in Historical Context," *Journal of American Folklore* 88 (1975): 254-65, gives a complicated but convincing visual model for variables that affect any folklore performance, including tradition itself, community structure, a performer's individual characteristics, family and significant others, the per-former's individual perception, and the immediate context in which all of these forces are brought to bear on each other in the actual folklore performance. Barbara Kirshenb-latt-Gimblett, "A Parable in Context: A Social Interactional Analysis of Storytelling Per-formance," in Ben-Amos and Goldstein, *Folklore: Performance and Communication,* 105-30; James Porter, "Jeannie Robertson's 'My Son David': A Conceptual Perfor-mance Model," *Journal of American Folklore* 89 (1976): 7–26, suggests a circular chart for demonstrating the relationship between the forces bearing upon the performer and the attitudes of the performer herself. Jarold Ramsey, *Coyote Was Going There: Indian Literature of the Oregon Country* (Seattle: University of Washington Press, 1977), insists that the entire range of Native American oral literature cannot be considered unless the reader is willing to try reconstructing the actual performance situations in which those stories and tales were originally carried out. Bruce A. Rosenberg, *The Art of the American Folk Preacher* (New York: Oxford University Press, 1970), studies the oral-formulaic composition of folk preachers in the performance situation of church services where variation on standard themes is *de rigueur.*

For important observations on everyday aspects of performance styles, see Erving Goffman, *The Presentation of Self in Everyday Life* (Garden City, N.Y.: Doubleday, 1959), 17-76; and Michael J. Bell, "Tending Bar at Brown's: Occupational Role as Artistic Performance," *Western Folklore* 35 (1976) and his book-length ethnology of cultural performances in the same bar, *The World from Brown's Lounge: An Ethnography of Black Middle-Class Play* (Urbana: University of Illinois Press, 1983).

Chapter 4

DIMENSIONS OF THE FOLK EVENT

In Chapter 3, "The Folk Performance," we concentrated on that identifiable, often carefully developed, pose that relates a performer to an audience when a traditional expression takes place. Now we move to focus on the event itself: When did it start? How and why did it come about? What were its principal parts? And when did it end? Essentially, a *traditional* event is a discrete set of actions and expressions that are motivated and directed more by group taste and demand than by the private idiosyncrasies of an individual. Life is full of events; some of them are folk performances.

Anthropologists are inclined to study all recurrent events in a culture (religious holidays, quilting bees, football games) because they all provide valuable data about the culture, its workings, and its tastes. Folklorists, on the other hand, are likely to concentrate on those traditional events in smaller, more cohesive groups within the larger society in which the performance is the realization or the conscious transmission of culturally important ideas.

INVENTORY

One way to describe any event is to inventory its principal parts in a sequential array from the beginning ("At what point did we notice that something else was starting to happen?") to the end ("At which point did we notice that something else was starting to happen?"). This method provides an observer's list of ingredients and may be helpful in breaking down a complex event into units discussable at a later time. However, this method has several problems: The inventory does not necessarily provide the inside view of the event or when it started or what parts are considered principal by those involved or how it may intersect or overlap with other events. It assumes that things happen one at a time, and it relies on a sequential time reference as the only connection between the principal parts, even though we may be aware of other dimensions.

As we shall see, these are fascinating problems, and they need not cause scholarly panic or despair. They do suggest, though, that we must develop a fuller way of seeing events so that we are able to perceive their variable dimensions.

What would be a good way of noting and studying the Navajo storytelling performance described in Chapter 3? Was it one event or several? Was the performance of Tina's proverb really an event or was it only one small part of a larger folk event, the party? Has the performance now assumed the feel of an event because it was singled out for discussion (both then and now)? To approach these questions, we need first to relax and to observe that the word *event* can cover anything from a phenomenon visible only through a microscope to an occurrence involving all of humanity. The range in folk events is hardly that great, of course, but there is the similar possibility of simultaneity and the probability of sharply varying dimensions. If we use for a working definition of a folk event "any actual realization or performance of a traditional expression" (keeping in mind all we have said previously about tradition), we will be focusing properly on those aspects of the tradition that are actually articulated, and not on comparatively superficial considerations of genre or chronology. The singing of a ballad, not the remembering of it, would be the event; the communal building of a barn, not the memory of it, would be the event—though the narrative retelling of the memory might be seen as another kind of event. The observance of a custom, the use of a proverb, the employment of an ethnic recipe—these are fully understandable only when we can see them realized and articulated in their home contexts. How to register the event, then, is our first concern: what happened, and how do we know it?

A Navajo Inventory   Thin description

A sequential inventory of identifiable "happenings" at the time the Navajo story was told (recounted in Chapter 3) might look something like this:

1. Opening of the occasion: their own arrival begins, for the visitors, a sequence of observable events. Something was happening before they arrived, and they have now become a part of it, but as far as their ability to observe is concerned, the sequential list must begin here.
2. General framework: observable folk events in progress as scrutiny begins.
   a. Children are playing.
   b. Mother is weaving.
3. Subsequent discrete events:
   a. a round of string figure performances
   b. an offering of legendary and belief-oriented explanations
   c. a string figure/folk astronomy performance
   d. a string figure/caricature performance
   e. a folktale narration

f. a discussion of traditional elements in the tale (metafolklore)
g. another folktale narration (artificially cut off in the previous chapter for the sake of discussion)

As we admitted in Chapter 3, the Navajos involved in this sequence did not abstract each kind of performance from the others. For them, the evening itself was a single experience, perhaps enlivened by visitors but dictated mainly by their own seasonal customs in the aggregate. As far as the naturalness of this family setting is concerned, a person may well hesitate to dissect into antiseptic pieces an obviously holistic phenomenon. Yet it is through such theoretical dissection that we can understand the full nature of what we have observed. Thus, along with the student of anatomy, we do not seek by dissecting to ruin our appreciation of the body, but to enhance our ability to know it more fully the next time we encounter it in the live state.

One thing we can clarify for ourselves in setting out a sequence of folk events like this is the extent to which our own predilections lead us to stress certain elements. For example, in describing these events within the Navajo family situation, I have shown them in such a light as to suggest that they led up to, or at least provided the context for, the storytelling performance. The assumption in such an approach is that I had gone there to collect some Coyote stories, and so I was naturally looking forward to those events that most closely approximated that genre. Thus, although perhaps the weaving was of greater economic importance to the family at that moment, although the string figures were perhaps more centrally important to the children at that moment, although perhaps the Navajo philosophy was closest to Yellowman's interest at that particular moment because of his concern for his children's education, the quarry, from my point of view, was the folktale, and all other items were subordinated to it. A weaving specialist in the same group of visitors could have placed such emphasis on watching the mother weave that we might never have moved to the kitchen for storytelling. A scholar interested in string figures might have focused such attention on those expressive events that even if all the other kinds of expression had taken place they might have seemed peripheral to that activity. Since we did not try to push the evening's activities in any particular direction, we can be relatively sure that what we witnessed was a natural set of occurrences; just as obviously, my description of them reflects my own scholarly interests.

Inventory "on Film"

There is no point in hoping that a folklorist—or anyone else, for that matter—should be able to see and appreciate all traditional phenomena simultaneously with equal clarity. We will always be interested in one kind of event more than another. Yet in order to understand even one small part of a folk event, we will want to understand its relationship to the other elements in the whole context.

How can we approach this problem, at least hypothetically, in order to train ourselves for such a demanding task? One method might be to imagine filming the entire event: Where would we place our cameras? How many cameras would we need? When would we begin filming? What would we need to film so that the eventual viewer might understand the event and what led up to it, how it came about, how it related to other contextual elements, and how it ended? The benefit of carrying out this exercise hypothetically, of course, is that we can use more imaginary cameras than we could ever hope to in real life; moreover, with an imaginary camera we do not run the risk of entirely changing the family's pattern of life while we set up lights, sound systems, and other equipment to record what might by that time become a very self-conscious performance. For purposes of discussion, how would we want to film the situations described on this one evening with that Navajo family?

Ideally, we would want a camera fixed into the ceiling of each room so that an objective record could be made of all activities and movements simultaneously. We would also want to have a camera operating before the visitors arrived so the effect of their entry upon the normal events of the evening could be noted (this is an unsolvable dilemma in real life since the very presence of a camera would have constituted an intrusion already). Other obvious positions would be a fixed camera on the mother while she weaves, augmented by close-up shots of her technique and pattern. At least two cameras would be needed to film the children's string games activities: one to pick up the entire group as the string is passed from person to person so that the interaction among the participants can be noted; another to move in close to the string figures themselves in order to see how they were made and to provide a record that could be compared with other string figures in other cultures. We would want to have at least one camera that could sweep across all these activities to show where the focus of the group's attention might shift from one moment to another. At least one camera would have to be mobile to follow us all out into the kitchen while we prepared to hear stories. Perhaps the same camera could also follow us outdoors and show the alignment of the one string figure with the Pleiades (since we are using imaginary cameras, there will be no problem of light source on this shot). During the tale-telling activities one camera would be needed to hold on the narrator to record not only the story but his style and mannerisms in telling it, while another camera would focus on the entire group to show their responses.

Now in reality, as filmmakers, even if we had all these cameras at our disposal, we would want to consolidate some of the shots and some of the work. At what point could we use one of these cameras for another shot? The technical question is a good one to ask for our hypothetical purposes, for it requires us to consider when certain actions stopped, if indeed they did. Did the mother continue weaving at her loom intermittently while the tales were being told or not? If so, a camera would be needed to register that ongoing event, even though the immediate audience was in the kitchen listening to a story. Since all

Helen Yellowman weaves a *Yé'ii* rug in her yard in Blanding, Utah (1970s).

the children moved into the kitchen with their father, we could assume that we would no longer need the cameras originally used for their play and for the string figures.

Understanding the Inventory: From Within and Without

With all this imaginary footage on hand, we would need to decide how we might best show the films. We can assume, I think, that we would show them all uncut so that we would not miss any detail of the events. But we would need to devise some way of showing which events overlapped with each other; perhaps a split screen or multiple projections would work. We would still be left with the dilemma of whether we had in fact captured the events in such a way as to lead efficiently to an understanding of them. We will wonder, for example, if the Navajos would have filmed these events in the same way, whether they would have focused on the same items, and whether they would have handled them the same way. It is too easy to say that an event is an event, and that anyone present would see it in the same manner. Sol Worth and John Adair brought forth some striking examples of this in their experimental work with Navajo filmmakers. One twenty-minute film made by Susie Benally, *A Navajo Weaver,* showed only about four and a half minutes of weaving, and most of that is at the very end of the film. Only two or three inches of a fairly large rug are shown being woven at that. There are several extremely brief shots of the weaver holding up different completed rugs, but the main interest in the film seems to be in people moving over the landscape herding sheep, gathering the various plants to be used for washing and dyeing the wool, preparing the wool by carding, dyeing, and spinning, and not in any sequential order. We may well wonder why a Navajo making a film of a Navajo weaver would show only a few minutes of weaving and instead focus about three-quarters of the entire film on other activities. By asking Navajos about it, we would learn that the live processes involved in the weaving are of the greatest traditional interest to the Navajos, while the final product, the finished rug, is an item usually traded for food or cash. From a Navajo point of view the rug and its physical pattern are not of greatest importance; the interaction with animals, landscape, plants, the mastery of preparation procedures, the knowledge of dyes, and the creative imagination that brings forth the patterning are the central elements. One's involvement with these processes, moreover, comes in a non-sequential manner through the year, with herding and gathering plants occurring while the weaver spins some wool for a future rug, dyes other wool, weaves, and shears sheep.

Going back to our hypothetical film, we may guess in retrospect that the part we filmed of the mother weaving at her loom, holding the camera there as long as she was weaving, might have been thought highly unusual by the Navajos present, because it would seem to focus on only one element of a much larger event, and perhaps one of the least meaningful elements at that. What can we say, then, about the rest of our filming? Are the other events open to the same kind of esoteric correction? We should always hold out this possibility, for the outside observer, even armed with a hundred cameras, will not be able to get a full view of the folk event without the help and direction of the participants themselves.

Margaret Mead has called attention to the preference shown by folklorists and anthropologists for verbal materials—both for texts to study and for ways to describe the items under scrutiny. She suggests that this has blinded us to other kinds of expression and communication and has encouraged us to overlook, or subordinate, other kinds of description such as those that might be afforded us by photography, whether still, video, or movie. In this discussion of hypothetical filming, I have not given proper exposure to the real technicalities and promises of the cinematic instrumentation, which is surely, as Mead and others have eloquently shown, an indispensable means of observation in folklore and anthropology. I have introduced the idea of hypothetical filming only to suggest a set of considerations that must be kept in mind as we seek to register a folk event fully. Imagining that filming or videotaping is going on encourages us to see our subject matter in a richer way than a mere lineal sequence would suggest. It is said that good and bad movies are made in the editing, in the cutting room; the same thing may be said of scholarly articles and books on folklore and anthropology, for one always wonders how much was left on the cutting room floor and how much even the most well-intentioned editing and analysis alters our perception of what actually happened. And with all our enthusiasm for picturing an event (fueled, perhaps, by our love affair with television and the Virtual Visuals of Internet), let us assume that we will still need careful observation techniques and careful use of the language in our analytical processes. As Walter Ong has said, if it is true that a picture is worth a thousand words, why do people keep *saying* so?

STUDYING THE EVENT

A Check List: Apparent and Esoteric Dimensions

Considerations such as those just cited should encourage the student of folklore to keep in mind the following topics when studying a folk event:

1. Context and occasion
2. Framework
   a. apparent beginning and end (Yanagita's level 1)
   b. esoteric beginning and end (Yanagita's levels 2 and 3)
3. Participants and their roles
4. Sequence (the normal or typical order of events)
   a. apparent sequence (Yanagita's level 1)
   b. esoteric sequence (Yanagita's levels 2 and 3)

5. Simultaneous or overlapped elements and intersections with other events
6. Weight and dimensions of components in the event
   a. apparent inventory (level 1)
   b. esoteric inventory, including value judgment and rationale (levels 2 and 3)

This checklist cannot be followed serially, but must be adjusted to each particular event. It simply asks us what items we might have forgotten to consider. Most important, its topics recognize that there may be at least two strands of any observation of a folk event. There will be those occurrences that are apparent and obvious to any onlooker, and there will be those that are noticed and valued variously by the insiders. Both elements are needed for a full understanding of an event, for the insiders, even though they may have complicated rationales for what has happened, may overlook similarities between their customs and those of others, while the outsider, lacking the system of values of the insider, may fail to appreciate—or even to see—important details of the event. The apparent inventory of items and actions in a folk event may therefore be far longer than the esoteric inventory, for the insider may see only a few of the actions as centrally related to the event while the outsider has no way of knowing which actions or items are typical or obligatory.

For an example, take any well-known folk event and imagine how an outsider might approach it, then how an insider might clarify the ingredients. A commonly celebrated holiday like Thanksgiving provides a good place to start. We might easily agree that the central part of Thanksgiving as an event is the usual turkey dinner "with all the trimmings." We might decide in advance to set up our hypothetical cameras just before a Thanksgiving dinner takes place and then note how it starts, who comes to it, how the participants comport themselves, what they do while they are at the table, and whether other things are going on in the house that seem directly related, and we would want to focus on those items that seem to be centrally involved. If we did so, however, without asking the advice of the insiders in the family under scrutiny, we might find later that we had not been able to film the entire event.

The women in the family who prepared the meal might insist that Thanksgiving had actually started early in the morning with the preparation of the food. At the turn of the century, and up through the 1930s, when it was typical for many families to provide their own meat and poultry, we might find someone insisting that Thanksgiving had begun the previous day with the killing of the bird. In other words, by focusing only on the most obvious aspect of the event, that element most recognizable to everyone, we would be dealing only with the apparent framework and the apparent inventory, not with the full dimensions of the event as seen by those who carry it out.

Moreover, if we set our imaginary cameras over the table and record all the items that are there on that occasion without asking the participants to identify them and their relation to the event, we might have no way of determining which of the foods and utensils relate to the event of Thanksgiving alone and which ones relate to the daily event of eating. Thus, while our film might be full of colorful items and actions, it would not necessarily be full of cultural meaning; perhaps, more accurately, it might be full of data that remain generally unusable because of our lack of a system by which to focus on the primary elements of the event. Our picture might indeed not be worth a thousand words.

Folklorist Sharon Sherman illustrated this extremely well by making a videotape of her family's Seder meal, which had been arranged for two nights in a row to accommodate a large number of family members. After Sherman "shot" the first night's Seder from an adjoining room so the camera would not intrude, the family viewed the results and decided that the depiction did not look right. On the second evening, the camera was placed near the head of the table; by "becoming" one of those seated at the table, the camera was able to provide a culturally more accurate view of the Seder traditions, from the standpoint of the participants themselves.

Comparative Inventories

I asked the members of two extended families in widely separated parts of the United States to describe what they considered the obligatory elements in their celebration of Thanksgiving in terms of the topics listed earlier. Although each family considered its Thanksgiving customs to be unique for various historical and geographical reasons, I found them very similar in many respects. The Kimball, Damon, and Howland families, related by marriage, are primarily rural people in central Massachusetts. The Wodtli and Tabler families, related by marriage, live in Foster, Oregon, in the foothills of the Cascade Mountains. Their recollection and current celebration of Thanksgiving are also essentially rural in character; for example, they recall Thanksgiving as a harvest holiday that separated the active outdoor work of the year from the indoor winter maintenance and restricted dairying of the winter.

The Kimball Thanksgiving

The apparent framework of Thanksgiving in these New England families would be Thanksgiving Day itself, most obviously the dinner at which members of these and other families related by marriage gather. However, the members of this family said that Thanksgiving actually began for them at least a week before the actual date, when in school they were obliged to write essays on why they were thankful. On the surface, this might seem to be an essentially nontraditional aspect of the event, but it is so solidly a part of the participants' concept of Thanksgiving that it cannot be overlooked. Among other things, it testifies that Thanksgiving, for all its traditional elements, is also a part of the formal calendar of holidays in the United States and is therefore to be encountered in formal as well as informal settings. The participants in the Kimball family Thanksgiving are family members and their spouses and children; rarely is someone outside the immediate family ever invited to Thanksgiving dinner, although such is the practice at other times of the year.

Central arenas of focus during the actual development of events during Thanksgiving Day are the kitchen, where most of the women prepare the food, and the den, where the men gather for conversation and sometimes a smoke. The central person in the kitchen is the woman whose house is being used for the dinner; the same woman presides over the table during the meal itself and usually requests someone else present to say grace, most often a younger person. Since there are two particular arenas of activity, the kitchen and the den, two entirely separate kinds of conversation have developed by the time dinner is served. These conversations are brought as far as the table, but dropped there in favor of a generalized set of recollections, mainly of family and regional history.

Our hypothetical camera over the table would reveal at a Kimball family Thanksgiving dinner of today a large turkey, various kinds of vegetables and condiments, and, eventually, a number of pies served with coffee and tea. Conversation with family members indicates, however, that the turkey is a recent arrival; up until the mid-1940s, the family usually enjoyed a chicken or capon, sometimes a duck. The turkey, thought by many to be so traditional at Thanksgiving, was not an obligatory tradition for this family until the last twenty-five years. Having some kind of bird on the table is the obligation. Of the vegetables that appear, only some are traditional: sweet potatoes must be present (in more recent years, yams have been added, but they are considered a modern frill), small stewed onions, squash, and usually peas. Two kinds of cranberry sauce are necessary, fine and chunky. Regular potatoes may or may not be present, other vegetables may or may not be present, pickles of any variety may be present, and usually there is at least one kind of salad. Gravy is obligatory. The stuffing used to fill the bird when it was cooking is excavated and placed on a separate dish, and all are expected to take some, whether or not they like it.

The "oysters," two small hollows of tender meat along the back of the bird, are always given to the senior people present (in a smaller Thanksgiving event in an immediate family, they always go to the parents). Everyone around the table usually takes a small helping of each kind of food offered, and each makes a request for light or dark meat. In earlier years, this helped to avoid references to embarrassing parts like breast, thigh, and leg. Usually the legs, the drumsticks, go to the children—to the fussiest ones if there are more than two present.

Dessert is served after the dishes of the main meal are cleared away. Four kinds of pies are obligatory: mince, pumpkin, squash, and apple. Other kinds of pie may also be offered as long as those four are present. After the meal, the women return to the kitchen and wash dishes and divide up the leftovers to be taken to the various homes. The men return to the den or the living room for further conversation and napping. From this point on, as families begin to leave for their separate homes, Thanksgiving itself is considered over. The turkey and some of the other foods may survive a day or two in the form of sandwiches and leftovers, but they are no longer considered directly to be aspects of Thanksgiving.

Clearly, for this family, the Thanksgiving event centers on the gathering of family members around a traditional meal. The event is separated in some of its aspects into the same sex roles found prominently across America at the turn of the century. The communal performance of the event, then, is at least in large part a symbolic re-enactment of those factors that the family sees as part of its history: clearly divided sex roles, traditional handling of food, discussion of family history, invocation of a religious perspective at the beginning of the meal, hierarchies of relationships in the parceling out of the food supply. It is doubtful, however, that particular members of the family would describe Thanksgiving in these terms. Rather, they would insist that they continue to celebrate Thanksgiving in large part as a memorial to their cultural heritage: since both the Howland and the Kimball families descend from Mayflower pilgrims (Howland and White), the re-enactment of Thanksgiving is also a family reassertion of lineage.

Moreover, in the 1930s the families were removed from Quabbin Valley in central Massachusetts, where five towns were obliterated to make way for the reservoir that now helps supply Boston with drinking water. The sense of having been dispossessed of the rural basis of its heritage is also evident at the Kimball family gatherings, where stories of "the Valley" and of people prominent in the family's past are brought forward as central topics that accompany the actual eating of the traditional foods, binding the family together in a communion with its past. Members of the family believe that theirs is a "good old-fashioned New England Thanksgiving," and that people in other parts of the United States probably do not celebrate the event in a similar way. Said one family member, "Well, sure, they probably all eat turkey these days, just like we do, but they probably wouldn't make much sense out of the rest of what we do when we get together for Thanksgiving."

The folklorist is in a position to follow up on such surmises by taking those imaginary movie or video cameras to another location and researching the same event with another family in another part of the country. What differences will we find? To what extent will we be dependent upon the insider again for pointed evaluation of obligatory items in the traditional performance?

The Wodtli Thanksgiving

The Wodtli and Tabler families are of Swiss and German background. Thanksgiving is for them also preceded by official notice of it in school. In the early 1900s, for example, the children always dressed up at school as Pilgrims and Indians and put on a public program. Thus, as with the New England Kimballs, official occasion ushered in the observance of the traditional event as celebrated within the home.

Thanksgiving Day itself begins early in the morning with the stuffing of the chicken. The stuffing, always a celery and onion mix, never varies; the chicken is stuffed on the same day it is cooked because it might spoil if it were prepared earlier. The typical bird is chicken or duck, although the family occasionally has had roast pork. In more recent times the family has used turkey because they are given away by the local logging companies to their men. Participants in the Thanksgiving Day event are principally family members, with a focus on the older people: Grandmother Wodtli always has to have a nice clean apron; Grandfather Wodtli always says grace, in German, in about the same words each year.

The apparent inventory of foods on the table is, as in the New England instance, larger than the obligatory, esoteric list: The family always has sweet potatoes, never yams ("the people around here were not yam people"), canned vegetables (the family did not have a refrigerator until the late 1930s), pickled crabapples, homemade pickles, hot rolls. In earlier years, there was no cranberry sauce ("we didn't even know about cranberries"), and liquor was not allowed ("wine and whiskey were medicine"). For dessert, homegrown pumpkin pie and mincemeat are mandatory, although recently chocolate and cream pies have been added.

Thanksgiving dinner is usually held at the home of someone on the maternal side of the family (at a Wodtli home rather than a Tabler). The women gather in the kitchen to prepare the food while the men move to the living room for conversation. Although alcohol is frowned upon, uncles occasionally gather outside on the porch for a couple of quiet drinks. Both genders gather together at dinner, and the conversation turns primarily to family anecdotes.

After dinner, the women go again to the kitchen to wash dishes and divide the leftovers while the men return to the living room for more talking and smoking. During the Thanksgiving dinner itself, children usually receive the drumsticks, and people around the table are expected to state their preferences for light or dark meat, which is served from a central platter. Thanksgiving as an event is considered ended when the people leave, taking the divided leftovers with them.

The family relates the holiday primarily to the harvest season, but sees the celebration of it as primarily an American event. Both Grandmother and Grandfather Wodtli were immigrants to America (from Germany and Switzerland respectively), and the family today believes that the holiday is in part a confirmation of their conversion to the American culture as well as a partial recollection of their own rural past.

The Beginnings of Questions (A Summary)

There are some distinct differences between the two Thanksgiving events discussed sketchily above, but it is also evident that these two families, although at opposite ends of the United States and from different national backgrounds, celebrate the holiday in very similar ways that they themselves are unaware of. If we were to discuss in depth only one of the similarities, we would notice that our understanding of it would depend both on internal evidence from the participants themselves as well as observations only an outsider would be inclined to make. For example, in both families the gender roles during the Thanksgiving event are clearly delineated: the women are in the kitchen, the men are in the living room, each group engaged in what would be called women's talk and men's talk. When the genders merge over dinner, the conversation turns to more general family affairs; then the genders separate again when the dinner is over. Is this a pattern we might find across the country at Thanksgiving time? Is it a pattern we might find in rural communities generally at any family gathering? Is it an event motif that indicates a deep conservatism about gendered roles that can be celebrated openly or perceived during festive occasions? Is it perhaps a female-centered holiday, coming as it does at the end of the harvest, which has featured essentially male labor? Is it thus a threshold festival, marking the transition of the agricultural year from the outdoor, male-dominated arena of work to the indoor, feminine domain?

These and other questions naturally arise in the mind of the researcher when confronted with comparative evidence such as presented here. Yet, these questions cannot be answered without considerable fieldwork among diverse families celebrating the same event across the country. Here, the researcher as an outsider develops questions and hypotheses for further pursuit that lie beyond the interests and inclinations of a particular family eating its Thanksgiving dinner. Without the aid of the insider's view, however, the researcher has only a generalized mass of evidence: a mixed batch of family members gathered together, a table loaded with food, various arenas of conversation. What *do* the women talk about in the kitchen while dinner is being prepared? What *kinds* of conversation are taking place among the men? Are the participants themselves aware of the propriety involved: Would a man feel at ease moving into the kitchen on such an occasion and taking part in the food preparation? Would it be likely for a woman in the family to slip quietly into the living room and participate in the men's conversations? In either case, would topics and vocabulary change abruptly? One suspects that these boundaries are not made of concrete, but that they are seldom crossed; such a conclusion cannot be stated firmly, however, until the event is studied further in all its multiform appearances across the country.

I discuss the Thanksgiving holiday here because on the surface it seems to be a simple example of a traditional event. People do not regard it with the same deep religious involvement inherent in some other holidays, and many who celebrate Thanksgiving shrug off questions with quick answers such as, "Well, of course we have Thanksgiving, but all the things we do are just things that the family has done over the years." In other words, people are aware that they share certain customs with others around the country, and they are aware that their own particular families have certain traditions that may or may not be shared by others. But no one is particularly inclined to make a deep-level study of it to see the extent to which these traditions are tied in with larger processes and ideas within the culture as a whole, or within a region, or among members of similar ethnic backgrounds. By asking only a few questions of inside participants, we quickly notice that Thanksgiving as an event has both official (national) and local family dimensions. For the family, Thanksgiving specifically begins with the preparation of food for the Thanksgiving dinner itself, and ends, at least in the case of these two widely separated families, when the participants leave the scene and begin their trip home. It thus has its own inner dynamics as far as the participants are concerned, and while its celebration is occasioned by a certain calendar holiday, its active parts are decided not by time constraints but by the internal scheme of the event itself.

A still larger set of perspectives can be obtained from the approaches of social history. David Hackett Fischer points out that the many folkways brought to America by immigrants from four distinct regions of England included their food traditions, among them a "special taste for frying in the south and west, for boiling in the north, and for baking in East Anglia." Since East Anglia is where the Puritans and most other New England settlers came from, it is no surprise to discover that their cooking preferences remained the same, and indeed even intensified, to the extent that the brick oven became the standard feature of New England cooking procedures. When we think of the usual foods served today at Thanksgiving dinner, we realize that they are predominantly those plants and meats native to the New World which were supplied by the Indians (the Puritans' supplies having been meager at best) and have since been transformed by Puritan oven cooking: poultry, squash, potatoes, and pies. Fischer quotes Harriet Beecher Stowe's enthusiastic claim that pies—especially the culture-markers for later New Englanders: mincemeat, squash, pumpkin, and apple—were the crowning achievement of New England oven cooking. Stowe, noting that American housewives were adapting "old institutions to new uses" (our conservatism and dynamism), saw the variation, decoration, and architectural richness of pies as attesting to "the boundless fertility of the feminine mind, when once let loose. . . ." We will discuss still more of this creativity in later chapters, but here it suffices for us to note the impact of these two streams of foodways—Indian ingredients and Puritan ovens—on our subsequent eating behavior at the folk event we now call Thanksgiving.

An Ethnic Event: The Japanese New Year

The celebration of the New Year by Japanese Americans seems on the surface to be very much like that of Thanksgiving: a nationally recognized, official holiday is the scene for a special meal which family members and friends attend. A visitor to a Japanese American home on the afternoon of New Year's Day would notice, of course, the distinctly ethnic character of the food, but might be inclined to classify this event alongside Thanksgiving as one in which a meal allows or encourages people to experience a sense of togetherness and thanksgiving. By asking questions, of course, we can try to determine whether indeed the meal is central to the event; by asking the hypothetical questions about the placement for our imaginary cameras in order to film the entire event, we can uncover information leading us to a clearer understanding of the event's dimensions.

Context and Occasion

While the occasion for this event in America is the transition from one year to another, in Japan this was originally a midwinter festival concerned with fertility. Great stress was laid on the delicacy of the earth at a time when rice was not yet growing, and concern was shown for the spirits and memories of departed family members and ancestors. In previous times, the New Year festival in Japan was celebrated at the same or nearly the same time as the Chinese New Year. Japanese people today generally celebrate New Year's with the rest of the Western world, and Japanese Americans in particular see this holiday as distinctly a New Year holiday, not an agricultural event. Nonetheless, it becomes evident in a close study of the inventory of the important items and actions of this event that there has been a strong carryover of concern for the relationships among family members, food, and community. Thus, while the occasion itself is recognized and celebrated by most Americans of Japanese descent, the particular meanings of the event follow an older, traditional Japanese set of assumptions. Part of the event focuses on the individual and his or her orientation to the larger family, represented by ancestors. Other elements celebrate the individual's relation to the immediate family, and the family's relationship to the community around it. Through all of these areas of focus runs the constant theme of sharing food, basically a ritual form of rice, the small cakes of *mochi* mentioned in Chapter 2.

Framework of Activity

The frame for the event would seem to be New Year's Day itself, apparently beginning—as we found with Thanksgiving—with the preparation of food, following through its consumption by visitors, and ending with the disappearance of the last guests. The esoteric framework, however, forces us to begin our consideration of the Japanese American New Year several days before January 1 and extend it in some cases for several days beyond. Typically, the community awareness of the New Year's festivities approaching comes almost immediately after Christmas, when people begin to discuss the making of *mochi*. In some communities, the *mochi* is now produced by machine; in others, it is still produced in the old way, using large wooden mallets that pound the sweet rice into a rubbery pulp, as described in Chapter 2. In either case, whether a group of families gather to make *mochi* for themselves (each bringing a quantity of rice and taking home *mochi* cakes in proportion) or whether a Buddhist church group makes it for sale among community members, this opening of the New Year's event is essentially a festive, community-oriented foodway custom. The *mochi* will be eaten not only by family members on New Year's Day, but will be given as gifts to others, will be offered as part of the food for visitors, and will be offered to ancestors symbolically at the family altar.

The *mochi* cake is made by turning a small ball of pounded, cooked rice dough around and around in the hands until it is smooth and almost flat, but with rounded edges. It symbolizes harmony, happiness, and peace. In the local Buddhist church, two large *mochi* are placed on the altar. Called *kagami mochi* (mirror *mochi*), they signify a doubling, a reflection of brightness, good fortune, and happiness. During the days before January 1, while the *mochi* is being prepared throughout the community, women are also doing extensive shopping for the particular foods required on New Year's Day, and many families are shopping for "dress up" clothing, especially for children. In the same period of time a thorough housecleaning is undertaken, going far beyond the usual compulsion for cleanliness and order.

Participants and Sequence

On New Year's Eve, the women of the family begin the extensive food preparation for the following day, an inventory of which follows. The preparation of food may take almost all night, and so it is rare for families celebrating the Japanese New Year to be free on New Year's Eve for the revelry that characterizes other Americans' celebrations, though sometimes the men of the family will participate in the New Year's Eve parties of other American friends. During New Year's Eve the women of the house may make an offering of *mochi*, usually two or three cakes placed on top of each other and topped with a tangerine (including stem and leaves), at the family altar to the spirits of any family members who have died.

New Year's Day itself begins at breakfast, with the family gathering to eat *ozoni*, a soup made of fish stock that has a glutinous *mochi* cake in the bottom. Parents pay respects to the deceased members of the immediate family by lighting incense and bowing at the family altar, which may be decorated with the written names of recently departed relatives. All dress in their Sunday best, children are alerted to be on their best behavior throughout the day, everyone is reminded that it is improper to become irritated for any reason during the day, and food preparation and final arrangements for serving the food are carried out.

Beginning in the early afternoon of New Year's Day, some members of each family will begin circulating to other homes in the Japanese American community, stopping off to visit, sharing some of the traditional foods, and wishing friends and relatives a happy New Year. Usually the women in each family stay home to continue offering hospitality to others in the community making their rounds; children and adult males do most of the visiting. Among

Japanese immigrants who take part in this custom, a typical New Year's greeting would be, *"Akemashite omedeto gozaimasu!"* ("Congratulations on the opening of the New Year!"), followed by, *"Honen mo dozo yoroshiku onegai shimasu"* ("Please take care of me this year as you have done during the past year"). Other, simpler greetings, such as "Happy New Year," both in Japanese and English are used, but it is clear that the sense of the event is a renewal of reciprocal relations among members of the community, not simply a matter of making a social call.

Dimensions of Esoteric Value

The foods offered to visitors at this time are primarily the typical festive foods one might find at a Japanese picnic: various kinds of sushi, teriyaki chicken, deep-fried shrimp, and so on. There may also be raw fish and a number of different condiments. Alcohol is usually available in abundance, primarily in the form of warmed *sake,* and typically a variety of beers is offered, including Japanese brands. The drinking of hard liquor is rare, but a bottle of whiskey may be brought out at the arrival of a Caucasian visitor. The outsider, then, would notice a table absolutely groaning with a wide variety of identifiably ethnic Japanese foods but might not be aware that only some of these are obligatory on this occasion: Somewhere near the center of the table will be either a *tai* fish (a large reddish-colored fish cooked so that the fins and tail are raised upward as if the fish is swimming), or perhaps a lobster, and certain other foods that feature the colors red and white. These colors indicate good luck and prosperity—hence the central focus on these foods—and their use at this season corresponds to a wish that anything done on this day will presage the nature of things to come in the ensuing year. In addition, many of the foods are seafoods, which are connected to the concept of fertility in Japanese folklore. These dishes, in conjunction with the rice that is the staple of Japanese food custom, bring together the main concerns for a bountiful food supply during the coming year and for prosperity and good fortune in the community.

As the menfolk circulate from one home to another on New Year's Day, they may pay off personal debts; some prefer not to do this on New Year's Day but to handle it over the next day or so after the holiday. In Japanese custom, usually seven full days are required for the celebration of the New Year, each day given over to some particular custom such as the paying of private debts. The precision of this seven-day event has generally faded in America, with much of the observation and celebration being focused on New Year's Day itself and the preceding days of preparation.

It is important for us to ponder whether the previous days of preparation should be included as part of the event in our use of that term: are these important dimensions of the event itself, or are they only aspects of getting ready for the event? We need to know what the event is and what it means before we can answer this question, for if we answer it from the outside, we are likely to view these elements sequentially as items leading up to an event largely because that particular observance we can most fully identify as an event, the New Year's Day dinner, is that part of the observation most open to our scrutiny (as outsiders) and most familiar to us (because it resembles our own traditions). We may therefore incline, unintentionally, to subordinate other aspects of this celebration to the one feature we think is central. If we are going to take our human subjects seriously, we need to listen when they say, "Oh, of course New Year's begins with the making of *mochi,* and with housecleaning." And we need then to find out what making *mochi* and housecleaning have to do with the central aspects of a celebratory event.

One approach in this case may be for us to take a close look at the Japanese word for New Year: *shogatsu.* This word is usually translated "New Year's" or "January." The word *gatsu* means "month;" the first part of the word, *sho,* taken separately can mean "just," "punctual," "right," "righteousness," "justice," "redress," "straighten," "amend," "correctly," "surely," "proper," "natural," "lawful," "healthy," "moral," "straight," "straightforward," "perfect." Thus, while *shogatsu* means on one level a simple reference to the beginning of the year, all of its connotative meanings suggest bringing things to a recognized norm, celebrating things that are natural and just and proper, in other words, setting things straight for the New Year—hence the use of an honorific prefix: *oshogatsu.*

Everything done at the time of the New Year is done with the intent of realigning the individual and the family to the requirements of normal community custom. This is obviously more than just the occasion for merriment that another year has passed or another has begun; it is a sense of personal and communal obligation to maintain the reciprocal interactions necessary to the proper, natural continuation of one's family and culture over the coming year.

It features, basically, a very private personal and familial kind of preparation for straightening things out and making the world regular: the extra housecleaning, the intensive efforts to dress up and behave correctly, the personal rededication to act properly in one's family context. The responsible older members of the family are expected to rededicate themselves to their family lineage at this time, which is done privately and out of the sight of visitors at the family shrine. The family gathers for a specific, symbolic, traditional meal as the very first family action of the first day of the New Year, and for many Japanese Americans this observance is the central feature of the whole event.

The afternoon of New Year's Day opens out this tight concern with propriety and familial obligations into its application to the community at large, the larger family with whom Japanese Americans must relate during the public parts of their lives. This part of the day is less intense and somewhat more social in nature. The outsider might conceive of it simply as an ethnic holiday and entirely miss its larger relationship to the specific and very intense breakfast that was shared earlier, out of sight of the observer. To treat this event accurately with our imaginary movie cameras, we would want to understand the communal preparation of the *mochi* and the private preparation of home and person as the opening coefficients of a very complex cultural observance. They start the sequential framework from the insider's point of view; from this joint concern with the individual and community the event then moves to a focus in the privacy of the family late New Year's Eve and early New Year's Day morning, then widens out again to community participation later that afternoon.

The Japanese American New Year might be diagrammed as an hourglass with community and personal concerns at each end and the focus on the nuclear family at the center. Obviously, any one aspect of this event would be difficult to understand apart from the others. Yet, as outsiders, we would be most likely to have noticed and to have been able to film only one end of the hourglass had we not asked for the help of insiders in guiding us to the full sequence of events, which, taken together, allow us to discover a cultural meaning in the continuation of an important ethnic custom.

Induced or Recalled Events: Mrs. Judkins's Cante-Fable

One particular kind of folk event recurs continually in the study of folklore, yet it is one of the most difficult to deal with. When a collector of folklore goes into the field and elicits performances from a chairmaker, a barn builder, a ballad singer, a storyteller, and others, the researcher is trying as far as possible to bring forth a normal traditional event that can be studied as a text of a particular performance. Modern folklorists always try to collect tales and ballads and barn raisings in their home contexts so that all the details will be reliable in the tradition and not simply brought forth because of the presence of the collector. Nonetheless, it is inevitable that the presence of the collector, which is often limited by time and money, is a certain urgent factor in many performances, and hence a force in any related folk event. Observations thus generated should not be discredited for this reason, but they need to be carefully scrutinized for exactly what they can and cannot tell us about the traditions observed.

On the positive side, as we have already noticed, it may always be true that the researcher will be able to bring to the experience comparative knowledge of other folk performances that will allow for a fuller perspective on an event than might be provided by the single event itself. This is particularly the case when the performer does not (or cannot) do a proficient job. On the negative side, it may place unfair focus on some traditions over others (Cecil Sharp, the British folklorist, combed the U.S. Appalachian communities for songs and ballads, virtually ignoring the tales which were more typical and more numerous there), and it may also elicit poor texts from a performer who might have been a fine resource some years earlier but whose repertoire has remained in hibernation long enough to make awkward an event that otherwise could have been carried forward with alacrity and articulation. Since these dilemmas cannot be predicted in advance, the folklorist must always be ready to sense in any fieldwork situation the limitations and the promises presented in each event/ performance.

Mrs. Clarice Mae Judkins was said to be at one time the leading traditional singer in Lane County, Oregon. Her family was among the pioneers to the area, and she herself had married the son of one of the more prominent local pioneer families. Her repertoire was estimated to be in excess of 250 songs, which included old traditional ballads, folksongs of the westward movement, Civil War songs, and popular songs of the late 1800s and early 1900s. She was often invited to sing at the meetings of pioneer societies, clubs of old-timers, and at family picnics. In her elderly years, she was visited by a number of local folksong collectors who found her an inexhaustible source; invariably on second, third, and fourth visits she would bring forth songs she had not remembered earlier. I am certain that no one ever heard her entire repertoire. In her eighties she was still being invited to parties and old folks' homes to entertain, so when I visited her on numerous occasions to get her to sing for the tape recorder, although we lacked numbers in the audience, I thought I was not getting essentially different texts than might have been heard had she been singing for a large audience of friends or family. Nonetheless, eventually I realized that she was trying to recall those songs that had not been in the most active part of her repertoire.

On one occasion she began singing snatches of a song I had never heard before, interspersed with spoken narration. Since this was one of her ways of recalling the words of a song she had not often sung, I thought nothing of it at first and simply requested that she try to recall what the song was in its entirety so we could tape it. (Under these circumstances I usually start the tape recorder and leave it on so the mechanical manipulations do not in and of themselves become part of the opening and closing reference points for performance events.) A transcript of the tape reveals the following interchange between us, in which she tried to recall how another traditional singer she had heard in her youth had performed the song. In her estimation, the earlier singer had not known the song very well, for he could only sing parts of it. The induced event, in the case of this one fragmentary text, went as follows:

Toelken: Can you remember how that one, that one you were just sing-ing, goes all the way through?

Mrs. Judkins: I don't think I've ever heard it all the way through. I think that he would say that this man lost his horse and somebody'd sto-len his mare and they didn't want to give him any information about it, so they told him, "Yes, I saw your mare, she went wavering through the air." So the fella finally became con-vinced that that was where his horse was. They kept telling him, "In yonder cloud I see thy mare—she goes wavering through the air."

Toelken: Finally convinced him.

Mrs. Judkins: Finally convinced him. He'd asked a shepherd, and he'd asked a farmer, and everyone would tell him the same thing. They didn't want him looking for a mare. He, probably someone, had stolen it, but they didn't want to give him any information. They got tired of his questions so they told him that the mare was up in the clouds, which is another way of telling him they didn't know.

Toelken: Well, how did the tune go again?

Mrs. Judkins: Oh, let's see. This man would tell the first of it—tell the incident, so apparently he didn't know all the song, uh, the words. And, uh, so but every now and then he burst out singing it, and then everybody'd look disgusted and say, "There's that man with the old gray mare going wavering through the air." But the first he sung and all the others he just talked about.

[She sings:]
Oh tell me, shepherd, tell me truly,
Have you seen a man a-riding?
A man and a mare with coal black hair,
Methinks he is not far behind me.

Oh naddle doodle dow ridden, naddle doodle day,
Oh naddle doodle dow ridden, naddle doodle day.

Oh yes kind sir to my surprise,
A man and a mare went into the skies.
A man and a mare with coal black hair,
I can see him yet, I can see him yet.

Oh naddle doodle dow ridden, naddle doodle day,
Oh naddle doodle dow ridden, naddle doodle day.

[Speaks:] And then the other man was so convinced that he began saying,

[Sings:]
In yonder cloud I see my mare,
As she goes wavering through the air.

[Speaks:] And that seems to be about all of it.

Toelken: And then the man would go on once more telling parts of the story?

Mrs. Judkins: Yes, telling part of the story, and then stopped for the chorus. So all the music part of it was that, and the other people would say, "Well there goes that old gray mare, wavering through the air again." That was an old song, and that was all he knew of it.

What Mrs. Judkins did not realize—and what I did not realize until much later, listening to the tape again—was that the event she and I had shared was an attempted recounting of a genre folklorists call *cante-fable,* a narrative that alternates a spoken story with a verse or chorus sung to a tune. Since Mrs. Judkins did not understand that it was a particular kind of performance, she had assumed that the man did not know all the song, that he sang only the part he remembered. But her constant reference to a repetitious chorus with highly formularized wording and tune, and to what seems to have been a repetitious and perhaps rambling story told in prose, indicates pretty clearly that the real event, which took place long ago, was a performance of a well-known genre of folklore that may have been recognizable to others in the audience but apparently not to young Clarice Mae.

In this case, it seems that the event witnessed by the folklorist, induced by the attempt to research and recover old songs, was really in the category of an anecdote, a memorate, or to some extent a recitation of oral history; and yet within that somewhat codified event lay the remnants of another event that could lead eventually to some research on the *cante-fable* there suggested through partial recollection. Here the role of the researcher, the outsider, has become almost more important in the generating of meaning than was that of the insider whose familiarity with the material was not conducive to a full sense of the traditional meaning. Hypothetically, it will be possible for a researcher eventually to come up with a more complete text than Mrs. Judkins was able to do.

There is also ample evidence of traditional awareness and articulation even in events induced by a folklorist. For example, Charles Cultee, almost the last of his people—the Kathlamet Chinook—narrated several striking and powerful myth texts to Franz Boas at the turn of the century. Boas took the texts down phonetically and then, interrogating Cultee in the Chinook jargon, provided an interlinear translation that can still be used by students today as a means of getting back to original elements of style and structure and meaning in the storytelling event, as Dell Hymes has brilliantly shown in his reconstruction of the full text of the Sun Myth. Even so, such a text cannot reveal to us all the details we need in order to understand a folk event fully and therefore to discover in it the actual meaning of a performance. Even the best of these texts remain powerful fossils of an even more powerful occurrence.

FOLK EVENTS: AN OVERVIEW

It should be clear by now that folk events are not all the same "size," that they may occur simultaneously with other folk events, and that some folk events may consist of smaller components that themselves may be dealt with as events. If we return now to the question posed earlier in this chapter about Tina's proverb—was it a folk event or does it take on the look of a folk event because of the attention we give it?—we can probably say that because the occurrence is extractable and discussable as a separate entity, yes, it can be dealt with as an event, and in so doing we are not denying that it was also one of several components of a larger folk event called a party.

Setting up our imaginary camera equipment under those circumstances, then, we would envision at least one roving camera taking in the small groups of people at the party as they told jokes and anecdotes, another camera in the kitchen focusing on the kinds of food considered appropriate on that occasion, another camera taking in the entire sets of components, and one at the ready (because hindsight is cheap and we might as well use it) to zoom in on the particularized event in which a proverb was performed.

Usually proverbs are not aimless observations on philosophical matters of general interest; rather, they are pointed applications of well-known, culture-oriented attitudes under conditions in which perhaps tension, indecision, or some other similar frustration has entered a human interaction, and in which specific personal advice might be embarrassing or intrusive. The fullest and most impressive account of such an event is given by Barbara Kirshenblatt-Gimblett. In her study of a parable in context, the entire situation in which the event took place is detailed, both by the collector and by the main participant, the teller of the parable. In many respects, a parable is a narrative proverb: both try to represent in formularized ways the wisdom of the community as applied to a particular instance in which easily recognized philosophy can solve a dilemma when personal intrusion would be doomed to failure.

Whether the event is a proverb that takes five seconds to recite, a parable that takes somewhat less than a minute to tell, a folktale that takes fifteen or twenty minutes to relate, an epic poem that takes a day and a half to be sung, a holiday that takes a week to celebrate, or a barn that takes a week to build, each will have some identifiable markers, some framework within which the occurrence is recognized by performer and audience as a communicative event, a realization of cultural values. In each case we find our attention focused on the particularized articulation of all those possibilities that lie dormant in the mind of a tradition-bearer at any particular moment. Even the custom of throwing spilled salt over the shoulder is only a potentiality until it is actually done by someone; when it is done, there will be some reason for it, which will often be stated in a phrase as the action takes place. There will be a beginning and an end to the action, and some framework within which it can be understood. Not all who know of the belief of throwing salt over the shoulder actually perform the custom when salt is spilled; therefore, we are distinguishing between beliefs and actions when we discuss folk events. For every traditional event, there may be any number of possible events that never take place; these may be discovered through discussions with members of inside groups, who can very often give us the typical dimensions of possible traditional acts, but it is only when the traditional act is made manifest within a natural context that we can actually study it as a folk event.

BIBLIOGRAPHICAL NOTES

If the active part of folklore can be called *performance*, then the actual total occurrence of that performance, including performer, audience, and context in a time-frame, can be called the *event*. Most of the references in the previous chapter thus apply inferentially here. This chapter parallels many of the considerations offered by Dell Hymes and others in the study of sociolinguistics: Hymes's division of topics into speech community, speech situation, speech event, speech act, and speech styles is an attempt to focus on the actuality of speaking in live context, not on the language, word, or grammar as abstracted phenomena. See Hymes, "Models of the Interaction of Language and Social Life," in *Directions in Sociolinguistics,* ed. John J. Gumperz and Dell Hymes (New York: Holt, Rinehart, and Winston, 1972), 35-71; nearly every essay is parallel to, or directly involved with, the dynamics of folklore discussed in the present book. In *Beyond Culture* (Chapter 6, "Context and Meaning"), Hall asserts that cultural code, context, and meaning are all different aspects of an event. For a succinct account of the dimensions of "event," see Bauman's *Story, Performance, and Event,* 1–10, and his "Verbal Art as Performance" (1984), esp. pp. 25–36.

Metafolklore is Alan Dundes's term for, among other things, the commentaries and remarks made by tradition-bearers about their own traditions, that is, folklore about folklore. See his "Metafolklore and Oral Literary Criticism," *The Monist* 50 (1966): 505-16. In "Toward a Definition of Folklore in Context," *Journal of American Folklore* 84 (1971): 3-15, Dan Ben-Amos asserts that "in the real habitat of all folklore forms, there is no dichotomy between processes and products. The telling is the tale; therefore the narrator, his story, and his audience are all related to each other as components of a single continuum, which is the communicative event" (10). Robert A. Georges in "Toward an Understanding of Storytelling Events," *Journal of American Folklore* 82 (1969): 313-28, suggests that storytelling must be seen "holistically rather than atomistically"—that is, as a total event (or series of events), not as a simple text. Folklore lies in the doing, according to Georges, in the performance-event, not in the artifact as a structural entity. The present chapter is obviously aligned with these sentiments.

Paul Hockings, ed., *Principles of Visual Anthropology* (The Hague: Mouton, 1975), presents a fascinating array of essays, several of which lend themselves to the filming situations hypothesized in this chapter. See especially J. Marshall and Emilie de Brigard, "Idea and Event in Urban Film," 133-45, and E. R. Sorensen and Allison Jablonko, "Research Filming of Naturally Occurring Phenomena: Basic Strategies," 151-63. The work of Sol Worth and John Adair is presented in *Through Navajo Eyes: An Exploration in Film Communication and Anthropology* (Bloomington: Indiana University Press, 1972); a brief synopsis of Susie Benally's film *A Navajo Weaver* appears here on page 162. Of a more practical bent, but still of value to our imaginary filmmaking, is John Collier Jr., *Visual Anthropology: Photography as a Research Method* (New York: Holt, Rinehart, and Winston, 1967). Margaret Mead's comments about the importance of film can be found in "Visual Anthropology in a Discipline of Words," in *Principles of Visual Anthropology,* ed. Hockings, 3-10. Sharon Sherman gives an account of her Seder videotaping in "'That's How the Seder Looks': A Fieldwork Account of Videotaping Family Folklore," *Journal of Folklore Research* 23 (1986): 53–70. Walter Ong's comment on the validity of "one picture is worth a thousand words" is in his "Hermeneutic Forever: Voice, Text, Digitization, and the 'I,'" *Oral Tradition* 10 (1995): 6.

For their willingness to share their family traditions with me for this book, I am deeply indebted to Mr. and Mrs. William Tabler and their daughter, Twilo Scofield. Even more profoundly am I obliged to my own Massachusetts relatives, Leslie and Virginia Howland (Granby), Alice Kimball, and Ada Collis (Pelham Hill), Kenneth and Alyce Damon (West Springfield), Leila and Homer Damon (Belchertown), and my mother, Sylvia Damon Toelken—all formerly of Enfield, before Quabbin Reservoir—for passing the traditions of Thanksgiving on through me. David Hackett Fischer's *Albion's Seed: Four British Folkways in America* (New York and Oxford: Oxford University Press, 1989) is an excellent example of how folklore can expand and enrich our historical sense of culture. See esp. pp. 8–9, 134–39, 164, 783–898; Harriet Beecher Stowe is quoted on pp. 138–39. An excellent survey of the annual round of traditional holidays in the United States is Jack Santino, *All Around the Year: Holidays and Celebrations in American Life* (Urbana: University of Illinois Press, 1994).

The Japanese and Japanese American people listed in the notes to Chapter 2 are my sources here as well; my special thanks go to Mrs. Chiyoe Kubota, an excellent cook, a serious conservator of family tradition, and an indefatigable source of cultural information as well as my vivacious mother-in-law. Further cultural backgrounds on rice and its relation to the New Year may be found in Toshijiro Hirayama, "Seasonal Rituals Connected with Rice Culture," in *Studies in Japanese Folklore*, ed. Richard M. Dorson (Bloomington: Indiana University Press, 1963), 57-75, esp. 73-74, and Ichiro Hori, "Mysterious Visitors from the Harvest to the New Year," also in Dorson, 76-103, esp. 83-88 and 97-98.

An article focusing on Mrs. Judkins's songs is Russell M. Harrison's "Folksongs from Oregon," *Western Folklore* 11 (1952): 174-84. The full text and commentary on the Sun Myth is in Dell Hymes, "Folklore's Nature and the Sun's Myth," *Journal of American Folklore* 88 (1975): 345-69.

Many folklore studies have indeed centered their attention on the event rather than on the artifact. The following studies provide some idea of the possibilities in focus for such work. James P. Leary, "Fists and Foul Mouths: Fights and Fight Stories in Contemporary Rural American Bars," *Journal of American Folklore* 89 (1976): 27-39, shows the striking correspondence between the structure of fight stories told in bars and the structure of the actual fight events. Instead of the story being treated merely as a text, or the fight dealt with as a mere chance occurrence, the two are seen as interrelated traditional structures, each deriving meaning from the other, which can be understood only by scrutinizing the entire traditional performance event. Richard Bauman, "The La Have Island General Store: Sociability and Verbal Art in a Nova Scotia Community," *Journal of American Folklore* 85 (1972): 330-43, rests its evidence on the continual series of evening sessions of traditional conversation events at a local community store. Seen as events, these culturally structured conversations reveal much of the local aesthetic sense. Alan Dundes and Alessandro Falassi, *La Terra in Piazza* (Berkeley: University of California Press, 1975) is a study of an event that captivates the lives and emotions of an entire city, Siena, Italy, as its annual horse-racing and related activities interweave in the most intricate system of event frames imaginable. An exceptionally sensitive account of a cultural event is Madeline Slovenz-Low, "On the Tail of the Lion: Approaches to Cross Cultural Fieldwork with Chinese-Americans in New York," in *Creative Ethnicity: Symbols and Strategies of Contemporary Ethnic Life,* ed. Stephen Stern and John Allan Cicala (Logan: Utah State University Press, 1991), 55–71. For a collaborative (Native/non-Native) account of a Native American social event, see Vanessa (Wanbli Ota Wi) Brown and Barre Toelken, "Pow-wow: Ethnic Intensification in Indian America," *Folklore Annual 1987* (Washington, D.C.: Library of Congress, 1988), 46–69.

Chapter 5

AESTHETICS AND REPERTOIRE

Choices from the Community Menu

JUST AS DOCTORS DO NOT TALK ABOUT THE BODY WITHOUT KNOWING ALL THE principal parts, just as a linguist cannot talk about language without a vocabulary of terms that describe words, sounds, and meaning, so the folklorist does not discuss folklore without a sound knowledge of its genres. And just as some doctors specialize in ears, or digestive tract, or feet, or in single processes like childbirth, and as linguists specialize in verbs, sounds, or whole languages, so do folklorists specialize in tales, songs, or in the traditions of a whole group of people. Without a generic terminology, we would have little hope of understanding each other, especially when, just like doctors, we try to see how the arm or leg, tale or belief, functions as part of the whole live phenomenon.

Unlike the human body, however, folklore—as a creature—may not always have the same structure on each occasion. The motifs and ideas of a particular item or performance of folklore are always changing (while humans usually continue to appear with one head, two arms, and two legs). That is to say, folklore is not *limited* by genre or by the repertoire of one person. Folk ideas and expressions have a way of appearing in several genres, and people in a close group are likely to know many genres and perform in more than one of them, making their choices on the basis of personal preference and a traditionally shared aesthetic.

One result is that we may find the same idea or motif here in a tale, there in a legend, here in a ballad, there in a news item. Another is that we discover the woman we sought out for her quiltmaking is also a great storyteller and a specialist in local foodlore, the man we started to collect ballads from is an even better whittler and blacksmith, while another person we gathered jokes from turns out to have nothing else to offer (from tradition) besides jokes. Cecil Sharp and Maud Karpeles, the British folksong scholars, made three extensive trips into the Appalachians collecting many hundreds of folksong texts in an area that we today realize is also one of the richest places for folktale tradition in the country. Take any one of their informants: Were the songs actually the central or most important part of that person's traditional repertoire? Were the motifs or the stories in the songs and ballads also found in local folktales? Was the song tradition in those areas actually more active than other kinds of folk tradition? Answers to such questions are difficult if not impossible to come by now, years later; in their understandable zeal for collecting folksongs, Sharp and Karpeles overlooked perhaps dozens of other related kinds of folk expression that might have afforded us a fuller view of folk experience, expression, and aesthetics in those areas not long after the turn of the century. Since the character of that region is now vastly changed, it is impossible for us to recover those patterns, and preferences could have been easily noted and studied by scholars who were actually there. This is not merely an antiquarian quibble, for the same myopia is possible for any folklore fieldworker who limits the field of vision to one genre, whatever the date.

GENRE AND FOCUS

While generic distinctions in folklore are important, we cannot let generic boundaries become ideational restrictions, especially when we seek to understand the live processes behind the categories of folk structures. The choices open to a traditional performer at any time will be encouraged or restricted by the traditional context of the event as well as by the community's taste in such matters as language, topic, propriety, and decorum. Over the long haul, ongoing community taste will help to condition the choices on larger matters, such as the forms a given idea may most likely take. These choices may come to our attention most clearly in generic terms, as when someone says, "That song you just sang is the same as a story I used to hear from my father." But the deciding factors are not generic details; they are instead those dynamic and constantly shifting canons of traditional taste that continually recombine to influence (and even to cause) any particular folk performance. In this chapter I propose to discuss some dimensions of folklore that seem unrestricted by generic categories: repertoires of traditional performers in which the same folk item may fall into different categories depending on function and context; folk ideas found in a number of genres without appreciable difference in meaning; matters of community taste, aesthetics, and decorum that help to determine who does what, when, and with what import for the close group. This chapter does not suggest, however, that genre is a useless term; to the contrary, genre allows us to group similar items together for purposes of analysis and discussion. But generic distinctions in and of themselves seldom lead us to clear understanding of traditional processes.

Multiform Repertoires

"Chris" Christensen, a retired teacher in Oakridge, Oregon, was known as a whittler. He carved fans, balls in cages, and chains; indeed most of the traditional items of the whittler's craft are found in his work. Probably in generic terms a folklorist's category for Mr. Christensen's work would be *craft*, or *whittling*. Yet, when Mr. Christensen talked about how and where he learned whittling, we found that he picked it up from other commercial fishermen years ago: it was customary to whittle when work fell off and the men were bored. Now, is his whittling a craft or a custom? Obviously both, and this can be accommodated (in an archive collection for example) by cross-referencing. But what the cross-reference does not indicate is the relative importance of the genres mentioned. Seen as only one small part of a fisherman's repertoire of folklore (folk speech, popular belief, occupational custom, song, story, gesture), whittling is an insignificant—or at least a subordinated—activity ("we used to just throw them away, back then"). Seen as a craft later practiced quite often by Mr. Christensen, when he was no longer a fisherman, it appears central. It related him to neighbors and friends to whom he gave (never sold) the carved items. Moreover, his own dedication to the aesthetic and personal details of whittling, though modestly understated, were strong: he was very careful to choose the right wood (Alaska cedar, when possible) and to treat it properly by soaking it in water before beginning his work. Usually he had a few pieces "a-soak" for those moments "when I feel the whittlin' comin' on." We might suggest, then, that even though the whittling remained an interest for Mr. Christensen, its generic focus had changed in weight: had we "collected him" years ago we might have called his whittling a custom, while now we might call it a craft since it had been singled out by him, excerpted, so to speak, as something he particularly liked to do. In this case, since the tradition-bearer himself has done the excerpting, the theoretical problems are comparatively few.

All too often, however, it is the folklorist who unwittingly does the excerpting and presents a vivid record of what is thought to be a genre without providing a sense of where it stands in the traditional repertoire of the informant. An example of such an omission is provided earlier in this book: the case of the New England family that sings "Rolling Home" at Thanksgiving. I did not supply the observation that for only a few people in that whole family is it part of a repertoire of songs. For the others it is a custom, performed on a particular date because "we've always done it." Most people in the family remember only the chorus, and they do not sing it at other times of the year. Without this information, we might easily suppose that the family is one with a rich song repertoire, so active that they even sing at the table. Then is "Rolling Home" not to be placed in the genre *folksong*? Of course it is a folksong, when considered separately and when seen in terms of its own form, transmission, development, and variation in oral tradition. But the situation is more complex when we consider where and how the song lies in the particular repertoires of its various singers. An item once a part of a song repertoire passed on by sailors and fishermen for use at times appropriate to their traditions has become an occasional item within another context. In both instances, custom plays a role, of course, but in

"Chris" Christensen of Springfield, Oregon, whittles a fan for his grandson. Photo by Suzi Jones.

A fan and a tower of
balls-in-boxes whittled
by "Chris" Christensen.
Photos by Suzi Jones.

the case of the New England family, custom, not musical considerations, seems to have the upper hand. It is evident that judgments about whether a given folk expression can be called a tale, a song, or a custom must be based as much on its function in the live process as on its appearance when written out on a page.

Hugh Yellowman lived in a small town in southern Utah, just north of the Navajo reservation. He was known locally as a moccasin maker of great talent; the people of his town brought him their deer hides and commissioned him to make Navajo-style moccasins for their families. Proprietors of nearby tourist shops and trading posts sold his moccasins when they could get them. His wife, Helen, is still a well-known weaver who occasionally sells her rugs through a local trading post. Both of these activities would no doubt be classified as folk crafts or "material folklore: hide work, weaving" by most folklorists, for the kinds of performance under scrutiny here require manual formations of culturally recognizable items, in culturally transmitted ways, from material goods. Yet, the weaving of a Navajo rug is only part of a larger set of culturally important actions: herding sheep (animal lore, folk science, custom, belief), gathering plants and herbs for washing and dyeing (plant lore, belief, folk medicine), and spinning (craft, belief). And Yellowman's moccasins entail a set of hunting beliefs and rituals that go far beyond the manual dexterity required to produce the actual items: proper hunting and skinning of the animals must be congruent with the annual round of ceremonies, with the mental and physical preparation of the hunter, with the stories told before dawn each morning in the hunting camp, and so on. If the rug is the least important aspect of the process that produces it, if the moccasin is only a physical symbol of a larger set of abstract relationships, are we not warping Navajo reality if we focus chiefly on the physical nature of the items in determining genre? Do we not miss a great deal of meaning when we apply our generic concepts to performances of other cultures? The answer to both is yes.

On the other hand, how are we to understand anything unless we try to see clearly in the codes we already know? This may seem at first to be a dilemma sufficient to discourage anyone from studying folklore further, but it can be solved by admitting that genre designations are devices for clarity, not natural definitions in and of themselves. Genre may indicate something to us of structure and substance, as well as of import, meaning, and function. Since we can articulate generic distinctions and hold several of them in mind at one time, we should be able to approach even more fairly those traditional expressions that might otherwise puzzle us or evade our understanding.

The Basket As Folksong

Suppose an Indian woman from northern California says that we cannot learn to make baskets until we learn all the proper songs. Indeed, when Evalina Matt, a Yurok woman, was invited to teach a two-week basketmaking seminar at the University of Oregon in the 1970s, she spent the first week teaching songs to

Joanne, Helen, Hugh, and Mike Yellowman stand by the author's jeep in Montezuma Creek Canyon, 1955. Note Helen's *jaa'tl'ool*, used twenty years later by her husband as a pendant.

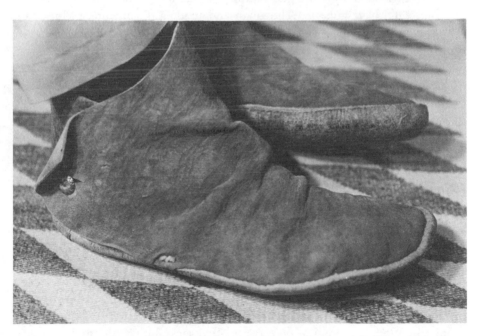

A pair of moccasins made for the author by Yellowman: raw cowhide soles, sacred deerskin (from a deer whose hide was not injured while being killed) uppers, split rawhide thread, and silver buttons made from hammered dimes.

the students. During the second week, the students were taken to the forest, where they were told to sing the songs while they gathered the appropriate plants. Then, back in the classroom, they were taught other songs which would be hummed quietly while the students softened the materials in their mouths, and finally, on the last day or two of the course, the students were shown a few of the basic practical steps in assembling the basket structure. When the students—in a mixture of awe and frustration—asked why they had been required to spend so much time singing in a course where they had expected to make baskets, they were told by Mrs. Matt, "The songs are basic to basketmaking; after all, a basket is a song that's been made visible."

In a parallel instance, N. Scott Momaday shows that an arrow is an aspect of both language and communication for his tribe: a brief description of how Kiowa arrows are made with toothmarks on them is superimposed on a story of an arrowmaker who recognizes the presence of an enemy (and shoots him with a newly made arrow, right through the buffalo hide tepee) because the unseen person cannot answer in the Kiowa language. In such discussions, we must have our generic concepts straight or we will not be able to articulate the wide variations in function, value, focus, and process that lurk behind all live performances of folklore. Holding two (or ten) genres in mind is confusing only if we make the mistake of thinking that they are, or should be, mutually exclusive.

We could have gone to Yellowman and made a documentary film about the process of producing a pair of moccasins. The film might have shown the hunting scene preceding the skinning, which would have preceded the tanning, which would have preceded the moccasin-making. But even so, the filmmaker might have left town totally unaware of the artist's ability to make silver and turquoise jewelry, his extraordinary talents at storytelling, his singing and dancing in the very important *Yé'ii Bicheii* ceremony, his making and use of bows and arrows, his extensive knowledge of plants, astronomy, medicine, mythic lore, most of which in fact intersect with the use and symbolism of the moccasins. Notice that it is not the live context that would be missing from such a documentary (for there might be plenty of contextual material), but the esoteric idea-context would be fragmented; thus the Navajo idea of what a moccasin is and how it functions would recede, leaving an image of the object *we* think the moccasin is. In practice, genres are difficult to separate, and this should be approached as a positive and exciting matter for speculation.

For example, some kinds of folk expressions absolutely require us to register the fact that one genre is being disguised in the format of another—often for humorous purposes. The famed jackalope of the Western Plains and Intermountain West is a physical object: a stuffed jackrabbit with antelope horns mounted on its head. But it is accompanied by legendary accounts of how potent jackalope milk is (if one can get it), how fast they breed (only during lightning strikes in a thunderstorm), and how they came to be (as a result of jackrabbit attacks on timid antelope). The same animal is often seen mounted

Yellowman stands by his wife's loom in Blanding, Utah, holding some of the items he uses when dancing the *Yé'ii Bicheii* dance (1970s). The pendants on his coral necklace are turquoise earrings (*jaa'tl'ool*, lit. "a looped cord through the ear") formerly worn by his wife.

on hunter's walls in Austria; called the *Hasenbock* (buck hare) or *Wolpertinger*, it has small deer antlers, and is surrounded with the same range of humorously improbable legends. The point is, of course, that there are no serious legends—that is, real belief stories—told about the jackalope, and even the mounted specimens are, in the zoological sense, phonies. In spite of a wonderful "documentary" on the jackalope presented on national television by Charles Kuralt and Roger (Himself) Welsch, there isn't any such thing. But there it is, hanging on the wall of many a western barber shop and hunter's den. What is its genre? Tall tale? Legend? Folk taxidermy? Joke? Regional parody of official state animals? I would say it is a visual joke disguised as a legendary animal, and that it is in the ambiguity of the disguise that much of its force and meaning lies. Many people outside the West took the Kuralt/Welsch program seriously, as did some recent Asian immigrants in the West. But the true westerner knows the jackalope to be an inside joke, and I would say that the joke is funny precisely because of its intergeneric ambiguity.

Another example of generic ambiguity is the Nebraska logging chain: a handcrafted iron chain with a hook on one end and a ring on the other (see photo p. 412). Logging chains are usually made to provide a simple, practical way of chaining up a large "boom" of logs for river transport (or to fasten them to the bed of a truck). The usual logging chain is 20 to 50 feet long—sometimes even longer—in order to accomplish its job. The Nebraska logging chain is only 9 inches long, because the trees in Nebraska are so few—or so small. Is it a real chain? Yes. Is it a real logging chain? Well, it depends on whether you mean "in existence" or "exactly accurate," for the Nebraska logging chain does exist, and in every way but one it is accurate. Its short length is a kind of hyperbole for the scarcity of large trees in Nebraska. Here again, the generic category could easily be material culture (folk craft/blacksmithing), and the designation would be entirely straightforward and accurate—but it would leave out *meaning*. The Nebraska logging chain is a visual Munchausen disguised as a tool.

The same kinds of ambiguity can be used in total seriousness as well. Some years ago, a Tututni woman gave me a beaded wristband she had made. The Tututni are a small Athabascan group living near the coast of southern Oregon. In former times they were skilled basketmakers, using principally the shoots of beargrass that come up the year after a fire. Because the coastal peoples had burned off the underbrush regularly to encourage the growth of small plants (to bring the deer closer) and to discourage the accumulation of underbrush (which made forest fires more likely), they had had no shortage of materials for baskets. With the White immigrants, however, came fire suppression, and today there are very few proper beargrass shoots to use for basketry. In order to preserve the basket designs, the Tututni weavers have continued to use them in other media, including beadwork (which was not, of course, an indigenous craft). And so I was told that my wristband might look like a beaded bracelet, but that in fact it was a basket, its design lurking in the beadwork until such

The wily western jackalope, said to be the offspring of jackrabbits that forcibly mate with antelope during lightning flashes on the high plains, may not actually exist, in spite of a half-hour television special on it by Charles Kuralt in the 1980s; but they persist in local anecdotes told to strangers, and they appear regularly on the walls of barbershops across the West (as here at Dick's Barbershop in the Utah State University Student Center). Photo by Ron Daines.

Ordinary wall ornaments often receive a Christmas touch, whether they be an unlikely jackalope or a very likely (but equally puzzling) African Ankoli cow skull.

time as the U.S. Forest Service might change its policies about fire suppression and once again allow a cultural art to flourish. By giving me the bracelet as a gift and urging me to wear it, the giver was not only making a generous gesture of friendship, but was effectively using an Anglo-American as the living medium for reminding our culture that Indian people are still waiting for us to get out of their artistic way.

Rather than focus, then, on a single presumed genre, we need to ask—at least to begin with—what is the range of vernacular meaning in this expression? On this occasion? In this medium? Are there elements of meaning, style, or structure that strike us as belonging to more than one generic category? We might, later on, excerpt the beadwork, say, for special focus, but we will not then have overlooked the other expressions and their relationships to the bead-work. And we will not have missed the real place of patterns in the total fabric of this person's (or group's or region's) normal traditions.

MULTILATERAL LEARNING

Another important aspect of traditional repertoires is that each item or genre or idea may come from a different source within the folk group. A person may have learned how to whittle from a grandfather, how to make willow whistles from an uncle, how to play the guitar from another uncle, how to sing songs from an aunt, how to know the traditions of crossing the equator from later buddies in the Coast Guard. For this reason, each tradition-bearer is a unique combination of folk expression. Equally so, we cannot conclude that because one person has only a partial recollection of a tradition that the tradition itself is dying out. Mrs. Mary ("Grandma") Spivey of Buckeye Cove, North Carolina, was the matriarch of a large traditional mountain family when I visited her in 1952. She was a walking treasure of mountain wit, traditional cooking lore, herbalism, folk medicine, stories and legends, beliefs, and folksongs. Even so, her fourteen-year-old granddaughter, Carolyn, had a far larger repertoire of songs and ballads—numbering in the hundreds. Clearly, Carolyn was the cur-rent carrier of ballads in the family, and she had learned them from everyone else (most of her relatives sang at least a few songs), including a deceased grand-father. We would surely be hasty to assume that all members of a community should know the same items and genres in the same quantities or that older tra-dition-bearers should normally "have" more folklore than younger ones.

The tendency toward multiplicity and overlapping assures that the total "quantity" of folklore in a particular person's repertoire will be highly variable, as will be the kinds of folklore in each repertoire; these variations will be as much a function of the person's own tastes as they are of differences in the peo-ple from whom the traditions were learned and the ages at which they were picked up. This condition is obviously an important component of the concept of dynamic variation brought up in Chapter 1: not only is each item of folklore subject to variation at every remove in tradition, but the traditions themselves and their roles in the lives of each folk performer are in continual flux.

Traditional Deference

In addition to such encouragements to generic variation as creativity, contextual constraints, memory lapse, source, and age, many folk groups feel a delicacy about intruding into any field of expression associated with a particular person. Thus, people in a family may all know of a certain tradition, but one particular person performs it for the rest. Grandma's reputation for a special pie usually ensures that others will not bring their versions of it to the Thanksgiving gatherings while she is present unless some arrangement has been made previously. Indeed, in some families, no one else will make that pie at all according to her special recipe until Grandma has passed away; at that juncture, someone else may step forward to fill the traditional slot. In the Spivey family of North Carolina, Carolyn was the acknowledged singer, although others also sang; earlier, Carolyn's grandfather had been the family singer. Bess Hockema, a grandmother living in Pistol River, Oregon, makes afghans for her grandchildren as her own mother once did for hers. Others in these families know the same traditions and perhaps can perform them as well, but the actual centrality of the performance focuses on a particular person because of age, talent, interest, or because of simple family custom. As one tradition-bearer dies or retires, several others are available to take that place in the generic spotlight.

One hears people say, "Oh, don't ask me to tell a joke; ask George over there, he's a scream." On logging crews, often one person is the chief trickster, is acknowledged so by his buddies, and relishes his position. On Indian reservations, we are directed to "the last basketmaker in this tribe"; some years later, when she dies, another person (who was there all along) becomes "the last basketmaker in this tribe." I have heard a quilter (a man) say, "Well, you know, I never did mean to become a quilter, but when there weren't any others left in the family it just didn't seem right to let it drop, so I just started doing what Mom did." Such attitudes testify to a kind of deference to recognized traditional performers by those in the close group who know the traditions. In turn this widespread deference—in the ways we actually encounter it in conversation—indicates an awareness of genre ("Oh, yes, he's the best storyteller in these parts.") and of a set of shared aesthetics. The aesthetics we will take up later in this chapter, but here it is important to realize that deference to tradition-bearers helps to determine who will perform in certain genres, and at what intervals in time. Keeping in mind that some traditions are more prominent in childhood while others blossom when we are older, that some traditions seem to skip generations in the family, that many traditions are learned from peers not necessarily older than ourselves, we see that almost any member of a close group is a potential performer in a great number of genres at different times and for different reasons. Meanwhile, as we will see more fully later in this chapter, many folk ideas can be and are expressed in any of several genres, and with varying focuses within genres. All of these possibilities make up the ideational context from which arises any particular articulation or performance of a tradition, and they inform the way in which the formulation is made, by whom, and when.

Such a range of variables can be better understood if we refer to a particular person and see how real situations actually bring forth the choices and performances that demonstrate the conservation of traditions in dynamically responsive ways. Even so, we should not allow ourselves to hope that in any one person, family, or ethnic, regional, or occupational group we will see all the possible interactive permutations of genre, motif, style, and performance. Rather, one clear set of examples can give us some insight into the tremendous richness of tradition in everyday life, a demonstration that for the tradition-bearers in a close group there exists a constellation of potential folk expressions that are not limited by generic differentiation and that seldom exist alone, even though they may be described separately for convenience in academic discussion.

The Integration of Genres in a Traditional Repertoire

Bess Hockema of Pistol River, Oregon, was a striking example of a multiple repertoire in action. As a farm woman, she performed daily in a wide variety of genres, most of them closely interrelated. Complicating the picture, however, is that the traditional performances were learned from different people (chiefly from her father and mother), who came from another part of the country. More complicated still is that her performances were geared to a sense of local and family decorum and deference so that they were shared with others in the family under rather solidly recognizable rules.

First, some background on this richly traditional family: Bess Hockema was born Bess Finley, daughter of Ed Finley from Tennessee and Genarah Beckham of Arkansas. In 1923 she married George B. Wasson, son of George R. Wasson (from Nova Scotia) and Adulsah, daughter of Gishgiu and Kits-un-jin-jn (of the Coos tribe, southwestern Oregon). Their five children (Wilfred, Susan, Bette, George, and John) are thus the inheritors of a richly mixed set of traditions. After the death of George Wasson, Bess married Paul ("Dutch") Hockema, whose son, Earl, subsequently married her daughter Bette. Four of Bess's children have children of their own, so she enjoyed the role of matriarch in a close-knit family group whose traditions, though they come from sharply varied sources, act as a unifying force.

The family gathers for special holidays like Thanksgiving and Christmas, for shared outings like hunting, fishing, picnicking, and camping, and for any other event that provides an excuse. On these occasions stories are told, songs are sung, and memorates and anecdotes about family history are shared among members of all ages.

Bess Hockema in a characteristic pose at her kitchen sink at Sundown Ranch, deep in Oregon's Coast Range and east of Pistol River. Photo by Suzi Jones.

The whole family possesses, and is the context for, traditions too complex to assign to one person. Yet if we look at where Bess Hockema stood in this traditional world—and how she performed in it—we will have at least one clear cross section of folklore dynamism. If we focus on any other person in her family (and we shall, briefly), we will find another kind of cross section, equally vivid, equally valid. In both cases we will find that some of the folklore in Bess's family is shared and performed by everyone, while other expressions are attached chiefly to one specific person, even though others in the family know the tradition and could probably perform it themselves.

In the case of Bess Hockema in particular, what are the genres through which she shared tradition with her family, and how do these categories relate or overlap? Her family considered the following to have been her chief areas of tradition. In discussion, they do fall into generally recognizable generic categories: planting and harvest customs, folk foods, animal husbandry, folk medicine, crafts, folksong, proverb, memorate, and family history, but in practice they interpenetrate so fully that generic boundaries seem almost irrelevant.

Putting in a Garden and Gardening

Bess was the primary family gardener, and although everyone who happened to be at home when the gardening was done was expected to help out, she directed the planting and decided the relationships and order of plants within the garden. The cornfield, a separate garden plot, was the full responsibility of Dutch until his death. During his illness and inability to plant corn, his own son, Earl, performed that duty in his father's behalf when Dutch determined the time was right.

Bess's gardening traditions came chiefly from her father (i.e., from Tennessee); she planted marigolds by the pole beans to keep aphids away, garlic next to other vegetables to discourage cutworms. Interestingly, even though Bess planted a good deal of garlic for this purpose, she used none of it in cooking, not in the smallest amounts—even though her mother was so fond of it that she ate it raw. This is a good example of how a traditional performer is not constrained to follow all aspects of custom; personal taste—in this case, Bess's distaste for the smell of garlic—plays a strong role in determining the precise details with which a tradition is or is not performed. Zinnias and other such flowers were placed strategically in Bess's garden to repel some insects and attract others.

A typical city gardener, used to keeping vegetables and flowers separate, might look at Bess's garden with puzzlement; although the plants were all presented in neat rows, they appeared to the outsider an odd combination. But here, surely, is where tradition exerts its influence, for Bess's garden was not primarily for show but for function, and a customary function at that, connected with old family practices. Within that function, the garden was of course expected to look neat and beautiful. While there was a central practical motivation for placing the vegetables and flowers, then, the traditions that dictated their placement were the result of culturally recognized aesthetic judgment. Clearly, these are not the high art aesthetics of formal gardeners, but they are easily "read" and appreciated by other western Oregon farm people.

Food Preservation

During the summer and fall, as vegetables, berries, and fruits ripened, Bess began the canning procedures she learned from her mother (from Arkansas). Here again, although she performed in the tradition, she elected to make certain changes of her own. For one, she canned her string beans whole, even though her mother had always "snapped" hers. In fact, Bess paid so much attention to beans, both string beans and dry beans (which others call "Bess's beans"), that it became a common family joke. In addition, of course, she canned other vegetables and fruits as well as meats such as beef, venison, tuna, and chicken. She made the usual jams and jellies from local berries as well as other kinds of preserves from beets and other vegetables, using crabapple and quince for pectin. She was famous in the family for her pickles and relishes, nearly all of them produced from recipes and traditions handed down to her from her mother's side of the family.

Animal Husbandry

Although Bess did not do the heavy work with the animals on her farm, she was considered the best milker in the family, and she also owned the milk cow. She delighted in her ability to wean calves and teach them to drink from a bucket, and she presided over lambing even in the most inclement weather. It was her traditional duty to select those calves that would be allowed to mature into bulls. Although her own busy schedule seldom permitted her to work more directly with the animals (in such matters as health care for livestock, paring horses' hooves, and so on), she was a fund of opinion and advice to the men who did.

Butchering

Bess knew how to do the killing of animals (*butchering*, it is called by the family), but usually deferred to the men in these matters. She enjoyed skinning an animal and was considered very adept at it; when time and occasion permitted she filled this traditional role with acknowledged talent. Her butchering, meat cutting, and animal husbandry were learned from her father while her ways of drawing chickens came from her mother.

Folk Cooking

Since Bess was the principal cook of the family and spent much of her time cooking, the breadth and depth of her lore in this category is far too extensive to treat fairly here. In this family, as we shall see, some of the recipes prepared traditionally by Bess have been taken over by various of her children, and there is now a traditional assignment of certain dishes to certain family members. Of those that Bess always prepared, and that therefore others would not think of preparing, were corn bread, sour cream biscuits, applesauce cake, and an ad hoc cake made from whatever ingredients might be available that is called simply *cake* by the family. "Mom's cake" was an inside family joke, for outsiders always asked, "What kind of cake is it?" The family members then replied, "Just cake." Bess's talents were such that she could simply lay hands on enough varied ingredients to come up with a fine cake under any circumstances. While perhaps other members of the family could also have done the trick, no one would have been so intrusive as to try it. Bess did not consider herself a good cook, however, and claimed her expertise was only the result of necessity. It will be interesting to see, now that Bess is gone, whether someone else in the family will make "Mom's cake."

Folk Medicine

Bess of course knew the various local herbs and teas that could be used for minor ailments. More particularly, in years past she was known as a local diagnostician for baby illnesses. Families who had already taken their babies to a doctor would come to Bess and ask what she thought. Bess would look the infant over, make some kind of deliberation and comment on what she felt the ailment might be, and then suggest the parents take the baby to a doctor. On at least one occasion the parents replied, "Well, we already have, but we wanted to check with you to see if the doctor was right." While not functioning specifically as a midwife, Bess served informally in this capacity on demand in the various rural areas where she lived.

Knitting and Crocheting

These particular crafts were saved for the long and dark winter months. As I mentioned previously, the crocheting of afghans for grandchildren had been a tradition carried on throughout her life by Genarah Finley, and Bess learned the traditions from her mother. After her mother's death, Bess moved into this role and supplied the expected afghans for her own children and grandchildren.

Quilting and Needlework

These crafts were also learned by Bess from her mother, but more important than the craft itself in this case is the manner in which it is carried out. Grandma Finley had made numerous quilt tops in her spare time throughout her life. The tops were put away, and when people in the family got married, they were given a quilt. Many of these quilt tops are still in the family, and, even today, when someone gets married, his or her top is quilted and given; the family gathers, as is traditional, and joins in the quilting. Thus, each quilt represents the handiwork of all family members. Here is a solid example of a case in which the craft in its manual aspects, or the item in its physical existence, comes

Bess Hockema working on one of the many afghans with which she regularly supplied her children and grandchildren. Photo by Suzi Jones.

nowhere near the connotative power that inheres in the quilt for the members of this close group.

Folk Narratives

Although her children perform extensive repertoires of folktales, most of Bess's narratives would be classified as memorates, family legends, anecdotes, and oral history. One of her favorite stories concerns an adventure she had as a young girl growing up in Texas. Early one morning, when she went out to get the cows, she heard some loud noises in the dry slashing above the road and concluded that one of her cows had gotten entangled in the dried brush. She tried and tried to call it out, but every time she stopped to hear where the cow was, the cow would stop moving so she couldn't hear it. After a while she gave up and went to get the rest of her cows and found to her surprise that they were all there. When she got home she told the details to her parents, especially how the cows had raised their tails and had run wide around that place on their way home. Someone went back out and found cougar tracks all along the road where she had passed. This personal anecdote came forth whenever there was a low drift of early morning fog hanging close to the ground on the farm; at times like these, undecipherable noises can be heard in the forest, and the stage was set for her recitation of the story. As with other personal accounts of this sort, the content of the story is recalled history, not transmitted lore, but the choice of what makes a good anecdote, the continued telling of a given story in a close group, the style, structure, wording, and context are all solidly traditional.

Bess also liked to relate her impressions on coming to Oregon by steamer from San Francisco in the early 1900s. Again, all the details of the trip were not mentioned; only those high points that related to her tastes and attitudes and that responded to the demands of the close group received special focus. She also recounted stories of humorous happenings in her family: A family favorite recalls the time Grandma Finley tried to administer a dose of Epsom salts to her daughter Verna, promising it would make her feel better. Verna steadfastly refused, an argument ensued, and Grandma got so angry that she took the dose of salts herself so as not to waste the proven remedy.

Other stories were memorates she recalled having heard from older family members who had lived back East: encounters with ghosts, meetings with strange creatures in the woods, stories told by her mother were all parts of her narrative repertoire. A few folktales were there, of course, but they were a small part of the whole. One favorite of the family today is the tar baby story, one of several Bess told that feature "Bur Rabbit."

Not confined to anecdotes from her own side of the family, Bess enjoyed passing on stories that concern the Indians and the Scots in her first husband's family. There were memorates about her husband's relatives being able to foretell deaths in the family; a recurrent story held in high regard by all members of the family tells of Great-grandmother Gishgiu's escape from the soldiers. The army had rounded up members of the small southwestern Oregon bands and tribes and had moved them at gun point up the Oregon coast, first to a spot near present-day Reedsport, then to Yachats. There the Coos, among others, were confined on a small promontory jutting out into the sea while a tiny reservation was being prepared inland for some of the others who had treaties (the Siletz Reservation, in later years "terminated" by the government). The people on the promontory were close to starvation, and they could barely gather enough shell-fish to stay alive; some drowned in the rough surf while gathering mussels on the rocks. Gishgiu would not put up with this degradation any further, and she dove into the ocean, heading south for home. She made her way down the coast, moving along the beaches at night, hiding by day in the dense undergrowth of the forest, and swimming out around the precipitous headlands to avoid meeting soldiers and other Whites who might be using the narrow trail above. She eventually made her way back to the South Slough country on Coos Bay, living for some time in a hollow cedar tree in the forest near her daughter's home. Here she remained undetected by the soldiers but in contact with her daughter's family at night. Finally, when she felt secure enough to move into the house, she resumed the duties of clothing mender even though totally blind by that time.

Somewhat later, an alarm was received that the soldiers were on their way to get Grandmother and return her to Yachats. The family hid the tiny woman under the bottom stair step by shoving boxes and sea trunks underneath the stairway behind her. An older child was sent to the woods where her son-in-law was logging with an ox team while the two soldiers ransacked the house, ignoring the youngest children who, unable to keep the secret, kept saying "Gekka, Gekka" (Coos for "grandmother") while pointing to the stairs. George R. Wasson, a large man, burst into the house, grabbed a soldier in each hand by the back of the neck, and heaved them into the front yard with instructions never to return. Gishgiu was able to live out her life close to the people and the land she loved.

For her descendants, the story is not simply an account of Great-grandmother's bravery, but an ironic and dramatic re-experiencing of the perils and frustrations that beset many of the families in the Oregon country who intermarried with Indians (a practice more common than is realized today). As the current family matriarch, Bess clearly enjoyed focusing on the adventures of the family's strong women.

Proverbs

Proverbs are used by nearly all the members of Bess's family, a clear indication of their involvement with traditional modes of advice. In addition, proverbs and proverbial phrases are often accompanied by a tag line identifying someone from a previous generation in the family who had been well known for using the particular saying. Having not seen one of her sons for a long time, Bess told him over the phone, "When you come home for Thanksgiving, we'll put the big pot in the little pot and make soup out of the dishrag; [pause] that's what I remember Grandma used to say."

Folksong

Bess's mother played a concertina and her father a fiddle. Her father, however, would not play for dances or even for play-parties for religious reasons. Her mother, Genarah Beckham, sang a good deal, and many of her songs are still in the active repertoire Bess used on those rare occasions when she had time to sit down among family members and sing. There are strong traditions surrounding two particular songs that are well worth mention here. For over fifty years the Finley family observed the tradition in the town of Coquille of going Christmas caroling after midnight on Christmas Eve. Their distinctive song on this occasion was "Song of the Angels," which people in the family had learned in full four-part harmony out of a very old book. In this case the song itself was not for them a folksong, but the custom with which the song was employed was squarely in the folk tradition. The tradition itself still survives, though in later years Bess lived on a farm so isolated from the rest of the community that the family did not ordinarily go singing Christmas carols to neighbors. In earlier years, when they lived in town, it was a standard occasion for the Finley family to go caroling at the houses of neighbors and relatives starting at about two in the morning, when everyone was sure to be in bed, and continuing until daylight. Those who were normally visited often lay awake, sometimes with their windows open for the special treat. This custom is so central to the family's sense of itself that it conjures up strong memories of family ties and of deceased relatives—so much so, that the family today can seldom finish singing the song without several people in tears.

Another folksong that has become central in the ongoing traditions of Bess's family is "Old Mister Fox," which Bess's mother sang to the accompaniment of her concertina. Although no one in the family now uses the concertina, the song is still sung with a pause at the end of one line where Grandmother had to stop and draw air into the bellows of her instrument. On almost any occasion when the family gathers, if there is a chance for people to sit around and relax, this song is sure to come forth. Everyone in the family knows it, and all the verses are sung in unison by everyone:

1. *Old Mister Fox on a moonshiny night,*
   Stood on his hind legs just about right; [pause]
   "I'll have some meat for my supper tonight
   Before I leave this town-e-o,
   Before I leave this town-e-o."

2. *He marched up to the farmer's gate,*
   There he spied an old black drake; [pause]
   "Mister Drake, Mister Drake, come and go with me—

You're the finest old fellow in this town-e-o,
The finest old fellow in this town-e-o."

3. *Mister Drake stood still and he replied,*
   "No, Mister Fox, I will not go; [pause]
   If you never eat meat 'til you eat me, oh,
   You'll never eat meat in this town-e-o,
   Never eat meat in this town-e-o."

4. *Old Mister Fox, he took his track back,*
   Grabbed up the gray goose by her back; [pause]
   Her wings went flip flop over his back
   And her legs hung dingle dingle down-e-o,
   Her legs hung dingle dingle down-e-o.

5. *Old Mrs. Flip Flop lyin' in the bed*
   Raised up the window and poked out her head; [pause]
   "Old man, old man, the gray goose is gone,
   For don't you hear her goin' crank crank-e-o?
   Don't you hear her goin' crank crank-e-o?"

6. *Old man raised up in a mighty, mighty rage,*
   Wiped out his mouth and it full of sage, [pause]
   "Old woman, old woman, just let them go.
   I'll make mighty music come-a-hime-e-o,
   Make mighty music come-a-hime-e-o."

7. *He marched on till he came to his den;*
   There were the young ones, nine or ten, [pause]
   The old ones eating up all the meat
   And the young ones gnawing on the bone-e-os,
   The young ones gnawing on the bone-e-os.

8. *"Daddy, oh daddy, when you goin' back agin?"*
   "Hope to the dingle dingle never to go agin."
   ("Why?") [in falsetto by youngsters]
   "Oh, don't you hear the music come-a-hime-e-o?
   Don't you hear the music come-a-hime-e-o?
   Don't you hear the music come-a-hime-e-o?"

Generations and Genres

Even though Bess Hockema remained proud of her first husband's dedication to his Native American traditions, it was obvious that she herself continued to live in an essentially White Anglo tradition. She illustrated as well as anyone the survival and maintenance of traditions that are shared with other people of the same ethnic background throughout the United States. If we close our account of Bess's traditions, however, without regarding those of the rest of her family, we will be forced to overlook some of the most interesting dynamic qualities of folklore being exercised around her, for her children have not simply accepted the traditions of their mother as is. For one thing, three of them (Wilfred, Susan, and George) are avid tellers of the Coyote stories they learned from their father and from his Indian relatives. Even though Bess did not tell these stories, they have nonetheless become a standard part of family behavior, and they condition to a large extent the interactions that take place at any traditional family occurrence. Thus, if we look only at Bess's traditions, we will fail to see the extent to which they affect and are affected by the Native American traditions once represented by her husband and now carried on by her children.

Moreover, the family members are so imbued with a sense of deference toward one another that they take quite seriously the roles into which they have moved in the family network. George was singled out by his father and other Indian relatives to be the special receiver and bearer of the Indian traditions in the family. Although his father died before George was able to assume this task fully, he takes the role with utmost seriousness and sees his position in part as an important aspect of tradition maintenance. Furthermore, so sensitive are the members of this family to one another's roles that the three who tell Coyote stories do not usually tell each other's favorites; each has a subrepertoire of stories known to them all but thought of as more or less under the proprietorship of certain persons.

Some members of the family specialize in certain foods: Bette is the one who makes lemon meringue pies, Susan makes mince pies and all the wedding cakes, and George makes the fresh apple cake. When I asked George if he would ever make lemon meringue pies for a family gathering, he responded, "No, Bette makes lemon meringue pies." When I asked if he would ever make a lemon meringue pie for himself at his own home, he responded with the same answer. When the family gathers for a salmon bake, it is usually George who is considered the salmon baker, and using his father's recipe he directs the preparation of the fish and determines when it is done. Wilfred, now deceased, was the one who dug the pit and prepared the fire. All the people in the family, with the possible exception of the youngest children, are brought up knowing all these traditions; they are also brought up with a sense of propriety and decorum that dictates that it is appropriate for some members of the family to specialize in certain genres. Under these circumstances, it would be difficult indeed to go back over the separate genres and excerpt them from their total family context, for just as some of them are based on manual production of craft items (such as quilts), they are also founded upon a rich background of custom and belief.

Old Mister Fox and Old Man Coyote

The Coyote stories told by these people, taken by themselves, would undoubtedly fall into our genre of folktale; at the same time, the customs that dictate the use of Coyote stories by the Wassons/Hockemas and the beliefs and attitudes that lie behind the Coyote tales among the Coos and related tribes are so strong that the story as a narrative stands only as one dramatization of cultural details far more complex than any single story itself could possibly show. The stories feature Old Man Coyote, a personage of extreme selfishness on the one hand and brilliant creativity on the other, who is depicted as gluttonous, underfed, oversexed, inquisitive, cruel, benevolent, witty, playful, and lazy. A good many of the stories have such a strong sexual component that early White people in the area were repulsed by them; the tales and their tellers were branded as pagan and evil. At the same time, the stories are excruciatingly funny, and many have lasted. People delight in telling them and in hearing them, but, especially with the older generations, there is a kind of apologetic embarrassment about their content. Thus, while they have survived, they have developed a certain kind of aura that can be handled only through a considerable exercise of decorum. If one announces that Coyote stories are about to be told, there is a ripple of excitement and smiling among the family. Nonetheless, the family custom is never to tell Coyote stories in the house, and they are not told before the youngest of the children for fear that they will not be able to cope well with the content. There is an attempt in general to tell the stories only at the proper time of year (in the winter) and in circumstances that approximate their earlier natural environment: while camping "upriver," or while hunting. Whenever possible, a further restriction is noted: the old Coos custom was that no one person could tell the same tale more than once during the same season. This ensured that other people in the tribe had constant practice in telling the various stories. Among the Wassons and Hockemas this has led to a minor problem, for while people would prefer to pass the stories around, some stories have become associated rather solidly with particular narrators.

On the other hand, "Old Mister Fox" may be sung at any time of the year, in the house or outside, and it is palatable in front of the youngest of children. It is not restricted in any way as to who its singers may be, and it comes of course from the Anglo-American background of the family. At the same time, Old Mister Fox in the ballad is, like Old Man Coyote, witty, crafty, and desirous of food. It is tempting to think that in this family of mixed heritage Old Mister Fox and Old Man Coyote exist in complementary fashion, each one representing a certain key part of the family's valuable traditional backgrounds. This might explain why, of all the songs sung by Bess's parents and relatives, it is "Old Mister Fox" that exists today among her children and grandchildren as the family song. Her children, participants in both cultural worlds, have experienced the kinship between the two characters as well as the cultural distinctions.

I think we can see how hazardous it would be to take any one of these genres or items out of its rich family context; we can sense how much would be lost in meaning. It is precisely this hesitation that the folklorist must develop into a kind of healthy cynicism about generic categories. The categories must never be allowed to seem more important or more solid than the live people and processes that produce them. We must note as well that although the Wasson-Hockema family has rather centered its attention on "Old Mister Fox" as a song, this does not indicate that singing or song traditions are dying out for them. Neither can we assume that Bess Hockema, being older, knew more folklore than her children; neither can we assume because her children do not practice all the genres she knew, or all the items within each genre, that her folklore is dying out in the next generation. Rather, I think we see a typical gravitation of people in a close group into certain traditional roles that satisfy them in relation to one another. Shortly before her death at 93 in 1995, she was described in her local paper, *The Curry County Reporter*, as "the First Lady of Sundown Mountain." Her family traditions are alive and well.

Bess Hockema's family is not unique; no doubt all our families and all our folk groups experience the idea of special roles or slots in tradition. If farm families seem to be more vivid examples of this phenomenon, it is most likely because they feature a necessary cooperation among members of a close group toward common goals. In the cities today, and among the members of that group often referred to as the middle class, individuation, individuality, independence, and competition have been stressed over cooperation with the close group, while allegiances to larger national or corporate groups have been encouraged. In addition, the rural life has become almost a mythic stereotype of the good old days for many Americans, and its images seem heightened in meaning when we encounter them. Nonetheless, we find many groups of people in the city and elsewhere that, for various reasons, have encouraged or thrived upon group interests rather than individual strivings; many ethnic groups and nationalities in America, many religious groups, many occupational groups, have stressed the individual's strong ties to the close group as a central issue in survival. Among these groups (among which we may number African Americans, Italians, Mormons, smokejumpers, and students) we will expect to find the kinds of traditional dynamics suggested here. Because a farm features such a close interaction of those traditions that have to do with getting, preserving, and preparing food, as well as those crafts and customs that totally relate to personal and cultural survival, the term *folklife* has come into wide use among scholars in referring to the overall rural life traditions. But we will find this dynamic interactive fabric of traditional performances in the settings of many groups not necessarily rural in nature.

MULTIFORM FOLK IDEAS

Stith Thompson's *Motif-Index* is founded upon the observation that some ideas have been so recurrent in tradition that we may encounter and recognize them in a great number of "texts." This is as good an indication as any that folk

performers are not bound entirely by generic distinctions as they help to conserve certain ideas that have become important to them or expressively useful
to their close group. Just as a ballad story or a folktale may be recounted in
innumerable ways within the same genre (the ballad or the story core being
conserved while the manner of singing or telling remains dynamic), so may an
idea be conserved through expression in several different genres. Moreover, the
same story can have a number of meanings.

Miraculous Fire Deliverances

Years ago, when I was working for the U.S. Forest Service, I was taken off my
normal work on the trail to help fight a fire. During one rest period, as we
tried to ignore our fatigue and sore muscles, a companion began telling a story
about a friend of his who had been on a fire crew somewhere in the Pacific
Northwest on "one of the biggest fires of the century." Working nearby had
been a small squad of Zuni Indians, firefighting "hotshots" who had been
brought in by the Forest Service to help on the fire line. The fire had suddenly
raced toward them at a tremendous speed, and most of the firefighters felt
lucky to be able to make their way quickly to a nearby stream and find pot-
holes where they could submerge themselves at the moment the fire would
pass over. Once assured of safety, they looked up to see the Zunis moving
calmly from tree to tree in a small perimeter around the area, carving curious
marks into the bark. "The fire swooped down on 'em, but it split and went
around, and never touched anything inside that circle of trees the Zunis had
put their marks on." Our companion went on to insist that this adventure
proved that the American Indians had greater than normal abilities to deal
with natural phenomena. The Whites on the crew, who might have been
somewhat disdainful of their Indian colleagues, were saved because the
Natives had obtained magical help that the Whites, even with their technological know-how, could not match.

   The story that a small busload of tourists, including three nuns, was once
trapped by an advancing forest fire is told in many parts of the United States,
from New England to the West Coast. While most of the tourists screamed and
panicked and ran in circles, the nuns calmly knelt to pray, and the bus and its
passengers were spared as the flames swept around them. In some versions of
the story a practical tour member who had run off for help or to find a phone
was the only one killed, while those who fell under the protection of the pray-
ing nuns were saved. In traditional terms, the nuns in this story are akin to the
Zunis in the previous legend: they represent contact with unseen powers that,
although perhaps not overtly believed in by onlookers, may be invoked in an
emergency to indicate the relative weakness of the technical system in times of
all-out panic and to illustrate that there is, after all, "something beyond."

   In the northwestern United States, especially in Oregon, a story circulates
about another forest fire, "the Tillamook Burn," a gigantic fire that swept

through the coastal range west of Portland and east of the coastal town of Tillamook in the 1930s. A group of visiting dignitaries from Washington were being shown through one part of the forest by a young ranger named John Pulaski. They were taken by surprise when the forest fire advanced toward them, and they were saved only by the ranger's superior knowledge of the surrounding terrain: he herded them quickly to a small cave he knew about from which issued a cold stream of air, presumably from a deep underground cavern. Cramming his charges in ahead of him, Pulaski protected them with his body, and all escaped unscathed, except for Pulaski, who suffered third-degree burns on his back. In recognition of his bravery, the Forest Service later named a special fire-fighting tool after him. In this recounting of the motif, it is not magic or divine intervention that saved people's lives, but thorough knowledge of the terrain.

The first story was told by someone who was a great admirer of American Indians; the second story was told to me at first by a devout Roman Catholic (but I have since heard it from believers of other faiths); and the last was told in a Forest Service meeting by a ranger trying to illustrate the necessity for a thorough knowledge of the countryside in which one worked. It would be beside the point to observe that no doubt the dates of the first two occurrences have never been established and that the Pulaski was not named in such a way. What we notice, rather, is that the same motif has been used in three legends but for somewhat different purposes and with different shades of meaning in each case. The motif is recognizable, the genre remains the same (assuming that by *legend* we mean the recounting of an occurrence that is believed by the teller to have happened); it is the context, the dynamic live situation in which each legend was told, that determines the real meaning in these cases.

The same motif, sometimes even in the same words, may appear in numerous expressions over a wide geographical area and have much the same meaning as well. Stories of Bigfoot, or Sasquatch, in the Northwest seem to be very similar to the motifs found in the eastern United States in such stories as "Yoho Cove," collected by Richard Dorson in Maine, and the story of the Yeahoh collected by Leonard Roberts in the mountains of Kentucky. Further, there seems to be a kinship of motif between all of these and the figure of Grendel in the old English epic *Beowulf* as well as the wild man of the forest featured in those widespread and curious woodcuts and stories from the Middle Ages. It is impossible to say that all these appearances of this motif have the same meaning; on the other hand, they all seem to appear in contexts that demonstrate or probe the fear people have of wild, unrestrained nature along a frontier or in the deep forest. When Jonathan Swift wrote of the apelike Yahoos in *Gulliver's Travels*, he was drawing on a complex network of associations and nuances.

Who Will Glove Your Hand?

Some years ago, in the mountains of western North Carolina, Clif Bushnell taught me a deceptively simple song:

Who's gonna shoe your pretty little foot?
Who's gonna glove your hand?
Who's gonna kiss your ruby red lips?
Who's gonna be your man?

Who's gonna be your man?
Who's gonna be your man?
Who's gonna kiss your ruby red lips?
Who's gonna be your man?

Papa's gonna shoe my pretty little foot,
Mama's gonna glove my hand,
Sister's gonna kiss my ruby red lips,
And I don't need no man.

I don't need no man,
I don't need no man,
Sister's gonna kiss my ruby red lips,
And I don't need no man.

In these sparse words a man seems to be inquiring of a girl whether she is being properly cared for in life, and she is responding that her family is doing just fine at that task. For years I assumed this song was "about" a young man who wanted to become the one who would take care of the girl, with the girl replying that she was not interested. On one occasion, however, when I was singing with friends who were about to leave the country, it suddenly occurred to me that the song could have an entirely different meaning: A young man leaving his sweetheart for a considerable length of time might inquire, in effect, "Who's going to take care of you while I'm gone?" to which she might respond reassuringly, "Don't worry about a thing, my family will do just fine, and I will not require the company of any man while you are gone." As with so many items in folklore, it is impossible for us to revisit the originator of these verses to find out if, indeed, either of these interpretations comes close to what the creator had in mind. But it is interesting to note in passing that the same words can have such different meanings depending on the implications deriving from various contexts in which the song may be sung and certain attitudes on the part of the singers or the audiences. In addition, these same verses, with some small differences, are the opening stanzas of one of the best-known Scottish ballads, "The Lass of Roch Royal," Child #76. Version E in Child's collection, written down from the singing or recitation of the famous Mrs. Brown in 1800, offers the following stanzas:

1. *O wha will shoe my fu fair foot?*
    And wha will glove my hand?
    And wha will lace my middle jimp,
    Wi the new made London band?

2. *And wha will kaim my yellow hair,*
   Wi the new made silver kaim?
   And wha will father my young son,
   Till Love Gregor come haim?

3. *Your father will shoe your fu fair foot,*
   Your mother will glove your hand;
   Your sister will lace your middle jimp
   Wi the new made London band.

4. *Your brother will kaim your yellow hair,*
   Wi the new made silver kaim;
   And the king of heaven will father your bairn,
   Till Love Gregor come haim.

Here essentially the same words have a very distinctive meaning, for Annie of Roch Royal is lamenting that her lover is not there to care for her now that she has or is about to have a baby. Someone, obviously a member of her family, offers help and protection until her love should come home, pointing out that God will protect her child. As the ballad progresses, however, she sets out to sea to find her lover, and when she arrives at his gate in the midst of a storm, she is not admitted by Gregor's mother, who manages to keep her outside until she and the baby in her arms die of exposure. The next morning the evil deed is discovered by Gregor, and he ends the ballad with a curse upon his cruel mother. It would be too easy to argue that these verses represent a mere commonplace that can be used whenever there is a concern about someone's proper care. Some might suggest that the version I learned from Clif Bushnell is one of those many examples of an "emotional core" to which a longer ballad had eventually distilled itself (or, as some might feel, degenerated). Both of these arguments would overlook that for whatever reasons we may assign to the case, the version I learned in North Carolina is a distinctly adequate lyric that can stand by itself and can carry at least two fully acceptable poetic meanings. It would be difficult to believe such a neat coincidence to be the background for a mere floating cliche.

Further, the way these verses are used in "The Lass of Roch Royal" indicates that the singers of this ballad have been aware of how it effectively poses the question of family protection for a young woman in such a way as to juxtapose very cleverly the warm concern of her own family to the cruel rejection of her potential mother-in-law. The contrast is too powerful to be shrugged off as the accidental effect of a cliche. The fact that these stanzas can exist by themselves as a lyric *and* be used as a strongly integrated part of a longer dramatic ballad indicates the extent to which this particular folk idea is not limited by generic categories. It is worth mentioning that the same stanzas were used by Huddie ("Leadbelly") Ledbetter in one of his several versions of "John Henry."

After the death of John Henry, others on the crew are interested in finding out who will have the attention of John Henry's girlfriend:

> *Now who's gonna shoe your pretty little foot?*
> *Who's gonna glove your hand?*
> *Who's gonna kiss them red ruby lips*
> *After that steel-drivin' man, oh Lord,*
> *After that steel-drivin' man?*
>
> *Papa's gonna shoe my pretty little foot,*
> *Mama's gonna glove my hand,*
> *Sister's gonna kiss my red ruby lips,*
> *And I can't use no man, Lord, Lord,*
> *Not after that steel-drivin' man.*

Here the stanzas function in the way I had originally assumed Clif Bushnell's song did: a man applies to watch out for a woman, and she refuses his advances. In this case the refusal is couched in some of the terms used in the song itself, and within those terms is the connotation of sexual vigor and potency as well as the general strength and ability admired on the work crew. Admittedly, the migration of this particular cluster of folk ideas must have been facilitated by the fact that these are, after all, songs. Similarly, the three stories of miraculous escapes from fires are all legends. But we will want to remember that stories about the wild man of the woods often appear in legends on the one hand, origin stories on another, and, at least in the case of *Beowulf*, in a sung epic—that is, in forms generically quite dissimilar from one another.

Sir Hugh and the International Minority Conspiracy

An outstanding example of the way in which a folk idea may be performed in a number of different genres is the widespread story whose principal ingredients seem to be the following: a young boy, about ten or twelve years old (that is, presexual in terms of maturity and experience, and therefore "innocent"), is attacked and mutilated by thugs belonging to the local, feared minority group. There are some variations in this cluster, but this is the most typical combination. Indeed, as several scholars have shown, it is quite an ancient story, and it has continually surfaced in cultures where minority groups of one sort or another have posed a threat to the security of the majority. There is sketchy evidence that the story circulated in Greece with the alleged culprits being members of the secret mystery cults; it was said they required the blood of innocent young boys for their rituals. In later times it appears to have been believed by the Romans about the Christians, who were thought to require the blood of an innocent lamb as a sacrifice, a central aspect of their religious ritual. In medieval Europe, the culprits were usually the Jews, who were believed to use the body and blood of an innocent young child, usually a boy, for their paschal ceremonies. We know from the medieval writings of Matthew Paris and others that the story must have had wide circulation in Europe as a legend, for nearly everywhere it is recorded, local names and dates and the testimonies of good citizens are provided. Chaucer used the story as the central feature of his Prioress's Tale, and the same cluster of ideas was used in song form (there are over twenty versions of the ballad "Sir Hugh, or, The Jew's Daughter," Child #155, collected from Scotland, England, and America).

The other side of this idea comes out in family histories, especially where immigrants to America use the story as a testimony of their family's escape from oppression. During the Easter season of 1977, the *Eugene* [Oregon] *Register-Guard* ran some interviews with local Jews in which one young woman noted that when her grandparents were still living in Russia they would cross the street when passing a Christian church. "In 1913, the Russians were still accusing Jews of murdering young Christian boys and using their blood for Passover," she lamented. It was clear that her family had suffered the persecution that resulted from such attitudes as those encapsulated and symbolized in this widespread idea. As abhorrent as the idea itself is, one cannot help but note its vitality and its geographical spread. While it may not represent the typical intellectual attitudes of people in the various places it has been found, it must certainly represent the inner, in-group feelings and tastes of many, or it could not possibly have survived in so many versions and in several genres. We can call such an idea *multivalent*, for like some elements or chemical compounds, it has the power to combine itself with other ideas in order to express powerfully a local, deep fear of minority "outsiders."

Among the legend versions of this story there is considerable variation, especially in details of time, place, and victim. In the dramatic ballad, there is much more attention to colorful detail and less to factual material. The young boy is usually lured into a garden by a Jew's attractive daughter; he is led into the castle or down into the cellar and there killed, usually with a knife. In some American versions, the Jews have been replaced by a jeweler, and in one version ("The Fatal Flower Garden") sung for me by an Ozark friend, the boy is lured into a garden by flowers, which then kill him.

My initial firsthand acquaintance with modern versions of this legend occurred when I had stopped to spend the night with friends in Boise, Idaho, and the town was tense because of an outrage that had occurred the previous night in a local drive-in theater. A young boy of ten was at the drive-in with his parents and left them to visit the restroom. When he did not return, an older brother went to check on him and found him bleeding profusely, having been castrated by a gang of teenage Indians. The evening I arrived, vigilante committees of parents were patrolling some of the drive-ins with baseball bats, looking for suspicious characters lurking in the dark. When I arrived in Salt Lake City a day later, my friends welcomed me, and the woman, a dietician in a hospital, burst forth with the news that a terrible thing had happened there just the evening before. A young boy of about ten had been castrated by Mexicans in a local drive-in and was now at death's door in the hospital. She had heard her colleagues talking about it, and everyone in town was quite sure that it was the first stage in a long-awaited racial conflict. On a hunch, I called the hospital where the young boy was said to be a patient; the woman at the information desk immediately recognized the case and referred me to another hospital. I called every hospital in town, in each case talking to someone who knew of the occurrence but who was absolutely certain that the boy was at another hospital. When I had contacted all the hospitals, I called the police to find out the details and was told that the incident had actually not taken place in Salt Lake City: "It happened down in Reno two weeks ago." Inquiries among friends since have convinced me that the story is a continually recurring rumor that develops quickly into legend and can be easily adapted to almost any locale where there is friction between a majority and a minority group.

Friends of mine went to a baseball game in Philadelphia a few years ago and heard the rumor that at the very game they were attending a young White boy of ten or twelve had been castrated in a restroom by a gang of Black thugs. My students have reported the same story as having been told in Los Angeles about "Pachucos," in various cities about Indians, and especially in the East with reference to Blacks. More recently, a student of mine collected in Portland, Oregon, the "true story" of a young boy, about ten, who had been castrated by hippies and left to die in an elevator in one of the downtown department stores. Still more recently, students from Salt Lake City, Portland, and Seattle have reported hearing accounts of girls who disappeared while shopping and were later found drugged, being carried out of the store in the arms of counterculture druggies.

The element of castration will be brought back for discussion in Chapter 8. It seems to parallel a number of similar themes in which the threat posed by minority groups is interpreted and responded to with sexual symbolism. Here it is sufficient to point out that the idea in this traditional cluster has remained the same, very likely because it provides a succinct and usable traditional dramatization for any majority group that wants to rationalize and vivify its symbolic fears of the minority group: in each case the person being attacked is young and innocent, usually a male (a potential leader in the culture), and he is attacked while doing something normal by somewhat older thugs who in effect take away the power of the majority by emasculation, slitting the throat, or drugging. This is not a common idea among minority groups; rather, it seems to be a kind of cultural paranoia among the majority, as if to say, "Watch out for those people, they're out to get us and they'll be likely to attack us in the most vulnerable places and most objectionable ways." The appearance of this idea as an active rumor, as a legend, as a ballad, as an ingredient in a modern novel (Bernard Malamud's *The Fixer* uses it prominently), and in memorates and family anecdotes testifies to its viability and its capacity to combine with other factors of expression to provide an important clustering of culture-specific ideas, performed in what can only be called a culturally meaningful way.

Good, Though!

Another example of multiformity, one in quite a different humor and key, is a song I heard in Wild River, Maine, in the summer of 1954. It is easily recognizable as a sung version of the moose pie story given in Chapter 2. The song features not only the well-known idea of the inedible pie used as an excuse for the current cook to get out of his chores, but it places that story within a local context that mentions a local character, Jigger Jones, said to be a local logger who in his later years manned a lookout tower for the U.S. Forest Service. Supposedly, when he was a logging foreman, he would not allow anyone on his crew who couldn't kick the knots off a frozen hemlock log with his bare feet. The song places this tough character in a situation where he has been trapped by having complained about someone else's unacceptable cooking. He at first seems to have found the answer to his dilemma, but even then he is outwitted by the fast-thinking comrade who gasps a compliment on his way to the floor:

Chorus: *Oh, the Wild River crew is a rough old crew,*
And I'll tell you the reason why:
We live on brew and cat-liver stew,
And a daily piece of moose-turd pie.

1. *Old Jigger Jones kicked the knots off logs*
With his bare feet, so they say,
But he hung around Wild River too long,
And it drove him nuts one day.

2. *Now old Jigger Jones he got pretty tired*
Of doin' all of our cookin',
So he says, "If I hear one more guy bitch,
For a new cook you'll be lookin'."

3. *Jones was out in the woods next day*
Chasin' a big deer herd;
Coming back to camp without any luck,
He slipped upon some fresh moose turds.

4. *He scooped 'em up in his old game bag,*
The grin on his face was sly;
He thought the boys would surely bitch
If they tried a piece of his moose-turd pie.

5. *The boys come in for supper that night—*
Their appetites were high;

> They chawed their way through a ten-course meal,
> Then they started in on the moose turd pie.

6. One by one the boys turned green,
    Their eyeballs rolled to and fro;
    Then one guy hollered as he sank to the floor
    "My God, that's moose-turd pie!

[Shouted]   Good, though!" [cheerfully, with eyebrows and one finger
            raised]

The song has been heard in many parts of the country, but I think it is not widely sung anymore; at least I have not found anyone who sings it all the way through. Occasionally someone will mention another punch line, such as "Just the way I like it!" or "Just like Mom used to make!" It is impossible to say, I think, whether the song was made up by someone who knew the story, or whether the story came about as a spoken version of the song. Most people today who are aware of this cluster at all have usually heard it as a story and not a song, but this proves little, for it parallels the general situation in the United States, where song traditions seem to have been on the wane while spoken narrative traditions have continued to develop.

For our purpose, however, it is enough to note that the idea has survived with clever articulation both in spoken narrative and in song. That it can be phrased in either way, according to the dictates and assumptions of each genre, indicates that generic matters are here part of the vehicle rather than central aspects of the expression itself; the concept we are discussing is the recurrent folk idea, the culturally understood ideational core, not its surface structuring in any particular kind of performance. In any case, generic terms are not mutually exclusive; take the making of Ukrainian Easter eggs. Is it an art? A craft? An aspect of folk belief and superstition? Folk symbol? Folk religion? Foodlore? Custom? Is it considered, potentially at least, beautiful? The answer is yes.

A MATTER OF TASTE: FOLK AESTHETICS

For many people, art is understood to be a conscious attempt on the part of an individual to produce an aesthetically pleasing expression in a form recognized by society. What is recognized and what is aesthetic are, of course, the cruxes of any tighter discussion of the subject. We are all familiar with comments like, "That's not art, that's junk!" and "That's too imitative to be real art." and "That's too ugly to be art" (which I overheard a woman say while looking at a Dali painting). True enough, no one has come up with a final definition of *art* and *aesthetic* acceptable to everyone (and we should hope that the day never comes when such a definition becomes possible). Nonetheless, several central concerns are almost always encountered in a discussion of art, at least of what people call fine art. For example, usually there is a concern about the artist as a unique individual developing his or her own vision within the possibilities of a recognizable genre (e.g., painting, musical composition, architecture). There is a concern for the genre itself, especially if it has classical and refined aspects within which the artist works and against which creative expressions may be judged. There is a concern for the judgment, which is informed by a refinement and education in the classical aspects of the art. Finally, there is the underlying implication that the artist is trying to elevate his or her art into the ranks of those whose unique visions have already been recognized as worthy of praise.

We are well aware that developments in the formal arts are more easily perceived from the present looking back in time, for many artists were not recognizably within the accepted canons of taste in their own eras, so far ahead of their contemporaries were they in their pursuit of their vision. We also recognize an attitude of exclusivity about art that suggests, for many, that the more popular something is, the less founded on refined tastes it must be. Thus, detective fiction, fantasy, science fiction, and westerns are not usually given much serious attention by literary specialists. Art historians often concentrate on the highest achievements in art, the most impressive and unique demonstrations of the artistic spirit combined with the highest examples of personal talent in the execution of an art object. The most beautiful examples, judged by educated taste, are put on display in art galleries, museums, literary anthologies, or musical programs. Usually, their innovative aspects are highly valued.

Folklorists, on the other hand, are interested in precisely those expressions that most members of a close group know and to which they respond. They are equally interested in the mechanisms by which the group develops and transmits its tastes over time and space in multiform ways. Thus, while many folklore studies focus on one person as the exemplar of a kind of folk expression, it is usually to the avowed purpose of revealing more about the tradition and about where the artist stands within the tradition that folklore addresses itself. Innovation per se is not important here except as an index of how dynamically the artist relates to the tradition.

Folk Art and Fine Art

For most folk artists, I think we can say that folklore represents the expression of the aesthetic factors central to their everyday lives. Folk artists are not unaware of their own aesthetics, as we shall see in the examples cited later in this chapter, so we cannot fairly call them naive (as many art historians do). Nor are folk artists untrained, for they often spend years, a lifetime perhaps, trying to learn and perform well their genres and styles. Bess Hockema knew what a good afghan is and worked years to be able to "perform" one well, yet she would have been the last to claim she had produced a perfect one—or a unique one, for that matter. Not a perfect one because first of all she was modest, and community decorum would have prevented her from bragging; moreover, it is the community's (in this case primarily her family's) taste, not her individual creativity running in its own direction, that informs the judgment. Not a unique one because the whole point in folk art is to produce an excellent performance within a customary form, not far out and away from it.

For this reason it is proper for Albert B. Friedman to say of folk ballads, "Any rare or subtle figurative expression in a ballad would make its genuineness suspect, for the language of ballads is a tissue of commonplaces, stock figures, stock symbols, and formulaic phrasing." Some students of the ballad have taken Friedman's comment to be derogatory, but of course it is not. It represents the plain fact that ballad aesthetics are based on a continually shared battery of expressions known and used by the ballad-singing communities, not on the *unique* poetic brilliance of particular recognizable composers. For this reason, ballads, afghans, and all the other folk expressions we have been discussing represent shared vernacular taste more than individual genius. It is not a comment on any lack of talent on the part of the folk performers, but a recognition of an entirely different dimension in aesthetic background.

Of course, some high art is elite in that it is produced for and bought by those with such large sums of money that it is out of the reach of average people. I once took a college class of Native Americans to the Oriental art museum on the University of Oregon campus. They were not moved by the delicate jade carvings, the immense thrones, the elegant Japanese lacquers, or the huge embroidered tapestries, but they were enthusiastic about prints by Hiroshige and Hokusai and ecstatic about an exhibit of boats, oars, and masks from New Guinea. Primitive? Naive? I think not. They were quick to point out to me that the Asian treasures were pleasing to the eye but "that's not really art," they said. "You can tell that it's stuff some rich man could afford to have made for him, to suit his own likes. This other kind, these pictures and these masks: you can tell that the guys who made these were expressing themselves and people who were just like them." My students might easily have made similar negative assessments of many of those paintings, musical creations, buildings, and sculptures that have been seen by historians as important formal steps in the development of western art. One cannot deny the impact and the importance of formal art in the development of any culture; equally so, one cannot deny the existence of various kinds of art, judged by different standards and addressed by and to differing audiences.

We have a tendency to see modern fine artists as gifted individuals making new, sometimes bold, aesthetic decisions independently and essentially alone in a studio or garret; similarly, we often view the folk or vernacular artists as unwilling (or unable) to free themselves creatively from the accumulated aesthetic opinions of their whole culture. The folk artist is thus easily stereotyped as culture-bound (however rich that experience may be), and the resultant art as mundane, repetitive, and everyday (though sometimes quaint and charming or pleasantly "naive" in execution). The fine artist, on the other hand, is as easily stereotyped as *avant-garde*, original, even potentially naughty and culturally dangerous, the art so unique that it may not be understood until the future, when—alas—the artist will have passed away in obscurity.

According to this view, fine art is elevated, urbane, sophisticated; folk art is common, rural, unsophisticated. Folk art reeks of smoke, paint, and sweat, while fine art is redolent with oils, papers, and inspiration. Now, while there may be a grain of truth (or at least a breath of perspective) in this view, the presumed differences between fine art and folk art need not be phrased or perceived in adversarial, mutually exclusive terms. After all, many of our greatest classics are based on folk themes—from the plays of Shakespeare (*Taming of the Shrew* is an enlargement of a pan-European joke) to the melodies of Bartok and Mozart to many of our contemporary musicals and ballets.

As William A. Wilson has pointed out, *all* art is art, and all good art persists because of its capacity to express important elements of meaning and design which others can respond to; and all art depends on the quality and seriousness of purpose brought to the task by both audience and artist. It will be easy to see that the Cajun fiddler, playing Cajun songs for his Cajun neighbors at local dances, will not be in favor very long if he plays tunes and tempos his local culture does not want or like; his art—both in origin and in performance—is culture centered in that his community exercises a tremendous influence on what happens in it. The sculptor working alone in her studio, on the other hand, may seem to be in charge of all the artistic decisions, but she, too, is "performing" for a culture of art aficionados who share a certain set of expectations about what has been done and what is new in the field. The culture to which she addresses her art is likely to be even more demanding, in fact, than the folk group, and even less forgiving when the art does not "work." In this sense, then, we could say that all art is culture centered, because all artists use the perspectives, languages, assumptions, and traditions of their cultures in the development of taste and articulation. What makes the folk artist different from the fine artist is the manner in which these cultural assumptions are engaged and organized.

If we see art as—among many other things—a field of tension between conservation of tradition and experimentation, between the solid maintenance of older ideas and the dynamism of new ones, then we see two distinctive tactics being employed by artists: the folk artist, who is usually allied to culture by ethnic, religious, family, or occupational ties, will tend to resolve the tension in the direction of group consensus, while the fine artist will follow the impulse to resolve it by doing something new and dynamic (nothing in this model suggests that one direction is qualitatively better than the other). Fine art thus often urges an expansion of future group aesthetic while folk art tends to reinforce past group aesthetic; the fine artist tends to work *away from* or *counter to* current cultural biases with the idea of testing and questioning them, while the folk artist works *within* cultural biases, confirming and strengthening them. Both kinds of artists, of course, strive for excellence in articulation, for certainly a poorly played fiddle tune can hardly confirm or nurture a culture's tradition, just as a poorly executed sculpture can hardly test the prevailing aesthetic winds.

Think about it for a moment: if a folksong, a carving technique, a fiddle tune, a costume, a weaving, an instrument, a dance step is not taken up and repeated by members of the culture where it originates, it will die out. The very fact that these expressions are vernacular is itself an observation on their significance, for by and large these arts do not show up (until recently) in museums or in books; rather, they exist in the doing of them in everyday life. Their continued performance through time can be seen as a basic cultural urge toward artistic expression. Each traditional tale, each pottery style, and each song is full of cultural meaning because it has been subjected through time to an accumulative process in which the transitory, the trivial, and the inessential tend to be changed or discarded. What survives expresses the soul of the group, because it carries within itself the compacted wisdom of the past and because it is phrased or designed in terms of the group's own ongoing aesthetics.

Folk art of whatever genre is not the uninspired or naive production of items which might have been done better had only the artisan been educated in formal art. It is not the humble outpouring of rural, backward, or underdeveloped genius, nor is it the coincidentally attractive making of practical items by people unaware of the aesthetics of their work. Nor are folk artists "untrained," for they often spend years, a lifetime perhaps, trying to learn and perform well their genres and styles.

As is the case with all serious artists, the folk artist is usually well aware of what is good and beautiful and is concerned about how members of the local culture will respond to his or her work. Thus guided by a community aesthetic which is usually unspoken because it is functional and not intellectualized, subscribing to a sense of decorum which prevents bragging and discourages the self-centered discussion of the obvious, the folk artist is likely to place more weight on the item or performance itself, or on the culture which informs it, than on personal talent. One hears, "Oh, I really like that song; my Dad always used to sing it—but far better than I can," or the opposite, "They say that's a good one, but I don't like it myself; I don't care for the tune to it, now."

Just leafing through the pages of Steve Siporin's *American Folk Masters: The National Heritage Fellows*, the reader encounters some of the most revealing statements from folk artists about their relationships to their art, their families and their cultures: Stanley Hicks, a dulcimer and banjo maker from North Carolina, says, "Here's my Dad's dulcimer . . . it still lives, it's still there. And . . . when I'm gone, there's some of my stuff for the young uns . . . you know, it still lives" (42). Clyde "Kindy" Sproat, Hawai'ian cowboy singer and musician put it this way: "I wanted to listen to the songs, stories, and watch the old timers doing their dances. . . . I hope and pray that someday I will find someone interested enough to learn these songs and stories . . . someone in whom I could impart this feeling that I have inside my heart and every fiber of my body of the love for Hawai'i, its songs and tales" (79). Cleofes Vigil, a New Mexican santo carver and musician, sees the arts as his own cultural history, and insists, "All this history has been passed to me by my ancestors and I have preserved it because to me, it is beautiful and it penetrates the heart" (89). The Santa Clara Pueblo pottery traditions carried forward by Margaret Tafoya are not hers, but belong to her community: "I was taught to stay with the traditional clay designs because that was the way it was handed down to my mother and me. I am thankful for my mother teaching me to make large pieces. I watched her and tried to do like she did. And, I did" (95). As Jeannie Thlunaut, the last Chilkat blanket weaver in Alaska, prepared to teach fifteen other women to weave (a year before she died), she said to them, "I don't want to be stingy with this. I am giving it to you, and you will carry it on" (105). Dewey Balfa, the famous Cajun fiddler, was convinced it was the interplay of creativity and tradition that provided his musical art with its force: "When things stop changing, they die. The culture and the music have to breathe and grow, but they have to stay within certain guidelines to be true. And those guidelines are pureness and sincerity" (161).

The folk arts are not excerpted from everyday life for elevation of taste or intellectual curiosity. To the contrary, what makes folk art important is precisely that it is based on the aesthetic perception, expression, and appreciation of community values *in* everyday life. Folk art is dynamic because it is totally integrated with the dynamics of life in a close group—a situation which encourages unspoken group awareness of what is considered pleasing. Folk artists are mediums of community concern and traditional standards; they know this and so do their audiences. It is evident from the comments of the Heritage Award winners that they want to be the kind of persons who bring the culture forward, pass it along, and savor it along the way—not old fashioned artisans who are dying out and going out of style. Their efforts are dependent on the cultural past but are trained on the cultural future as tradition bearers.

Even so, cultures change all the time, and much gets lost—even destroyed—along the way. Indeed, for many Americans their folk arts are all they have left of a once-complete culture: the immigrant, the Black, Native American, Asian, and Hispanic American (to name only a few out of hundreds of similar cultural groups) experience a sense of community and express their own position in it by focusing on certain living traditions and then intensifying them symbolically. African American quilts usually retain color and design concepts that can be traced back to West Africa even though the quilts use a fabric medium adopted from Anglo neighbors. The Navajos use the weaving they picked up from the Pueblos, along with geometric designs from Persian rug photos shown them by traders, to create two-way and four-way reciprocal patterns symbolic of Navajo ideas about harmony, balance, and life symmetry. Indians from various tribes, wearing items and colors which would never have appeared in everyday life a hundred years ago, use the contemporary powwow

"Chair Quilt" by African American quilter Annie Jackson of Pocatello, Idaho; the apparent irregularity of the pattern recalls African design features more than it reflects Anglo-American quilting conventions. Photo by Carol Edison, courtesy of the Idaho Commission on the Arts.

A "fancy dancer" at the University of Oregon Powwow dances with his child to acquaint him at an early age with Native rhythms, dances, music, and social dress.

A young participant in the annual University of Oregon Native American Student Union Powwow dances the energetic steps of the Shawl Dance, in which long fringes accentuate the rapid movements.

to dance together and show solidarity with people who would have been their enemies in earlier times. Japanese Americans incarcerated by their own government during World War II expressed their faithful citizenship by volunteering for military service, but preserved their cultural identity through concerts of Japanese song and dance, through flower arrangement and Japanese gardening, and by intense engagement in a wide range of visual arts. *Los Moros y los Cristianos*, the medieval Spanish folk play enacted annually in Chimayo, New Mexico, has come to be central in this small town's sense of itself in the New World—a function the play did not have in Spain.

Yet the intensifying of older themes does not preclude creativity within the tradition, as Dewey Balfa so eloquently pointed out. Hugh Yellowman's son Tom, for example, is a potter in Blanding, Utah; using Anasazi patterns and Sioux "dream-catcher" designs, he makes a kind of intertribal ceramic statement that is true to several traditions while articulating a contemporary way of being "Indian." On nearby White Mesa Ute Reservation, Aldean Ketchum (recipient of a Folk Arts Apprenticeship from the Utah Arts Council) carves traditional Ute love-flutes according to the teachings of 100-year-old Billy Mike, his mentor, while also making a new style of love flute decorated with beadwork by his Navajo wife. His discovery of a cultural kinship between the Utes and the earlier Anasazi has led him to incorporate some older symbols (like the hump-backed flute player as a decoration), and has given him the idea of experimenting with ceramic flutes patterned after fragments he has found in old ruins.

Not far away, in Montezuma Creek, Santo Domingo/Acoma silversmith Willie Tortalita lives with his Navajo wife Joanne. Willie may call your attention to a ceramic water bottle hanging on the wall and explain that its designs—a bear paw print and a set of deer tracks—represent the powerful forces of nature a hunter needs to keep in mind while far from home. Traditionally, a young man going on his first venture away from his village was given a specially made canteen which supplied not only the water he might need, but as well reminded him of his ritual obligations to nature and correct deportment. But the "canteen" hanging on Willie's wall has the animal tracks incised into the clay so that the object will not actually hold water; it has been intensified from a partly practical item to a wholly symbolic expression of his family's concern for him, living as he does among the Navajo, far from his mother's village.

The folk arts, which we may see as synonymous with what we have been calling folklore in general in this book, are not excerpted from everyday life for special scrutiny or elevation of taste or intellectual curiosity. On the contrary, what makes folk art different from fine art is precisely that it is based on the aesthetic perception, expression, and appreciation of the community constructions of everyday life. Folklore is dynamic in large part *because* it is totally integrated with the dynamics of life in a close group, a situation that encourages unspoken group awareness of what is considered pleasing and discourages individual

Ute flutemaker Aldean Ketchum plays his Hawk Flute, made in memory of a wounded hawk he nursed back to life. Photo by Randy Williams.

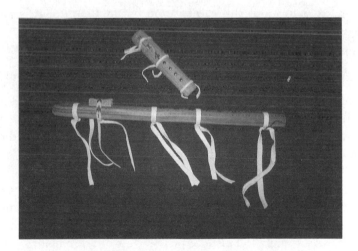

Ketchum's flutes are made from the core of desert cedar branches, following the patterns and procedures taught to him by 104-year-old Billy Mike, of White Mesa, Utah. The beaded bands and deerhide strips are made by his wife, Wanda, a Navajo from nearby Blanding.

(oddball) expressions of creativity. In a letter to John Greenway, folk singer Aunt Molly Jackson put it as well as anyone can: "This is what a folksong really is the folks composes there own songs about there own lifes an there home folks that live around them." And, we might add, "in there own words."

Beautiful Languages

A few more examples will show that folk aesthetics are far from naive or primitive for the tradition-bearers. We will notice also that aesthetic comments are not all based on the same sets of criteria: some are commentaries on function, some on content, some on style. All of them seem to recognize, some more overtly than others, the integration of aesthetic judgment with the processes of everyday life.

Ida Rodakowski Moffet of Springfield, Oregon, decorates Easter eggs in the Ukrainian tradition, having learned it from her mother while growing up in her Ukrainian family. Drawing fine lines of melted beeswax on an egg with a small stylus, she uses the batiklike process of applying continually darker dyes to the egg until, graced with a number of colors and designs, it is put on display for Easter. Her designs include the rose, the ram's horn, a fish, symbols of Lent and the Dead Sea, ladders to Heaven, the Blessed Mother's tears, eternity, the Holy Trinity, and sometimes animals (including three-eared rabbits). Probably her favorite single design is one she learned from her mother; it clearly has a deep meaning for her because it grows directly out of the circumstances of everyday life. For their family, wheat symbolized life, and Ida comments, "There's something about the wheat [symbol] that I like. Maybe it's because I remember Mother's scolding if we dropped a crumb of wheat on the floor, 'cause wheat meant a lot to people in Europe. That was life, and as long as we had wheat we had nothing to worry about. Mother always said it was life, 'cause wheat was life to her. 'Cause I know when we kids would drop even a crumb, we had to pick it up. We could not throw half a slice of bread away to the dog because she used to say, 'As long as you have wheat you can live.'" Who can doubt that wheat, as a family symbol for life, is not superimposed on Ida Moffet's eggs with the Christian concept of everlasting life symbolized by the wheat that is made into the communion wafer? And can we not suppose Mrs. Moffet knew that, in folk usage, wheat was a symbol? This interpenetration of art, religion, nation, and daily life is not rare in folk arts, and it is a fine example of the basic aesthetic of which we speak here.

"He uses those pretty languages." In these words, Helen, daughter of Yellowman, tried to explain to me the especially beautiful archaic vocabulary her father uses in the performance of Coyote stories. I was trying to solve the puzzle of why the Coyote stories told in Navajo seemed to be easily understood by family members of all ages, even the youngest, while non-Navajos with twenty years' experience in the Navajo language were often dumbfounded by the vocabulary. What I began to surmise through my conversations with some of the Navajo narrators was that there is a special old-fashioned-sounding vocab-ulary used in the Coyote stories, and because the stories are told so often dur-ing the winter months, everyone learns this special language passively but as fully as everyday Navajo. Whether the vocabulary is actually archaic or not I cannot say, especially since contemporary speakers of Navajo all understand and use it. At any rate, it is clear that the special vocabulary, which is consid-ered stylistically beautiful and fun to listen to, is an integral part of telling the Coyote stories.

On the practical level, this is of course one of the vexations in providing English translations of the Coyote stories, for the beauty of the vocabulary, its special feel, along with all the deep associations in the minds of the listeners, all disappear in translation. Since, as we have seen in Chapter 3, the meaning of the Coyote tales is seldom overtly articulated, we must assume that at least a good part of the meaning must reside in the style of the narration. And if we accept Yellowman's insistence that hearing the stories will help young people become good folks (while not hearing the stories will incline them otherwise), we may begin to perceive a hazy, perhaps undefinable, link between aesthetic response and meaning. The Navajo concept of perfection, often interpreted as long life and good health, is most fully summed up in the word *hózhó*, literally, "the condition of beauty" or "stability and balance." In other words, the most special condition imaginable by Navajos is described with a word that speakers of English would identify with aesthetics. It seems to me that the "pretty lan-guages" (by which Yellowman's daughter simply meant the especially beautiful words) of the Coyote stories may have a direct therapeutic relationship to the more all-embracing Navajo concept of well-being. Thus, the narrator of a Coy-ote tale, using beautiful language to express ideas conducive to a beautiful life (from a Navajo point of view), actually engages in that sense of well-being and applies it to the listeners as the story is performed.

Sometimes beauty can be a reflection on the aesthetic appreciation of the most common daily task. In his presidential address to the American Folklore Society in November 1974, Dell Hymes suggested that the truest exposure to aesthetic experience as a part of everyday life might be gained "by an accounting of the satisfaction in the voice of Mrs. Blanche Tohet of Warm Springs, Ore-gon, when, having finished fixing eels to dry one evening, she stood back, look-ing at them strung on a long line, and said, 'There, i'n't that beautiful?'" Eels are a favorite food of Indian people from the Columbia Basin and plateau areas, so part of Mrs. Tohet's assessment must reside in her recognition of the eels as a highly prized ethnic food. Obviously, too, something about their preparation is involved here, because her comment came when her job of preparing the eels was finished. In this, do we not see her own appreciation of herself as a compe-tent participant in traditional modes of food preparation? In addition to her comment that the object of her scrutiny was beautiful, we need most of all to remember Dell Hymes's plea that we account for the "satisfaction" in her voice;

the way she made the pronouncement, the style in which it was enunciated, was an expression of the aesthetics of what was being said.

Even though these are all provocative markers of folk aesthetics, it will be a while before the Museum of Art ever mounts a display of drying eels. And even if such an exhibition did take place, I imagine Mrs. Tohet would not find the result beautiful, for the item out of its traditional context would certainly not make much sense or provide much beauty. The same thrill of participating in a tradition in a meaningful way within its usual context was registered by an old woman who stopped singing in the middle of a song and seized Cecil Sharp by the lapel of his coat, saying, "Isn't it beautiful?" The referent of "it" in the old woman's urgent question, and the referent of "that" in Mrs. Tohet's sigh of satisfaction, are far more complex entities than a song text or a string of eels as physical objects can account for.

John Palanuk, the Ukrainian hammered dulcimermaker mentioned in Chapter 3, did not speak of his instruments themselves in any aesthetic terms. Rather, his comments ran toward the kind of wood used and its utility in holding its shape, the difficulty of finding iron rods that could be cut down to tuning pegs, the virtues of fishing wire versus piano wire for strings, and so forth. Mr. Palanuk was modest enough not to refer to the finished product as a beautiful instrument. On the other hand, he was fond of snapping a heavy fingernail down onto a set of strings to test the liveliness of sound projected by the instrument. If the volume and timbre suited his ear, he would say, "Now that's a pretty one, isn't it?" Since Mr. Palanuk did not himself play the instrument, his judgment was based on his perception of the ability the instrument would have in projecting its distinctive sound when it was played in a small orchestra at a Ukrainian dance. Where the crowd makes a good deal of noise, and where other instruments are often electrified, the ability of the ethnic instrument to hold its own and to provide a distinctive ethnic sound for a distinctively ethnic celebration is paramount. Thus when John Palanuk said, "That's pretty," he was singling out a particular aspect of his traditional art for focus.

It would be difficult to perceive how an art exhibit might handle such a matter, for in a gallery the instrument would be on display, not its distinctive sound. Of course, with this traditional art as with others discussed here, the central question does not come down to how an item may be best displayed in a museum. In the case of a hammered dulcimer, we might suggest that a museum display several of them and then hire a musician to play appropriate tunes for passers-by. Still, one suspects that John Palanuk would rather have heard one of his instruments played in a small orchestra at a Ukrainian wedding than to see it or its sound enshrined in a marble hall.

Sometimes aesthetic judgments in folk arts are based on evaluations of practical function, and it is possible for several aesthetic bases to be used simultaneously. Michael Owen Jones's chairmaker, Chester Cornett, referred to his grandfather's chairs as stressing one kind of quality over another: They "weren't comfortable, but one thing about it, my grandfather's chairs—if you could see one today—it'd be good an' stout. They didn't make for the beauty part, they made for the lastin' part, he did." His grandfather's chairs, he felt, "don't set good but they last good," and his uncle observed of the same grandfather, "Buddy, when he threw one together, hit was together." Here the aesthetic basis is not visual recognition of design or style, but rather a high evaluation for a piece of furniture that would last, obviously of considerable importance in a mountain culture in which the passing on of family heirlooms is important and in which money for continual buying of new furniture is limited. In distinguishing between his own chairs and his grandfather's, moreover, Chester made it clear by implication that while his grandfather's "last good," his own probably "set good." That is, two different criteria can be applied to the traditional chairs in this family, neither of which is based on surface beauty in design.

In the Pacific Northwest, one often hears traditional woodworkers and boatmakers refer to a particular kind of work in which surface aesthetics are subordinated to the practical necessity of an indestructible item (such as a small boat to be used in heavy surf or a cabinet to be used in someone's shop or garage): "It ain't much for purty, but it's hell for stout." Here, aesthetic considerations are openly admitted, as are their conscious subordination to pragmatic use. At the same time, language of a distinctly non-elite variety is used to show that the artisan is not trying to "talk over anyone's head."

Some folk aesthetics are based on recognition of the proper way of doing things. The logger's derogatory reference to a Coos Bay splice is based on the assumption that such a splice is made the way a seaman would do it, not the way "one of us" would perform the task. Even though the splice might be perfectly acceptable, perhaps even a superior job, by sailors' standards, the loggers' recognition that it is done by an outsider according to other rules provides the basis for a negative aesthetic judgment. A skilled Austrian yodeler, Hermann Koessner said at the conclusion of a very complex four-part yodel, "That's a good one—not long." Said one Norwegian grandmother to her granddaughter when asked her secret for lefse, "You must spend twenty years in Norway and bake it every day of every year for eighty years." This is, of course, a hyperbolic statement of the proverb "Practice makes perfect," and it is found as the basis for aesthetic judgment in many kinds of folklore. The point is that if you do not know how to do something right, if you have not had extensive experience in actually doing it among those whose taste is valued, you can hardly be expected to do it very well.

Some kinds of aesthetic judgment in folk art tend to be based on proper content. The following is a transcription, with only some minor excerpting and modification (interruptions by the telephone, by visitors at the door, by cats, and by pudding spilling over on the stove), of a conversation I had with traditional singer Clarice Mae Judkins. She was telling me about a young man she had met who had been collecting folksongs in the rural areas nearby and had found one that featured some wording she entirely disapproved of.

Mrs. Judkins: My sister taught at Crow, on the Siuslaw River, and that was where most of those songs came from. When this, uh, young man went looking for them several years ago. Well, he said there was one or two old men out there at Siuslaw. I remember arguing with him bitterly about one song that I had learned and it was about the, uh, corn and why of course, why corn was, uh, but anyhow, what was the line? Well anyway, it went to the effect that, uh, when he was harvesting, he wasn't harvesting corn. But anyway it was something you could only do to wheat or oats but not corn. I tried to explain to him I came from the Midwest where we raised wheat and corn. And I knew that, what was it now? That he, that line went—and this old fellow at the Siuslaw taught it to him. And, uh, but I said you don't, what was it now? You fallow and you husk, but you don't—

Toelken: Thrash?

Mrs. Judkins: No, the word wasn't thrash. It was just like something like mow, yes mowing corn. And that outraged me right entirely because I knew you couldn't mow corn. And I said the man's got it mixed—it's *hoe* corn. And, uh, no he said, he, he took the old fella's word for it. Boy, I said, you'll just be laughed at if you find anybody lived in the West and you go around singing about mowing corn. I said that's just foolish. But that was the way he learned it and he insisted on keeping it. But, uh, this is about this young man that, uh, and I knew the song anyhow myself. This young man went a-courting to his next neighbor's door:

> [She sings:]
> *Where he'd often been before,*
> *And then the subject came along,*
> *Asking if he'd hoed his corn.*
>
> *No, madam, no, and I'll tell you why.*
> *He bowed down his head and began for to cry.*
> *No, madam, no, and I'll tell you why,*
> *Truly my corn has grown up too high.*
> [laughter]

And so then she told him of course that he couldn't come courting. That she wouldn't marry a man that couldn't support her and he'd have to go home and hoe his corn. And so this old fellow in Siuslaw had the song but when he sung it he sung it "to mow his corn." And I kept telling, what was that young fella's name? Anyway, he had it all wrong, and people would sure laugh at him if he stuck to "mowing" his corn.

[She recites:]
He hung down his head and began to cry,
No, madam, no, and I'll tell you why:
I tried and I tried and I tried in vain,
And I don't think I shall have a single grain.

So why do you come and ask me to wed,
When you cannot earn your bread?
Single, I am and single I'll remain,
For a lazy man that won't maintain.

Mrs. Judkins was clearly unaware that the word *corn* in England refers to grains like wheat and oats, and the term *mow* would have been quite appropriate in English versions of the song. Thus she could not have known that the old man out at Siuslaw might have been maintaining a song tradition more directly related to England than that which she herself had participated in. She was probably even less aware that "mowing the corn" in English metaphor usually had a sexual nuance in folksong—more or less the equivalent to "cutting the mustard." A folksong scholar, using the great number of collected song texts from England and America, would probably see in this song the delightful possibility of ambiguity: on the practical level, the young woman rejects his courtship because he has not shown he can do the work to provide a family's daily bread, while on the sexual level, he is rejected because he apparently lacks sexual competence. Totally oblivious to all this, as far as I can tell, Mrs. Judkins was certain that in her understanding of the word *corn,* one could only hoe it, not mow it. Hence her negative value judgment on that version of the song, and her general contempt for anyone who would maintain those words even in the face of "proper" information.

In a parallel instance, I took my Coos friend George Wasson with me to visit Yellowman, that consummate narrator of Navajo Coyote stories, and after we had listened to a number of Yellowman's stories I suggested that George tell a few Coos Coyote tales to show the Navajos what kind of episodes Old Man Coyote experienced in the Coos tradition. George and I had previously noticed that many of his stories were very much like the Navajo stories. But when George told a fairly lengthy and humorous story from his tribe, Yellowman's question to me was, "Where did he learn that story from, missionaries? Or from a book? That's not a Coyote story." We asked why Yellowman did not consider the story proper, and he responded it was because Coyote was described eating fish. I explained that the Coos were fish-eaters, which brought an involuntary shudder to Yellowman and a grimace to his face. He politely changed the subject.

Still another kind of aesthetic judgment may be based on what we can call ethnic style. For example, the Japanese New Year foods described in Chapters 2 and 4 are often said to be beautiful, based on their arrangement, their color, the design of their ingredients, and the way in which they are laid out on the table. In this way, a Japanese person might enter a room and see all the proper items on a table but might recognize that they had not been placed there in an aesthetically pleasing way. In his books on urban Black folklore, Roger D. Abrahams notes the extent to which style forms the basis for personal evaluations. Calling someone a "cool cat" is actually an aesthetic value judgment based on the recognition that a person's actions and the style with which he carries them out are done so well according to esoteric standards that they require singling out for commendation. An African American friend of mine tells of an incident in which he and other Black musicians were "jamming" after hours in the back room of a San Francisco nightclub. Several prominent jazz men were there, including a very well-known jazz trumpeter. A White teenager begged to be admitted so he could sit in on the drums, and he was so sincere and so obviously interested in jazz that the group invited him in briefly, even though the presence of a minor in the nightclub environment was illegal. The young man took over the drums and impressed everyone with his virtuosity for the next couple of hours. At the conclusion of the jam session, the prominent trumpeter walked over to the young White man and said gravely, "You a *baad* motherfucker, Jim," at which the young man broke into tears—not tears of rage but of surprised pleasure at having been singled out for such high praise. In this case the material being performed was not folksong, but the style with which it was rendered in jazz improvisation was so traditional, so ethnic in its articulation, and the young man had mastered it so well, that the Black jazz players' only appropriate response was through their own folk speech. Such aesthetic judgments are to be found in all ethnic groups in America, and their focus may range from evaluations of personal action to styles of performance to distinctive ways of arranging furniture in the living room of a home.

We should listen closely and ask questions when such phrases as "That's a slick job" or "He's a good hand" or "That's just like Mom used to make" are used in what might otherwise seem to be casual conversation. In most cases, we will find that the evaluation is only seemingly a simple one; it is usually based on a perception of a style, or of content or of application and function, that is valued highly by members of a close group precisely because it is shared by many and because the particular person who is its medium at that moment has reperformed in a creditable manner, working from and within the familiar ideas and genres of the group.

The folk artist is, then, a medium for community concern, decorum, and traditional standards; the traditional artist knows this, as does the audience.

When a community sees excellence in one of its own folk arts, it is because the performer has exercised community taste in a recognizable and praiseworthy manner. The repertoires of the folk artist and of the fine art artist may occasionally overlap, of course, but the canons of taste by which they are fairly judged seldom do.

BIBLIOGRAPHICAL NOTES

The standard interest in genre as a basis for organizing the field of study in folklore is evident in such works as the Aarne-Thompson *Types of the Folktale,* Dorson's *American Folklore and Folklife,* Brunvand's *Study of American Folklore,* Ben-Amos's *Folklore Genres,* Wayland D. Hand, ed., *American Folk Legend: A Symposium* (Berkeley: University of California Press, 1971), and Hand's *American Folk Medicine: A Symposium* (Berkeley: University of California Press, 1976), as well as in articles such as Linda Dégh and Andrew Vàzsonyi, "The Memorate and the Proto-Memorate," *Journal of American Folklore* 87 (1974): 225-39, in which personal narrations are seen in both their generic and "pregeneric" dimensions.

An increasing number of studies have focused on the dynamics of tradition for a particular folk performer or a particular kind of folk performance. Out of them all, one should at least consult Roger D. Abrahams, "Creativity, Individuality, and the Traditional Singer," *Studies in the Literary Imagination* 3 (1970): 5-34, as well as his and Almeda Riddle's *A Singer and Her Songs. Almeda Riddle's Book of Ballads* (Baton Rouge: Louisiana State University, 1971), and David Evans, "Techniques of Blues Composition among Black Folksingers," *Journal of American Folklore* 87 (1974): 240-49, noting especially his comments on rephrasing on p. 248. For more extensive commentaries on whittling, carving, and the changes in meaning for folk crafts as their practitioners grow older, see Simon Bronner, *Chain Carvers: Old Men Crafting Meaning* (Lexington: University Press of Kentucky, 1985) and Patrick Mullen, *Listening to Old Voices: Folklore, Life Stories, and the Elderly* (Urbana: University of Illinois Press, 1992).

N. Scott Momaday's story about the arrowmaker is only one episode of many traditional vignettes in his important collection of Kiowa lore, *The Way to Rainy Mountain* (Albuquerque: University of New Mexico Press, 1969), 46. Another fascinating view of the interrelationships between items and language is Janet D. Spector, *What This Awl Means: Feminist Archaeology at a Wahpeton Dakota Village* (St. Paul: Minnesota Historical Society Press, 1993), which uses stories and personal recollections related to objects as ways of understanding and amplifying their cultural meanings. Bess Hockema's expression about putting the big pot in the little pot is a fairly common one in the South, but with a certain important difference: F. R. Smith and C. R. Smith, in their pamphlet "Southern Words and Sayings" (Jackson, Miss.: Office Supply Company, 1976), say that "put the little pot in the big pot" means "company's a-coming; water it down."

Walter McCulloch, *Woods Words* (Portland: Oregon Historical Society Press, 1958), says "Pulaski" is named for "Ranger Pulaski, U.S. Forest Service, famed for his lifesaving work on the big 1910 fire in Idaho," an equally vague derivation as the one mentioned here, though closer to the facts of history: Edward Pulaski, great-grandson of General Casimar Pulaski, did save the lives of a forest work crew in Idaho's historic

1910 fire and went on to work 20 years more as a forest ranger and develop the fire-fighting tool which carries his name. A version of the nuns and the forest fire is mentioned by Brunvand in *The Study of American Folklore*, 160. The legend of Yoho Cove is given by Dorson in *American Folklore* (Chicago: University of Chicago Press, 1959), 130-31; the Yeahoh story ("Origin of Man") is in Leonard Roberts's *South from Hell-fer-Sartin* (Berea, Ky.: Council of the Southern Mountains, 1964), 162. I discuss several other possible meanings of "Who's Gonna Shoe Your Pretty Little Foot" in "Ballads and Folksongs," in *Folk Groups and Folklore Genres: An Introduction,* ed. Elliott Oring (Logan: Utah State University Press, 1986), 158–62.

In his headnotes to ballad #155, "Sir Hugh, or, The Jew's Daughter," Francis James Child provides a rather full background for the medieval European version of the mutilated boy story. A briefer account of the legend, detailing Chaucer's possible source for his use of it in the Prioress's Tale, is given in Larry D. Benson, ed., *The Riverside Chaucer,* 3rd ed. (Boston: Houghton Mifflin, 1987), 913–14; a greater range of comment is given by C. Brown, *The Miracle of Our Lady* (London: Chaucer Society, 1910). An unusually detailed study of the whole complex, with reference to the employment of the legend by Chaucer, Joyce, and Malamud, is provided by Faith Hippensteel, "'Sir Hugh': The Hoosier Contribution to the Ballad," *Indiana Folklore* 2 (1968): 75-140. See also Florence Ridley, "A Tale Told Too Often," *Western Folklore* 26 (1967): 153–56. For an extended study of this story as it pertains to Jewish history, see Alan Dundes, *The Blood Libel Legend: A Casebook in Anti-Semitic Folklore* (Madison: University of Wisconsin Press, 1991).

In *The Ballad Matrix: Personality, Milieu, and the Oral Tradition* (Bloomington: Indiana University Press, 1990), William B. McCarthy discusses the repertoire, style, and mindset of Agnes Lyle, an elderly Scottish ballad singer of the 19th century, in terms that highlight her command of a ballad corpus and her control of aesthetic articulation within the genre. A brief but extremely helpful essay on repertoire is Robert A. Georges's "The Concept of 'Repertoire' in Folkloristics," *Western Folklore* 53 (1994): 313–23.

For further explorations on multiple or overlapped genres and repertoires, see Adrienne L. Keppler, "Folklore as Expressed in the Dance of Tonga," *Journal of American Folklore* 80 (1967): 160-68, in which traditional dance is described as existing simultaneously in other traditional dimensions such as cosmology, legends, heroic exploits, information and connotation about sacred animals, recollections of local events, and the like, all interwoven in a communal, gestural reaffirmation of cultural allegiance. William A. Wilson, "The Paradox of Mormon Folklore," mentioned previously in this book, demonstrates the existence of formal and "unofficial" religious stories side by side. Warren L. d'Azevedo, "Mask Makers and Myth in Western Liberia," in *Primitive Art and Society,* ed. Anthony Forge (London: Oxford University Press, 1973), 126-50, discusses creativity, magic, ritual, and art as mutually inextricable elements of cultural expression. Vivian De Sola Pinto and Allan Edwin Rodway, eds., *The Common Muse* (New York: Philosophical Library, 1957), suggest that the broadside ballads and traditional ballads of England were and are mutually invigorating and occasionally identical, even though their format, diction, and contexts were often quite dissimilar. Linda Dégh calls it *symbiosis* in "Symbiosis of Joke and Legend: A Case of Conversational Folklore," in *Folklore Today: A Festschrift for Richard M. Dorson,* ed. Linda Dégh, Henry Glassie, and Felix J. Oinas (Bloomington: Indiana University Press, 1976), 101-22.

For introductory purposes, the two most useful and informative pieces on the subject of folk art are Henry Glassie's chapter, "Folk Art," in *Folklore and Folklife: An Introduction*, ed. Richard Dorson (Chicago: University of Chicago Press, 1972), 253-80, and Holger Cahill, ed., *American Folk Art: The Art of the Common Man in America, 1750-1900* (New York: Museum of Modern Art, 1932). The latter work is probably the first book on American folk art to deal with the subject not in condescending terms of quaintness and whimsy but with direct recognition of its own status as a species of community-based aesthetics. Although Cahill occasionally uses such terms as *primitive, childlike, quaintness, innocence,* he admits the term *primitive* has inappropriate implications and finally insists that "the work of these men is folk art because it is the expression of the common people, made by them and intended for their use and enjoyment. It is not the expression of professional artists made for a small cultured class, and it has little to do with the fashionable art of its period" (6). Glassie points out that we usually assume if a traditional item has chiefly utilitarian purposes the artifact is called an aspect of craft, where if pleasure predominates in its production it is called folk art. We can see how easily genres can overlap under these circumstances, if we consider that many old hand-held and locally made plows have been later used as mailbox supports by the descendants of the original farmer. It may be the same plow, the same family, the same region, but clearly it is the aesthetic process involved in the local usage that determines the position of the item in the community at any particular moment. Glassie's study of Turkish folk art (*Turkish Traditional Art Today,* previously cited) is not only a stunning achievement in itself, but an exemplary articulation of how context, personality, repertoire, culture, and traditional taste operate together in the dynamic processes of artistic choice and execution.

Albert Friedman's comments on the lack of "subtle figurative expression" in ballads are found in the Introduction to *The Viking Book of Folk Ballads of the English-Speaking World* (New York: Viking Press, 1956), ix-xxxv, esp. x; his remarks have been mistaken by many to represent an elite view toward oral tradition. This is as good an indication as any of how difficult it is to speak of aesthetics in a language where that very discussion has been carried out chiefly by people of elevated social class. Unfortunately, the English vocabulary carries evaluative connotations about aesthetics that often impede the process of clear discussion.

The words of the National Heritage Award winners (and photographs of their work) are available in Steve Siporin's landmark book *American Folk Masters: The National Heritage Fellows* (New York: Harry N. Abrams, 1992). William A. Wilson's assertion that distinctions between "folk art" and "elite art" are based more on context and process than on art or aesthetic sense can be found in "The Deeper Necessity: Folklore and the Humanities," *Journal of American Folklore* 101 (1988): 157–67. Wilson holds that art is art and literature is literature; thus the prefix "folk-" can be too easily misunderstood as a qualification or an apology for expressions that really do not pass muster with intelligent audiences. Aunt Molly Jackson's clear and unpretentious definition of folksong is quoted by John Greenway in his *American Folksongs of Protest* (Philadelphia: University of Pennsylvania Press, 1953), 8. Anyone unfamiliar with Aunt Molly Jackson as a singer and songmaker may find remedy in Chapter 8 of Greenway's book.

Ida Moffet's comments and pictures of her work are in Suzi Jones, *Oregon Folklore* (Eugene: University of Oregon, 1977), 80–82. Further information on Yellowman's stories and their complex meanings can be found in the several articles mentioned in the bibliographies for Chapters 3 and 4 above. It is important to note that my work with Yellowman's stories spanned about 40 years, and was always being updated and corrected—as should be the practice in all thorough research. Nonetheless, some scholars still make reference to the first essay ("The Pretty Languages") instead of the second corrected translation and interpretation ("Poetic Retranslation"), and virtually no one has picked up on the warning (in "Life and Death") that from the Navajo viewpoint working with Coyote tales may be as psychologically dangerous as it is entertaining. Thus, readers of recent overviews (like *Folkloristics*, by Georges and Jones, cited previously) should be encouraged to consult the latest works of active folklore scholars quoted therein; they will discover more accurate texts and analyses (as in the case of the Yellowman materials), different—even opposite—critical interpretations (as in Roger Abrahams's work with African American street recitations), and entirely new fields of interest (as in the case of Elliott Oring, who now focuses more on humor and on Freud than on whaling songs). Blanche Tohet's comment on drying eels is quoted by Hymes in his article "Folklore's Nature and the Sun's Myth," *Journal of American Folklore* 88 (1975): 346.

Michael Owen Jones's *The Handmade Object and Its Maker* (Berkeley: University of California Press, 1975) calls attention more to the individual artist's own opinions and directions in vernacular art (in the production of chairs and rockers) than to the local traditions of chairmaking; a later revision of the book broadens its field of vision and takes advantage of the author's rich accumulation of vision on the subject of vernacular aesthetics: *Craftsman of the Cumberlands: Tradition and Creativity* (Lexington: University Press of Kentucky, 1989).

The fishermen's attitude toward the knotwork of farmers can be inferred from such comments as the following: Farmers "always think they're working in the 'lower forties' and they tie farmers' knots, which can't be untied in a hurry . . . they think the tree line at high water is caused by the sea cows' biting the twigs off, and they tie up the vessel like it was the *Queen Mary.*" This and similar attitudes may be found quoted and discussed by Suzi Jones, *Oregon Folklore* 16-23 ("The Oregon Coast"). The comment on the extended apprenticeship in making lefse was made by an immigrant Norwegian grandmother, Mrs. Helge Ledahl, in a collection made by a folklore student, Tamara Stenshoel; it is filed in the Randall V. Mills Memorial Archive of Northwest Folklore with the collections of December 1976.

A brief but fascinating consideration of an urban folk art form is given in Elaine Eff, "The Painted Window Screens of Baltimore, Maryland," *The Clarion* [published by the Museum of American Folk Art, New York City] 6 (Spring 1976): 5-12. For a few examples of the varying ways in which the aesthetics of folklore may be approached, one can consult the following pieces: Tristram P. Coffin, "Mary Hamilton and the Anglo-American Ballad as an Art Form," *Journal of American Folklore* 70 (1957): 208-14, reprinted in *The Critics and the Ballad,* ed. MacEdward Leach and Tristram P. Coffin (Carbondale: Southern Illinois University Press, 1961), 245-56; Daniel J. Crowley, *I Could Talk Old-Story Good: Creativity in Bahamian Folklore,* University of California Folklore Studies, no. 17 (Berkeley: University of California Press, 1966); Warren L. d'Azevedo, "A Structural Approach to Esthetics: Toward a Definition of Art in Anthropology," *American Anthropologist* 60 (1958): 702-14; Alan Dundes, "The Henny-Penny Phenomenon: A Study of Phonological Esthetics in American Speech," *Southern Folklore Quarterly* 38 (1974): 1-9; Michael Owen Jones, "The Concept of 'Aesthetics' in the Traditional Arts," *Western Folklore* 30 (1971): 77-104; Jones, "'There's Gotta Be New Designs Once in Awhile': Culture Change and the 'Folk Arts,'" *Southern Folklore Quarterly* 36 (1972): 43–60. (Since folk art is a manifestation of culture and a direct outgrowth of the tastes of both artist and audience, it changes in response to ongoing cultural developments; therefore folk art does not cease to be "folk" when modern machinery is used, as long as the traditional aesthetic system of performer and audience is still intact.) Jones, "Violations of Standards of Excellence and Preference in Utilitarian Art," *Western Folklore* 32 (1973): 19-32; Jones, *Exploring Folk Art: Twenty Years of Thought on Craft, Work, and Aesthetics* (Ann Arbor: UMI Research Press, 1987), esp. Chap. 9, "Aesthetic Attitude, Judgment, and Response: Definitions and Distinctions"; Alan Lomax, "The Good and the Beautiful in Folksong," *Journal of American Folklore* 80 (1967): 213-35; Robert Jerome Smith, "The Structure of Esthetic Response," *Journal of American Folklore* 84 (1971): 68-79, reprinted in *Toward New Perspectives in Folklore*, ed. Américo Paredes and Richard Bauman (Austin: University of Texas Press, 1971), 68-79; Simon J. Bronner, ed., *American Folk Art: A Guide to Sources* (New York: Garland, 1984); Kenneth L. Ames, *Beyond Necessity: Art in the Folk Tradition* (New York: Norton, 1985); John Michael Vlach and Simon J. Bronner, eds., *Folk Art and Art Worlds* (Ann Arbor: UMI Press, 1986); Vlach, *Plain Makers, Making Sense of American Folk Art* (Washington, D.C.: Smithsonian Institution Press, 1988); plus anything else by Henry Glassie, John Vlach, or Michael Owen Jones.

Kenneth S. Goldstein's essay "Notes toward a European-American Folk Aesthetic: Lessons Learned from Singers and Storytellers I Have Known," *Journal of American Folklore* 104 (1991): 164–78, focuses on the idea of "bigness" as a working aesthetic category among performers, ranging from their high estimation of the "muckle songs" to their admiration for performers with large repertoires to their pride in performing long songs or stories. Whether size is really an aspect of beauty or moving articulation is an idea difficult to prove, but it makes Goldstein's long-standing position clear: just because everyday people do not have an extensive aesthetic vocabulary, and just because they often misunderstand the aesthetic queries of folklorists, there is no justification in the view that folk performers exercise no aesthetic judgment. Rather, if we listen carefully to what they say about their arts, we will be able to extrapolate their aesthetic system from their actions and comments and, of course, from their performances.

The Navajo wedding basket, made of split strips of the desert sumac, is made mainly by a community of Paiute-Utes who have married into Navajo families in the vicinity of Navajo Mountain in southern Utah. The patterns are variously interpreted as cloud formations, mountains, and gendered colors; the basket is thought to invoke harmony, fertility, and ceremonial stability. The opening in the circle represents the direction east, and is analogous to the hogan's doorway as well as to the birth canal of Changing Woman, principal Navajo deity.

Chapter 6

FOLKLORE AND CONNOTATION

ONE OF CHAUCER'S MOST INTERESTING CHARACTERS IS THE WIFE OF BATH; somewhat overdressed and proclaiming loud her interest in and abilities at sex, she is described as riding along on a religious pilgrimage with one eye open for a potential husband. When Chaucer says, "She had passed many a foreign stream" and "She knew a lot about wandering by the way," we feel fairly secure in assuming that he is speaking metaphorically—that these are not only denotative records of her geographic travel but that they are simultaneously connotative of her sexual wandering. When Chaucer mentions her knowledge of remedies for love and says, "She knew the old dance of *that* art," we can be confident, again, that the author wishes us to register *dance* with a somewhat wider and deeper application than the word normally would suggest (saying "She danced a beautiful waltz" would surely miss Chaucer's intent).

PLAYING WITH LANGUAGE

Yet, we may ask, how do we know Chaucer's intent? Is this not an example of reading something into the author's work? After all, Chaucer himself said *wandering* and *dance;* who are we to come along six hundred years later and be so certain of what he meant? And if he meant something else, why didn't he just come out and say so instead of being suggestive? These are common questions in folklore and literature classes; they are often asked by people who believe that the authors themselves do not know (or remember) what they meant, by those who believe the world's problems would be solved if all communications were denotative, and by those who do not like to play. Some people will interrupt the first line of a travelling salesman joke to demand the salesman's name and company, the date and place of the occurrence, then—when you have made up an answer to get on with the story—state triumphantly that the Filstrup Brush Company did not sell in Oklahoma until 1952. The question is often asked by serious students who have been brought up to believe that texts are sacred and who are just finding out that one may indeed ask into such matters. At the other extreme, others are ready to assert that a piece of literature can mean anything a given reader feels it means, which may indeed stretch the author, the work, and shared knowledge of the culture to unreasonable limits.

First of all, connotation (the attitudes, value judgments, and implications associated with words) is a common aspect of language. Many animals communicate; as far as we know, only human beings use connotation. Some have argued indeed that connotation, especially in the use of metaphor, is more basic to human language and meaning than is denotation (the dictionary meaning of a word). In our daily conversation we are more likely to use words like *pig, cow, monkey, cherry,* for their figurative power than for their regular definitions. And we are not confused when others do it; we are ready to perceive the *real* meaning via implication because usually we are talking of matters that are not susceptible to denotative discussion.

Consider: "That party was a real blast!" First, unless a bomb went off, it probably was not a *real* blast. Was the party, then, noisy? Well, that is part of it, perhaps. What else lurks in the meaning that is not part of the denotation but that is central to the declaration? The idea of fun. The term is a value judgment as well as a description, and the effects of both levels are meant to be simultaneous, with a stress on the connotative, not the denotative, level.

Pigs and Red Stockings

Consider this complaint overheard in a school hallway: "Sam fixed me up with a real pig last night." A real pig? Not unless Sam is a practical joker. More likely it means, "A friend of mine arranged an evening engagement for me with a young person [perhaps of the opposite sex] whose physical, moral, intellectual, and habitual attributes struck me as being objectionably on the negative end of my scale of values." Yet I know of no high school student who would make the latter statement in the hallway (at least not seriously). Not only is it stuffy, but it omits the personal revulsion easily suggested by the word *pig.* Now, in recent years, it might be that a marijuana smoker had been fixed up with a police informant, and was complaining about that, still using the connotative power of the language to carry the value judgment. Thus, while the declaration can have a number of meanings, the one we assign to it will be the one we see as obvious in the particular context, using the terms as members of the group would use them. The denotation has little to do with the real meanings here.

While denotation is easily translated into other languages, connotation is not; this should be a clear signal to us that connotation is a strong part of a shared sense of "we" as it is found in language usage. And this is true in larger national and cultural terms as well as in the very local setting of a close folk group. Remember that *lumberjack* is a positive, masculine term in some parts of the United States, but among Northwest *loggers,* the same term may be used in derision.

One of my own experiences in teaching a Chaucer class may give an example of the cultural differences in connotation. I had given a quiz that asked students to speculate briefly on why Chaucer had described the Wife of Bath as wearing red stockings—neatly tied, at that. Everyone came up with something: if other pilgrims could see how neatly tied her stockings were, she must have had her dress pulled up immodestly; *red* stockings might suggest sensuality, passion, sex, maybe even danger. Two very good students from Taiwan, however, sat totally puzzled by the later conversation. How could we assign those meanings to red stockings? What is wrong with displaying a woman's legs? We started giving analogies for our connotations of the color red: red light district, sins as scarlet, *The Scarlet Letter*, I saw red, and so on. The Taiwanese students were still puzzled. "What do you think of first when I say *red*?" I asked. "Good luck," they responded. "Would a bride in Taiwan wear a red dress?" "Of course, what else?"

Now, of course, my students had no way of knowing whether red had exactly the same connotation for Chaucer as it had for them; in fact, most of their analogies were quite recent. Yet we can speculate that, since the color and its meaning do seem to enjoy widespread connotation in the society on the informal, folk, level, *perhaps* it may be traced back through a considerable time to the Middle Ages. In this case, we do not know for certain that Chaucer so intended the color of the Wife's stockings to register on the.reader, but we can use the data we have to speculate on the matter, bolstered by the knowledge that such a construction is congruent with the rest of the Wife's description. Our shared connotations can lead us to fruitful questions about how meaning is shared by members of a close group, and they cause us to recognize how culture-specific connotation is: we can share it more easily with Chaucer in spite of a great span of time than we can with contemporaries from a distinctly different culture.

Connotation is not limited to spoken or written language. Any communicative event can—and no doubt will—have a connotative level, whether everyone is aware of it or not. Eye contact during conversation can be seen as an observable fact; as connotative meaning, it may be registered positively (as in most Western cultures, where it is interpreted as a sign of interest, integrity, assertiveness) or negatively (as in many American Indian tribes, where it is read as insolence, mistrust, intrusion). A hand held up, palm forward, may be a cheerful greeting in one culture and an obscene gesture in another. Not only may the meaning be different, but the associated emotions and responses may be sharply opposed.

The Connotative Moose Nose

Sometimes an entire situation carries such a strong set of understood meanings (especially in a high context culture) that the mere presence of someone will come to have a connotative function, especially if the person is a visitor who does not fully share the context. One snowy December evening I had enjoyed a sweat lodge ceremony with some Indian friends on the Umatilla Reservation in eastern Oregon. As we left the sweat lodge behind, someone suggested we visit an old man who enjoyed singing the old traditional songs. A previously "sick" drum was being returned to daily use, and we would surely be welcome to join in the singing. I was told not to worry about not knowing the songs; I would catch on to them easily.

We received a warm welcome at the old man's small frame house, where an extended family was engaged in sharply defined traditional activities: a middle-aged woman gathered the children together on the far side of the room and led them in beadwork; the men and older boys sat in a circle around the drum, had a cigarette and told a few jokes, then began singing; the old man's wife stayed by the stove and kept everyone in the room supplied with coffee.

Each singer held a drumstick; the group sat around the drum, drumming and singing simultaneously. The old man sang the first phrase of a song, which provided everyone with the tempo, the tune, and the words or vocables, then everyone joined in on the next phrase, singing in a strong falsetto. I was able to pick up the tunes easily enough, but I could not sing as high as the others, so I settled on an octave below. As the singing went on, the old man was becoming visibly more and more amused, although I could not tell whether he was smiling because I was joining in with them, or laughing because I could not sing in falsetto tones. I was sure that I was doing all right, in any case, because I was catching the tunes successfully.

The old man called for a break, and, after mopping the perspiration off his face (partly to hide some further chuckling), he said, "You know, this reminds me of the time a few years ago when one of our girls here got married to a guy from another tribe from down south on the coast somewhere. They got married up here, you know, and they decided to go up to Canada moose-hunting for their honeymoon. So, anyway, the girl's father decided to go along, too, and he really liked moose hunting. So they went on up there and they were camped out up there in Canada someplace, and they started in hunting for moose. Well, after about two or three days, they caught sight of a real big moose, a bull you know, with a real big rack on him. So the son-in-law drew a bead on him and let him have it. Got him with one shot. Fell flat right there. And before the kid knew what was going on, the old man ran right up to the moose and started kicking it in the nose. As hard as he could, just kicking that moose's nose. And the kid ran up to him and says, 'Hey Dad, what are you doing that for?'"

General heavy laughter in the room indicated that we had reached the end of a funny story, but I sat puzzled. "I guess maybe you didn't understand that joke," the old man offered, trying to stop laughing. "Absolutely right," I said. "Well, it's like this. This kid was from another tribe, see, where they didn't know about eating moose nose. You have to soften it up—tenderize it, I guess you'd say—while the moose still has some blood in his head. You have to bash it with a rock, or kick it, or something, and it gets all swollen up. Then you cut it off, and—boy!—it's a real delicacy. But, see, this kid didn't know all that. So all he could say was something dumb like, 'What are you doing *that* for?'" More laughter from the old man, echoed by everyone in the room.

"Oh, I guess I see, then," I said cautiously. "It's a joke about how dumb outsiders are, right? And here I am an outsider, too, right?" "It's nothing personal," he said, "but it's just that outsiders don't know what they need to know. It's not their fault. You might even like them—like that kid that married our girl. But there are just some things you don't know." Trying to be objective, I asked if my singing had been off. The place collapsed in laughter. What remained unanswered was the question of *how* I'd been off: was it that bad to sing an octave below everyone else? And what was the relation of the moose nose story to singing; that is, why did the old man choose that particular story to dramatize what was happening?

For a while I had no answer to these puzzles of meaning. Clearly, the members of that group had understood and had enjoyed something keenly based on their response to the meaning of the story as it was felt to be congruent with the immediate situation. But just as clearly, the totality of meaning did not reside denotatively in the story or in the situation, for I had been there and had heard it, and had not understood. Some weeks later, when I shared the anecdote with some Native American friends in another town, they doubled up with laughter, and one remarked, "Boy, they really put one over on you, didn't they?" And to my baffled silence he added, "Nobody over there eats moose nose!"

At this point I was now sure that I had been originally told a story about how "dumb" outsiders are, one that was so ludicrous that it could be told to an outsider who would then be so naive as to think people really ate moose nose and who actually would believe that he had been able to understand the nature of the joke. In recognizing myself as a parallel to the young man from another tribe, and by articulating it there in front of insiders, I had become an embodiment of outsider naiveté, made the more funny by the fact that I had swallowed the explanation of the joke along with the joke. In this hypothesis I was partially correct. Subsequently, I found out that among the several tribes on that reservation there were long-standing differences in food customs, and that moose nose was one of them. Some tribes had eaten moose nose, some had not. Those who had enjoyed moose nose felt that those who had not were somewhat backward; those who had not eaten it felt that anyone who would must be warped. The group I had been singing with had been eaters of moose nose in the past; my friends who had later explained the joke to me were from the abstainer tribes. Still further, I found that in the tribe who had been my hosts at singing, moose nose had been primarily a food prepared by women. Now what emerged was the possibility of a double joke: It was as funny that the *father-in-law*, acting like a woman, ran up and began preparing the moose nose for eating as it was that the young man had no idea what was happening. The old man in the joke had been playing a joke on his son-in-law, who had not understood. But still, what had all this to do with singing?

The last piece of connotative evidence came into place about four years after the original situation. I was retelling the anecdote to some old women from that same reservation as we spoke of singing styles. I asked what would have been so funny about my singing an octave lower than the other men. They considered this for a few minutes, then said, "Show us how it went; we'll sing, and you join in." As we sang they suddenly began laughing, and one stopped to say, "Oh my, you made them sound like women!"

In the customary singing styles of some of these tribes, the women sing an octave above the men. Apparently as I had been singing with the men, they had suddenly realized that they were an octave above me and felt very odd about singing the "women's" part. The moose nose joke not only broke the tension by allowing the outsider to be singled out as the unwitting cause of the dilemma, but it also provided an extremely accurate depiction of the entire episode: the naive outsider takes a masculine role (shooting the moose, singing in a lower register) and the knowledgeable insiders are put in the role of women (preparing the moose nose, singing in a higher register). The laughter, we may suspect, was directed at themselves as much as toward me, which makes the joke a complicated one indeed. Yet, for all its complications, it was immediately understandable to members of the in-group, for whom all these strands were already parts of a total context of custom, attitude, food lore, and esoteric contrast.

Sharing these ideas through multifaceted traditions of the folk group (in this case tribal) constitutes a dynamic reservoir of potential meaning that can be brought forth and focused by someone skilled in those traditions. We justly call this kind of meaning connotative, for it resides not as manifest content in the item or text or in the denotation of the words, but in the feelings and associations people share about the items, situations, and words. Since these attitudes are usually culture-specific, the deepest meanings seldom arise openly from the text but need to be extrapolated from ethnographic evidence as well as from further discussion with the tradition-bearers themselves.

What my Indian friends understood and relished in a few moments took me over four years to understand. Yet it was only one joke. In order for us to perceive the enormity of the folklorist's task, we need to multiply this incident (theoretically) by all the texts, genres, and situations possible within that folk group.

The possibilities for connotative richness are enormous in high context folk groups, where closely associated members are in constant touch with each other, sharing the nuances of continual references, attitudes, and information. Among such groups the most basic statement or performance may elicit a tremendous depth of meaning. As a Papago singer remarked to Ruth Underhill, "The song is very short because we understand so much."

INTENTIONAL CONNOTATION: IMAGERY

While some kinds of connotative events may take place inadvertently, as in the last example, we also have abundant evidence that the evocative powers of connotation are commonly used consciously by succeeding generations of tradition-bearers. The following ballad circulates in oral tradition in many parts of the English-speaking world; it seems to have had its origins in England in the Middle Ages, at least as far as its ballad formation goes (it is based on a far older apocryphal story, which no doubt circulated in oral tradition long before anyone made it into a song). Denotatively, the song tells a very simple story about a brief episode in the lives of Joseph, Mary, and Jesus; it is the moment at which Joseph discovers that Mary is expecting a child. Although Joseph is at first doubtful about his wife's announcement, the unborn Jesus speaks miraculously from his mother's womb to certify her story.

The Oxymoronic Cherry

We notice that the ballad is phrased, however, in one of the stereotyped situation comedies of the Middle Ages: an old man married to a young beautiful woman discovers by chance that his wife is pregnant and, doubting that the child can be his own, becomes sarcastic about it. As we listen to the song, we are confronted with an odd juxtaposition between the standard religious seriousness of the moment from a theological standpoint and the potential comic misunderstanding inherent in the situation from a medieval literary and cultural perspective.

1. *Joseph was an old man, an old man was he;*
   He married pretty Mary, the Queen of Galilee.
   He married pretty Mary, the Queen of Galilee.

2. *While they were out walking, said Mary so mild,*
   "Go gather me some cherries, for I am with child.
   Go gather me some cherries, for I am with child."

3. *Then Joseph got angry, so angry grew he:*
   "Let the father of your baby get your cherries for thee.
   Let the father of your baby get your cherries for thee."

4. *Then out spoke little Jesus, so loudly spoke he:*
   "Bow down low to my mother, bow down, oh cherry tree.
   Bow down low to my mother, bow down, oh cherry tree."

5. *Then the cherry tree bowed low down, so low to the ground,*
   And Mary gathered cherries while Joseph stood around.
   And Mary gathered cherries while Joseph stood around.

6. *Then Joseph, he took Mary all on his right knee,*
   Saying, "Tell me, little baby, when your birthday it'll be."
   Saying, "Tell me, little baby, when your birthday it'll be."

7. *"On the sixth day of January my birthday it'll be,*
   And all the stars in heaven will twinkle with glee.
   And all the stars in heaven will twinkle with glee."

Folklorists will notice almost immediately that part of the action in this ballad turns on a well-known item in folk belief: pregnant women crave certain foods that they must often ask their husbands to provide for them. Yet, curiously enough, the particular food craved in this ballad is a fruit, and the craving for fruits in folklore seems widely connected to the idea of sex and self-indulgence (examples of this attitude are to be found ranging from the widespread folk notion that it was an apple that was eaten in the Garden of Eden to the famous and sensuous banquet scene in the movie *Tom Jones)*. Moreover, it is interesting to speculate why the cherry, over other possible fruits, has been maintained as the key object of craving in this ballad. Proving that the cherry was commonly used in the Middle Ages as a metaphor or symbol for virginity (as it has been in more recent years) may be impossible; but it is also impossible to ignore the tenacity of this one fruit in this particular ballad, knowing the constant variations that can occur in orally transmitted poetry. We are justified, for this reason, in suspecting that the cherry has something to do with the idea of the song as it has been passed along in tradition. What might explain this, and how can we account for the function of the cherry?

First of all, we note Joseph's surprise when he learns of his wife's pregnancy through her craving for fruit. He assumes he is not the father, and he thus responds to her request with sarcasm: "Let the father of your baby get your cherries for thee." If we work from the premise that the reference to cherries carries an implication of virginity, we see an even greater irony in the scene, for of all foods a young pregnant wife could crave, certainly the symbolic virginal fruit would be the least appropriate under the circumstances. In this light, of course, Joseph's reference to the "father of your baby" becomes doubly rich, for the audience realizes that the father of Mary's baby is God; the listener is therefore prepared for some sign from God to that effect. When the unborn Jesus speaks from the womb (and of course in the medieval view Jesus, God, and the Holy Spirit are one), not only is Joseph's sarcasm carried out on a serious level (father = son), but if cherry = virginity, there is implied a direct relationship between the father, the unborn Jesus, and Mary's virginity.

At this point it should occur to us that according to the Christian view Mary is both pregnant and a virgin: both the pregnancy and the virginity are central to medieval Christian theology. When Joseph is described as so dumbfounded that he can only stand around while his wife gathers cherries from the bent tree, we can imagine that his astonishment derives as much from the contemplation of a miraculous virgin birth as it does from the miraculous movement of the tree. It seems to me that no other fruit is available in English folklore that could so powerfully stand for both aspects of Mary's situation, and that may be precisely why the cherry has remained central to this ballad.

The potentially funny cliché of the *senex amans,* the old man married to the beautiful woman, is used as an ironic setting for Joseph's enlightenment. We, the audience, know something about the potential outcome of the story because we recognize the names of the participants. If their names were Jim and Maizie, for example, we would have no grounds upon which to understand the miraculous behavior of the unborn child and the tree. The medieval setting of the garden in which fruit trees grow is, of course, a well-known parallel to the Garden of Eden, and it reflects the common medieval notion that the earliest of gardens was itself a scene of an essentially sensuous event. Thus, even in Chaucer's working of this motif, the Merchant's Tale, where Old Man January and young May stroll through a walled garden that encloses a pear tree (that in turn conceals a lover), there is the same possible double level; even though the garden is the scene of sexual activity, the event itself causes enlightenment as the old husband regains his sight through the actions of a man in the tree. This juggling of physical and spiritual imagery is well known in medieval European poetry, and we see the same kinds of juxtapositions running through this ballad. Certainly, such complex uses of sexual and spiritual connotation cannot be explained away by chance or coincidence. Rather, they testify to an ongoing concern for the evocative properties of shared language. Making such an observation does not require us to believe that every ballad singer who has ever sung this song understood the delicate relationships; on the other hand, enough primary singers of the ballad must have had some strong notion of the real meaning of the song, or there could not have been such a faithful retention of the central connotative elements.

Connotative Word Play: The Double-Entendre Cherry

In the summer of 1952, I was invited along with some friends to a southern mountain family picnic held in Grassy Branch, North Carolina. In addition to a fine, old-fashioned "dinner on the grounds," there was a good deal of singing: old, traditional songs people had learned from their grandparents, hymns old and new, and a few popular "country" songs from the radio. I was particularly struck by a song I had heard hundreds of times before, however. "The Riddle Song" was being widely sung on the radio by Burl Ives and other professional singers, but it was sung on this occasion in Grassy Branch in such a distinctive way that it popped into another focus for me. A young couple newly engaged to be married sang the song as a duet, with much nudging of each other to the accompaniment of knowing looks from their relatives in the audience. I had never heard it sung in this manner before, and I have never encountered it in this fashion since. It would be attractive to suppose that they were carrying on an old tradition that maintained some striking connotations inherent in the song; on the other hand, perhaps their performance was their own attempt to insinuate their own situation into the obvious connotations of the song for local effect. In either case, the resultant song was far more meaningful than the sum of its denotative parts:

> She: *I gave my love a cherry that had no stone;*
> He: *I gave my love a chicken that had no bone;*

She: *I gave my love a ring that had no end;*
He: *I gave my love a baby with no cryin'.*

He: *How can there be a cherry without a stone?*
She: *How can there be a chicken without a bone?*
He: *How can there be a ring without an end?*
She: *How can there be a baby with no cryin'?*

She: *A cherry when it's bloomin' has no stone;*
He: *A chicken in the egg has no bone;*
She: *A ring when it's rollin' has no end;*
Both: *A baby when it's makin' has no cryin'.*

We know that the song has existed for a long time on both sides of the Atlantic not entirely innocent of implications of pregnancy; Sharp, for example, notes that a Mr. Thomas's version had for the last line, "When the baby's in the belly, there's no cry within." Thus, even though the denotative message of this song seems quite innocent, we are justified in looking further to see if there are not, on the connotative level, other possibilities that may add to the total meaning. We see, of course, the cherry, with its possible connotation of virginity; there is the egg, a widely used fertility symbol; the ring is often found as symbolic of sex, fertility, and, of course, marriage. In addition, many other versions of the song include other words and refrains that are themselves suggestive of sexual processes and anatomical parts; the periwinkle, mentioned in some versions, has been used both as an aphrodisiac and as a colloquialism for the vagina. It is, of course, impossible to say that all these possibilities have been present in the minds of all the singers of this ballad; on the other hand, given the common understanding of these terms in colloquial language and folk speech, given that they all seem to relate somehow to sex and marriage, it would be rash to dismiss them as a coincidental cluster. And, knowing the courting customs of the rural Old World and of the American frontier, who would suggest that the sequence cherry (virginity), egg (pregnancy), ring (marriage), and baby is an accidental combination? We should note that if indeed cherry here is meant to connote virginity, it is an appropriate gift for the woman in the song to give; similarly, if the egg refers to impregnation, it is an appropriate gift for the man to give; if the ring refers on the physical level to a metaphorical or anatomical view of sexuality, or of the inception of a family circle, certainly it makes a fitting gift for the woman to give the man as a physical counterpart of the wedding ring; with the reference to the baby in the final line, of course, both levels of the song come neatly together.

Yet, on the surface level of the song, the questions and answers are phrased in such a way as to resemble riddles, so that the person answering uses an innocent word that satisfies the demands of propriety and yet at the same time implies the meaning of the song. It is not accidental that such riddles can be humorous, for of course one of their literary functions is to bring up at least two possibilities at once in the minds of the audience, yet to solve the dilemma with an answer that everyone recognizes but does not outrage public sensibilities.

The connotations discussed thus far have been seen as the workings of shared associations about a word or an image by people in a close group. In the case of the moose nose incident, a particular event gave rise to the use of a connotative joke in which the meanings shared by the close group about moose nose were focused in such a way that the story had a rich meaning for them (and almost no meaning at all for the hapless outsider who had unwittingly triggered the episode). At the same time, had the old man simply said "moose nose," the meaning might not have been so clear to the insiders. So in addition to our understanding that colors like red and fruits like the cherry may have splendid connotative power, we need to recognize that occasion and custom and narrative structure may also function as determiners of appropriate meaning.

CONNOTATIVE STRUCTURE

A good part of the connotative meaning in "The Riddle Song" derives from structural position. The riddles are juxtaposed and given meaning by being parts of a dialogue; by themselves they would mean little, while in combination they reflect meaning on each other. Connotative structure can be found on even more complex levels: whole parts of long narratives may have the same reflecting capacity, and entire tales in a cycle may reflect on other entire tales (as when a Native American Coyote tale is told, for it assumes the audience has heard all the others as well). In *The Red Swan*, John Bierhorst suggests that many Native American myths are double, that is, they tell the same story or incident twice, the second telling adding a connotative dimension to the narrative that provides a depth of meaning it did not have before.

Double Structure in Myth

Bierhorst sees the Arapaho tale "Raw Gums and White Owl Woman" as one of these double myths: a monster baby born with teeth sneaks out of the lodge at night to eat old chiefs, and, later in the story, as a young man he saves his people by killing the spirit of winter. In Bierhorst's view, these are complementary retellings of the same story, providing the listener with two enactments of the same struggle: the overpowering of older, deadly forces by youthful energy, first in frightful physical fashion by using the mouth for chewing human flesh, second by using the mouth in a battle of wits with White Owl Woman. There is a clear distinction between the earlier, fierce oral urge by the baby to *consume* human flesh (an analogy to breast feeding?) and the later, socialized urge to save the people from winter by *speaking* judicious answers to culturally important riddles. Looking at the story sequentially, there is indeed a development from infantile to adult processes; but looking at both halves simultaneously there is a further impact: a deep and complex enactment of the normalcy of violence, qualified by context. For the youth who saves his people from winter in the second part does so by bashing out White Owl Woman's brains after she has treated him with food and hospitality. Is there a difference in the quality of the killings? Only by bringing both halves of the story together, reflecting on each other, can we have the "proper" cultural meaning of the story—a meaning that, although we as outsiders may never fully comprehend it, clearly resides not in praise of actual bloodshed but in a kind of mythic metaphor, a sacred equation perhaps, about youth and the production of food. The baby had consumed fellow human beings; the youth he grows into brings about the season of vegetation by vanquishing the killing effects of winter. Like so many myths, this one says more in its simultaneous enactment than the commentator can say in summary, and more than the structure will reveal by itself. Probably this is one key to the function and survival of myth.

Be that as it may, I want to suggest that this double structure is a prominent feature of Northwest Indian myths and that our appreciation of that fact can help us to derive even fuller meaning from the grand myth achievements of the American Indian. Here I would like to focus on a particular matter that goes beyond structure: the folkloric process in which structure is but one mechanism for transmitting connotative meaning. In the case of double myths, for example, I think it is of the utmost importance to recognize that the story would seldom have had an unknowing, naive audience. Not only would the typical listener have heard the particular tale many times, perhaps often through his own narration of it, but the listener would also have been familiar with the same formulas, attitudes, motifs, numbers, sequences, colors, characters, and other expressive narrative features from innumerable other tales.

This interdependence—well known to folklorists—has been recently called "intertextuality" by literary critics, who apparently have the notion that it is the *texts* which interact; but in fact it is the people who interact, using their accumulated experiences with ongoing narrative articulations in their culture. Thus, while the modern intellectual *reader* of a myth text might certainly register it as a linear story, the native *auditor* could hardly avoid applying the "second half" of the well-known story to the "first half" while the story was being told, allowing for a simultaneous perception of complementary qualities rather than a single string of events. For a parallel (though far less moving) example, we might recall that it is only the first time we hear "The Three Little Pigs" story that we are in doubt about its outcome; on subsequent hearings, we automatically contrast the stone or brick house we know is coming in the third part with the insubstantial straw and stick houses in the first two parts, making their fragility (and the poor or lazy planning of their builders) even more striking than before. The result is therefore quite similar to the perception of metaphor: two (or more) concepts are juxtaposed in such a way as to create a mutual reflection and enrichment of meaning that is fuller than the single concepts taken separately.

One result of perceiving a metaphor is the creation of an emotional response or an evaluation of the quality of things as suggested by the reflection.

The Sun Myth: Structural Connotations of Morality

In his presidential address to the American Folklore Society in November 1974, Dell Hymes presented a scholarly landmark: the rephrasing of a Native American myth in a way that restored as much as possible the style of presentation lost when an oral narrative is translated and presented in written prose. The myth Hymes used is a Kathlamet Chinook text narrated to Franz Boas in the 1890s by Charles Cultee, one of three surviving Kathlamets at that time. The myth is a very powerful one, not the least for its spare style and stark imagery. It concerns the destruction of a people through the selfishness of a chief whose fascination for a bright object clouds his sense of responsibility to his people. Hymes is convinced that for Charles Cultee the story must have been a chillingly real re-enactment of the demise of his own tribe—perhaps through their own ruinous fascination with the bright and powerful things of the new world around them. That topic—the destruction of a people because of someone's attachment to a bright and overwhelming object—has been, of course, a matter of universal interest in western literature from the story of Pandora's box to the abduction of Helen of Troy to the theft of the dragon's treasure in *Beowulf* to the preoccupation with money and power in modern literature.

However, we want to find out what the connotative meaning of this narrative might have been, aside from modern literary perceptions. Can we see in the myth some suggestive reference to forces or attitudes that had sacred power for the Kathlamets in earlier times, long before the Whites brought about a new physical reality, a sudden, terrible congruency between myth and daily life? Approaching the narrative as a double myth may afford some clues, although the analysis here is uninformed by any extensive ethnographic data on the Kathlamets. These speculations are thus subject to correction; they are based primarily on suggestions drawn from the text itself, using the hypothesis that the two parts may represent equivalents rather than (or at least in addition to) a linear episodic progression.

The broad outline of the story may be summarized quite simply: A chief leaves his home, arrives at another place, and stays. Later, he leaves that place and returns to his home. Hymes divides the story into two parts, which may be recounted as follows:

1. a. A chief is so fascinated by the sun that he wishes to travel to look for it.
   b. His wife remonstrates with him, scoffing at the idea.
   c. Nonetheless, he is determined to go, and, in spite of her reservations, she equips him for the journey.
   d. He travels for ten months, using up as many moccasins and leggings.

e. He reaches a large house.

f. Inside, a prepubescent girl is surrounded by tremendous wealth that is to be given away when she is mature enough to be married. The many items are listed in gorgeous detail.

g. He "takes" her, and settles down there to live.

h. Among the things in the house is a shining object that he likes.

i. An old woman (the Sun) daily brings them gifts.

2. a. The man gets homesick, and the old woman notices he wants to return home.

b. She tries to offer him proper items for the trip.

c. Nonetheless, he is determined to have that shining thing, and after showing him everything else the old woman finally hangs it on him and gives him a stone ax, making it clear that taking this item (which is never named) is his own responsibility.

d. He travels for an undetermined time.

e. He reaches his home.

f. There, as he approaches his uncles' towns, the stone ax begins to shake, and one by one he utterly destroys the five towns and their inhabitants, the last one his own village. Great detail is provided, with fivefold repetition.

g. He tries repeatedly to rid himself of the ax; to no avail.

h. The old woman appears, takes the shining thing from him, and leaves.

i. Alone, he builds a house, a small house.

Hymes suggests the following gross structure:

> *Part 1:* Desires (a, b, c)
> Travels (d, e)
> Discovers (f, g)
> Stays (h, i)

> *Part 2:* Desires (a, b, c)
> Travels (d, e)
> Discovers (f, g)
> Stays (h, i)

A careful reading shows that these are not simply sets of parallel structural elements, they are just about homologous. For example, both parts begin with the man at home restlessly thinking of going away. In both, a shining thing which is not his to own is the single focus of his attention. In both, women represent the forces of cultural reason: in Part 1, the chief should have been attentive to family and tribal needs, not to a selfish curiosity; in Part 2, he should be sensible enough to take the proper items (skins, blankets, armor) offered him, not the shining object that the old lady (the Sun) obviously does not want to part with. Both parts end with the man settling in a house.

However, the second part does bring in some differences that indicate that something qualitative is suggested. In the section referred to by Hymes as "Discovers," Part 1 shows the man obtaining goods by creating a family relationship (marriage), while Part 2 shows him destroying his own goods and family; in the section labeled "Stays," he is given gifts in Part 1 and has the shining thing taken away in Part 2; in that same section he settles in a large, wealthy house in Part 1, in a small and obviously poor house in Part 2.

	Desires	*Travels*	*Discovers*	*Stays*
1.	Sun	ten months	acquires goods, takes girl	marries, inhabits large house
2.	"Shining Thing"	presumably same distance, but travel is compact in description	destroys towns, kills relatives (including wife)	is alone, builds small house

The contrast between the two houses is perhaps the easiest to deal with because of the obvious irony. A chief has devastated his own life and those of his people through selfishness; the small house at the end is a fine image for the loss he has brought about. Especially since his selfishness was focused on the goods in Sun's opulent house—in particular on the shining object—the small house he builds for himself at the end seems a fitting moral comment. The image would have suggested a considerable contrast for the Chinookan people, in whose society the chief would normally have enjoyed a large house, complete with extended family, surrounded by the rest of the village. So the small house not only provides the stasis necessary to the end of the story, but it epitomizes the condition of a man brought low by his own willfulness.

The section labeled "Discovers" is probably, on both levels, the center of mythic meaning in this story. In both Parts 1 and 2, this section is the richest in detail and repetition, and it seems to be the most important aspect of the story. But can the amassing of goods on one level be equated with the destruction of relatives and their towns on the other? I think so. Hearing the two levels together, one is struck by the idea that what the chief does in his personal selfishness is, in fact, destructive to family, fortune, and the whole social fabric, and this is consistent with our sense that the chief has abandoned social obligations by leaving his family and tribe in the first place.

In taking the young girl, he has apparently appropriated to himself the many items that should have been given out to others at the time of her maturation. He has thus intervened in the normal social order of delicate gift relationships.

This certainly puts his earlier search for the sun in sharper focus by confirming in specific terms his great selfishness: first the dereliction of cultural duty, now personal acquisitiveness outside the normal means of distribution—in fact, even in direct denial of custom. Moving from this stage to his almost hypnotic attraction to the shining thing (which is never precisely named) is only a matter of still sharper focus. It is important, I think, that this attraction is mentioned right at the end of Part 1 and the destructive consequences of it are followed up in Part 2. The shining thing seems to be thus the link between the two levels. It is the epitome of his lust for treasure in Part 1 and the driving force behind his killing of relatives in Part 2. For this reason I think the equation is justified. There is also the possibility that taking a prepubescent girl as his wife is another factor in the total sense of social deterioration, but I have no direct ethnographic evidence of this. We do know that among the Clackamas Chinook the highest bride prices were paid for the girls who were at puberty. This may bring in another possibility for a moral or social flaw: Why does the chief not offer a payment for the bride? Is he in the wrong in this? Why does he marry a prepubescent girl? Clearly for her goods. Since the Chinook were acquisitive people, I think we can assume that amassing a fortune is not in and of itself bad, but the methods and propriety of obtaining goods were of extreme importance, and that is the connotative focus here. I think that even in the absence of fuller data, we can infer that something is totally amiss in his trip to begin with, in his taking the girl, in his selfishness generally. And the meaning of equating these defects with his willful destruction of relatives in Part 2 is that such actions, undertaken by a chief, will destroy the society utterly. The equations, then, suggested by the chart above, might be stated as follows:

1. Desiring the sun is equivalent to wanting an object that is not proper for you to have.
2. Arduous travel toward such a selfish goal is the surest way to come directly into conflict with your family.
3. Acquiring goods under these conditions is destructive to the society.
4. Being married improperly, even though in prosperity, is really personal, moral, cultural impoverishment.

But, as I observed earlier, merely stating these meanings is far from approaching the real power of the myth. One would have the same sense of inadequacy in hearing *King Lear* summarized with the statement, "Things aren't always what they seem." It is of course the dramatic interplay and connotation made possible by the mutual reverberations between levels that provides the actual power of the myth. What we have in this myth is a cultural *performance* of an abstract concept about human behavior and the morals of individual deportment. Even if we have picked up only a few of the culturally loaded connotations, we have had a dramatic experience with a set of ideas made palpable by the narrative. And we note that this cluster of ideas does not dramatize the same set of values we find typically in the hero tales of Europe and America in which the protagonist is *expected* to leave home, *expected* to confront dangers, *expected* to gain the prize and bring it home, and *expected* to arrive home tougher and wiser than when he left. The same plot, clearly, does not always mean the same thing; without the implied meanings and shared connotations supplied by cultural context, we may very well have a coherent text whose meanings are totally misapprehended. This is one of several points missed by those who believe "archetypes" are universal in their meaning: it led Joseph Campbell to argue in an otherwise brilliant book that there is a universal hero myth—an assertion that can be maintained only by suppressing thousands of stories like "The Sun's Myth" in which culture is threatened and destroyed, not stabilized and renewed, by the egotistical actions of a powerful male seeker.

Conclusions and generalizations on the basis of such material must necessarily remain guarded and tentative. Here are only two stories out of many thousands. Nonetheless, certain particular "architectural" details are prominent in these stories, and a check of numerous other myths indicates to me that these details, as features of dramatic meaning, are quite common in Native American narratives. Bierhorst has written (in private correspondence) that he feels the double structure may be a regular feature of American Indian narratives generally, unnoticed by scholars because the halves may not be obviously congruent (in length or meaning) to outsiders.

In any case, the feature seems widespread, and it may be—as I have suggested—far more complicated than mere doubling would suggest. Whether there are two or more simultaneous levels of meaning, their function seems to be a direct outcome of ongoing oral tradition, not a matter of prodigious memory feats. The listener, steeped in continual myth recitals using the same or similar features, having heard particular myths numerous times previously, would have been able to apply several possibilities of meaning to each part of a myth. Such devices as were catalogued by Melville Jacobs and others (number, time of day, sequence, personalities) are the particularizing items that focus the listener's attention on meaningful clusters within the tale in contradistinction to all other possible meanings for the action.

Without ethnographic evidence of the fullest sort (so we can approximate the cultural meanings of these items on the idea, word, and phrase levels and hence the people's likely response to them), without an appreciation of the mechanics of oral tradition, the prose narratives left to us by scholars like Boas must remain stark skeletons. We can say, I think, that at least as important as order, sequence, and structural patterning are the inevitable effects of evaluation and qualitative response that occur when two related concepts are brought into each other's sphere of influence in a performance. Most of the real meaning in these myths seems to take shape "between the lines," in the dramatic tension set up between congruent layers of narrative.

March on, Second Grade

This kind of "tension" need not be absolutely serious in nature, either. In parodies, the whole point is to juxtapose one level of understanding with another in such an *appropriately congruous* way (to bend Oring's term a little) that the result is a larger burst of meaning than the listener could get from either level by itself. The following schoolyard song sung to the tune of "The Battle Hymn of the Republic" suggests that even second graders have school-related stresses that loom as large as the Civil War and the freeing of the slaves:

> *Mine eyes have seen the glory of the burning of the school,*
> *We have locked up all the teachers and we've broken every rule;*
> *We've burned down the office with the Principal inside,*
> *March on, second grade, march on.*
>
> *Glory, glory hallelujah,*
> *Teacher hit me with a ruler;*
> *I shot her through the door with my trusty forty-four,*
> *And I ain't seen the old bat since.*

In spite of the chilling resemblance of the *words* to the scene in many an urban school today, the singing of this revolutionary expression to the tune of the Civil War song usually connotes humor to those who sing it (though not always to the teachers and principals who overhear it). Yet, there is nothing manifestly humorous about the words, or the music, taken separately.

Similarly, the early American song, "Springfield Mountain," which details the death of a young man by rattlesnake bite on the slopes of a hill near Wilbraham, Massachusetts, was originally sung to the hymn tune "Praise God from Whom All Blessings Flow," setting up the connotation that everyday events are providences from God, as we shall see in greater detail in Chapter 10.

A story told in several formerly polygamous families in Utah describes how Great-Grandpa broke the news of his upcoming second marriage to his first wife, a recent convert who wasn't convinced of her commitment to the ordinance. He told her she could retire, let the younger woman take over the bulk of the housework, relax a little, and take some time to do the quilting and embroidering she so loved. Why, Great-Grandpa renovated a room for her, up in the attic right over the master bedroom, where she could retreat and do her own things. But somehow, Great-Grandma couldn't take the strain, and she got a little quirky and clumsy; and most nights, when she got up to use the chamber-pot, why she just kicked it over.

It does not take too much imagination to see this story as a connotative dramatization of Great-Grandma's attitude toward polygamy, expressed in an action image which says more than she probably dared to say. And why is the story told by women in a number of families unless that same connotation about being displaced by a younger wife is shared by a number of women in the society? Though polygamy officially ceased with the issuance of a manifesto in 1890, there was no revelation on the matter, and some Mormons continue to feel that the change was only because of political pressure applied by the U.S. government. Some continued the practice, but nearly all Mormons were affected by it, if on no other grounds than the massive kinship system that relates most of the leading families in the state to this day. Modern L.D.S. women who would not relish being plural wives nonetheless live in a culture deeply affected by the earlier practice. Thus, the range of connotations in the story, all of them suggestive of disapproval voiced by women in an essentially patriarchal system, can be powerful for cultural insiders.

"Born in the Grave"

In Japan, one of the favorite themes in folktale and legend is death and ghosts. In a typical story, a pregnant traveller falls dead in front of a Buddhist temple far from her home town. The priest of the temple takes pity on her lonely death and has her buried behind the temple. Shortly after that, the old man who runs the town's sweet shop is awakened late at night by a woman dressed all in white, with flowing hair; she demands to buy some *ame*, a kind of candy, and then leaves quickly. After several such nighttime visits, the shopkeeper decides to follow this strange woman to see where she lives. He watches as she glides into the burial ground and disappears in a shower of sparks. Next day, he tells all this to the priest, who orders the freshly made grave dug up. In it, the villagers find the dead woman with her live baby, who was born after his mother was buried. Surrounding her are the wrappers from the *ame* she had bought. When they try to take the baby from her arms, however, the corpse clutches the boy even tighter, until a nursing mother bares her breast and promises she will raise the boy as her own. The dead mother relaxes her hold, the baby is taken out of the grave, and the mother is reburied to the accompaniment of sutras chanted by the priest. The boy grows up to be a strong runner and local wrestling champion, and later becomes a Buddhist priest. You can still visit the temple where this happened (where of course the candy wrappers are still on display).

This story is loaded with suggestive images and connotations for the Japanese, many of which can be read out of the text by any careful and sensitive person. White kimonos are worn in Japan only by corpses, and the long flowing hair is also associated with death, since in older times the normally coiffed hairdo was let down straight for burial. Ghosts in graveyards are often accompanied by sparks or flames—will o' the wisp, foxfire, jack o' lantern these lights are called in England and America. So it is easy to believe that the Japanese audience will recognize from very early on in the story that the nighttime shopper is a ghost. The more delicate connotations have to do with the Japanese concept that the bond between mother and child never ceases. Proper fulfillment of parental obligations, according to stories like this one, result in strengthening the social and religious order. The story does not mention—but any traditional Japanese person would know—that the obligations also run the other way: we living people are expected to fulfill our responsibilities to our departed relatives by offering prayers and memorial services (these are done in seven-month, seven-year intervals, in some cases up to one hundred years after the death of a relative). A person's spirit, properly ritualized, becomes a *kami*, a kind of local deity whose concern it is to nurture its family by promoting luck, fertility, success, and stability from "the other side." Since Buddhist priests in Japan are mostly employed in chanting sutras for departed souls, we can suspect that the young man's movement into the Buddhist priesthood is the natural counterpart of his mother's earlier dedication to saving his life: she nurtured him with food and he now nurtures her with prayers. But all of this is suggested by the connotative images and actions of the story, not overtly stated anywhere in the text. As in most of our examples in this book, the living tradition exists not in the *form* of texts and barns and quilts, but in a shared set of cultural propositions which are set off—triggered if you will—by the culturally constructed performance.

This chapter has dealt mainly with connotation in verbal performances, but the inquiry cannot end here. What of textural and structural connotation in other traditional genres and folklore events: Are there connotations in an unpainted New England barn? In a Japanese woman wearing a red dress or white kimono? In a Slavic woman showing the soles of her feet while dancing? In the number of ingredients in *sushi?* In a wink?

BIBLIOGRAPHICAL NOTES

The standard single-volume text for university-level work in Chaucer is Larry D. Benson, ed., *The Riverside Chaucer*, cited previously (Chap. 5); this is the modern updating of F. N. Robinson's *The Works of Geoffrey Chaucer*. Incisive notes on the Wife of Bath's Tale and the Merchant's Tale are on pp. 863–74, 884–90. Chaucer's description of the Wife of Bath appears in lines 445-76 of the General Prologue. Because Chaucer uses a great number of puns, and due to the delicate nature of connotation itself, anyone interested in Chaucer's connotative use of language should read the material in the Middle English, not in modern English.

Munro S. Edmonson, in *Lore: An Introduction to the Science of Folklore and Literature* (New York: Holt, Rinehart, and Winston, 1971), argues that folk groups can indeed be defined as those peoples who share culture-specific connotation: "the connotative meanings that constitute a lore grow up in patterns held in common by populations with an intensively shared history" (3). Pointing out that the color yellow implies mourning in Russia, sanctity in Thailand, maturity in Yucatan, and cowardice in England, he suggests that the entire expressive output of any culture can be considered its lore as long as it is phrased in the codes understandable mainly to insiders. Recognizing the culture-specific aspect of connotation, Edmonson says that "it is a basic feature of lore that it is not easily communicated." I would add, "to people outside the close group." Geoffrey N. Leech talks of the importance of connotative power to poetic expression in a very tightly condensed but totally lucid statement, *A Linguistic Guide to English Poetry* (London: Longmans, Green, 1969), 41.

Although I present the moose nose story as if I have arrived at a final explanation for it, there are a number of details in the story that beg further study. Alan Dundes has pointed out to me privately that we may expect to find further meaning in the fact that the incident occurs on a honeymoon, suggesting that father-in-law and son-in-law are shown in a competitive relationship. Is there a parallel between the father kicking and severing the bloody nose and the new son-in-law's implied defloration of the bride? Why does the father want to go on the honeymoon in the first place? These and other questions may indeed bring up other levels of connotative meaning for the joke, each of which should be properly accounted for in terms of its relationship to the singing situation that occasioned the joke in the first place. Edward T. Hall's concept of the high context group certainly comes to mind in this discussion as a way of describing the intensity with which unspoken meaning is shared by people who operate in a long-standing cultural system. The remark to Ruth Underhill by the old Papago woman, Maria Chona, may be found in *The Autobiography of a Papago Woman*, ed. Ruth Underhill (Menasha, Wisc: American Anthropological Association, 1936), 23. To experience the esoteric richness of what the Papago lady meant, one might consult Donald M. Bahr, *Pima and Papago Ritual Oratory* (San Francisco: Indian Historian Press, 1975); in this work, Papago texts are presented in direct, line-by-line translation. A phrase like "then reached the sun-drinking water" (43) is not shrugged off as a mere awkwardness in translation, but recognized as representing tremendous connotative power for those who know the language and its cultural references.

The story of "The Cherry Tree Carol" derives from the apocryphal Pseudo Matthew Gospel, Chapter 22. Francis James Child gives a brief account of the story and its background, along with several texts, in *The English and Scottish Popular Ballads;* "The Cherry Tree Carol" appears as #54 in the Child collection. The text for the version cited here was sung to me by Daniel Hoffman near Black Mountain, North Carolina, in the summer of 1952. For an even more complicated usage of double-level sexual riddles, see "Captain Wedderburn's Courtship," Child #46, in which the sexual connotations of the riddles themselves are placed within a structural situation featuring an aggressive courtship and an eventual sexual domination by the male character. See also my article "'Riddles Wisely Expounded,'" *Western Folklore* 25 (1966): 1-16, as well as my *Morning Dew and Roses: Nuance, Metaphor, and Meaning in Folksongs* (Urbana: University of Illinois Press, 1995). For examples of the way in which folksong collector Cecil Sharp felt obliged to translate sexual connotation into something more acceptable to the Victorian taste, see James Reeves, *The Idiom of the People* (New York: Norton, 1958). For interesting connotative riddles in Old English see G. P. Knapp and E. V. D. Dobbie, eds., *The Exeter Book* (New York: Columbia University Press, 1936), especially riddles 25, 44, 45, 54, 62.

John Bierhorst's anthology of Native American narratives, *The Red Swan: Myths and Tales of the American Indians* (New York: Farrar, Straus, and Giroux, 1976), is an excellent collection containing a number of tales that are almost intimidating to us because of our inability to respond to the connotative suggestions. "Raw Gums and White Owl Woman," an Arapaho myth, appears on pp. 141-48. Bierhorst's comments about double myths appear on pp. 10-14. See also his article "American Indian Verbal Art and the Role of the Literary Critic," *Journal of American Folklore* 88 (1975): 401-8. The full reference for Dell Hymes's article on the Sun Myth is provided in the bibliographical section of Chapter 5. Joseph Campbell's work on the hero archetype is brought together in *The Hero with a Thousand Faces* (New York: Bollingen Foundation, 1949; numerous reprints by Meridian books), and has almost a cult following, especially among nonfolklorists. Jarold W. Ramsey's brilliant article "The Wife Who Goes Out Like a Man, Comes Back as a Hero: The Art of Two Oregon Narratives," *PMLA* 92 (January 1977): 9-18, is a landmark in scholarship on Native American traditional expression, not the least for the very fact of its appearance in a journal that has seldom if ever paid attention to Native materials. It is based almost entirely on the sensitive perception of culturally constructed connotations.

For more discussion of song parodies and legends which express complex attitudes about the westward movement in America, see my "Folklore and Reality in the American West," in *Sense of Place: American Regional Cultures,* ed. Barbara Allen and Thomas J. Schlereth (Lexington: University Press of Kentucky, 1990), esp. pp. 14–27; and "Folklore in the American West," in *A Literary History of the American West,* ed. Thomas J. Lyon et al. (Fort Worth: Texas Christian University Press, 1987), 29–67. A number of anecdotes and legends about Mormon polygamy are provided by Austin Fife and Alta Fife, *Saints of Sage and Saddle: Folklore among the Mormons* (Bloomington: Indiana University Press, 1956), 162–79. The ways in which Japanese ghost stories are used as dramatizations of complex cultural abstractions are discussed in Michiko Iwasaka and Barre Toelken, *Ghosts and the Japanese: Cultural Experience in Japanese Death Legends* (Logan: Utah State University Press, 1994); the story discussed in this chapter can be found on pp. 66–71 in two different versions. Ilana Harlow proposes that supernatural legends like ghost stories function to connect, articulate, and make sense of local tragedy, personal experience, and cultural assumptions; see her "Unravelling Stories: Exploring the Juncture of Ghost Story and Local Tragedy," *Journal of Folklore Research* 30 (1993): 177–200.

Other works that relate to this chapter are Benjamin Lee Whorf, *Language, Thought, and Reality* (New York: Technology Press, 1956), which deals with cultural connotation as real meaning; Marcel Griaule, *Conversations with Ogotemmeli* (London: Oxford University Press, 1965), which discusses the function of metaphor in the Dogon culture; James Fernandez, "The Mission of Metaphor in Expressive Culture," *Current Anthropology* 15 (1974): 119–33, plus discussion, 133-45, in which the author holds that metaphors convert "pronouns" from inchoate references to distinct concepts with large social and cultural identities; Peter Farb, *Word Play: What Happens When People Talk* (1974; reprinted New York: Bantam, 1975), 99ff., for a discussion of obscene puns.

For a delightful demonstration of how culturally based connotations are used by Shakespeare, see Eric Partridge, *Shakespeare's Bawdy* (New York: Dutton, 1960; originally publ. 1948). Chaucer's use of certain kinds of connotations is taken up in Carolyn Dinshaw, *Chaucer's Sexual Poetics* (Madison: University of Wisconsin Press, 1989). The connotative suggestiveness of metaphors is discussed in George Lakoff and Mark Johnson, *Metaphors We Live By* (Chicago: University of Chicago Press, 1980). See also Victor Turner, *Dreams, Fields, and Metaphors* (Ithaca, N.Y.: Cornell University Press, 1975).

Chapter 7

FOLKLORE AND CULTURAL WORLDVIEW

"WORLDVIEW" REFERS TO THE MANNER IN WHICH A CULTURE SEES AND EXPRESSES its relation to the world around it. While earlier students of culture were certain that similar conditions would impress any human eye and soul in similar ways even in widely separated circumstances, there is now evidence to the contrary; that is, objective reality (as we like to call it) actually varies widely according to the viewer's means of perceiving it. Often those means are affected by cultural and linguistic factors that have been so deeply engrained in the mind that they have actually become a method of thinking which includes a logical system and a set of evaluative assumptions. For example, a UCLA research team working on the Hopi reservation found by brainwave analysis that Hopi children use the right hemisphere of the brain for speaking and hearing the Hopi language and the left hemisphere for English. The researchers concluded that there is solid support for the concept that people speaking different languages "may perceive things in basically different ways." Such an observation does not waste time on the comparatively superficial idea that people in different cultures may disagree with those of other backgrounds; likewise, it does not take up the common occurrence of disagreement in conscious personal opinion among people of the same culture. The point here is that each culture has a distinctive way of thinking that it passes on to its young, and this way of thinking is made up of codes so deeply represented in language that they become, as Dorothy Lee pointed out some years ago, the primary way in which people of that culture can understand anything.

CULTURE AND MEANING

The same kinds of codes found in language are also found in the way we experience things visually, even under the most "objective" circumstances. In *Patterns of Discovery,* Norwood Russell Hanson says, "We are set to appreciate the visual aspects of things in certain ways. Elements in our experience do not cluster at

In Austria, Germany, and the culturally German parts of Alsatia, people pride themselves on the neatness of their woodpiles, which are often seen as external expressions of the owner's care for household and family.

random. . . . Seeing is not only the having of a visual experience; it is also the way in which the visual experience is had." In the area of linguistic theory, this idea has been heavily discussed by Benjamin Lee Whorf, Edward Sapir, and more recently by Edward T. Hall. The linguistic discussion is far from settled, and so it is not possible for us to do more than develop a general notion about cultural worldview. However, taking some leads from that linguistic debate, and drawing our observations from a great variety of traditional expressions, we may still be able to gain important perspectives on the ways in which insiders of a culture see, understand, and express their responses to the world around them through their folklore. Beyond the world of language, although not totally divorced from it, we find a great variety of human behavior and expression that is culture-specific. For example, in *The Hidden Dimension,* Hall points out that "significant evidence that people brought up in different cultures live in different perceptual worlds is to be found in their manner of orienting themselves in space, how they get around and move from one place to the next."

The researches of Hall, John Adair, Sol Worth, and many others indicate that the members of any given culture perceive reality in terms of culturally provided sets of ideas and premises, and that the world of reality is processed differently from culture to culture. Not only are the incoming data interpreted according to the pattern of a particular culture, but expressions and communications with others are based on those same perceptions and premises. The human mind keeps producing—in miniature, as it were—the worldview that has formed its conception of reality by creating analogs and parallels on all levels of human expression, from houses to myths. Thus, the artifacts and artistic expressions of any culture will reflect rather strongly the codes which that culture utilizes to represent the premises of reality.

Since folklore is comprised of those artistic expressions most heavily governed by the tastes of the group, we should be able to find in folk performances a continual tableau or paradigm more revealing of cultural worldview than we might find in the expressions created independently by individuals. Nonetheless, as students of culture have shown, in terms of worldview the distinctions between formal culture and folk culture are not as sharp as one would have imagined; apparently, little is exempt from the functionings of cultural worldview. In this chapter we will not be able to take up all the ramifications of this idea, for they need to be followed into philosophy, history, architecture and art, music, and literature on all levels. Here, our focus on folklore will ask us to consider those aspects of cultural worldview transmitted and performed in the same manner as the other kinds of folklore we have been discussing.

Worldview and Tradition among European Americans

The  Primal Context

As remarked in Chapter 1, every child grows up surrounded by a number of cultural, personal, and physical features that provide its first—and perhaps its most lasting—set of perceptions about the world and its operation. In the earliest years, the child is learning more about its language than it will ever learn again, and at this time of life just as much is learned about cultural context and physical surroundings. For our purposes, we need to know which aspects of this learning are culture-specific. That is, what might be experienced by a child in one culture at this age that would not be universal to all children? We might suspect that every child has some kind of family surrounding that could be called fairly universal; at the same time, we must recognize that the concept of what a family is and who comprises it varies widely from one culture to another, and therefore the effect of family meaning upon a newborn child varies considerably as well. We can assume that in most cases around the world the child will have some kind of physical context that may be called a home, some kind of shelter provided by the family. Just as quickly, however, we realize that not all these shelters look alike, and so their visual impact on a newborn child will vary from one culture to another. If we were to take a look at several key contextual features for the European American child, what sorts of physical and cultural surroundings would we find that might be considered formative of cultural worldview?

First of all, for physical surroundings, most babies in America find themselves lying alone in a room made up primarily of straight lines. The child may be placed face up or face down during sleeping but is almost invariably placed face up during waking hours. Above the child, the ceiling provides a large flat surface with corners. Around the child, closer at hand, are the vertical and horizontal slats and corners of the crib. How early the child notices the presence of these straight lines is probably not possible to determine, but it is a moot point, for there are few other things for it to look at. Presumably, the setting impresses itself upon the mind as the basic surrounding for the individual. It is also difficult to say at what point a baby begins to be aware of aloneness, but the situation must be a basic element in the growing sense of individuality.

Contacts with other human beings at this early age are chiefly with parents, who must seem to come from some invisible place above as they hang their faces over the edge of the crib to investigate the condition of the baby. Often these visits from above are unannounced, but more often they come in response to the appeals of the child. Many doctors feel that within a few hours of birth a baby can learn how to make these appeals and make them work in bringing comfort and succor from above. This ability is developed still further when, as a growing child, the individual learns to compete for attention among other siblings or playmates.

If language is being learned so quickly at this time of life, it would be strange indeed if these other visual and interactional patterns were not also being absorbed as basic sets of human experience. It does not take a great stretch of the imagination to suppose that these experiences, perceived as normal ways of life, must provide a strong basis for certain ideas found in more sophisticated form among adults in this culture: the idea, for example, that the individual is the basic unit of society, that straight lines and grid patterns constitute a sense of order, that help from interested personages above can be had if the proper appeal is made, that competition is an indispensable and praiseworthy means to confront the problems of life.

These ideas not only provide a foundation for action, but as the individual grows older and has children they become almost basic philosophical necessities: for example, the insistence that a baby should have his or her own room and the later encouragement of the child in competitive endeavors that are thought to "build character." As we will see more fully in this chapter, these ideas also become ways of judging other people who act differently: consider the opinion widespread among many European Americans that families who do not provide separate bedrooms for each person must be overcrowded, underprivileged, immodest, or even backward.

Yet we know from the vernacular architecture of earlier American periods that home spatial arrangements were once quite different. Even when people had the means and the materials to build larger cabins, they retained the one-room design—in which nearly all social and private functions were carried out in one area, focused on a fireplace—for a considerable time. Roger Welsch and Henry Glassie have suggested it was not because of architectural dullness or blind conservatism, but rather because the family was defined differently: it was inwardly focused on itself—a centripetal mode, E. T. Hall might call it—and its space was arranged in such a way that indoors everyone was practically in arm's reach of everyone else. Indeed, as Welsch points out, the government had to force homesteaders on the plains to install windows in their cabins, for their preference had been not to look out on the forbidding horizon but at each other when the day's work was done.

Glassie notes that as the United States began to move toward concepts of individuality and individual rights, vernacular homes began to be articulated: the cooking was moved out to an adjoining room (separating the cook from the everyday conversation), the bedrooms were attached in another room (separating first the adults and children, then eventually the children by gender—usually upstairs). Obviously, the vernacular concept of individual/family has been in flux all along, even when people were not articulating it philosophically; a child growing up at any given period in United States history thus lives in a physical model of the cultural constructs animating the contemporary vernacular culture. No wonder that people in different ethnic, economic, and regional groups have the feeling that they live in different perceptual worlds: indeed they do.

In addition to physical surroundings and human interactions that have their foundations in cultural attitudes, the young child is also bombarded with a number of orally performed traditions. Folktales provide examples of how some younger brother was able to compete with wit and valor and gain the hand of a princess; proverbs teach the merits of culturally appropriate ideas or behaviors; lullabies may help to relax the child for sleep. But what are the deeper messages of some of these traditions? To whom, for example, is the lullaby addressed? Bess Lomax Hawes has shown convincingly that a good many lullabies sung in America are really laments about the mother's fear of losing the child or her husband. We might add that some other lullabies seem to stress the father's continual obligation to support the child ("Papa's gonna buy you a . . ."). Through these subtle means, the child is educated in the underlying cultural "facts of life" that separate people into distinctly individual categories of obligation and hierarchy.

All of these observations are typical of the basic contexts experienced by European American children. I have not considered the more complex ideas of Freud and Jung here because I want to stress those aspects of the cultural scene that we can observe clearly through vernacular artifacts and performances. If we add those inborn tendencies discussed by psychologists, the subject becomes far more complicated, but not contradictory: Freud's patients dreamed in symbols that represented their own (and their culture's) concerns; they did not dream of Chinese dragons or Lakota Sioux eagles.

Individual Orientation

By using the basic patterns learned in the earliest childhood context, a child in any culture learns how to get oriented in space and time. Among European Americans, the concepts of orientation are simply extensions of the rudimentary straight lines and grid patterns experienced in the nursery. From a child's knowledge of the crib and its placement in the room, it develops an expanded sense of the placement of rooms within a house (along with their specialized functions, which are not to be confused). On a still larger scale, one learns the arrangement of houses and streets in the neighborhood, the pattern of streets and avenues around an entire city; in rural areas one learns about boundary lines, acres, range and section coordinates, and so on. On a smaller scale, one also learns the typical expression of these concepts in material traditions; the similarities between a patchwork quilt and a view of rural America from the air are more than coincidental or superficial, for as cultural designs they are based on the same premises of evenness, order, symmetry, predominance of straight lines, distinctive measurements. Jagged edges, disparate measurements, asymmetry, and incompleteness are considered intolerable in both areas of expression. There is something deeper than a pun in the statement made by the old New England farmer to his wife: "I'm glad I don't reap the way you sew."

Ways of orienting ourselves in space can be both imaginary and physical. In the wilderness we can use a compass line, and the imaginary course set for us by straight lines projected over a map can bring us safely to our destination (even if in actuality we come out of the woods down the road from where we expected to). In a physical sense, our cities, classrooms, graveyards, and football coliseums all use straight lines and symmetry to order the relationships between people by use of regularity in discrete spaces, whether they be large vertical spaces for people storage, arenas for great numbers of people to focus on a single occurrence, or final "places of rest." The effect of these grid patterns on our behavior will be discussed later in this chapter; at this point we need only note that using coordinates such as these, most of us can find our way even in a city we have not visited before. These are assumptions about the use of space that are so ingrained in our culture that it is ludicrous when someone gets lost. Yet getting lost is a common occurrence, especially when one moves from one set of grid assumptions to another. New Yorkers laugh about strangers who don't know the difference between uptown and downtown, and farm people the country over love to make fun of the wandering tourists who can't find their way back to town ("Come to think of it, you can't even get there from here").

The coordinates we recognize in keeping time are very similar to those we use to measure space. Our very interest in arriving on time, our concern about wasting and saving time, our penchant for eating meals at measured intervals, and our continued anxiety about "what time will bring" are strong indications that we see time as a lineal structure, a path along which we move (preferably ahead rather than backward). The cultural conviction that we move forward on a single line of time has led to a concept of future, the anticipation of future events, and a high evaluation of anything that lies in the future. Conversely, since time is for us single-stranded, it does us no good to look backward and "cry over spilled milk."

Even the study of history is justified by many, not in terms of its inherent value, but because of its capacity to teach us what to avoid in the future. Alan Dundes has followed this topic through a study of the aphorisms, figures of speech, metaphors, proverbs, and customs that saturate American life: our demand for happy endings, our concern with the future of children ("What do you want to be when you grow up?"), our concept of a person's worth in terms of potential (categories like "rookie of the year" or "most likely to succeed"), membership in clubs like Future Farmers of America and Future Homemakers of America, our interest in the news, the number of shopping days before Christmas, future rewards in heaven, and future payments on credit accounts. One might also add matters ranging from the sophisticated to the everyday: financial investments, weather forecasts, and greetings like "What's new?"

The grid patterns of space and time have become so important for European and American culture that they dictate nearly everything we do. It may well be that some of these patterns had their origins in practical necessities or as helpful aids for the interests of the culture or particular people in it. But it is interesting to notice that in our zeal to measure lineal time, we have found that our principal model of time—earth's rotation around the sun—is a slippery computer to go by, if we are interested in accuracy. Astronomers distinguish between six different ways of computing how long a year "really" is: the *anomalistic year* is 365 days, 6 hours, 13 minutes, 53.1 seconds long; the *sidereal* (or *astral*) *year* is 365 days, 6 hours, 9 minutes, 9.54 seconds long—which is a whole 20 minutes and 23.5 seconds longer than the *tropical* (or *solar*) *year*, which is 365 days, 5 hours, 48 minutes, 45.5 seconds long; the *lunar astronomical year* is 354 days, 8 hours, 48 minutes, 34 seconds long, while the *common lunar year* (refreshing in its simplicity) is 354 days long; the unadorned *lunar year*, as its name suggests, measures not the days and the minutes, but the rotations of the moon around the earth—it is just 12 lunar cycles long, no more, no less. You might want to remember these differences the next time someone accuses you of being 10 minutes late for an appointment, for the *real* answer to the question "What time is it?" is, "It all depends."

Nonetheless, as Thoreau pointed out, after the discovery of fire there arose the necessity to stand by it; similarly, after the development of the clock there arose the necessity to go by it, and one now finds widespread in western culture the general assumption that there is such a thing as accurate time, that it moves forward, that it is measurable, and that people must relate the events of their lives to the clock. So deep is this assumption that if clocks are taken away from people anxiety results. On the positive side, using these coordinates, any number of us could agree to meet on the corner of First South and Second West in Salt Lake City, at 3:30 P.M. on July 24 of any specified year, and we could all find our way there on time even though we had never been there before. As we shall see, however, there are cultures in which such precision of time and space would be meaningless (even ludicrous), and this capability would not necessarily register as a positive advantage. Lineal time was developed by cultures who had developed the idea of a creation, a development, and an ultimate destination in their physical and religious affairs. The line leads straight from "the Beginning" to "the End," from alpha to omega.

Individual Deportment

As I have indicated, much of our deportment in life as individuals is based on "where" we conceive ourselves to stand in time and space, for our concepts of appropriate behavior rest on these perceptions. One thing a grid pattern seating arrangement provides for a group of people in our culture is a behavioral set. The audience is in its place, and the speaker or entertainer is in another place before them. If the members of the audience leave their places, they are considered unruly or unmanageable; through this we can see a direct relationship between the use of space and a sense of appropriate regulated behavior; and we can surmise that the grid pattern seating found so often in school classrooms is as much related to pre-established concepts of behavior and predictability as it is to the practical seating of a certain number of people in a limited space. In fact, many teachers who have "broken" their classrooms up into circles have found that the janitor has come through afterwards to "put the room back in order." Even though the individual may be the basic unit of American society, he or she must still learn the appropriateness of behavior in time and space with respect to other individuals. Part of this behavior has to do with a sense of order, and the grid pattern seating arrangement helps to provide a stability of behavior in which whole crowds can be more or less predictably disposed toward appropriate behaviors.

On the personal level, we want younger people to "know their place," we expect people to be "direct," we hope they are "up front," we admire a young man who knows where he is going, and we advise people to be logical enough to take one thing at a time. We expect a person to show up on time for an appointment, and we expect everyone to be concerned about personal identity. We are encouraged to "do our own thing," and to "look out for number one." We are thus encouraged to extend the competitiveness learned in the nursery, and to measure our worth in progress against or alongside others' progress by besting them or being bested by them. We measure the length of our lives very carefully and we celebrate a long succession of birthdays, some of which have special significance in determining our entrance into larger spheres of activity (twelve years old, eighteen years old, twenty-one years old) that involve development, independence, or activity, and later in life (sixty, sixty-five, or seventy) our entry into a condition of "reduced" usefulness to the society, the retirement we have been encouraged to look forward to and plan ahead for.

Because we are expected to be direct and forthright, in our conversation we are supposed to move directly to the point and make our lines of reasoning clear, often by using parallels. Eye contact and body gesture are important. If proximity forces us into very close (for us, amorous) distancing, we compensate for it (because of the demands of law and order) by facing the same direction as the other person (on crowded elevators or movie lines or buses, in which body contact can occur as long as people are not looking into each other's eyes). But in a personal conversation, the speakers are expected to maintain eye contact most of the time in order to indicate sincerity and attention. In a classroom or church, the speaker makes contact by looking down at the audience; they signify their attention as well as their subordinate role by looking up at the speaker, ordered carefully by their seating. To break up these patterns is to create, for the typical European American, a sense of disorder in which the predictability of human thought and action is considerably lessened, and in which the responsible individual then is guilty of suspicious behavior.

Cultural Deportment

In addition to general support for these ideas through the various rewards given an individual for excelling in them, there is a broader corporate use of such premises as the basis for society's actions and as an explanation for its history. For example, in America there has been a high priority for subduing the wilderness, driving back the frontier (that place characterized by disorder), the bringing of law and order to the Wild West, and the establishment of townships and governments all subject to similar rules of time and space. Modern government planning, the establishment of timetables by railroads and airlines, the idea of "standard time," the setting of deadlines for applications to granting agencies, and so on, are applications of these concepts. Within the culture, they are perfectly sensible modes of operation.

Nature, on the other hand, is often dealt with as if it stands quite separate from our created systems. Spring comes and goes when it pleases, not by the clock or by government schedule. Thus, much of our cultural deportment is aimed at the regularization of nature, the reduction of its "hazards," the harnessing and directing of its energies, and the utilization of its "resources." It often seems as though nature, to fit into our system, must be subordinated to our values. Even during wartime, when armies try to camouflage themselves, they often give themselves away by maintaining a grid pattern on a larger scale; it is said that German fighter-bomber pilots were told to bomb anything they found in a straight line, for where there is a straight line there are bound to be human beings. This cultural recognition, that the straight lines in time and space are means by which we can prove our presence, our validity, or our domination over nature as well as over people, is testimony to the extent these premises are exercised throughout our cultural existence.

European American tradition values time and space in proportion to the ways in which they can be ordered, measured, planned, timed, and thus weighed and sold. Actions that are "off the wall," statements made "off the top of the head," enterprises undertaken at the "spur of the moment" are generally less seriously taken than long-range impact statements, 2001 plans, prospectuses, well-planned activities, and completion of work by deadline, even when the substance of the former group is exciting and creative or the content of the latter group is totally boring or inconsequential. The individual who wants to get along in American society is therefore encouraged to plan the future, not to daydream.

Cultural Philosophy and Folklore

As Alan Dundes has pointed out, we see multiform examples of folk ideas being expressed through cultural traditions. Folktales very often transmit for the members of a culture a set of unstated yet obvious rules for the kind of deportment leading to success within the value system of that culture. More overt are the various proverbs and figures of speech we use to express our cultural attitudes toward the behavior of others rather than our own assessment. Phrases like "First come, first served," "The early bird catches the worm," "He who hesitates is lost" are ways of asserting the positive cultural value of rapid movement along the linear path of time. Related to this, Dundes feels, is our great interest in youth and staying youthful, along with our abhorrence of old age and of getting old; our wish to be avant-garde rather than "old hat" and our not wanting to run out of potential; our fascination with new frontiers, new directions, future promise; our feeling that death and old age are something to be confronted and coped with rather than features of life in which we are fully and naturally involved.

Beyond this, we recognize that the very concept of logic and practicality in our society is based on this same set of notions. In logic usually a + b = c, and in mathematics certain linear relationships in algebra are felt to be basic to learning more advanced computations. The linear order in spelling and alphabetical systems, filing systems, essays (usually with an introduction, a body, and a conclusion), novels with linear plot structure, marching (the most unexplored folk dance of our society) and square dancing, linear concepts of productivity (resource, production, product/waste), and assembly lines are all examples of linear use of time and space to achieve *ends* considered practical and logical by society at large. Indeed, if we construct anything from an idea to a vehicle by just putting stray bits of important items together, the product is considered haphazard, shoddy, crazy, or incomplete.

Similar ideas are experienced and expressed further through the use of common expressions like "keeping things straight," "getting straight," "staying in line," "toeing the line," by keeping our thinking "level-headed," our "quarters" "squared away," and our behavior "on the straight and narrow." When we want to indicate that someone else is crazy, it is often by making a gesture directly opposed to the linear perspective, that is, by making a circle around the ear with the forefinger.

This well-known gesture may be one of the most important examples of the issues raised in this chapter, for it is the conscious employment of a folk gesture in a "different" pattern to indicate not simply disagreement with another person but total negative evaluation of the other person's approach or behavior. Conversationally, we may say, "You're talking in circles," "You're crazy; your logic is circular," or "That idea makes me dizzy" (recall that dizziness is described in cartoon form by a spiral drawn over the affected person's head). It is in this matter of folk expression that worldview studies can be of tremendous importance to our understanding of cultural stresses in the modern world. For one thing, we cannot fail to recognize that many of the patterns discussed here as European American are found primarily in northern Europe, several parts of the Middle East, and in America.

Not all people who are American citizens, however, share these patterns equally, for their transmission goes more closely along ethnic, folk, and familial lines than through the channels of formal citizenship. Others, from cultures organized "along different lines," do not share these patterns at all, and still others recognize them but value them differently. If it were simply a matter of recognizing diversity in the world, if one could approach these dissimilarities on the intellectual level of curiosity only, the problem would not be so complex. Perhaps it is unfortunate that our own worldview gives us such a secure sense of logic in our daily encounters that our sense of normalcy is shocked when we encounter something radically outside its pattern. In such a situation we react emotionally rather than intellectually, often as if we had been deeply and personally challenged.

As Hall has pointed out in the case of proxemics, if an Arab (coming from a culture that encourages close body contact among people of the same gender in conversational situations) approaches an American (who comes from a culture that discourages physical body contact except under amorous or sports conditions) each one will feel something has gone wrong. The Arab is likely to feel offended by the American, who seems "totally disinterested in what I am saying or who I am," while the American may feel that there is something sexually aberrant about the Arab and recoil in disgust. The least likely occurrence on such an occasion is the intellectual; the participants will not say to themselves, "This is very interesting indeed; that other person there seems to exercise a different set of proxemic customs than I have been brought up with." Rather, each one will say to himself, "My God! What's wrong with that guy?"

People being interviewed on their front doorsteps would perhaps give their own intellectually formed opinions on their concepts of other cultures. It is precisely because the members of each culture consider their worldview to represent normalcy, a system of reality that can be experienced in all traditional forms from proverbs and tales to physical artifacts, that folklore provides us with one of the most valuable and reliable ways of entering the subject. If suddenly plunged into a circumstance in which deeply seated traditions are suddenly juxtaposed to those of another culture, however, people's expressions, attitudes, and actions will reveal more fully the emotional dimension of their assumptions.

Worldview and Traditional Material Artifacts of the Navajo

The Primal Context

The widespread creation of folk artifacts by a broad segment of the population is not as prominent among European Americans today as it is among some other peoples. Even though I have tried to make the point that all productions within a culture bear strong relationships to the cultural worldview, a study of vernacular artifacts and how they represent the basic premises of the culture is easier if we can refer to a group of people where traditional artifact production is more common, and where the premises may therefore be seen more often and through a wider variety of expressions. There are many such cultures, but I choose the Navajo because of my deeper acquaintance with them than with most other groups. Before looking closely at a few typical Navajo artifacts and their relationship to the Navajo worldview, however, I would like to mention the basic circumstances in which a Navajo baby first perceives its surroundings, so that the objective world in which a Navajo grows up can be seen in contradistinction to the one described for a typical White American earlier.

The Navajo child, at least one brought up traditionally, is not only born at home but begins life within and among the family, not alone. The traditional one-room Navajo hogan, made of mud, stones, and cedar poles, surrounds the entire family in circular fashion. The baby spends much of its time bound up in a cradle board, which is thought to provide the feeling of being held. In addition, the baby is often held or placed upright within the family group; its earliest views of other people, then, are of being surrounded by family members, not separated from them in space. Lying on its back, looking upward, the baby's view is of the domed inner roof of the hogan rather than a flat ceiling.

Most of the family's activities within the hogan are related to the center of the room, where a fire burns almost continually for warmth in the wintertime and where most cooked meals are prepared. Family members often group themselves around the fire, aligned to certain cardinal directions by gender. The door of the hogan always faces east, and so, as the child learns when somewhat older, the family is oriented to the movements of the sun and the cosmos. Traditional Navajos believe that the hogan represents the womb of Changing Woman, their principal deity: the smoke hole above is analogous to her navel, the eastward-facing doorway the birth canal through which they emerge anew into the world each day (and a reminder that Changing Woman was impregnated by the sun and by water as she lay down to rest with her lower torso oriented to the east).

Living space and ritual space are not rigidly separated from each other as they are in the European tradition; rather, the sacred healing ceremonies take place in the same hogan where the patient lives. The fire is extinguished and its place in the center of the hogan is taken by the sand paintings that depict the holy people, the *Yé'ii*, who, although depicted with long rectangular lines, are arranged to reciprocate each other by color, direction, arrangement, and function. In short, nearly every patterned experience coming to the young Navajo child, whether featuring round or straight lines, is described in essentially circular rather than linear terms.

The Navajo concept of time is most similar to European concepts of space; insofar as the Navajos talk about anything like time at all, it is not seen as a pathway along which one passes by but a context in which things move about. The flowering of a plant, the birth of a horse, the maturation of a tree, the building of a home, all have their own time surrounding them and are not measured off against each other on a single scale. For this reason, ancestors who might be considered remote by Europeans are often discussed as if they are near at hand by Navajos. One Navajo confided to me that he thought the Whites were unfortunate because they lived "so far" from their ancestors while "ours are all around us."

Individual and Cultural Orientation

The individual craftswoman, instead of standing on a straight ribbon of time leading from the past to some future point, stands in the middle of a vortex of forces exerted in concentric circles upon her by her immediate family, her extended family, the clan, the tribe, and the whole living ecological system within which she lives and functions. Instead of planning the future as if she were separable from nature, she negotiates with those forces presently around her; instead of looking toward a future product, she looks to the past for patterning, for advice and wisdom. As we might expect, her expressions, whether oral (religious or secular) or material (artistic or practical), are created according to the circular reciprocating designs that are models of her concept of the human position in nature. Time surrounds her, as do her dwelling place, her family, her clan, her tribe, her habitat, her dances, her rituals. The Navajo feel that one's proper position with respect to nature has to do with one's reciprocal responsibilities to it, and that maintaining balance and harmony in this proper position in turn maintains and occasions good health, which is the central part of Navajo religious concern.

Individual and Cultural Deportment

Because of this reciprocal model of reality, each person is brought up to act in ways that are not only harmonious but that match the concept of how life actually operates. For example, Navajos avoid competing with relatives and peers; they avoid any aggressive actions or gestures which might cause undue focus to fall on them; they relate to the world around them as if it were made up of interlocked, concentric circles beginning with the immediate family, surrounded by the clan of the mother (and, peripherally, the clan of the father), the people who live in the locality, other Navajos in general, and, finally, "other people."

As in any culture, deportment includes all of those things people do which are considered culturally recognizable modes of action. Many of these modes are what we would call expressive in nature: they articulate in various ways those models and systems which "make sense" to the people who share that worldview. The various genres of folklore could hardly exist unless in their expressiveness they participated heavily in references to those ideas, philosophies, attitudes, and logical patterns which are held in common by the group for whom the folk performances take place.

Cultural Art and Artifact ✳

In order for an item to be recognized as Navajo by a Navajo, it needs to reflect the Navajo circular, reciprocal, negotiating view; but the word *reflect* does not fully describe the Navajos' own recognition of artifacts themselves as "models" of worldview, because the Navajo language is based on movements, not on objects. Perhaps the juniper seed necklace provides one of the best examples of their values.

The brown seeds in these necklaces are found inside the blue juniper berry. The tree drops the berry to the ground, where it is picked up by chipmunks and other ground animals and taken to underground burrows. Navajo children, mostly girls, search for the hiding places and take those seeds with one end chewed off, carefully replacing the rest so the animals will have their normal food supply. The seeds are taken home, where the hole in one end serves as a guide for punching a hole in the other end with a needle. Colored beads are obtained from a nearby trading post or mercantile store, and the results are necklaces sometimes called "ghost beads" by the Whites who buy them. One Navajo term for them, however, is *gad bi naa'*—literally, "juniper's eyes." Because the seeds represent a partnership among the trees, the animals, and the humans, they stand in the Navajo mind for the active interrelationships between the various aspects of nature whose harmony assures good health. A Navajo will say that one who wears the juniper seed necklace will not go astray in the fog, get lost in the dark, or have bad dreams.

However, Navajos have assured me that they do not believe the necklace itself actually has magical properties; that is, the necklace as a physical item does not produce the condition of harmony necessary for good health. Rather, it epitomizes it in such a way that it acts as an external, physical representative of an internal frame of mind that the Navajo considers absolutely necessary in maintaining natural harmonies. A person who lives harmoniously with the natural world will be healthy. One who is healthy will not get lost or have bad dreams. In this respect, the necklace is primarily symbolic, or it acts as what a literary critic might call an objective correlative; in and of itself it is a physical reminder of some deeper reality, one of actions more than of beads, one that operates in our own interactive relationship to our living natural context.

The beads are strung in sometimes simple, sometimes complex, ways, but always with the same meaning for the wearer. Another dimension is sometimes added: in those juniper seed necklaces that feature circles with pointed figures, there is a representation of the cosmos, the stars, which deepens further the physical reference to total context for a Navajo. Recently, the people have added a circular rosette of beads representing the Navajo wedding basket, that vital accompaniment to virtually every Navajo ritual. But whether in the form of a simple or complex necklace or a wristband or a key ring, the juniper seeds are carried by almost every Navajo I know who lives in Navajo country. Making these necklaces for sale, especially featuring brightly colored beads from the trader, is probably an innovation learned from the nearby Utes, who have used beadwork more prominently than the Navajos. It seems also to be based on the widespread Navajo belief that Whites "just love those bright colors."

Another expression of worldview is seen in the weaving of Navajo rugs or blankets. Usually, the Navajos do not weave rugs for their own use, but produce

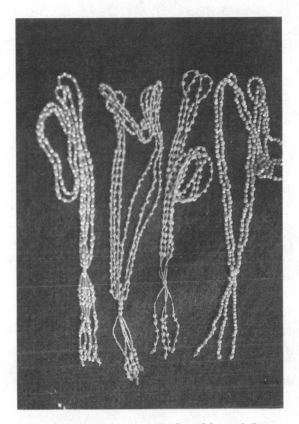

Juniper seed shells, called *gad bi naa'* (lit. "juniper's eyes") by the Navajo, are combined with colored glass beads in necklaces, suggesting cooperation between plants (who give the seeds), animals (who gather them), and humans (who collect them and string them together).

Round rosettes in Navajo jewelry suggest star constellations, sun and moon, the cosmos, or reciprocal relations among parts of nature.

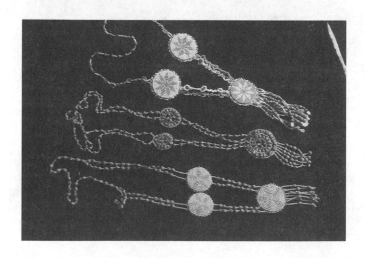

In recent years, the pattern of the Navajo
wedding basket, ubiquitous accompaniment to Navajo rituals, has been incor-
porated in the juniper seed necklaces.

them to trade for food or to sell directly for income. Thus, the Navajo could conceivably produce rugs in ways that do not distinctively represent their worldview. But in this craft, as in others, the Navajo way of doing things is very much a part of their total processing of data through their worldview, showing that their concern is with familiarity of process more than with products.

In Chapter 4, I referred to the incident in which Professors Sol Worth and John Adair gave movie cameras to a group of Navajos and asked them to produce their own films. In Susie Benally's film, "Navajo Weavers," there were only the briefest glimpses of someone actually weaving and only a few minutes devoted to full views of a finished rug. This seemed rather puzzling to those Whites who first viewed the film, but in fact it represented very well the Navajo attitude toward weaving: the rug itself is the least Navajo part of the production. Rather, the interaction of people with plant life in the gathering of herbs for dyes and the movement of people and animals across a familiar landscape are matters that deeply absorb the Navajo as aspects of their interactive relationships with the environment. The reciprocating geometrical designs in the rugs (suggesting a balance of the four cardinal directions) are also a reflection of a basically circular attitude produced on a flat plane, but they are as well functions of a style of weaving done on slants by counting so many vertical strings across for each movement in the pattern. A visible slanted line in the weaving is sometimes called a "lazy line" by Whites.

Some years ago, my adopted Navajo sister, Helen Yellowman, wove a rug that she gave to my family as a gift. It would probably be termed a *Yé'ii* rug by many buyers. (*Yé'ii* in Navajo means something like holy people, or spirits, or something approaching the idea of department heads of nature.) The figures in this particular rug, however, do not represent generalized holy spirits; rather, they are *na'ashó'ii*, or holy reptile people. The weaver would rather have used four figures (the Navajos' special number is four, as compared to our three), but she wanted to let these figures represent my five children: The two on each end are alike because my oldest and youngest are both female. The next two are alike because they represent my twin boys. My fifth child, who is actually the second oldest, is depicted in the middle as different from the rest because he has no one else in the family who matches him; he is set apart by four feathers on his head.

But why should the weaver depict my five children as lizards? It is because reptiles in general, and lizards in particular, are symbols of longevity and good health, and by superimposing on the idea of my children a concrete expression of longevity and health, my sister was creating an articulation of an abstract health concept, offering it as a gift that reflects her attitude toward my children. But the rug goes far deeper than that; as we talked about it, I found that she considers the wool in and of itself an important interaction between the sheep and the human herder, as well as between the sheep and the shearer, the spinner of the yarn, and the weaver of the rug. In addition, nearly all the colors

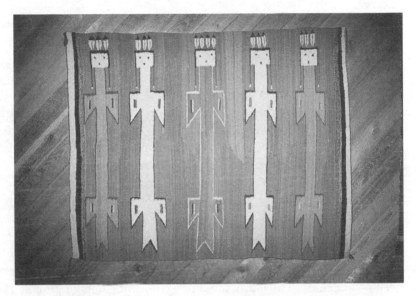

A *Yé'ii* rug woven for the author's family by Helen Yellowman. The *Yé'ii*, personifications of sacred forces of nature, are
invoked mostly in healing and agricultural ceremonies. These
are the Reptile *Yé'ii*, who represent longevity and family stability; they are woven in colors taken from plants and minerals
used for medicines, thus expressing hopes for the health and
longevity of the author's five children (suggested by the five
figures). Photo by Ron Daines.

in this rug are taken from plant and herb dyes that had to be gathered over the span of an entire year because some of them are from the same plants, whose roots produce different colors in different seasons. Thus the rug itself represents not only the interaction of humans with animals and of humans with plants, but of humans with the continuing cycle of natural seasons, and all of these, too, should be applied to the total concept of longevity and health for my children.

Further, some of the plants used are associated with particular medicines. The design, as I have suggested already, also represents an interaction between all of these factors and the human agent, the weaver, who held all of these possibilities in mind as she conceptualized the rug. Moreover, in spinning the yarn, the spindle must be turned in a sunwise direction (we call it clockwise), for it represents the circular movement of living things. Indeed, to spin the yarn by turning the spindle "backward" would be to produce yarn that represents the reverse of the normal state, yarn that will "come unraveled," "won't stay in the rugs," and "might cause sickness." It matters little whether the yarn might really physically unravel, for Navajo health beliefs are ritual and psychosomatic: the *idea* of unraveling is a greater reality and therefore a greater threat to health and stability than mere physical fact.

It is important to note, also, that in Navajo tradition it is from the woman that fertility and power emanate. The woman owns the hogan, the children, and most of the livestock, and weaves the blankets and rugs. This particular rug, given by one mother to another, is a powerful and eloquent articulation of human and natural relationships that language can only begin to describe. An artifact that we might normally say reflects the tastes and artistic premises of a culture actually embodies far more deeply the whole set of beliefs underlying the weaver's cultural worldview, thus ordering and giving power to her traditional expressions. Indeed, so central to her reasons for weaving is the concept of balance and harmony for others, that a few years ago when another Navajo woman got angry and ripped her own weaving from a loom in frustration, Helen Yellowman ceased weaving for more than two years.

The production of Navajo moccasins is an analogous expression of human responsibilities to relations in nature. When deerskin is to be worn as part of the clothing, such as in moccasins, shirts, and cradleboards, or when it will be used in ceremonies, according to older custom the deer's hide should not be punctured in the killing. Accordingly, the hunter must find a deer, chase it into open country, and pursue it until it is exhausted. While a deer will run in great bursts of speed for short distances, it cannot endure very long in the open or semi-open desert. The hunter eventually catches up, throws the deer over onto the ground gently, and holds its nose and mouth shut, suffocating it (often with sacred corn pollen) while singing a chant that apologizes to the deer for taking its life and hide and that thanks it for giving its substance to the support of people. Other more complicated ritual acts follow, but I have been

Made for the author by Zonnie
"Grandma" Johnson of Blanding, Utah,
in 1955, this Navajo rug contains mostly
natural shades of wool (the white is
enhanced by a clay powder). To person-
alize the rug, the weaver used a number
she had seen in a trading post, not knowing its meaning.

Grandma Johnson spinning yarn sunwise (clockwise) so it will not come unravelled (1950s).

Grandma Johnson and the author flirting (1970s). Photo by Van E. Porter.

asked not to share them. The resulting naturally tanned hide is called a sacred deer skin.

Yellowman told me that not long ago most traditional Navajos would have tried, at least, to obtain hides to be used for any kind of body cover in this way. Yellowman himself still occasionally got his deer in this manner, but after he developed back trouble, he was more inclined to use his bow and arrow. This did not pose a traditional dilemma for him, for the moccasins made were chiefly bartered to a local trader for sale to White tourists. Apparently the same rules of responsibility need not be so efficiently carried out when one is producing clothing for non-Navajos, just as brighter commercial dyes are often used in rugs for trade when the buyers ask for them. Yet, in Yellowman's earnest discussion on these matters, one can see that his role as hunter and moccasin maker were still very deeply imbued with cultural attitudes running far deeper than the practical aspects of simply killing and skinning a deer and producing footwear.

Yellowman said that the moccasins (made of animal skin) and the dye (some of the ingredients of which come from plants) and the tanning process (which uses the brains of the same deer) and the person's foot inside represent a living combination of cooperation among plant, animal, and human. The word for moccasin is exactly the same as the word for foot (ké); in the Navajo mind, the moccasin becomes a part of the individual wearing it and partakes of some aspects of the person's physical being, the most noticeable of which are the indentations of the toes and the shape of the foot that develop distinctively inside each moccasin. The old adage of not criticizing others until we have walked a considerable distance (I think we have added the mile) in their moccasins is widespread in many tribes, including the Navajo, and carries more meaning than our comparatively superficial metaphor, "If the shoe fits, wear it."

The bow and arrow are still another complex of cooperative elements. The bow is made of wood, of course, and the bowstring of braided animal hide (in his bow Yellowman used cowhide). The arrows, too, come from the plants, but are guided by the feathers of birds and are tipped by arrowheads made by man. The arrowheads today are made of nails pounded out between rocks and then shaped. (Stone arrowheads are made by reptiles and are left on the ground by them for us to use in medicine.) On the arrow, at the end grasped by the fingers, are two bands of color; one of them is always red, from herb dyes, and represents danger and death. Inscribed on each arrow are lightning designs, which represent both speed and death.

Arrows are straightened by two means. One is a ram's horn through which two holes have been pierced in such a way that they provide a strain on the arrow being passed through them. The arrow is soaked and is then continually bent through these holes until the original crooks and bends are worked out of

Yellowman stands in his corn garden to be photographed with his self-made bow and arrows because he considers corn, corn pollen, hunting, and deer to be parts of the same category.

it. The older method, used in conjunction with this helper from the animal world, is the human mouth; the arrowmaker makes minor adjustments in the arrow's straightness by biting it with his teeth. Thus on the arrow itself are the toothmarks of man, the feathers of birds, lightning from the cosmos, colors derived from the vegetable world, all applied to a piece of wood.

Yellowman, describing the workings of the bow and arrow, refered to all these things as necessary points of interaction, not only in the production of the arrow itself, but in the development of an instrument to be used carefully in one of the most delicate arenas of man's interaction with his ecological environment. One further gestural dimension should be noted here: when Yellowman shot his bow, it was not held vertically, but horizontally; the hand drawing the arrow was brought back to the front of his chest, where it touched his heart before the arrow was released. In this way, in addition to all the cultural considerations mentioned, the hunter makes one final gestural commitment to his task, which, if all other ritual aspects have been successfully completed, is reciprocated at the other end by the entrance of the arrow into the heart of the pursued animal. The arrow is thus an active link between man and animal, a form of communication and communion.

We could make similar excursions into nearly every aspect of Navajo material culture, and we would find that in most cases the premises upon which each artifact is made are also found vividly in the myths, tales, and religious commentaries. Not only is the hogan the living space for the Navajo, it is where rituals occur. It is created in the shape of rituals, its round floor and east-facing door functional parts of the total alignment of human beings with the world of nature to which their rituals are addressed. Ritual space is not separated from daily life but integrated into it. The hogan, not surprisingly, is made of a combination of plants (trees and branches used for the internal structure), animal substances (like rawhide) used in the lashing of materials together, dirt from the earth covering the outside, corn pollen rubbed along the main beams inside when the hogan is blessed, and the whole combination created for, and lived in by, people whose concept of their position in the world is expressed in terms of circles and interaction with those various aspects of nature. During some ceremonies, the great sand paintings on the dirt floor of the hogan provide what appears to be a two-dimensional diagram for the forces of nature. But when the patient walks on the sand painting, the ritual creates a four-dimensional world where one is surrounded by and related to the holy powers; the same ideas are found in connection with the juniper seed necklace, the rug, and the moccasin.

It is safe to say that it would be unlikely for a Navajo woman to take a close look at any of her own artifacts and not recognize in it the epitome of the larger realities governing the world about her. Similarly, it would be unlikely for her to look at any natural scene without seeing each plant and color as potential symbol or helpful substance.

During part of the *kinaaldá*, the Navajo girls' maturation ceremony, older women who have had children have a chance to pass on their fertile influence and creative power to the new adult by "molding and straightening" her—kneading her arms, back, and legs while holding weaving implements, which are also suggestive of women's creative power. Note the wedding basket in the right foreground. Photo by Lore Erf.

Sonya Starblanket Brown pauses for a moment while grinding white cornmeal for the *kinaaldá* cake, which is baked overnight and distributed to those in attendance after dawn on the last morning of the four-day event. Photo by Lore Erf.

Women presiding over the *kinaaldá*
pour cornmeal batter, which has been
"sweetened" by the saliva of small
children in attendance, into the corn-
husk-lined pit in which the cake will
bake overnight. Photo by Lore Erf.

Sonya's mother, Vanessa Brown, helps to put the cornhusk covering over the cornmeal batter before it is baked. Photo by Lore Erf.

Sonya, holding her wedding basket, distributes pieces of her cake to those in attendance at her *kinaaldá*. Photo by Lore Erf.

The study of material culture can give us access to the deeper levels of any culture's premises and worldview if we are willing to go beyond the artifact itself into the set of abstract data it reflects. Our considerations are best guided, of course, by the people who are most intimately involved in the expressions. Let us go back to the rug briefly. Many, not all, Navajo rugs have a border. In many, not all, cases, this border is interrupted by a gap, called, in Navajo, *ch'ijdii bitiin,* "evil spirit's pathway." Some rug specialists claim that the Indians believe all rugs must have a "flaw," that every blanket needs such a road for its evil spirit to escape. But I have asked many weavers about it and have received this reply: there is no spirit in the rug and thus nothing to be let out. Rather, there is a bad condition in the mind of any weaver who believes a design can be finished off, completed, circumscribed. If a mistake occurs, it is left there as a good sign; if not, a "spirit road" can be provided. For it is the mind of the weaver, not the rug itself, that remains the Navajo concern. Never the same from rug to rug, the designs fluctuate as reference points to the weaver's continual reperformance of premises that reflect the basic worldview. The rug is an item, a product, and when it is completed it is sold. The "flaw" is a reference to the active process of the weaver's unclosed mind.

What we are speaking of, then, is a cluster of cultural and artistic codes that occasionally reach expression in a rug (or string figure, hogan, moccasin, bow/arrow, necklace) but that really exist primarily as traditional assumptions. So the real tradition is not the artifact itself, for it is a particularized statement of traditional premises and assumptions. The tradition is that dynamic process by which these premises are shared, performed, understood, and transmitted through time and space among members of a close group. This is particularly so of Navajos, for whom verbs are always more central than nouns. While many Navajos today live in frame houses, they tend to gather in circles within rooms like the kitchen and living room for social interaction, and most reservation families maintain a hogan next door to be used in ceremonies that require the shape. Urban Navajos either make a circular, eastward-facing area in their largest room when ceremonial needs arise, or they travel back to their home communities where proper facilities are available. Some younger Navajos have become very active in the intertribal powwow circuit and have thus learned the dances of tribes which might have been considered enemies in older times, but when their families and friends require their presence for healing ceremonies, they will become part of the insider audience or the performers in the *Yé'ii Bicheii* or fire dances. Like the members of most cultures today, the Navajos make their accommodations to life in school and on the job, but try to maintain the worldview assumptions formed by their traditions about movement, language, custom, and shape.

We must learn to look beyond the thing, beyond the rug, the turquoise, the moccasin, for there—with proper visual and aural training—we will begin to perceive another reality. This reality will not be discovered through recreational chemicals or Sunday witch-hunting trips to obscure mountain villages, but through the rather more difficult path of language acquisition and sensitivity to a culture's most delicate expressions of itself. We may find many separate realities along the way, for each culture will yield its own, and we will perhaps have the good fortune, then, of better witnessing the dynamic kaleidoscope of traditional thought and expression.

WORLDVIEWS IN MULTICULTURAL AMERICA

Every group that has shared a distinctive ethnic or national background for a considerable period of time will have a correspondingly distinctive worldview. Its premises are expressed in a number of ways, ranging from terms of relationships, customs in proxemics, the use of gesture, the arrangement of furniture in a room, attitudes on the proprieties of food and food consumption, and designs of houses, settlements, and cities.

Ethnicity and Worldview: African Americans

In any discussion of worldview, we need to remind ourselves continually that we are not looking for stereotypical behavior (where every individual is assumed to act and feel like all others in the group, and where those actions are judged according to the values of the outside observer). At the same time, we must remember that most ethnic groups do indeed have widespread ideas about themselves and about how other ethnic groups seem to act, think, and relate to the world, and that these ideas are very often accompanied by value judgments. For the purposes of study, we need to avoid those value judgments ourselves, but it would be foolish to overlook the unfortunate presence and vitality of ethnic prejudices that are transmitted and maintained in folklore.

We cannot say that every European American is highly motivated to compete, is continually interested in the evaluation of the passage of time, or that each European American believes himself or herself to be a distinctly independent individual. Nonetheless, those elements are widely encouraged and believed in by members of that very large category of people in America. Similarly, many African Americans share some distinctive traditions about human interactions and performances that, although they may be said to be distinctively "Black" and thus perhaps represent a distinctive worldview, cannot be used to define the roles or attitudes of any particular Black American.

As Roger Abrahams and others have shown, there is among urban African Americans a distinctive use of a style of interaction that some have called the conflict model. This term is unfortunate, for it implies a negative evaluation of this interactive style. I prefer the term *antiphonal,* or *call-and-response,* for it is based on the recognition of a responsive interaction between two or more sides in every performance frame. In the urban folklore of Black males, as Abrahams has shown, there is the custom of "playing the dozens," in which a series of insults is traded by two participants, beginning with aggressive remarks about each other and escalating to derogatory comments about each other's mother. Such an interaction ends, in the words of a Black acquaintance, in "fight or flight." Certainly, under the conditions of stylistic interaction encountered on an urban street corner, this behavior would seem like a conflict model to an onlooker. However, we must realize that the same principles of interaction can be seen in many kinds of African American expression, ranging from rural to urban, from secular to sacred. For example, it is an integral part of many Black Protestant church services, in which the congregation responds continually, in many cases to each single line or phrase, to the preacher's sermon. It is also found in many kinds of Black music, perhaps most distinctively in blues, where a line or phrase of human singing is responded to by an instrument or another voice. It is found in many of the Black work songs and jail songs that use the call-and-response style. One detects the rhythmic application of this idea in much of modern jazz, with its strong attention to the upbeat of a song (as compared, say, to White fiddling, and its prime attention to the downbeat).

Some people have suggested that the conflict model is prevalent in African American folklore because African life in America started in disequilibrium and that the Black rhythms of life ever since have reflected that formative stage. While this may certainly be true on psychological and sociological levels, it is also true that many of the African tribes themselves use a call-and-response style for all kinds of interaction. In fact, this particular stylistic tradition may be one of the few Africanisms to survive the horrible processes of kidnap, transportation, murder, and slavery that characterized the beginnings of Black life in America.

These comments of course only scratch the surface, but the reason for making them here is to point out that such a distinctive style, which can be meaningful to our understanding of the expressions, customs, and attitudes of a group of people, may be registered by other groups as a defining feature as well; in many cases, the exoteric perception of such a style can result in a stereotypical value judgment of it. For example, among European Americans, who believe that one thing should occur at a time, who want each person "to have the floor in order to speak," where we tend to submit rather readily to the deliberations of legal groups (committees, juries, regional legislatures, and so on), the Black style of immediate interaction, with all its exciting antiphony, may be seen as talkativeness, interruption, aggression, argumentation, or simple lack of manners. That is, the very device that may be positively distinctive to those who share it may be thought of as negatively distinctive by outsiders.

A high school principal once confided to me that he would be able to get along perfectly well with his African American students if only they would "not shout at me all the time." I learned that he was altogether unaware of the antiphonal style in Black music and conversations, and equally ignorant of the custom among African American males to use a wide variety of intonations during conversation. Conversations with Black friends have convinced me that many Blacks are equally unaware of the custom among White Americans to use modulated tones in formal conversation in order to avoid any variation in volume that might imply the speaker is "losing control." This broad difference in the daily application of traditions concerning culture-specific speech events has led many Whites to believe that Blacks lose control of their tempers easily, that they won't let another person finish a statement, that "they just won't listen." It has convinced many Blacks that Whites are not interested in conversation (or in the issues represented therein), that Whites never really get committed to anything conversationally, and that "they just won't listen."

If we add to this the common ingredient found in worldview contrasts—a kind of fear or paranoia concerning those who process reality and human expression differently—we get a faint glimmer of how the study of folklore relates to racial and social dynamics in a multicultural country such as America; for whenever fear enters such relationships, especially when that fear is founded upon and nourished by folk traditions that believers feel represent normalcy and stability, merely rational or political approaches will not suffice for the discussion and resolution of conflicts and problems.

Ethnicity and Worldview: Spanish Americans, Mexican Americans, Latinos

An equally brief (but I hope not unfair) look at Hispanic American custom and lore reveals a distinctive set of expressions that mirror cultural attitudes about the world and the way we must cope with it. In addition to the retention of the Spanish language, which of course favors maintaining an esoteric system, Hispanic Americans place a very high value on family ties and community obligations. There may be occasional strife between families in a community, but in general there is the widespread assumption that traditions hold a village or a barrio together against the onslaughts of the outside and aggressive world.

Sickness may come about when another person threatens us by coveting something we own. The condition brought about by this situation is called evil eye, and an insider knows enough to touch the other person when paying a compliment to take away the possibility of causing illness or death. Other kinds of evil can be visited upon a community or a family from without; *susto,* "shock," is only one of several kinds of malevolent effects of witchcraft. The community deals with these matters by its own internal means: there are traditional ways of trying to ward off evil, evil eye, and shock, just as there are traditional ways of curing their effects when contracted. *Curanderos* or *curanderas* are folk healers who know the language, the customs, the medicines, and the attitudes of the people. Many Mexican Americans would prefer to go to a *curandero* than to a licensed physician precisely because the folk healer knows more about the psychosomatic elements of the malady and knows how to deal with them in culturally recognized and accepted ways. A member of your close group is more likely to cure you than a stranger who scoffs at your ways. Many Hispanic Americans visit both a physician and a *curandera* when they are ill.

There are now several examples of clinics or other services that have been set up by Anglo-Americans to aid Mexicans (for example, in migrant labor camps) and that have failed because the physicians or the lawyers or the social workers did not know enough about Mexican folklore to keep themselves from slipping into the category of an outside threat. For example, a Mexican worker with an injury comes to see a doctor at a free clinic. Following his tradition, he brings his entire family with him, and they wait patiently in the outer lounge while the doctor provides his services. When the doctor and patient emerge, the doctor attempts to show how friendly he is toward Mexicans by complimenting the worker's children on their good looks or health or pretty clothes. In the usual Anglo manner, he does not circulate among them and touch them as he makes his complimentary remarks, and thus he unknowingly exposes them to the effects of the evil eye. Later, when one of the children has an accident or becomes sick, the family may feel that it was brought about by the strange actions of the doctor. When several such incidents occur, word gets around that the clinic is not a good place to go if one wants to stay healthy; business falls off; the clinic closes.

For the doctors involved, who have selflessly donated their time in addition to their regular duties, this is easily interpretable as lack of appreciation on the part of the Mexicans, or it may be attributed to anti-Anglo feelings, political designs, or laziness. In other words, the conditions are "logically" judged from the observer's cultural point of view. Even if the Mexican attitude is explained to these doctors, they may very likely become contemptuous and respond with something like, "Well, if they're going to let their superstitions stand in the way of good health, then they get what they deserve." Similarly, the Mexican people involved will interpret it according to their own worldview traditions and will see that their own avoidance of the clinic has protected them and their families from potential illness brought about by outsiders. Each group may end up resenting the other for what has happened.

Ethnic Folklore and Cultural Terminology

The study of varying worldviews among ethnic and national groups in America remains one of the most important unfinished tasks for folklorists and anthropologists, for these cultural patterns are very seldom expressed when people give rational, personal answers to questionnaires, surveys, and other formal attempts to gauge people's opinions. Rather, since cultural concepts are shared most fully with those people we have the greatest identity with, they tend to become integral parts and premises of our folk performances and beliefs. Thus the folklorist and the anthropologist are much more likely to discover their forms and meanings as they exist in the events of traditional life than are other investigators.

And, as shown earlier, in even the most brief discussion of these elements of culture we see that they are of more than passing interest: they seem to underlie the daily events that determine our political, economic, educational, and—in many cases—personal decisions and conflicts.

We find we get along best with those folk groups whose worldviews most closely approximate our own on problematic issues. Asian Americans have a reputation for being quiet and law-abiding citizens largely because their strong concept of family identity and filial piety, coupled with an apparent reverence for formal authority, seem to make them the epitome of behavioral character-istics we would like to see in all "law-abiding citizens." One juvenile judge confided to me that he almost inevitably awarded probation to offenders of Asian backgrounds because he considered them exceptions, and because he knew their families would take care of disciplinary matters properly; at the same time, he bragged rather forcefully that it was typical for him to give stiff sentences to Black youths because he believed they were typical of their group, that they had no family context, that they were basically aggressive and insub-ordinate, and that for those "reasons" the larger community needed to make an example of them. In a case like this (and such instances are not rare in this country) justice is based not as much on the individual or on the crime as on feelings generated by similarities or dissimilarities in vernacular worldview. That they can be rationalized so neatly is a demonstration of how central folk-lore is to our daily "rational" behavior.

One finds them multiformly on an international level as well, such as in the famous argument at the Paris peace talks at the end of the Vietnam War: The North Vietnamese required that a round table be used so that negotiation could take place, and they interpreted American resistance to this plan as a sure sign that the Americans would not sit down in good faith. The Americans, on the other hand, insisted on a square table, taking the Vietnamese resistance to this "logical" proposal to indicate that surely the Vietnamese had not come with serious intent. It is easy to imagine that the diplomatic, economic, and religious history of the world is more fully characterized by cultural squabbles over the shape of tables, the nature of time, the ownership of land and water, the exist-ence and nature of God, than it is by famous names and "rational, objective" thinking. It is probably not the job of a folklorist to unscramble and solve all these matters, but certainly it does seem within the reach of this field to help us understand the dynamics and the social, political importance of traditional worldview more fully than we have in the past.

For one thing, we will not make the mistake of thinking that the names by which different groups want to be called are only some kind of nonsense. Afri-can American people are no doubt weary of puzzled White people whining, "Well, I just don't know what to call you people these days," as are Hispanic Americans tired of hearing, "Last year it was Chicano, and now you want us to call you Hispanic; what's going on?" Once we realize that each of these terms has a function and a meaning—many of them political—we can ask how those meanings might point us to shared cultural factors. For example, Americans of Brazilian ancestry have Portuguese as an inherited family language; for them, the term "Latino" suggests a sharing of geographical and linguistic affinity with other folks from south of the border without limiting that association to descendants of *Spanish*-speaking cultures. The term "chicano" for many activist Mexican Americans of the 1960s called attention to the Aztec dimension of their heritage, which for many in turn provided fuller acknowledgment of their *mestizo*, thus their down-to-earth, culture—in contradistinction to the elite nuances of "Spanish American." On the other hand, for the descendants of Spanish colonists in what was then the Northwest of New Spain (New Mexico, Arizona, California), the term "Spanish" feels more accurate than "Mexican"—even though the area was also later a part of Mexico before it eventually became the Southwest of the United States.

For many of our recent arrivals, tribal names (like Hmong and Lao) are markers of custom and language which animate most of their cultures in ways that political or geographic labels like "Vietnamese," or "Southeast Asian" do not. Moreover, we are aware that among the groups who may have language affinities (such as Spanish) there are other associations that are culturally just as important: many Spanish-speaking people are also Black; many Black people (in Haiti, for example) speak French, while others from the West Indies speak British English.

In America (both North and South), we have a wide variety of peoples from Asian backgrounds, hence the term "Asian" gives us only a very general idea of the geographical family origins of an immensely varied range of people. Chinese Americans often associate with and identify with others whose families came from particular parts of China, maintaining regional food preferences and dialectal variations. Japanese Americans usually identify themselves according to their generation, counting from the immigrants, the "first people," called *issei* (the second generation—newly born in the United States—are called *nisei* [*ni*-means two or second], and the third generation are the *sansei* [*san*-means three or third]); although these terms are Japanese, they are seldom used in Japan, where immigration sequences are not central to cultural identity.

North of Mexico, it is estimated that we have more than 150 Native American languages in daily use: not dialects, but languages. This in turn means that there are more than 150 different Native cultures alive today in North America, to say nothing of the many others which died out or were killed off. This is arguably more cultures than exist today in western Europe, yet we commonly refer to them in a lump—using Columbus's mistaken identification of his position—as "Indians." Obviously, this term is about as useful, culturally, as the term "European."

If we want to learn what effects the variety of worldviews may be having on the world we live in, it is incumbent on us to determine who the cultures are, and on what basis their assumptions are formed and transmitted. Noting—and taking seriously—how a group calls itself at any point in history will tell us a lot about that group's sense of identity in their own terms, not in the technical jargon of the sociologist or the fearful labels of the political analyst.

The overview of cultures given here is necessarily meager and superficial, and my comments have only addressed a few noticeable features. Obviously, there is much more to Euro-American culture than time and technology, much more to Navajo culture than rugs and moccasins, much more to African American culture than the call-and-response model, much more to Hispanic culture than *curanderismo*, much more to all our Asian cultures than food, festival, and dance. The reader is urged to take these comments as provocative and suggestive (in the academic sense), and build on them by careful observation of these and other cultural groups—including one's own—as they perform their folklore for each other in everyday contexts.

TECHNOLOGY AND WORLDVIEW

Although technology and machinery in general may not seem at first blush to have much connection with folklore, in a general way we may see the function of technology (in the way it is used, in the extent to which it means something) as a larger analogy to the observations made earlier about the Navajo production of material items reflecting certain cultural attitudes. Technology does not arise simply because one culture is smart enough to invent a helpful or useful item while another culture is not. Rather, items are developed that fit into the assumptions of worldview. It would be absurd for a culture to devise a machine to perform some function that the culture thought abominable. It is no coincidence, for example, that the tremendously sophisticated technology of modern warfare has been under continual intensive development precisely in those cultures where physical property has been considered valuable (and therefore its destruction would be a meaningful act) and in which occupation and ownership of another's land constitutes a meaningful resolution of a culture's dilemma. In cultures where such questions are settled more satisfactorily by bashing in someone's head, the instruments of war that provide that particular function are articulated with brilliant inventiveness. Those cultures that have more recently become interested in land acquisition or power have of course become more interested in the technology with which to accomplish their ends; in such cases, no doubt because of the good offices of American and European education, there seems to be more worldwide interest in almost any usable airplane than in the most beautifully articulated war club. But as I hope to point out, such technological borrowings are not often accomplished without a heavy price being exacted from the stability of the recipients' culture.

From Corn God to Tractor in Northern Europe

Technology as we know it in Europe and America is in part an extension of some common worldview features once shared by many people. If we imagine trying to face the demands of agriculture in northern Europe in early times, we can appreciate how beautiful the earliest agricultural machines must have seemed. The growing season is short, the winter long. Food supplies must be laid up for a long and intense winter, yet planting and harvesting must be carried out under the most limited and trying circumstances. Work itself must have been highly valued simply in terms of survival. Future planning would have become absolutely necessary as an increase in the number of people placed continually greater demands on those involved in agriculture. People would certainly have looked forward to the winter solstice as that magical hint of eventual return to warmth and fertility. Under these circumstances, almost any invention that would have made plowing, planting, fertilization, and harvesting more efficient would have been considered something close to a religious blessing. From what little we know of the mythological evidence of those early days in northern Europe, we know that fertility of plants was one of the most central concerns. Just as the priests of the river cultures in the Middle East gained stability for their cultures and power for themselves by learning to predict the annual floods, so must any inventor of an agricultural implement have gained personal prestige and an added margin of survival for his people in those dark grainfields of northern Europe.

But as in all traditions, the conservative element tends to dictate what is maintained. Thus there has always been a driving compulsion to develop a better plow, very likely because the plow was considered basic and necessary. So even though soil experts have recently concluded that plowing earth is one of the more certain ways to reduce the longevity of the soil, we continue even today to build larger plows and larger, more powerful tractors to pull them. In the modern tractor and plow we can see a physical, technological extension of a set of ideas that really reflect folk attitudes and worldview concepts of a culture that has survived through the development of agricultural processes which allowed people to deal aggressively with nature for survival.

"I'll Be down to Get You in My One-Eyed Ford"
(From a 1930s Navajo Song)

Another example of how technology may extend a cultural idea rather than conflict with it can be found in the current use of pickup trucks by Navajos. Despite their stalwart ethnocentrism, Navajos have always been quite willing to adopt other cultures' items that can be used in a Navajo way or that can extend one's

Traditional methods of stacking loose hay outdoors in the arid West vary by locality and culture.
In "Mormon   Country"—Utah, southern Idaho,
southwestern Wyoming, northeastern Arizona,
and eastern Nevada—the "Mormon Derrick" has
become the icon of local ranching custom, though
the owner need not belong to the Mormon church.
In other areas nearby, the "Overshot Stacker" and
the "Beaver Slide" are more common. Photos by
Austin Fife.

capabilities of being Navajo. One of the most central ideas in Navajo grammar, folklore, and religion is the metaphor of movement. Central to almost all Navajo conversational expressions, it receives heightened attention in healing rituals, in which the patient is described as moving in various ways among the holy people. The Worth and Adair experiment, mentioned previously, produced several movies in which the Navajo filmmakers had used movement of people and animals across a landscape as the basic framework for an entire idea. The well-known Navajo ritual phrase for completeness, beauty, longevity, and good health is phrased as a wish that beauty may be ahead of us, behind us, on both sides of us, above us and below us, as we go along. In former times, the Navajo riding on horseback provided the physical counterpart of this religious image: the self-contained harmonious individual, related to other live elements of nature, taking reality along with him as he went. Today the pickup truck provides an extension of this metaphor in everyday Navajo life. Thus, even though a given Navajo may choose to retain Navajo hair styles, clothing, and language, he may feel no hesitation at all in buying a pickup truck as a means of transportation, for it is much more than the practical element that makes it functional in his life. Additionally, the current widespread use of citizens band radio in Navajo trucks allows for an even more significant extension to take place. Tourists driving through the Southwest in recent years have tried in vain to contact aloof Navajos on their CB radios. But those who have monitored bands in that area have noticed that when a Navajo call goes over the air, the channel comes alive with Navajo responses. The pickup truck allows for an extension of the Navajo metaphor of movement into the realities of the modern world; the CB radio allows a similar extension of the Navajo language across space, but primarily for Navajo-style contacts and interactions with other Navajos.

The Ax, the Alphabet, and the TV

The borrowing of other cultures' technological devices does not always have a salutary effect on the borrower, however. There is the now well-known and melancholy story of the introduction of steel axes into Australia by missionaries and shopkeepers. In a culture where stone axes were produced by painstaking labor over long periods of time, they had been for many tribes the symbol of a patriarchal system, the basis for family stability, the center in many cases for religious meaning. When steel axes became widely available, all of these important cultural features were demolished within a few years for the tribes concerned. Even more extensive than the advent of the ax itself, of course, is the desire and demand it creates for other implements, such as sharpening stones, scabbards, extra handles, and the like, which create the need for further and more articulated contacts between the cultures. Since in a case like this the advantages are almost always on the side of the culture that controls the technology, such contacts can result in corrosion or downright destruction of the worldviews of the recipient of technological charity.

The pickup has become the successor to the horse for many Native Americans; this one, parked at the annual Crow Fair in Montana in 1979, bears markings suggestive of the Appaloosa (developed by Native Americans from a breed brought by the early Spaniards) and a warrior's hand stamp. Photo by Michael Crummett, courtesy of the American Folklife Center, Library of Congress (Montana Folklife Survey 1979).

This seems to have been the case for many of the Indian tribes of the northeastern United States and Canada. Formerly restricted in their killing of animals by rigid taboos and regulations which provided that certain animals could be killed only by certain means at certain times of the year, the Micmacs had enjoyed for generations untold a constant food supply ready to hand. When Whites interested in beaver pelts began to supply the Indians with firearms, when the local medicine men were at the same time so incapable of curing the new European diseases that they and their religious views were easily subordinated, and when this considerable bombardment to the local sense of stability was strengthened by Christian missionaries preaching individual salvation and hard work, it did not take long for the Indians to begin competing with each other for beaver pelts, driving the animals almost to extinction, and unwittingly sealing the fate of their own cultural worldview. Without the beaver to maintain them, ponds and bogs drained, depriving moose and other related animals of their normal habitat. Food animals vacated the area; poverty moved in.

Not many years ago the government of Malaysia decided that it might communicate more readily with the widespread villages in the countryside by installing small TV sets in a central public location where announcements could be made, helpful programs could be aired, and a sense of national togetherness could be fostered. In these villages there was already an institution, a place called a *wakaf*, which is a small, verandalike structure in the middle of the village where different groups of people could meet during the day, usually separated in their timing by gender and age, to discuss various important subjects. Many of the people in Malaysia are Moslems, and the sexual separation on these occasions reflected for them a religious as well as a secular custom. The installation of small TV sets in the village coffee shop did provide the government with almost instantaneous contact with its own villagers. At the same time, however, it attracted people away from the traditional communication system provided by the *wakaf*. And, since TV watchers are all facing in the same direction, not talking to each other, the presence of males and females in the same room was found to be tolerable.

Thus began not only the gradual disintegration of a village communication system that had operated since ancient times, but also a secularization of human relationships within the village that had been regulated by religious precepts. Additionally, TV programs depicted the human body, something that orthodox Islam has always opposed as a kind of sacrilege. Because the item through which this irreligious experience occurred was not of their own making, the villagers apparently had no way of working out for themselves the impact it was creating subtly in their own lives.

More recently, Malaysian communications experts have lamented that while the TV program has been useful in the strictly technical sense, it has endangered, rather than strengthened, the sense of unity that authorities had hoped would be a foundation for national pride and development. A Malaysian professor pointed out bitterly at an international conference on traditional communications that "we have had to learn that we cannot expect to adopt the machinery of the Western world without adopting the philosophies and world-views upon which that machinery is predicated." He went on to warn other nations to recognize that a technological object is not merely an object, but an item of cultural communication; he asked fellow participants to scrutinize the concept that technology itself is benign, that it can be utilized the way the user sees fit. Along with the thing comes its idea, and the idea is often culture-specific. Without the idea, without the worldview it represents, the object is often of little value or use.

Educational TV systems had been offered to the Malaysian government as positive elements to help them build a stronger culture, as devices to aid them as independent participants in the world community. Instead, many Malaysians now feel that the introduction of village television may be only a thinly masked intrusion of American political philosophy into Southeast Asia. Whether or not such an effect was intentional, we may see in this example the beginnings of the kind of fear and resentment that I have suggested are common when world-views intersect. We may expect them to be especially strong feelings when it seems as though one worldview is trying subtly to obliterate or modify another. We have no right to congratulate ourselves for wiping out patriarchal systems in Australia, "primitive" hunting and "pagan" religion in America, or sexual segregation in Malaysia, even though such ends may be consonant with our high moral concept of ourselves and our sense of advanced liberation. Wanton destruction of other cultures, for whatever lofty purpose, should be added to the list of deadly sins and capital offenses.

The tensions, frictions, and outright wars that have characterized the history of Africa, Ireland, the Balkans, the Middle East, and many other places are as much the outgrowths of conflicting cultural worldviews as they are of conscious political, religious, and economic factors. For this reason, they are not susceptible to easy resolution through the objective application of political, religious, and economic principles. The study of folklore will not produce an immediate resolution to these conflicts either, but it may certainly help reveal the foundations of ethnic and national malaise, and, more importantly, it can help us see that in each case a worldview is internally valid, consistent among its parts, and effective as a means of relating the mind of the individual to those larger occurrences of the world around. From fist fights to international war, conflicts seldom occur between Good Guys and Bad Guys, or between Right and Wrong; more typically, battles occur between two parties who are both right in their own estimation. Insofar as folk tradition, in the form of ethnic or national worldview informally transmitted among members of close groups, constitutes the background or matrix of situations arising around us in the world, these matters do indeed become important aspects of our field of study.

BIBLIOGRAPHICAL NOTES

The study of cultural worldview is far more complex than the scope of this chapter. These references are therefore grouped into the areas of concern brought up in the chapter; I assume the reader will take the subject far beyond the meager suggestions offered here. The minority peoples discussed in this chapter are perhaps the easiest to see; but the same considerations must be applied to the immigrants from European cultures, to the tremendous variety of Indian tribes, to the varying Black and Hispanic communities, to the different Asian groups, and so on. I have referred to the peoples and studies I am most familiar with; you must do the same: study the urban Greek community, the Russian Old Believers, the Irish in New York, the Italians in Chicago, the Scandinavians in Minnesota, the Basques in the Great Basin, the Spanish colonial descendants in New Mexico, as well as the later immigrants from Mexico. Each group is likely to exhibit a distinct worldview that may be encountered in its language, customs, proxemic rules, folk arts, jokes, and songs. Florence R. Kluckhohn and Fred L. Strodtbeck show how differently five close groups in the American Southwest perceive and express their relationship to the same ecological surroundings in *Variations in Value Orientations* (Evanston, Ill.: Row, Peterson, 1961). The importance of this kind of observation cannot be underestimated.

Some general comments on worldview, especially as it relates to topics of concern to folklorists, may be found in the following works: William Bascom suggests, in "Folklore, Verbal Art, and Culture," *Journal of American Folklore* 83 (1973): 374-81, that in a nonliterate culture, folklore is synonymous with the culture; this might provide a beginning for the discussion of how to approach aliterate cultures like ours (in which many people are literate, but in which we continue to transmit many of our cultural views orally and gesturally). Ruth Benedict, *Patterns of Culture* (New York: Penguin, 1934), while somewhat outdated now, is a basic study. Alan Dundes, *Every Man His Way: Readings in Cultural Anthropology* (Englewood Cliffs, N.J.: Prentice-Hall, 1968), presents an outstanding array of essays on cultural differences, most of them related to matters of worldview. See especially Dorothy Lee, "Codifications of Reality: Lineal and Non-Lineal," 329-43; Alan Dundes, "The Number Three in American Culture," 401-24; Horace Miner, "Body Ritual among the Nacirema," 433-38; Laura Bohannan, "Shakespeare in the Bush," 477-86. The works of Edward T. Hall are almost all related to the topic of worldview, and they contain innumerable comparative examples; his books *The Silent Language, The Hidden Dimension,* and *Beyond Culture* (Garden City, N.Y.: Doubleday, 1959, 1966, and 1977 respectively) are basic and uncomplicated. His three-level system, put forward in the first book, is illuminating, but probably oversimplified. In *Patterns of Discovery: An Inquiry into the Conceptual Foundations of Science* (Cambridge: Cambridge University Press, 1958), Norwood Russell Hanson shows the extent to which even our most scientific observations are channeled and defined by worldview. Harry Hoijer, ed., *Language in Culture* (Chicago: University of Chicago Press, 1954), presents a series of essays on the relationship between cultural worldview and language. Johan Huizinga, *Homo Ludens: A Study of the Play-Element in Culture* (Boston: Beacon Press, 1955), shows how a particular kind of expression—often one overlooked because of its everyday aspects—relates to cultural views. Benjamin Lee Whorf, one of the principal proponents of the hypothesis that language shapes and is shaped by culture, presented his views in *Language, Thought, and Reality* (New York:

Technology Press, 1956); most scholars today do not accept the whole argument, yet many, including Hall, have based their theories on the general proposition brought up by Whorf (and discussed by Lee, above): individuals see chiefly what their culture (including their language) has trained them to see. A fair and insightful review and reassessment of Whorf (and of subsequent scholarship) on language and worldview is provided by Jane Hill and Bruce Mannheim, "Language and Worldview," *Annual Review of Anthropology* 21 (1992): 381–406.

Relationships between worldview, culture, and childhood are discussed by Erik H. Erikson, *Childhood and Society,* 2nd ed. (New York: Norton, 1950); see especially his comments on the tenacity with which Native American schoolchildren retain customs and attitudes formed at home in spite of the well-intentioned efforts of both teachers and parents to change them when school problems arise (131). The effects of the lullaby, both in function of music and content of words, are discussed by Bess Lomax Hawes in "Folksongs and Function: Some Thoughts on the American Lullaby," *Journal of American Folklore* 87 (1974): 140-48. See also Mary Knapp and Herbert Knapp, *One Potato, Two Potato: The Secret Education of American Children* (New York: Norton, 1976) and Ione and Peter Opie, *The Lore and Language of Schoolchildren* (London: Oxford University Press, 1959), especially Chapter 8, "Code of Oral Legislation," 121-53. Both books deal with the powerful ways in which children learn an entire way of life from their peers through the dynamic processes of tradition. Although the Opies omit reference to "crude" materials, which they consider unrepresentative of the good child, the Knapps apparently have had better advice from their young informants. For other examples and analyses of children's folklore, see Simon J. Bronner, *American Children's Folklore* (Little Rock, Ark.: August House, 1988), which is drawn from collections and archives nationwide and offers an excellent bibliography; Jay Mechling, "Children's Folklore," in *Folk Groups and Folklore Genres,* ed. Oring, 91–120 (also includes a solid bibliography); and follow the discussions brought out by specialists in *Children's Folklore Review* (published twice a year by East Carolina University for the American Folklore Society Children's Folklore Section).

For discussions of folk ideas and their relation to custom, behavior, and culture, see at least the following: Alan Dundes, "Folk Ideas as Units of Worldview," *Journal of American Folklore* 84 (1971): 93-103, reprinted in Paredes and Bauman, *New Perspectives,* cited previously, and Dundes's "Thinking Ahead: A Folkloristic Reflection on the Future Orientation in American Worldview," *Anthropological Quarterly* 42 (1969): 53-72.

Edward T. Hall, who originated the term *proxemics,* discusses the traditions of where we place ourselves in relation to other people in space in "Proxemics," *Current Anthropology* 9 (1968): 83-108 (including discussions and a valuable bibliography); his "impressionistic" observations on Arab and American proxemics (Arabs stand closer to each other than do Americans) is confirmed in Michael O. Watson and Theodore D. Graves, "Quantitative Research in Proxemic Behavior," *American Anthropologist* 68 (1966): 971-85. The idea of leaving a flaw in a rug (Navajo) has parallels in related crafts among other cultures: Suzi Jones found the same idea among quilters in Oregon, where there is a common notion that perfection in a quilt would be presumptuous, for the quilter would not be humble before God. See *Oregon Folklore,* 113. Jones notes that the construction of a quilt is so complex that the quilter does not need to strive for humility.

For an elucidation of how the African American worldview is expressed in folklore, see, of course, Roger D. Abrahams, *Deep Down in the Jungle* and *Positively Black,* both mentioned previously. Also illuminating are the many essays in Alan Dundes, *Mother Wit from the Laughing Barrel: Readings in the Interpretation of Afro-American Folklore* (Englewood Cliffs, N.J.: Prentice-Hall, 1973). For more texts of the "toasts," along with perceptive remarks on their meaning and context, see Bruce Jackson, *Get Your Ass in the Water and Swim Like Me* (Cambridge, Mass.: Harvard University Press, 1974). Langston Hughes and Arna Bontemps, *The Book of Negro Folklore* (New York: Dodd, Mead, 1958), and J. Mason Brewer, *American Negro Folklore* (Chicago: Quadrangle, 1968), are both fine collections of Black folklore assembled by Black scholars; they omit much of the "obscene" folklore that characterizes the traditions of most young urban people of all groups today, with the result that the collections seem slanted toward the older kinds of folk performances. A good collection of Black folktales is Richard Dorson, *American Negro Folktales* (New York: Fawcett, 1967), although, since it contains tales collected by a White from Black informants, it is difficult to determine how fully representative it may be of the Black worldview; there is always the possibility that the stories are those that Black people felt most like sharing with an ethnic "outsider." Other scholarship on African American folklore demonstrates both the retention of earlier African expressions and the dynamic development of Black American traditions in a variety of communities. See Harold Courlander, *A Treasury of Afro-American Folklore* (New York: Crown Publishers, 1976); Daryl Cumber Dance, *Shuckin' and Jivin': Folklore from Contemporary Black Americans* (Bloomington: Indiana University Press, 1978); Bessie Jones and Bess Lomax Hawes, *Step It Down: Games, Plays, Songs, and Stories from the Afro-American Heritage* (New York: Harper & Row, 1972); Beverly J. Robinson, *Aunt [änt] Phyllis* (Berkeley: Regent Press, 1989); Patricia A. Turner, *Ceramic Uncles and Celluloid Mammies: Black Images and Their Influence on Culture* (New York: Doubleday, 1994), for a wide-ranging and incisive look at stereotypes in material form; Turner, *I Heard It through the Grapevine: Rumor in African-American Culture* (Berkeley: University of California Press, 1993); Gladys-Marie Fry, *Night Riders in Black Folk History* (Knoxville: University of Tennessee Press, 1975); Lawrence W. Levine, *Black Culture and Black Consciousness: Afro-American Folk Thought from Slavery to Freedom* (New York: Oxford University Press, 1978); John W. Roberts, "African American Diversity and the Study of Folklore," *Western Folklore* 52 (1993): 157–71; Roberts, *From Trickster to Badman: The Black Folk Hero in Slavery and Freedom* (Philadelphia: University of Pennsylvania Press, 1989); William H. Wiggins, *O Freedom! Afro-American Emancipation Celebrations* (Knoxville: University of Tennessee Press, 1987).

Folkloric studies of Hispanic American culture are relatively rare. The reader might start with the "Southwest Mexicans" section of Dorson's *Buying the Wind: Regional Folklore in the United States* (Chicago: University of Chicago Press, 1964), 415-95, along with the companion section in Dorson's *American Folklore* (Chicago: University of Chicago Press, 1959), l0l-12 ("Spanish New Mexico"). Sylvia Ann Grider studies a particular form of urban Chicano folklore in "Con Safos: Mexican-Americans, Names and Graffiti," *Journal of American Folklore* 88 (1975): 132-42. Joan W. Moore, *Mexican Americans* (Englewood Cliffs, N.J.: Prentice-Hall, 1970), provides a succinct and compelling account of Mexicans in America with a considerable focus on traditional customs and beliefs, though folklore, by name, is not overtly discussed. In the foreword and the introduction to his *Folktales of Mexico* (Chicago: University of Chicago Press, 1970), xi-lxxxiii, Américo Paredes provides a most helpful account of major themes in Mexican narrative folklore that distinctly mirror culture-specific views. Irwin Press, "The Urban Curandero," *American Anthropologist* 73 (1971): 741-56, demonstrates the vitality and function of urban folk healers in Bogota, Colombia. There are many studies of folklore in the countries of Central and South America, of course, but few of them are available in translation. Until North Americans shake off their reluctance to learn our most prominent neighboring language, these works will remain essentially beyond our reach—as will most of the traditional performances of the Mexican Americans, who now make up the largest "minority" group in most of the western states. See also Richard G. Del Castillo, *La Familia: Chicano Families in the Urban Southwest 1848 to the Present* (Notre Dame, Ind.: University of Notre Dame Press, 1984); James S. Griffith, *Beliefs and Holy Places: A Spiritual Geography of the Pimería Alta* (Tucson: University of Arizona Press, 1992); José E. Límon, "Folklore, Social Conflict, and the United States-Mexico Border," in *Handbook of American Folklore*, ed. Richard M. Dorson (Bloomington: Indiana University Press, 1980), 216–22; Américo Paredes, *"With His Pistol in His Hand": A Border Ballad and Its Hero* (Austin: University of Texas Press, 1978); Stanley Robe, *Hispanic Folktales from New Mexico* (Berkeley: University of California Press, 1977); María Herrera-Sobek, *Northward Bound: The Mexican Immigrant Experience in Ballad and Song* (Bloomington: Indiana University Press, 1993); James S. Griffith's *Southern Arizona Folk Arts* (Tucson: University of Arizona Press, 1988) contains an entertaining chapter on Mexican American art, especially celebrative.

Books on the Native American have appeared as regularly as stacks in the local pancake parlor, and most of them are as hastily produced. I do not have the space here to evaluate the many frauds and the few triumphs in this area. For some guidance in the area of worldview, the reader should consult Walter Holden Capps, ed., *Seeing with a Native Eye: Essays on Native American Religion* (New York: Harper & Row, 1976), and Dennis Tedlock and Barbara Tedlock, eds., *Teachings from the American Earth: Indian Religion and Philosophy* (New York: Liveright, 1975). For revealing accounts of particular tribes, see Joseph Epes Brown and Black Elk, *The Sacred Pipe* (1953; reprint ed., New York: Penguin, 1971), which discusses the seven sacred rites of the Oglalla Sioux in relation to the Sioux worldview; Alfonso Ortiz, *The Tewa World: Space, Time, Being, and Becoming in a Pueblo Society* (Chicago: University of Chicago Press, 1969); Edwin Wade and David Evans, "The Kachina Sash: A Native Model of the Hopi World," *Western Folklore* 32 (1973): 1-18. Popular among Indian faddists have been Hyemeyohsts Storm's *Seven Arrows* (New York: Harper & Row, 1972) and Frank Waters, *Book of the Hopi* (New York: Viking, 1963). Both have been repudiated by the tribes concerned. More substantive are works like Gary Witherspoon's *Language and Art in the Navajo Universe* (Ann Arbor: University of Michigan Press, 1977), which details the logic and verbal richness of the Navajo language so that non-Navajos can almost understand it (for example, showing how the language has 356,200 conjugations for the verb *to go*); Richard K. Nelson, an anthropologist who has lived extensively among the Alaskan Athabascans, has written a series of very sensitive and illuminating books: among them are *Hunters of the Northern Forests* (1973) and *Make Prayers to the Raven: A Koyukon View of the Northern Forest* (1983), both by University of Chicago Press. See also Rodney Frey, *The World of the Crow Indians: As Driftwood*

Lodges (Norman: University of Oklahoma Press, 1987); Trudy Griffin-Pierce, *Earth Is My Mother, Sky Is My Father: Space, Time, and Astronomy in Navajo Sandpainting* (Albuquerque: University of New Mexico Press, 1992).

The relation of cultural worldview to our concepts of environment and to the way we deal with the environment (as in farming) can be profitably studied by noting how our European ancestors felt about nature and fertility: see Sir James George Frazer, *The New Golden Bough,* ed. Theodor H. Gaster (New York: Criterion, 1959). With regard to plowing, *National Geographic* 45 (July 1976) shows studies that indicate that eight inches of topsoil will last an average of 36 years if plowed in straight lines, about 104 years if contour-plowed, and about 2,224 years if the seeds are "drilled" through unplowed turf. Yet one expects that many tractor companies and the farmers will not want to give up what they consider to be normal practices in order to "go back" (note the linear concept) to what they consider primitive farming methods. Our cultural romance with tractors has developed so far that they are often viewed as old friends or pets: see Roger Welsch's *Old Tractors and the Men Who Love Them: How to Keep Your Tractor Happy and Your Family Running* (Osceola, Wisc.: Motorbooks International, 1995). For further remarks on worldview and the way we register our environment, see David Lowenthal, "Geography, Experience, and Imagination: Towards a Geographical Epistemology," *Annals,* Association of American Geographers 51 (1961): 241-60, reprinted in *Man, Space, and Environment,* ed. Paul W. English and Robert C. Mayfield (New York: Oxford University Press, 1972), 219-44, esp. 233-40. Equally important is Wilbur Zelinsky's fuller treatment of cultural patterns in relation to patterns on the land, *The Cultural Geography of the United States* (Englewood Cliffs, N.J.: Prentice-Hall, 1973); Zelinsky makes some pointed remarks about American linearity in time and space. Two other works already mentioned in other chapters bear repeating in this list: Yi-Fu Tuan, *Topophilia,* and Lewis Mumford, *The City in History.* In Chapters 1-4 of the latter, Mumford provides an exciting view of religion, ritual, and worldview as they relate to the concept of early villages and cities. For an illuminating survey of the ways in which material objects and technology express and intersect with cultural constructs, see Thomas J. Schlereth, ed., *Material Culture: A Research Guide* (Lawrence: University Press of Kansas, 1985).

In the area of culture "contact," acculturation, colonization, or direct friction between worldviews, the following are enlightening. Of course, to begin with, the reader will want to become reacquainted with William Hugh Jansen, "The Esoteric/Exoteric Factor," reprinted in Dundes, *The Study of Folklore,* 4–51. In addition, Don Adams, "The Monkey and the Fish: Cultural Pitfalls of an Educational Advisor," *International Development Review* 2 (1960): 22-24, reprinted in Dundes, *Every Man His Way,* 504-10; John H. Bodley, *Victims of Progress* (Menlo Park, Calif.: Cummings, 1975); Pertti J. Pelto, *The Snowmobile Revolution: Technology and Social Change in the Arctic* (Menlo Park, Calif.: Cummings, 1973); Robert Tonkinson, *The Jigalong Mob: Victors of the Desert Crusade* (Menlo Park, Calif.: Cummings, 1974); Calvin Martin, "The European Impact on the Culture of a Northeastern Algonquian Tribe: An Ecological Interpretation," *William and Mary Quarterly* 31 (1974): 3-21; Francis E. Dart, "The Cultural Context of Science Teaching," *Search* 4, no. 8 (August 1973): 322-27. Dart, a physicist, found that different cultural views of nature and knowledge, different cultural organizations of evidence, affected the learning process of students forced to think, perform, and compete academically in a system not their own.

The colonial role of television in Malaysia came to my attention in a fascinating paper given by Mohd. Dahlan HjAman at an international conference on traditional media held at the East-West Communication Institute, Honolulu, July 7-August 1, 1975; Dahlan's presentation was entitled "The Sociocultural Significance of Traditional Gathering Centers in Peasant Fishing Communities in Malaysia." A hint of the psychological aspect of cultural differences may be gained by reading "Language Differences," by Warren Ten Houten, in *Behavior Today* (March 3, 1975): 407, which gives a brief account of the UCLA study on Hopi children (right brain-centered). For solid folkloristic perspectives on everyday issues in today's society, see Jay Mechling, "On Sharing Folklore and American Identity in a Multicultural Society," *Western Folklore* 52 (1993): 271–89.

At the beginning of a Navajo wedding, David Doctor leads bride Mary Gray (carrying cornmeal and pollen in her wedding basket) into the hogan where the ceremony will take place.

Chapter 8

SURROUNDED BY FOLKLORE

EVERYFOLK

Since we are surrounded by folklore from cradle to grave, nearly everyone must be a folklorist; some are professionals at it. To put it another way, although some people choose to study folklore and obtain the training necessary in that profession, all of us, to one extent or another, must learn, collect, and use folklore as a natural consequence of being members of close groups. The mill worker needs to learn and use the hand signals that allow communication in a noisy shop; the college student needs to know how long to wait for a late professor; we all learn how late is late—at a cocktail party, a wedding, a class, a picnic; we must know what connotations are available to us in our language (or else risk not understanding most of what is said to us); we need to know what a joke is and where the punch line goes (or risk exasperating our friends and losing out on fantasy and enjoyment); we learn the proper food for breakfast and the proper dress for supper or for eating out ("No shoes, no shirt, no service"). All of these and many more "rules," customs, mores, observances, and communicative traditions we learn and use through the dynamics of folklore. Indeed, unless we "collect" and "perform" the folklore of our close groups, we may be thought of as nearly outsiders. Just to belong to a close group we need to be amateur folklorists then; how rapidly we become members of new close groups and how deeply we remain members of others stand in direct proportion to our command of the group's folklore.

Levels of Folk Involvement

There are two kinds of involvement with the processes of folklore: cultural and intellectual. By cultural involvement I mean that gut-level personal relationship to the close group felt and acted out by the individual in the very performance of folklore under normal circumstances (Yanagita's level 3). The performances and responses in this kind of involvement are geared more to the group—the culture—than to the individual. In the intellectual, intentional engagement with folklore, we stand aside with some objectivity, actually studying and analyzing those dynamic processes that, as members of a close group, we may have participated in culturally without self-consciousness.

Unfortunately, the jump from cultural to intellectual involvement is farther than we may suspect, and many people are not willing or able to become objective about actions and assumptions so closely related to their own sense of cultural propriety, personal stability, or ethnic identity. For this reason, people are often more willing to study the folklore of others than the traditions of their own group. Until recently, folklorists and anthropologists had an inclination to run off to the South Sea Islands, to Africa, to the Native American reservations in the United States, and to immigrant colonies to study their folklore. Probably this is related to the continued interest in rural folklore by urban-bred and university-trained folklorists, too. And it probably relates to the terminology one finds until recently in the study of religion: ours is religion, theirs is myth—with the corollary that we can be objective about them and their myths while we simply accept our own as truth.

Folklore and Emotion

I bring up this interesting dichotomy for two reasons. First, some people resent it when an outsider analyzes their folklore because they suddenly sense that their views are not as unique or as universal as they had assumed. Moreover, to many, just the conscious discussion of assumed values implies criticism. Professional folklorists need to recognize that they run the risk of offending people by being objective about matters which are normally registered on the subjective level.

These attitudes are obviously opposite sides of the same coin, and they represent one of the greatest potentials for misunderstanding in the field of folklore: people often become angry when their own unexamined cultural involvement is held up for intellectual scrutiny. This means that people who seek to become intentional, professional folklorists must realize that they will be dealing with the most delicate and potentially volatile of human expressions: those that relate the individual solidly and emotionally to a close group—those that can therefore undergird such dynamic matters as the frictions between Celt and Saxon in Ireland, between Arab and Israeli in the Middle East, between soldier and marine on leave, between logger and mill worker on weekends, between Black and White in the inner city, between feuding mountain families, between Hopis and Navajos, between "the U" and "the Aggies," between kids and adults, between men and women. For, regardless of other psychological, economic, political, or historic factors, membership in any of these groups is also a matter of involvement with that group's folklore, and a demonstration of belonging lies in the expression of shared tradition as much as it does in intellectual pronouncements of philosophy and personal opinion. Question these deep allegiances, or be condescending about them, at your own risk.

The Cultural Cement Truck Driver

During our friendly discussion of contemporary legends, a university administrator told me he knew of a similar story which was "actually true," for it had

At Utah State University, anyone who is kissed on "the A" by a True Aggie becomes a True Aggie as well and can induct others into the group in the same manner. Some conduct the ritual in private on any night of a full moon, while others accomplish it in droves at Homecoming as the bell in nearby Old Main tower tolls midnight. Photo by Ron Daines.

happened in his home town. He told me of a cement truck driver who returned home one morning to have a cup of coffee with his wife. To his surprise, he found another car there and, being a suspicious sort, he assumed his wife was having an affair and filled the strange car with concrete. The car could still be seen at a certain gas station in his town, but, more importantly, the episode demonstrated how men in his community dealt directly with a marital intrusion. "He didn't see any more of her after that," he concluded proudly.

I made the mistake of responding on the intellectual, not the cultural, level. Instead of registering the story as an amusing confirmation of a man "in the driver's seat," I cheerfully pointed out the widespread occurrence of that story across the United States and noted the various outcomes I had heard. I also commented on the ironic image: a frustrated husband dumps a large load down the chute and into the car window in a dramatic enlargement of the presumed sexual scene taking place between his wife and the interloper. My acquaintance immediately felt that in front of his own colleagues his honesty had been questioned (along with the integrity of his home town, I now believe) and became very irate, insisting that we step outside to settle the matter. I narrowly avoided a fight by apologizing and noting the possibility for coincidence. I told him I would love to get a picture of the "real car" so that I could put it in along with other versions of the legend that I had collected, and he loudly promised one— "by God"—before the end of the month. Now, years later, I have begun to lose hope. Perhaps he forgot. But I have not forgotten the lesson: he was telling me the story not because I was a folklorist, but because I was a man and we were sitting with a group of men. I had awakened the legend in his mind by referring to some similar anecdotes, but he was clearly telling me the story because he believed it and thought I would be interested in what it represented. He was operating on the cultural level, I on the intellectual level, and the immediate result was outrage.

The folklorist must demonstrate a personable interest in the traditions being shared by any folk performer, but to analyze those traditions in front of the performer is to ask for trouble, not because the performer is intellectually incapable of such discussion, but because analysis and comparison seem to bring the veracity of the tradition-bearer into question.

Cultural Psychology and Folklore

Because folklore operates primarily on the cultural level, because its aesthetics, choices, and performances are dictated more by the group than by the individual, the expressions themselves reveal more of group values and assumptions than of consciously framed individual opinions—as I have already suggested. In fact, a person may even disagree on the intellectual level with something he or she is used to expressing on the cultural level. Some years ago I myself passed on the cement truck driver story to a number of people because I was totally convinced by a close and trusted friend that it had actually occurred in Moscow,

Idaho. Why did I tell that story so many times? On the intellectual level, I do not believe that filling someone's car with concrete necessarily resolves a marital problem, especially when it is done without checking on the details. What if, as one version tells it, the car actually belonged to the man's boss, who came over to arrange for a surprise party celebrating twenty years of faithful service to the company? In my own mind, I realize that if I saw a strange car in front of my house, I would not seek to damage it, even if I were suspicious.

Nevertheless, I recognize that on the cultural level I belong to a society in which marital infidelity by women is considered a massive threat to masculine pride and power. Thus, for the cement truck driver to triumph in a symbolic way represents, on that cultural level, a successful resolution to the psychological threat posed. I think when I told that story with relish to a number of friends, of course adjusting the corroboration of the story a couple of steps so that the anecdote related an event that had happened to a friend of a friend of *mine,* I was participating psychologically with my culture, not expressing my own opinion on how a rational male should deal with a situation he does not understand. One aspect of the intellectual approach to folklore is that now, having heard versions of this story all over the country, having seen cute advertisements for cement companies illustrated by a grinning truck driver loading an old jalopy with concrete, having read of numerous pranks in which people's cars were filled with concrete, I am in a position, as a student of folklore, to make some analytical remarks about that story that I never would have thought of back when I believed the story represented something that had actually happened in a nearby community.

But everyday people usually do not feel the inclination to amass variants of an interesting story going around; if they hear of other versions they assume the one they heard from their own trusted friend is likely to be more reliable than others. Folklorist William A. Wilson discovered this when he tried to use a contemporary legend recounted by his dean at an evening dinner party as a good example of folklore (the dean had asked for an appropriate illustration). Feeling that his own story had been branded unreliable in front of colleagues, the dean simply resolved never to share anecdotes with a folklorist again.

In Utah, there are numerous legends about Mormons in distress being saved by the supernatural, or certainly extraordinary, interventions of deceased relatives, small voices, or beings called the "Three Nephites." Mormons and non-Mormons alike are inclined to think, however, that the existence of many versions of the same story must mean the story is false (a Mormon neighbor calls them "faith-promoting rumors"). But the folklorist knows that whether the legend recounts a remarkable occurrence of healing brought about by a Nephite, or a local case of food poisoning caused by a batter-fried rat, or an exploded poodle in a microwave, or an overcooked young lady in a sun-tan parlor, *all* of them are true dramatizations of anxieties and concerns and beliefs which are indeed shared intensely by a close group of people. Looking at a number of variants is not a way of disproving the event or even questioning its likelihood, but of trying to account for the fact that the story is told tenaciously among the members of the group. Legends and jokes are among the most accurate barometers of cultural psychology, for they are the eager, unmediated, unrehearsed, unbleached constructions of shared values and fears.

The Black Elephant

Folklorists Alan Dundes and Roger Abrahams once made a study of the designs, topics, and categories of the well-known elephant joke craze of the early 1960s. They noticed that if all available versions of elephant jokes were compared, certain broad categories emerged, such as the supersexual elephant, or the elephant who tries to disguise himself by an absurd use of color (Why do elephants wear red tennis shoes? So you can't see them hiding in the cherry tree.), or the intrusive elephant (whose tracks are found in the peanut butter, or whose presence is felt in bed or in the bathtub). Clearly, all of the elephant jokes depended for their effect on a basic set of absurdities: elephants were always described hiding in places that could not possibly hide an elephant, being found in places obviously too small for elephants, being attracted by totally impossible sexual partners, and so forth.

At least one element of the elephant joke that anyone would recognize would be its play on absurdity. However, Abrahams and Dundes felt that there were a number of other features that were too prominent and too timely to be overlooked. For example, they wanted to know why the elephant joke craze had swept the country at that particular time. They wanted to know why certain categories were so prominent. They wanted to know, in short, what the elephant might symbolize for those who were telling the jokes at that time, for certainly there were many other absurdities available in the world.

They noticed that the categories of the elephant joke matched very accurately the categories found in comments and feelings about other races, especially about Blacks; for example, the absurd disguise with color seemed to parallel the widespread White notion that Blacks are absurdly interested in lightening their color, straightening their hair, buying cars associated with White affluence, and, in short, acting the "wrong" role. The supersexual elephant with gigantic anatomical parts and eclectic tastes seemed to mirror the widespread sexual folklore about Blacks encountered commonly among Whites. The intrusive elephant, described as being found in the refrigerator, bed, and bathtub—in all the most personal and private places—seemed to be an analogue to the widespread fear by Whites that Blacks were moving into areas of housing and employment that were not "proper" for them. Another category, one in which we are asked how one takes power away from elephants, usually featured some aspect of castration: "How do you keep an elephant from stampeding? You cut his stampeder off." This category seemed an obvious counterpart to the fear-inspired castrations, in reality and in story, in which Whites symbolically took power away from Blacks who threatened them.

Using Freudian psychology, Abrahams and Dundes argued that humor often functions in such a way as to allow a joke teller to bring up a topic of some anxiety among the members of a group and then to demonstrate or experience superiority over the implied threat by reducing it to something laughable. In other words, jokes may well represent traditional symbolic experiences with precisely those matters that bother us on the group level.

If that is so, how can the elephant possibly symbolize White anxieties about Blacks? And what does that have to do with the timing of the elephant joke fad? First, the authors noted that in the popular imagination of Americans, elephants come from Africa (even though, in fact, the elephants we see at circuses mostly come from India). They also noted that the elephant joke craze took place precisely at the height of the civil rights movement across the country. They argued, cogently, I think, that the elephant jokes provided an articulation of fear and anxiety among Whites.

In order to find out for myself whether this interpretation was noted by people on the cultural rather than the intellectual level, I asked a friend of mine from Philadelphia (which has a large Black population) whether he had heard Black people of his acquaintance telling elephant jokes during the civil rights movement. His answer was both curious to me and supportive of the Abrahams and Dundes hypothesis. He said, "You know, that's really an interesting question. I have a Black secretary, and when I came in one day and told her a really funny elephant joke I had just learned from a friend, she said to me—really sarcastically—'You folks used to call us monkeys; how come you changed it to elephants?'" Of course, this one bit of testimony does not prove the theory, but it does indicate a certain validity that the authors could not have known. I do know that the elephant jokes are not particularly funny or even understandable to people of other ethnic backgrounds. For example, once when I was struggling with the problem of what was funny about a certain Navajo joke, one of my Navajo friends said in exasperation, "I'll tell you what's funny about this if you can tell me what's funny about elephant jokes."

What *is* funny about elephant jokes? Is it only their basic absurdity? If so, why did they start during the civil rights movement and fade as that era faded? I think Dundes and Abrahams go a long way toward explaining what happens in ethnic, esoteric humor; it is all the more valid because it resonates with other kinds of joke fads in our culture. And it is important to know that different groups of people find different things funny; therefore we cannot make the simple assertion that these jokes are universal.

Nonetheless, my experience in mentioning this theory to people is that they immediately become offended and deny that it has any validity. "Well, I told lots of elephant jokes during the sixties, and I myself was involved in the civil rights movement!" In other words, we will find that the very people who

were telling those jokes are not only not in a position to analyze them according to any larger system such as that suggested by Abrahams and Dundes, but
they also resent, on the intellectual level, any implication that they might have
been joking about a subject of such passionate philosophical meaning to
them. But of course this is exactly the point. As intellectual individuals in a
culture that encourages individuality, we consciously articulate those personal
opinions that represent us in public, among friends, and professional colleagues. When we are acting or performing as members of a folk group, our
expressions will be less self-conscious, less geared to the personal, intellectual
statement than they are to the feelings of the entire group. The country was
gripped by excitement and anxiety over the civil rights movement during the
1960s, and the elephant joke illuminates the fact that regardless of our intellectual orientations, we did not escape in any way the ramifications of membership in a larger culture that was very much threatened by the equality
issues. Moreover, the civil rights struggle itself was saturated with emotionally
laden "subtexts" of race, power, gender, class, region, and politics: small wonder that a joke cycle could function powerfully by uniting clusters of these
concerns in distilled performance. More recently, Elliot Oring has argued that
the constellation of cultural and social factors to which the elephant jokes
referred should be enlarged to include all the other frictions and movements
which characterized and animated the emotional climate of the 1960s in
America: sexual revolution, psychedelics, political intrigue, and other issues of
power, gender, authority, and creativity.

If we were to list the most common jokes told in our culture, I believe we
could relate most of them to anxieties, threats, and concerns felt by different
groups at different, noticeable periods of time in our history. Probably the bulk
of American jokes concern sex, politics, religion, and ethnicity—just the very
subjects that cause us continual malaise in conversation, the topics our mothers
told us never to discuss in public. I think it is too much to place on the shoulders of coincidence that all these joke topics continue to parallel the ongoing
emotional concerns of society. Can it be coincidence that moron jokes were circulating among adults in the 1940s just as IQ tests were becoming so common
that they were almost obligatory in every child's life? Is it not possible to see the
moron jokes as an expression of anxiety among parents about where their children would fall on the grand chart?

What about the dead baby jokes that were being told, even at the table,
during the 1970s by pre-teenage children? When I became incensed at my own
children for telling these "jokes" at supper, I was told indignantly by one of
them, "Why do you care about dead babies? Nobody wants babies anymore." It
suddenly occurred to me that dead baby jokes, as told among children, might
well have been a similar kind of symbolic playing through of anxieties occasioned in children by the sudden adult discussion of contraception and abor-
tion, terms which were not even mentioned in public in earlier years. Similarly,

when disabled children began to enter the regular school system in some numbers, we were flooded with Helen Keller jokes, "MR" jokes, and others ("Mrs. Smith, can Billy come out to play?" "No, of course not, you know he doesn't have any arms and legs!" "We know! We want him to play second base!"). And who is the travelling salesman but perhaps the symbol of that marital threat felt by many men, also experienced to some extent in movie characters like Shane and serial heroes like the Lone Ranger? These homeless wanderers move into other people's towns, sometimes solving the local problem, often threatening the men and entrancing the women. It is important to note that the travelling salesman is outrageously "funny" only insofar as he remains in the joke; if he arrives on our front doorstep, the joke is over.

The Racial Polack and Other Shared Concerns

Not long after the elephant joke cycle came the so called Polack joke, a kind of ethnic slur focused on one particular group, but made up of attitudes and phrases found throughout Europe and America wherever esoteric-exoteric ethnic factors exist. One finds the same jokes today in former Yugoslavia, where the Serbs use them in referring to people who live in other parts of the country ("Bosnian vanilla" refers to garlic, for example). The Germans tell them about the *Gastarbeiter* (guest workers), the Danes tell them about the Germans, the Romanians tell them about the Russians. In the United States, the people in Montana tell North Dakota jokes, the people in Texas tell Aggie jokes, and so on.

If we keep all these things in mind, and if we remember that the word *polack* has existed long before it became American slang for "Polish" (in the Slavic languages it refers to a person who lives out on the land, a country bumpkin), if we recall that a good many of the Polack jokes were told in the 1930s as "nigger" jokes, and if we make the same category analysis as suggested by the Abrahams and Dundes study, we may be able to see that the Polack joke is not about Americans of Polish descent but probably about ethnic minorities in general. The main categories are stupidity, strength, and dirt. These are the most recurrent topics in ethnic slurs across America; they are commonly applied by European Americans to non-European Americans, sometimes to any immigrant group.

Thus, just as the travelling salesman joke is not about salesmen, so the Polack joke is not about Polish people; rather, it is a symbolic ethnic slur, the ingredients of which call up, on the cultural level, stereotypical assessments of groups outside the majority. Any number of ethnic groups could have been named in these jokes; I suspect that it is because Polish Americans have become so Americanized that it is clear to most people that the reference to the Polack is only on the most superficial joking level, while the more serious levels of the joke, which may indicate anxiety and tension about an unskilled "foreign" labor force "threatening" jobs in industry, do not represent matters of concern about Polish people.

A few years ago, when a NASA shuttle blew up in front of everyone on the television screen, the situation was not remotely funny; yet within twenty minutes I heard a joke (Where did Christa McAuliffe spend *her* summer vacation?—All over the coast of Florida.), which was followed in the next few days by hundreds of jokes all over the country—most of them focused not on the professional astronauts but on that personable teacher who was killed before our eyes. In addition to the wordplay (Why was Christa McAuliffe a perfect teacher?—She only blew up once in front of her class), there was an overwhelming attention to that trusting civilian who represented the concerns of the everyday people, not the rocket scientist.

In Germany, one of the most common jokes in 1984 was the *Türkenwitz,* "the Turk joke." Workers had come to Germany from Turkey, Yugoslavia, Greece, Spain, and Italy after World War II to help rebuild the country and by the 1980s, their children were going to German schools and the workers were expecting to be treated like fellow citizens. In addition, most of them had attained a solid level of employment in industry (one German social scientist estimated that if all the "guest workers" were sent back to their original countries, the national railroad would have to be shut down for two years in order to find and train Germans for the job). The Germans, who are very guarded about who can be considered a German, were beginning to feel pressured into sharing the employment market and the social scene with people they considered lesser than themselves. Yet it was particularly the Turks, who are mostly Moslem, who came in for the greatest amount of scorn, ridicule, and embarrassment—probably because they more readily dramatized the concept of the outsider. Jokes focused on the clothing of their women (How can you tell which horse is a Turkish mare?—She's the one with a kerchief.), some of them even suggesting efficient ways to commit rape. But most of the jokes dramatized injuring or destroying Turks:

> What's the difference between the white line [on the highway] and a Turk?—You're not allowed to drive over the white line.

> What do you get when you put a Turk through a meatgrinder?—Achmet [a Turkish name, but also "Ach!-hamburger"].

> Have you heard? The Turks are now allowed to carry a knife. Between the shoulder blades, 10 cm. deep.

> What sits in a tree and is black? A Turk after the fire.

> What sits in a tree and is red? One that's still glowing.

> Have you seen the latest microwave oven? There's room for a whole Turkish family.

> If you throw a Turk and a Jew into the furnace, which one will reach heaven first?—Ashes are lighter than crap.

> A Turkish train, totally full, leaves Istanbul and arrives in Frankfurt without anyone on board. Why? It went by way of Auschwitz.

A Turk and a Jew jump out of a plane at the same time; which will reach the ground first?—What difference does it make?

What's the difference between the Turks and the Jews? The Jews already have it behind them.

A number of interesting—if bothersome—issues come to light in even such a small sampling as this. One is the recurrence of destructive imagery, especially of dismemberment and fire. Another is the clear indication that for many modern Germans, the Turks represent the same kind of ethnic anxiety previously blamed on the Jews, who—like the modern Turks—were referred to as *Ungeziefer*, "vermin." In more recent years, since the "reunification" of East and West Germany, it is significant that openly expressed nazism, including the desecration of Jewish cemeteries, is again on the rise. Even more to the point, by 1994, Turks were being attacked openly on the streets with knives, Turkish women were assaulted, and their houses set on fire—in a macabre enactment of the jokes' themes from ten years before. Another way to look at these jokes is to realize that ten years before physical violence had broken out so widely, Germans were expressing the images of their anxieties and hatred more accurately in their jokes than in more formal venues.

For contrast, it is interesting to look at the kinds of jokes told by Turkish guest workers in Germany at the same time. Their shared concerns reflected their frustration at being exploited by a system which held them down while expecting them to work harder and perform better than anyone else:

> Three workers—a Turk, a Greek, and an Italian—are employed in a small German factory in Berlin, where each operates a small machine. The Turk works harder than the others, so the boss decides he can run two machines. So he dismisses the Italian. By using two hands, the Turk not only manages to operate both machines, but increases the factory's productivity. So the owner reduces his expenses by getting rid of the Greek and giving the Turk the job of operating all three machines. The Turk succeeds, but he has to use his feet, and he has to rush back and forth from one machine to another. One day the owner comes in and is surprised to see the Turkish worker with a broomstick thrust into his anus. When asked about it, the Turk replies that his anus was the only part of his body not working for the boss. Now, while running from machine to machine, he can also sweep the floor.

Obviously, for the Turk, the broom in the anus is an expression of the loss of masculinity due to exploitation by his boss. Is there anything funny about the situation, the imagery, the phrasing? In this case, as in most instances, the joke is a dramatization of something which is decidedly not funny, in terms which allow us to experience frustrations and shared anxieties along with the ambiguities of culturally loaded imagery and the pleasure of wordplay.

Currently, as this book is being revised, one of the hottest joke cycles focuses on O. J. Simpson, on trial for allegedly killing his estranged wife and her male companion. Simpson is African American, and a famous football player—as well as a familiar face in television commercials. His former wife was Anglo-American. The joke cycle foregrounds people's concerns with the proprieties of interracial marriage, with concerns about spousal abuse, with questions about whether a Black man can get a fair trial or whether a famous personality can find an impartial jury, with concerns for his children, and with a general malaise about potentially violent people on the loose among us (Have you heard O. J.'s getting married again? He wants to take another stab at it).

From these and many similar examples, we can suggest at least one hypothesis about joke cycles and cultural psychology: when an event happens or a topic emerges that touches off culturally shared sets of concerns in an arresting, meaningful way, people will often respond not simply by discussing the subject but by articulating the psychologically loaded or emotionally ambiguous dimensions of the topic in jokes, legends, rumors, and anecdotes. If we look carefully at the themes and images of these expressions, we will see that they very accurately dramatize and make palpable the abstract norms and assumptions on the basis of which people are feeling confused, frightened, or threatened.

Often, the sense of the unknown is underlined by the rhetoric of the question-and-answer joke (Why did. . . ? Have you heard that. . . ?) which forces the listener to say, openly, "I don't know." The hypothesis that an arresting event or topic can have the capacity to galvanize a culture's assumptions and stereotypes and doubts to the extent that they will be performed in the format of jokes and legends suggests in turn that we can provisionally take any joke cycle that comes along as a signal that something is "bothering" enough people in such a complex way that only a joke has the multiplex capacity to articulate it.

Just as the shuttle jokes were not *about* the shuttle, it is fair to surmise that the O. J. jokes are not about O. J. Simpson but probably about race and spousal violence in combination with celebrity status. Probably the "dumb blonde" jokes of the 1990s were not aimed at blondes per se, but constituted part of a dialectic on issues relating to women. In the jokes, blondes are presented as willful and demanding, oversexed, and so lacking in brains that they require basic directions—all of which arguably respond to the feminist movement as well as to the heated discussion of women's choices in childbearing. Probably the Turk jokes in Germany are not about Turks in particular, but about complex assumptions, fears, and ambiguity with regard to the concept of "ethnic purity." Thus, we miss something about the psychological dimensions of our own time if we do not take jokes seriously.

The Ethnic Threat

The story of the castrated boy mentioned in Chapter 5 is another good example of how folklore represents the feelings of a culture. One aspect of that story is its ability to exist in a number of different generic frameworks while still passing on the same ethnic information: one of "our" innocent people has been mutilated by members of the locally feared minority group. One need not ever have heard of Freud to be aware that castration has been widely used as a symbol of taking power away from someone. We have stories in which other people's aggressions toward ourselves are described in terms of castration or sexual assault, and there are stories, legends, and even factual occurrences that detail how castration has been used in retaliation to such perceived aggression. Moreover, the accounts of cavalrymen and American Indians from the frontier days of the United States tell us that castration of enemy dead and dying was a standard procedure. Yet we can assume, I think, that castration is more common in story and song than in reality. Again, without even inquiring of the standard works on psychology about the nature of this symbolic action, we can assume from the records available in folklore that such an image as castration may stand as a startling kind of tableau scene that expresses for a close group the most striking fears of interracial friction by projecting the blame for aggression onto the "other."

It is often the case that feared ethnic groups are depicted as being "out to get us" sexually. One hears the urban legend, sometimes circulating as rumor, that all the illegitimate children in a local high school had non-White fathers. One hears that Blacks, Indians, and Jews want nothing more than to cause someone from "our" group to become pregnant. The pioneer story about the family whose then pre-teenage grandmother was almost bought by an Indian chief is not found in any family journals but is told as true by at least a dozen unrelated pioneer families. And of course the image is often used in popular literature and in the movies: the young, innocent, light-skinned heroine is threatened, tortured, or even sexually attacked by an animallike, darker, aggressive male.

The story has been encountered less often in the United States in the 1990s than in the 1960s, but in its Jewish focus it is still widespread in Europe. Alan Dundes, in his *Blood Libel,* suggests that the legend provides an excellent example of "projective inversion," in that a concept abhorrent to one group is projected on another and they are held to blame for it. The idea of Jews requiring blood to drink in religious ceremonies flies directly in the face of the fact that Jews are prohibited from consuming blood. Indeed, one of the main reasons for kosher slaughter is to drain as much blood as possible from the animal when it is first killed. Christians, on the other hand, do drink "blood" during their communion ceremony, even though the act of consuming human blood would normally be considered cannibalism in their society. The resultant friction produces a mixture of ambiguity and guilt, argues Dundes, which is conveniently passed off on a feared or hated minority.

Projective inversion may be one of the reasons for the existence of many legends, in fact. Westward-moving pioneers, intruding into Native American territories, took possession of land and began to exterminate languages, cultures, and religions; their legends speak of Indian attacks which put the *settlers* in danger (actually, Indian attacks were relatively rare, in any event far rarer than pioneer legends would suggest). In the 1960s and 1970s, young men planning to penetrate their girlfriends on lover's lane told stories of cars being penetrated and boyfriends being slaughtered—by strangers lurking in the dark. As we have seen, Germans, who pride themselves on hard work and high mechanical abilities, tell legends and jokes about lazy and foolish Turkish guest workers, who in fact do much of the mechanical work in factories and railroads today in Germany. Just calling it "blaming the victim" does not acknowledge the complex way in which live vernacular tradition provides vivid dramatizations of our own social-psychological processes.

In the psychology of ethnic folklore, the majority group symbolizes its anxieties about minority groups by seeing them as sexual threats to "our" innocent males and females. The virtue is on our side, the aggression on theirs, even though historically it may have been more accurate that they were socially the victims. One is motivated to inquire into how these themes can be so vitally and continually passed on in oral tradition if indeed it is true that "nobody believes them." Here, I think, is the confirmation of the double level of the folk involvement I suggested previously in this chapter. As our culture has become increasingly intellectual in the way it educates its members, we are reared in at least a double view of reality; one is constituted of all those codes, attitudes, connotations, and traditional patternings that we pick up as members of our ethnic, familial, regional, and occupational folk groups, and the other is made up of all those individualized intellectual patterns and philosophies that we have been encouraged to develop for our own private view. These two kinds of involvement exist simultaneously in most of us; being a folklorist does not exempt anyone from the effects of both levels, for as individuals we may not consciously espouse a philosophy which nonetheless exists in our unstated cultural assumptions.

Being a folklorist involves recognizing that one cannot escape from tradition merely by studying it. One belongs to a particular ethnic group and perhaps has deep connections with the regional, occupational, religious, and national groups of parents and relatives. Being a folklorist on the level of cultural involvement is a simple matter of participating in those expressions and customs that relate to the group's sense of being. Being a folklorist on the intellectual, intentional, level of involvement thus does not imply that one can in any way claim an intellectual superiority over other bearers of tradition. We need to be able to realize that we are at one and the same time participating members of a culture in which the elephant jokes "made sense" a few years ago and as individuals who can, because of our particular interest, stand back and scrutinize our own position in those traditional networks. Anyone is free to hold a personal opinion on such matters as race, gender, politics, and human rights; at the same time, it would be naive to deny the effect traditions have on any society in exactly such matters as these. The folklorist therefore needs to distinguish between personal opinion and the powers of tradition. The larger importance of this can be grasped only if we are capable of noticing that the two kinds of involvement exist daily side by side, very often with each informing and confirming the other.

Currently, there is a strong move toward equal rights for women; many people have spoken out forcibly on one side or another. Regardless of the particular position taken by individuals, however, we still live in a society that tells jokes about mothers-in-law, that relates jokes and legends of women's alleged inability to understand mechanics or money, that thinks it funny to ask someone, "Have you stopped beating your wife?" and in a society whose members still laugh at ballads like "The Farmer's Curst Wife" and "The Wife Wrapt in Wether's Skin," (in which a farmer, not daring to beat his wife directly, places a sheepskin across her back and says, "I guess I can tan my own sheep skin"), as well as ancient jokes like "That's Once," which Shakespeare apparently used as the basis for his *Taming of the Shrew*. In addition, joke cycles about "dumb blondes," forceful first ladies, and mate mutilators circulating in the 1990s are testimony to the tenacity of gender stereotypes which continue to condition how people act, live, and vote.

It seems clear, considering these powerful elements of tradition, that the final determination of women's rights will very likely not be made quickly on the basis of politics or philosophy or on the opinions of individuals but on the development of another sense of traditional propriety within the culture. Such changes come slowly and the folklorist is in a position to see and appreciate how cultural involvements impinge upon timely matters that might otherwise be thought of as entirely political, personal, or philosophical.

Folk Measurements

A less ominous example of how we all participate in a cultural and intellectual use of folklore is in our traditional measurements. Even though we want to believe that our measurements are exact and reproducible, and even though we may believe they are used only for scientific exactitude, it is interesting to know that our most commonly used measurements are based on rather inexact foundations that reveal more about our culture's earlier attitudes than about scientific precision. For example, our *foot* seems to have been based originally on the average size of a man's foot. Similarly, a *rod* was the length of the left feet of sixteen men in the 1500s. Our word *mile* comes from the Latin *milia passuum*, one thousand paces. *Yard* comes to us from the Old English *gierd*, by way of the Middle English *yerde*, a rod or staff. A *furlong* was the customary length of a farmer's single furrow in a field.

In due time, of course, these measurements became standardized, and once they became formal entities within the intellectual framework of science they developed a sanctity that is now almost impossible to shake loose, for the foot has become so believed in as an actuality in nature that recent attempts to change over to the metric system have been greeted with suspicions of an inter-national conspiracy against our culture. Moreover, most of our measurements are based on human factors like those noted above, while the metric system removes the human element—presumably on the pretext that an objective sys-tem based on decimals is more accurate and useful for mathematical computa-tions. But removing the human dimension, especially when the basic assumptions are culturally constructed, has the effect of removing a culturally familiar mindset, and people feel threatened, though few are conscious enough about the reason to be able to articulate their malaise. But if we test the case by rephrasing some well-known proverbs and figures of speech, we can get a small glimpse of the friction between mathematical exactitude and cultural opinion: "a miss is as good as 1.57 kilometers," or "give him .3937 meter and he'll take 1.57 kilometers," or "I've come kilometers to see you," or "she's 1.8288 meters under." These expressions indicate that our vernacular uses of measurement are not usually about exactitude but about perspective and propriety; changing our measurement system would be registered as a loss in culture.

These measurements are therefore a part of our cultural bearings as well as building blocks in our intellectual connections as we study the formalities of weights and measurements. This is a good example of how folklore and formal culture interpenetrate continually, as well as grounds for the folklorist to realize that we live in a world in which people share traditions the intellectual use of which can be developed to a science.

Many scholars have pointed out how concepts of time in Western culture developed in pretty much the same way. We are aware that there was not even a future tense in Anglo Saxon (Old English), the forerunner of modern English, which was spoken from about A.D. 700 to 1000. Not only did northern Europe and some cultures in the Middle East develop the concept of measurable time, but some of these cultures became exceedingly interested in future time. We are now so intensely involved in measuring time that we actually believe that time exists as a separate entity in and of itself, that it can be counted upon, that it can be followed like a ribbon. Yet the concepts leading up to this current situation, in which we can and do measure microseconds, are based on cultural attitudes and traditions.

It is illuminating that our folk speech today contains a great number of measurements that may seem basically inaccurate or inconsistent to the scien-tific eye, and yet we use them on a daily basis perhaps more readily than we use more specific measurements. For small quantities we have just a tad, a smidgen, a touch, a skosh (no doubt brought back from Japan after the Second World War, for in Japanese the word for a small quantity is *sukoshi*), a dab, a dash, a thimbleful, a splash, a pinch, a bit, a little bit, and, for evenly distributed but sparse objects, a smattering.

A small, undetermined period of time is referred to as "just a minute"; the implication is that although some time will elapse, the person waiting is not to take it seriously. This can be contrasted with the statement, "It took hours for you to get here." A short distance can be referred to as "only a whoop and a holler down the road." Terms like "just a little ways," "a little bit farther," and "pretty soon" indicate measurements whose precise dimensions are not required in order to gain the knowledge we need.

Some particular occupations have what might be called hyperbolic folk micromeasurements. In logging, when gigantic logs are being loaded onto railroad cars or logging trucks, it is often necessary for the person guiding the loader to indicate how much farther the log needs to be lowered or placed to one side or the other. In order to indicate tiny movements of the log, measurements such as the triad BCH, YCH, and RCH are used, based on the supposed difference in diameter of female pubic hair. The colors black, yellow, and red, indicating increasingly fine measurements, are used by loggers in preference to such terms as "eensy-weensy" or "just a teeny bit more," either of which might bring gales of laughter from one's colleagues or, worse, aspersions cast on one's masculine credentials. Measurements for larger amounts include such terms as scads, a gang, a whole bunch, a whole raft, a pile, the whole shooting match, and the whole kit and kaboodle. In Ireland one sometimes hears the term "a clatter of people," an appropriate measurement that indicates not only a large group but also the noise it makes.

As people who are culturally involved in our own folklore, we use such terms as these every day, even though we like to think we are very precise and practical. As folklorists looking to intellection as a way of interpreting some of these expressions, we may be in the somewhat more complicated position of being able to study such measurements further, making complete lists and definitions, and finding out how our culture actually uses the concept of measurement on a day-to-day basis. These measurements convey *something* accurately or they would not be used, and as with the jokes mentioned earlier, daily concepts of measurement may differ from what people think they think about measurements.

The next step, of course, is to compare the measurements used commonly by our own culture with those used by others, and an interesting way to start is to look at measured situations we have experienced in other cultural settings. The Reverend Baxter Liebler, a long-time Episcopalian missionary to the Navajo, told of his first adventures in Navajo country when, riding an old bony horse across the desert, he tried to locate a certain area where he thought he might establish a mission. He met a Navajo riding nearby and inquired if the man could speak English. He said he did, so Liebler asked him how far it was to the place he sought. The Navajo sat his horse thoughtfully for a while, looking at Liebler's skinny nag. Then he said, "It's about five miles; on that horse of yours, about ten." Our first inclination is to smile at the well-intentioned inaccuracy of the measurements. Yet it is clear that the man had learned that a mile was some unit of distance, and in this situation he probably had said something far more meaningful than if he had been able to give the precise distance to Liebler's destination.

I tried once to show a small group of Navajo friends exactly what a mile was. We got into a jeep and I asked them to note where we were at that moment. I then drove as straight as I could across the desert until the odometer told me we had gone one mile. I stopped and announced, "Well, here we are. This is one mile." My friends sat silently for some time, then one asked politely, "Where?" "Right here," I said. "This is a mile." "Oh," they said politely. "We were way over there and now we are right here," I prompted. "Yes, we know," they said, "but where is it, this mile you are talking about?" Of course, at the time I was exasperated at my friends for not understanding me, but I had failed to recognize that the distance we had travelled, the place where we started, and the place where we ended were all irrelevant in the world they lived in, and there was no reason at all why they should have seen this arbitrary distance as important or worthy of any kind of measurement. In fact, so various is the Navajo understanding of our word *mile,* that the term *Navajo mile* has come to have a meaning all its own in the southwestern United States. When used by Whites, it means any great distance. As far as I can tell from my older Navajo friends, their understanding of the term is "way down the road and out of sight." Travellers in Navajo country looking earnestly for a gas station or a restroom, or who pick up a Navajo hitchhiker, would do well to be aware that "Oh, about a mile," is not a sign that the goal is near at hand.

I had lived with the Navajo family of old Little Wagon for several months before he politely asked me early one morning what kind of noise I was making on my wrist every day. I tried to explain to him that my watch was a means of measuring time, but of course since the Navajos have no word for time as we know it, and because I was still learning the Navajo language, I had no way to explain it to him. My first impulse was to believe that I could simply describe what time was like and why it was important to know it and where I was in relationship to it, but I was brought up abruptly by my realizing that nothing I could say to the old man made any sense to him at all. I pointed out to him how the hands went around a dial that was marked off in equal sections. I then told him that by watching where the hands were I could determine what kinds of things I should be doing. "Like what?" he asked in Navajo. "Well, eating. It tells me when to eat." "Don't your people eat when they are hungry? We eat when we are hungry, if there is food." "Well, yes, we eat when we are hungry; that is, no, we eat three times a day, and we are not supposed to eat in between times." "Why not?" "Well, it's not healthy." "Why is that?" And so on. I tried another tack. I said that this machine told me when I needed to do those things that were necessary in order to make my living (I knew of no simple Navajo term for measured, salaried *work* that sets it apart from other useful and normal things a person might do). The old man asked, "Aren't those things that you do anyway? What is it that this tells you to do that you wouldn't do anyway?"

"Well, it tells me when to go out and look for rocks [there was no Navajo word for uranium at the time], and then my company will know how much to pay me." "Do you mean if you lost that machine, you would stop looking for rocks?" "Well, no, I guess I wouldn't." Finally, in exasperation, I said that the watch actually was my reference point to some larger ongoing process outdoors, and this seemed to satisfy the old man. But later, when we were outside that afternoon, he stopped me and held me by the elbow and asked, "Where is it? That which is happening out here?" Even more frustrated, I said, "Well, the sun comes up and goes down, doesn't it?" "Yes, I know," he agreed expectantly. But then I was stuck. "Well, I guess I can't explain it to you. It's nothing, after all. It's all inside the watch. All it does is just go around and make noise." "I thought so," he said. A few weeks later, I threw the watch away, not anticipating the shock that would occur two years later, when I returned to a culture in which 8 A.M. was believed to have a very precise meaning.

In these adventures, although I didn't know it, I was being asked to be a folklorist in function if not in title, and I'm sure every person who has worked among the members of a distinctly different culture will have similar stories to tell. The point is that when we experience the people of another culture, even to understand them and to encourage them to understand us, we must operate through the worldview codes that are expressed in everything from art to science. When we find ourselves among people whose codes and systems are so different from our own that almost no understanding can take place without further study, we are forced to become applied folklorists and anthropologists even to survive. What many people do not realize is that we are also obliged to be applied folklorists in direct proportion to the extent to which we try to exist fully within our own close group as well. We may not be so overtly aware of it, not so painfully cognizant of it because of dislocations in meaning, but we are forced to study, learn, and use folklore nonetheless or be labeled oddballs in our own group. In this sense, we are all unintentional folklorists. By noticing what kinds of everyday measurements we have and do not have, and what kinds other people have and do not have, we become aware of codes by which we navigate in a multicultural nation and world. Similarly, by knowing what is and what is not funny in a culture we have one more avenue of relating ourselves to that culture, whether it be our own or someone else's.

THE INTENTIONAL FOLKLORIST

As I have suggested, the purposeful, intellectual involvement in folklore, at least for clarification, can be seen as that objectified scrutiny of tradition that is brought about by our interest in the existence of many versions of a story, the many ways of telling a joke, the variety of barn styles, and so on. In short, once we are cognizant of how tradition functions in all close groups, we can make an intellectual approach to the subject as well as maintain our own personal cultural involvement with the folklore of our own group. There are at least two kinds of intentional folklorists. For our simple purposes here, we may describe them as amateur and professional, but perhaps untrained and trained would be closer to the dichotomy many professional folklorists feel between themselves and others in the field.

Amateurs

There are two kinds of amateur folklorists: good and bad. The good amateurs are those who, in spite of a lack of professional training, have developed and maintained a real appreciation of the depth and importance of vernacular traditions. Their attempt is usually to contact the real bearers of local traditions, to interview them in depth, to record their expressions, and to bring their works forth in book form or in educational TV series, commercial records, and the like. In fact, a good many fine records of folk music have been produced by amateurs in folklore who, armed with a personal knowledge of folk music and proper equipment, have been able to make public a tremendous range of traditional musical art the likes of which most people are not in a position to experience firsthand.

One example has been the Foxfire project, begun in Rabun Gap, Georgia, by Eliot Wigginton as a class exercise for his high school students. Typically, the students combed their neighborhoods for local traditional artists of all kinds, those with special talents in everything from hog butchering to cabin building, to chair carving, to singing songs and telling anecdotes. The Foxfire project, and the great number of imitative progeny across the land based on it, are exciting not so much for their analytical brilliance as for the obvious local commitment and rededication to those vernacular traditions that might otherwise have gone unrecognized without the strong attention and interest of the younger generations.

Among the most stalwart and tireless of those who have elevated our awareness of the traditions of their regions without first obtaining academic credentials was Vance Randolph, the venerable Ozark folklorist. Long before folklore became a big publishing business in the United States, Randolph was publishing small collections of Ozark tales, retold according to the vocabulary demands of the publishers. *Who Blowed Up the Church House?* and *The Devil's Pretty Daughter* are simple retellings of Ozark folktales and jokes. *Ozark Superstition* is a somewhat more formal gathering of beliefs and customs from the Ozark area, gathered by Randolph over a lifetime of active participant observation. His *Pissing in the Snow,* a collection of Ozark folktales that could not have come into print until recently, is a fascinating compendium of anecdotal and narrative material, much of which can be traced back to its European origins. An indefatigable collector of folksongs, Randolph also produced the four volume compendium *Ozark Folksongs*—on practically no budget at all—and amassed field notes and recordings which are still being worked over by scholars some years after his death. His collection of "unprintable" Ozark folksongs is now in print after all, in a two-volume tour-de-force edited by Gershon Legman and titled after a line from a famous song: *Roll Me in Your Arms* (vol. 1) and *Blow the Candle Out* (vol. 2). Vance Randolph valued his Ozark heritage enough to want to share it with others not of the same close group. Without a formal degree in folklore, without the benefit of grants and government foundations, sometimes in the face of grinding poor health, he showed us the richness and beauty available in regional folklore when one is dedicated to the conscientious amassing and interpreting of personal traditions.

The bad amateurs are easily identifiable, and I do not intend to name any of them here. They are the ones who coo over local whimsies and absurdities, pointing out the backward quaintness that "still survives" in the nooks and backwaters of rural America. They would be embarrassed about folklore if it were not possible to describe it in demeaning terms. For such people, folklore is the stuff of children's stories, of cutely reworded anecdotes, of "local color" uninformed by the richness of live tradition. The materials they concentrate on are often romanticized or given an odd focus; the traditions they mention, insofar as they are recognizable as traditions at all, are usually comfortably juxtaposed to modern times, as if to say: "This is what folks around here were like, back before the highway came through" (implying relief that they are no longer that way).

There would be no harm in this kind of amateur except that such work tends to confirm the misconception many people hold of folklore: it is backward and quaint, it is held chiefly by people of low intellectual ability, it is found mostly in the rural areas where the blessings of technology have penetrated only slowly. Any record or book that portrays local people as hicks who ought to know enough to apologize for themselves is essentially an insult to serious tradition-bearers and an impediment to our understanding the most dynamic aspect of our culture. The worst possible effect in this category of folklore is that sometimes the folk themselves will hear such a record or read such a book and concur in the sentiments it projects.

Professionals

Probably the most common employment for professional folklorists today is in the academic setting. A number of major universities in the United States have folklore departments and institutes, but it is more common to find a folklorist teaching a few classes in an English, history, or anthropology department. Usually the scholar is interested in a particular genre of folklore, often one related to the specialty of his or her department: English department folklorists stress genres such as the ballad and the folktale, while anthropological folklorists often focus on linguistics, custom and belief, Native American oral literature, and so forth.

Most university folklorists spend at least some of their time doing field research, writing up their results for the professional journals, and when travel money is available, reading short papers to each other at regional and national meetings of the various folklore societies. Because the press of academic business and paperwork is always great, however, many folklorists in academe find that they do their research through surrogates—their students. Students in folklore classes are usually required to do some field research rather than library term papers. A typical folklore class features some kind of field project, some theoretical research in the library, and considerable discussion in class as the professor tries to make clear to students from a variety of academic departments what folklore does and how. Collections of folklore made by students are usually kept either in the professor's own files or in a larger folklore archive of the department or university.

Thus, it is a fact of the modern academic approach to folklore that much of the basic field research has been carried out by students. Indeed, this may be one of the few subjects in which a student can do a term paper that does not end its days in the wastebasket or rotting among the discarded Coke bottles, sandwich wrappers, and freshmen themes in the professor's desk drawer. Students who took a folklore course because they thought it might be an interesting way to fulfill a general course requirement have found their own research being used by scholars worldwide. This is fortunate for everyone, for it not only causes students to witness and document the dynamics of tradition and the idiosyncrasies of tradition-bearers directly, but it also allows professional folklorists access to a far wider range of traditional examples than they could ever make contact with themselves. It can have a sleazy side, however: some professors are known to use the fruits of their students' labors without appropriate acknowledgment.

Professional folklorists who work for public and private agencies usually document regional traditions, develop and coordinate festivals, assist social and educational programs, or perform research in applied folklore. The American Folklife Center in the Library of Congress was established by congressional action (Public Law 94-201) on January 2, 1976; it employs professional folklorists who archive and study folklore in the United States as well as others who engage in the ongoing field collection of folklore—often by hiring folklorists in particular states and regions to mount survey projects lasting from a few weeks to several years. The Smithsonian Institution employs folklorists in its American Folklife Program; they provide educational outreach projects, document and study family folklore, film occupational and ethnic traditions, and they sponsor the annual Festival of American Folklife on the Mall in Washington, D. C. The National Endowment for the Arts employs professional folklorists in its Folk Arts Program, a small office that (until the reshaping of the Endowment in 1995) has encouraged the maintenance of folk traditions and promoted greater public access to them as well as greater public appreciation of them through modest grants. Cities have employed folklorists as coordinators of ethnic heritage programs. Some states have established the position of State

Folklorist or State Folk Arts Coordinator. Some companies hire folklorists to train management officials for overseas assignments. Indian tribes have hired folklorists as consultants for heritage maintenance and cultural retention programs. The U.S. Park Service and many state parks and recreation services employ folklorists to plan and manage historical museum facilities and to provide culturally rich exhibitions at parks and monuments. In addition, many folklorists form their own consulting firms and make themselves available to businesses, health delivery corporations, legal offices, and school districts where folklore is used as a way of understanding cultural differences and resolving problems that arise when different cultures intersect.

The job of the professional is construed, then, not as an attempt to show how quaint folklore is or used to be, but to research, discuss and analyze its place in the ongoing culture, to provide greater recognition of its role in our lives, to encourage people to be more articulate about their traditions and about tradition's role in their lives—and to be more aware of the connections between their own customs and the codes and worldviews of others in their society and in the world around them.

RESPONSIBILITIES

Keeping in mind that the intentional folklorist is dealing intellectually with material the tradition-bearers themselves use personally and culturally, the folklorist presents not only a set of positive functions for tradition (to study, preserve, and provide status for folklore), but also the possibility of a negative impact by intruding upon or mishandling those very personal and gut-level codes that members of close groups share so solidly. Thus, the professional folklorist takes on some conscious responsibilities that inevitably condition what will get studied and documented, and should determine how, when, and where the collection will take place, and *whether* it will become available to others.

First, there is a distinct possibility that folklorists might unwittingly become cavalier about other people's lore. Indeed, since it is not our belief, or our song, we may not feel the need to approach it with the reverence accorded it by someone in the close group. In fact, until very recently folklorists and anthropologists assumed they had an inalienable right as fieldworkers to a proprietary interest in the materials they generated. Very seldom in a collection of tales or myth texts does one find an overt statement by the tradition-bearer giving permission to publish the account or providing an indigenous analytical voice. Seldom is the tradition-bearer listed as the author of such a book, either; usually the scholar gets the credit for producing the work. Because of this, and because some groups have distinct restrictions on how materials ought to be used and disseminated—restrictions that are not recognized in the print-oriented culture of the scholar—folklorists and anthropologists have earned, to some extent justly, the reputation for taking things away.

Some of my Navajo acquaintances have become very reluctant to share their Coyote stories with anyone who plans to publish them. These stories should be told only in the winter, and telling of them under proper circumstances enables the Navajos to take part in the annual round of seasonal events on a cosmic level. To tell these stories out of season is to challenge the stability of this cosmic system, yet to have the stories available in print makes it possible for them to be read at any time of the year. My friend Yellowman was convinced that this might be one of the reasons why sheep do not produce as much wool anymore, why there is not as much grass as there used to be, and why people are being bitten more often by rattlesnakes. Non-Navajo researchers might well laugh at these concerns in a cheerfully condescending way and assure the Navajos that, indeed, printing a story has nothing at all to do with rattlesnake bites. But in fact the Navajo family I have worked with over the past forty years has experienced a number of deaths and accidents which they do indeed interpret as having something to do with our joint interest in recording their father's Coyote stories, and they have come to expect me to sit as a patient in a Blessing Way ceremony each year to rebalance the family in their natural and cultural environment. Our culture's assumption that an objectively, respectfully produced piece of written scholarship should not be threatening does not address the premises of their culture, and it is they who have their psychological stability (not scholarly reputation) to watch out for.

Should we stop publishing Navajo Coyote tales? We could, of course, but there are already so many in printed circulation that perhaps action at this time would be fruitless in reducing the fears of Navajo storytellers. Should we suppress those already in print, burn all books with Coyote stories in them? This course of action runs against our feelings about freedom of the press and access to information. This is a good example of an entirely irresolvable dilemma, one that has grown more acute through the years *because* folklore and anthropological field researchers have assumed the right of access to traditional materials and have assumed the right to publish or disseminate those materials however they saw fit without regard to the hesitancies, codes, taboos, and ritual concerns of the real owners of those stories. We are now in a position where we cannot retreat or advance without doing injustice to the people who provided the riches of their culture, perhaps too willingly, for our scrutiny. That they feel dislocated and hurt while we only register embarrassment is a clear indication of our differences in worldview. It is also testimony to the abuse of power.

Ownership

One thing that should be made clear both in the mind of the folklorist and in the perceptions of the tradition-bearer is that even though individuals cannot usually obtain copyright for folk materials, they should be considered owned to some extent by the tradition-bearers or by their community, not by the folklorist. Folklorists, especially those working in archives, have the ability to translate the stored materials of others into a repository of facts and data to be disseminated to any interested party at the discretion of the archivist. However, they should not overlook the fact that dissemination of some materials may be embarrassing or shocking or dangerous to the community that considers those expressions their own. In some cases it may be a matter of simple impropriety, in others a matter of religious outrage.

Albert Lord observed that some Yugoslavian singers perform certain stories so well—or by special personal inclination—that they are thought by others to "own" them. Similarly, in many Indian tribes (e.g., the Tlingit) particular storytellers or their families are thought to own certain stories and songs by virtue of having been given them by a previous narrator. Even within the person's own village, in a case like this, the story would not be told by anyone else without special permission. This necessarily means that any folklorists or anthropologists who wish to collect and transmit the stories of such groups as the Tlingit need to be sure that they have been given permission, literally given the tales, before they can feel free to disseminate those narratives. It is impertinence for folklorists to assume that once the materials are collected the choice of sharing is up to them.

I once talked to an archivist who presided over a collection of Native American anecdotes, reminiscences, tales, and myths being amassed by a fairly large tribe; he insisted that the tribe had no right to tell him which materials could be shared with outsiders and which required special protection and secrecy. He felt obliged as an archivist to disseminate any and all materials to those people he felt were bona fide scholars in search of the kinds of information his archive could reveal. Why else have an archive? The tribe, frightened that it might lose control of some of its precious cultural property and ritual information, concerned that older tradition-bearers might not cooperate with the project if they felt their stories would come into the hands of strangers, asked for the archivist's resignation. But of course there could have been a compromise between the two in which the tribe recognized that some of its materials were of great scholarly value and might be shared while the archivist recognized that part of his job was to encourage and protect the tribe's special cultural information. Such compromises are not corrosive to folklore; rather, they ask the folklorist to join forces with the tradition-bearers to make sure that the materials are not squandered, misplaced, misunderstood, or mishandled. Surely those who can most accurately delineate the concerns in those areas are the tradition-bearers themselves.

One culturally destructive situation arose because of a well-intentioned field researcher sharing secret information with outsiders. The folklorist had been accepted warmly into a small tribe on one of the islands in the South Seas. He had become so familiar with the tribe and its people, so trusted by them, that he was inducted into one of the men's societies. While he lived there he participated fully in the ritual life of this small tribe; he was even allowed to take photographs where none had been allowed previously. Obviously, the people trusted him with these photographs, as they might one of themselves, because as a ritual brother he could be expected to act and respond the same way as others in the group. After his return to his home country, he was urged by colleagues to put out a small book of limited circulation describing the rituals of his adoptive tribe. This he agreed to do, apparently in the belief that the data were so full and rich that the only result would be a positive one: a few scholars interested in this particular tribe and its ceremonies would have a fuller picture and a deeper understanding of the beauty and complexity of those rituals. But as can happen, the book was listed in an international bibliography and came to the attention of a schoolteacher on the home island. Thinking the students would be interested in reading a book about their own tribe, the teacher ordered it for the school library. When eventually—and inevitably—a young girl from the tribe checked the book out and took it home, disaster struck: there, laid out in pictorial detail, were all the secret ceremonies of one of the central men's societies, secrets that had never before been revealed to the eyes of women or of people outside that ritual group. For one thing, the people believed women would go blind if they saw the ceremonies. But none did. Shock and apostasy followed, and the result of this episode was the near-total dissolution of the tribal religion. One of the practical effects of this misadventure has been that folklorists and anthropologists have since been barred by the people of that island.

This is not a case of a sinister, calculating folklorist with grave-robber mentality, striking it rich with shocking photographs for coffee tables across America. Rather, the researcher tried, perhaps beyond his ability, to limit the circulation to the eyes of those who could best understand those people. Nonetheless, the result was chaos and cultural destruction for the people so innocently betrayed. Of course, we might congratulate the scholar's unintended liberation of the women in this tribe, but can we feel fortunate about his inadvertent—shall we not say careless?—destruction of their culture? Our politics over their spiritual well-being?

It reminds us of the Korean story of the monkey and the fish: the monkey, having saved himself from a violent flood, notices a fish under the surface of the water and "saves" him by pulling him up on shore. Such attempts by outsiders at saving cultures other than their own are more and more being rebuffed by traditional communities. During August of 1995, the Hopi Cultural Preservation Office, with sponsorship of the Heard Museum in Phoenix, held a conference billed as a dialog on cultural copyright, but the centerpiece of the meeting was a three-page document declaring Hopi jurisdiction over any project, research, publication, presentation, or documentation concerned with Hopi cultural materials; anyone doing research on the Hopi, according to this declaration, must obtain permission from the Hopi, deposit raw data with the tribe, allow Hopi review and input on the project at all stages, and be ready both to post bond and to share revenues. While this action, if enforced, will probably cut down on the scholarship about the Hopis, it is clearly the end result of years of outsiders' appropriation of Hopi materials to their own ends. The Hopis now reserve the right not to be studied by others.

The folklorist and the anthropologist may be contemptuous of such tribal views if they want, but they cannot avoid responsibility when it comes to the effects of the dissemination of material outside the control of its usual owners and proprietors. If folklorists are to expand cultural awareness and not be "con artists," we must keep the delicacy of these responsibilities constantly before us in our research. Leading folklorists today are therefore moving away from the stance that implies they (or their models and genres) are in charge of interpreting the living vernacular expressions of their informants. Although they may disagree in some of their approaches; for example, Charles L. Briggs and Linda Dégh have published extensive studies in which the resource people are centrally involved with the interpretation as colleagues. Working from new perspectives suggested by postmodern critics like James Clifford, George Marcus, Jay Ruby, and Stephen Tyler, Elaine Lawless has developed a reflexive, reciprocal ethnography which she has used in her work with women Pentecostals. Larry Evers has worked with his Yaqui colleagues for years as reflexive collaborators in translation and analysis, and is currently co-editing an entire book of essays on the translation of Native American texts in which each essay was produced by a Native tradition-bearer and a scholar working as equal collaborators. The films of Alaska Native life created by Leonard Kamerling have always contained the images desired by the subjects, and have been edited and translated by Native people of the village being documented. Not only are the days of cultural strip-mining behind us, but we have discovered (to the surprise of some) that better ethics and fuller intellectual inclusiveness have resulted in better texts, richer performances, and more honest records of the traditions we seek to understand.

BIBLIOGRAPHICAL NOTES

In my estimation, the finest modern statement about the field of folklore, its promises, and its responsibilities was given in Dell Hymes's presidential address to the annual meeting of the American Folklore Society at Portland, Oregon, on November 2, 1974. It forms the first part of an article already referred to several times, "Folklore's Nature and the Sun's Myth," *Journal of American Folklore* 88 (1975): 345-69; see 345-56 especially.

Several notes and queries about the cement truck driver story have appeared around the country in regional journals and newsletters. Louie Attebery brings the strands together in "It Was a De Soto," *Journal of American Folklore* 83 (1970): 452-57. William A. Wilson's account of his legendary encounter with a suspicious dean is given in his chapter "Documenting Folklore" in *Folk Groups and Folklore Genres*, ed. Elliott Oring, previously mentioned, 225–26. A special issue of *Western Folklore* (49, no. 1 [January 1990]), edited by Bill Ellis, is dedicated to emergent legends, and of course Jan

Brunvand's many books on the subject have chronicled the liveliness of legends in the contemporary scene. We should not forget that many of these narratives come to us from a considerable antiquity, as the "Blood Libel" story shows. The well-known case of the mouse in the pop bottle or can, which surfaces continually in oral tradition as well as in court cases, is at least as old as medieval times, as illustrated by recorded church rules which provide a penance of three special fasts for anyone knowingly serving liquor in which a mouse or a weasel is found dead. See William R. Cook and Ronald B. Herzman, *The Medieval World View* (New York: Oxford University Press, 1983), 138; I am indebted to a student, Mike Thomsen, for calling this reference to my attention. The well-worn family legend referred to as "Goldilocks" was first discussed by Francis Haines, "Goldilocks on the Oregon Trail," *Idaho Yesterdays* 9 (Winter 1965–66): 26–30; I discuss its themes in "Folklore and Reality in the American West," in *Sense of Place*, ed. Barbara Allen and Thomas J. Schlereth (Lexington: University Press of Kentucky, 1990), 14–27, esp. 18–21.

I have already referred several times to the Abrahams and Dundes article on the elephant jokes *(The Psychoanalytic Review* 56 [1969]: 225–41); the piece contains a very succinct summary of Freud's approach to joking behavior. Elliott Oring's expansion of the reference field for the elephant jokes is "To Skin an Elephant: On the Presumption of Aggression in Humor," in his *Jokes and Their Relations* (Lexington: University Press of Kentucky, 1992), 16–28. Dundes explores other more recent jokes stemming from racial friction in "Jokes and Covert Language Attitudes: The Curious Case of the Wide-Mouth Frog," *Language in Society* 6 (1977): 141–47. In still another article, Dundes notes that the transference of what is painful, unacceptable, or taboo from "us" onto "them" suggests the psychological term projection; see "Projection in Folklore: A Plea for Psychoanalytic Semiotics," *Modern Language Notes* 91 (1976): 1500-1533. Of special application to this chapter are his comments on the mutilated boy (1524-25), dead-baby jokes (1525-26), and streaking (1526).

Other references to the mutilated boy are mentioned in previous sections of this book; consult, at the least, Hippensteel, "'Sir Hugh': The Hoosier Contribution to the Ballad," *Indiana Folklore* 2 (1969): 75-140, and Florence Ridley, "A Tale Told Too Often," *Western Folklore* 26 (1967): 153-56. A fine set of precautions for those who want to use the terms and approaches of psychology and psychiatry is suggested by David Hufford in "Psychology, Psychoanalysis, and Folklore," *Southern Folklore Quarterly* 38 (1974): 187–97. Hufford notes that many nonspecialists are inclined to misuse terms like *anxiety* and thus lose the force of what they could have shown in their studies. Dealing with psychological realities, such as real dangers and uncertainties on the job, Patrick B. Mullen shows that one need not use a Freudian approach to make the case for a clearly functional set of beliefs and practices based on shared tensions and group dynamics; see "The Function of Magic Folk Belief among Texas Coastal Fishermen," *Journal of American Folklore* 82 (1969): 214-25.

A number of folklorists have focused their attention on the ways in which particular joke cycles bring together a constellation of shared concerns and anxieties in the contemporary scene; among them, see Alan Dundes, "The Dead Baby Joke Cycle," *Western Folklore* 38 (1979): 145–57; Dundes and Thomas Hauschild, "Auschwitz Jokes," *Western Folklore* 42 (1983): 249–60; Willie Smyth, "Challenger Jokes and the Humor of Disaster," *Western Folklore* 45 (1986): 243–60; Elizabeth Radin Simons, "The NASA Joke Cycle: The Astronauts and the Teacher," *Western Folklore* 45 (1986)

261–77; Elliott Oring, "Jokes and the Discourse on Disaster," in *Jokes and their Relations,* ed. Oring, cited previously, 29–40; and Toelken, "'Türkenrein' and 'Türken, raus!'—Images of Fear and Aggression in German *Gastarbeiterwitze,*" in *Turkish Workers in Europe,* ed. Ilhan Başgöz (Bloomington: Indiana University Press, 1985), 151–64. The joke about the hardworking Turkish machinist in Germany was told to me by Professor Başgöz, who had heard it from Turkish friends; Gabrielle Hamilton, a graduate student in Utah State University's American Studies Program, has collected the same story among nurses in the United States, showing that the metaphor of being violated and victimized through one's own hard work is not rare in the world.

For a lighthearted example of how far the naming of animals and people in groups can be carried, see James Lipton, *An Exaltation of Larks, or, The Venereal Game* (New York: Grossman, 1968). For the cultural background of our folk measurements, see Hall's three books mentioned previously, especially *The Silent Language.*

Vance Randolph's *Pissing in the Snow and Other Ozark Folktales* (Urbana: University of Illinois Press, 1976) is introduced by Rayna Green and provided with extensive annotations (which do not overshadow the tales) by Frank A. Hoffman; it represents a brave foray against the kind of stereotypification that prefers to view the quaint hill folk as harmless churchy clods with dull wits. Randolph's posthumously produced work on bawdy songs, *Roll Me in Your Arms* and *Blow the Candle Out,* edited by G. Legman, appeared in 1992 (Fayetteville: University of Arkansas Press); his *Ozark Folksongs,* 4 vols. (Columbia: State Historical Society of Missouri, 1946) is a classic of regional collecting. Other works by "amateurs" would include *One Potato, Two Potato,* by Mary Knapp and Herbert Knapp—already referred to previously as a fine collection of real children's lore—and that of Eliot Wigginton (and his students), whose Foxfire project, for all its focus on their own rural scene, captured the imaginations of people all over the country. On the snobbishness that has sometimes reared its head in spite of these clear examples of valuable work by nonspecialists, read John O. West's impassioned but succinct statement, "The Professional-Amateur-Popularizer Feud in Folklore," *Journal of American Folklore* 88 (1975): 299-300.

For comments, advice, and good examples of the relationships between folklore researchers and their live resources, see the following works. Richard M. Dorson, in the introduction to his *Buying the Wind: Regional Folklore in the United States* (Chicago: University of Chicago Press, 1969), provided some very helpful remarks based on his own field experience ("Collecting Oral Folklore in the United States," 1-20). Dorson's comments in the introduction to his *American Negro Folktales* (New York: Fawcett, 1967), 12-64, are also illuminating, for they describe, among other things, the dilemmas faced by a White collector trying to get people of another ethnic group to share their favorite anecdotes. Alan Jabbour and Carl Fleischhauer, in their work on the Hammons family records referred to previously, provide us with a high performance to emulate: working with several members of an isolated family over several years' time without flagging and without alienating the family. George Carey gives some thoughtful reflections on our ethics, and on our professional debt to "informants," in his deceptively simple "The Storyteller's Art and the Collector's Intrusion," in *Folklore Today: A Festschrift for Richard M. Dorson,* ed. Linda Dégh, Henry Glassie, and Felix J. Oinas (Bloomington: Indiana University Press, 1976), 81-91. While Carey is not completely sure about the effects his published articles have had upon the lives and reputations of his informants, their effects upon him are clear: they have been instrumental in establishing him as a leading folklorist. Here is a rare and moving example of why vertical distinctions between scholar and folk simply make no sense.

Michael Owen Jones provides another, equally important consideration in "Folk Art Production and the Folklorist's Obligation," *Journal of Popular Culture* 4 (1970): 194-211, when he warns us of the possible distortion of both art and scholarship by the very nature of intrusion and special focus on a traditional performer. John J. Honigmann argues that relations between researcher and subject need not be restricted to objective, formal modes, however, and he suggests, moreover, that the researcher need not remain totally outside the phenomenon being studied or aloof from its eventual description. In "The Personal Approach in Cultural Anthropological Research," *Current Anthropology* 17 (1976): 243-50—plus discussion, 251-61—Honigmann puts forth the idea, already well accepted by most folklorists, I think, that the personal approach recognizes the importance of the investigator's own account and evaluation of an event, his interpretation of it, and his conclusions about it (matters often dismissed as too subjective by social scientists). These concerns are close to those of Yanagita Kunio, mentioned earlier, but they have been taken to a new level of sensitivity by postmodern ethnographers, whose approach includes—not simply allows for—reciprocity and reflexivity in observation and analysis. My own ongoing account of ethical problems in fieldwork among the Navajos is traced in "Life and Death in the Navajo Coyote Tales," in *Recovering the Word: Essays on Native American Literature*, ed. Arnold Krupat and Brian Swann (Berkeley: University of California Press, 1987), 388–401, and in "Fieldwork Enlightenment," *Parabola: The Magazine of Myth and Tradition* 20 (1995): 28–35; I have been struck by how many colleagues have argued that ethics should never get in the way of learning all we can from our informants, but I continue to believe that the exploitative model is losing ground. Witness collaborative works such as Charles L. Briggs and Melaquias Romero, *The Lost Gold Mine of Juan Mondragon: A Legend from New Mexico* (Tucson: University of Arizona Press, 1990); Linda Dégh, *Narratives in Society: A Performance-Centered Study of Narration* (Helsinki: Suomalainen Tiedeakatemia, Academia Scientarium Fennica, 1995) [distributed by Indiana University Press]; Elaine J. Lawless, *Holy Women, Wholly Women: Sharing Ministries of Wholeness through Life Stories and Reciprocal Ethnography* (Philadelphia: University of Pennsylvania Press, 1993); Larry Evers and Felipe S. Molina, *Yaqui Deer Songs/Maso Bwikam: A Native American Poetry* (Tucson: University of Arizona Press, 1987). The many films of Leonard Kamerling ("On the Spring Ice," "The Drums of Winter," among others) are monuments of intercultural work in the production of culturally valid documentation. More precise than the Hopi concept of cultural property is the Tlingit term *at.óow*, which means "an owned or purchased thing"; in Tlingit tradition, *at.óow* can refer to a design, a place, a geographical feature, or a story. In the latter case, single stories are considered the property of those who culturally "own" them; such stories may not be told by others without permission, unless they are given the story as a gift. See Nora Marks Dauenhauer and Richard Dauenhauer, *Haa Shuká, Our Ancestors: Tlingit Oral Narratives* (Seattle: University of Washington Press, 1987), 24–29.

If you want to meet folklorists and participate in the exchange of views at any regional or national meeting, you can find out how to join the various folklore societies by looking at the fine print in any *recent* issue of any folklore journal. Usually, subscription to a professional journal includes membership in the organization; in cases where it does not, the details for application are usually spelled out, often inside the front cover.

The annual meeting of the American Folklore Society draws professional folklorists (most of them college professors), other interested academics, graduate and undergraduate students, local history buffs, and, on occasion, some of the folk, from throughout the United States and from many other countries. Many of the best papers and reports are given by students, and many of these, in turn, become published papers, theses, dissertations, and books. Suzi Jones's *Oregon Folklore,* already mentioned several times, is one of several good examples of a book researched and written by a graduate student in folklore, using her own fieldwork as well as that of many previous undergraduate students at the University of Oregon. A whole issue of the *Journal of American Folklore* (January-March 1975), devoted to the topic of women and folklore, was edited by a graduate student at the University of Texas (and several of the articles were written by graduate students). *Folklore Forum,* a journal of contemporary folklore studies, is put out entirely by graduate students at Indiana University (some of whom also help edit the prestigious *Journal of Folklore Research,* also published at Indiana). There are similar examples of other folklore centers around the United States and Canada, but it is unnecessary to mention them all; the point is clear, I hope. Being a folklorist, on the international level, is a collegial activity involving the professional and the apprentice in an exciting partnership of discovery that would be totally impossible to carry off without the aid, charity, and interest of the tradition-bearers themselves, among whom we must often number ourselves.

Harry Fleming of Leadore, Idaho, hand-braiding his own rawhide riata (lariat). Photo by Gary Stanton, courtesy of the Idaho Commission on the Arts.

Chapter 9

FOLKLORE RESEARCH

EVEN THOUGH INTRODUCTORY STUDENTS AND OTHER NEWLY INTERESTED persons may not become directly involved in folklore research, they should find the details of fieldwork directly related to their understanding of how the dynamic expressions of folklore become available, intellectually palpable, to audiences outside traditional habitats. Were it not for folklore field research, there would be little of substance for folklorists or their students to discuss. While at first sight such a statement seems a careless admission that there is a field of study only because we have dredged one up, it is actually an assertion that as a discipline folklore—like marine biology—is a study founded on items "brought up" for scrutiny. Although folklore surrounds us all the time, it is so enmeshed in all we do and say that we seldom take the opportunity to regard it separately. Folklore field research does just that by focusing on those particular performance activities that can be seen as traditional.

FOLKLORE FIELDWORK

Research in folklore can be (naturally) divided into three main categories: gathering, storing, and pondering, or as they are more commonly referred to in the profession, collecting, archiving, and analyzing. In collecting, the main participants are the collector (the folklorist out in the field looking for—and recording—folklore) and the tradition-bearer, often called the "informant" (the possessor of folklore, whose role is to inform the collector). In archiving, there are the archivist (whose role is to protect and codify the collected materials as they are accessioned and stored) and the scholar (who wants to study these materials). In analysis, there are the collector, the archivist, and the scholar, trying together to make critical judgments on the meaning, function, and importance of folklore materials. Increasingly, the informants are being engaged in the analysis as well, sometimes as consultants, sometimes as collaborators.

Collector and Informant

Throughout this process, it is easy to forget that in folklore—in ongoing tradition itself—it is the tradition-bearer, not the collector, archivist, or scholar, who remains the important person. Notice how the terms *collector* and *informant* suggest a certain kind of one-way relationship: one takes and the other gives. If we are to view the field of folklore seriously, we must realize that the collector is doing something far more delicate than capturing rare butterflies, and the informant is giving out something far more difficult to share than an antique chair. Since folklore is made up of the expressions most closely related to personal identity within a close group, its possessors do not simply throw it up on command. Folks do not give out family recipes to just anyone, do not share songs with people whose reactions might be hurtful, contemptuous, or careless.

More knowledgeable folklorists have found that they must first establish some kind of warm relationship before people are willing to share their traditions. And once the traditions have been shared, the relationship must not be canceled. The givers of folklore are the basis of our whole enterprise, yet potentially they are placed in the most extraordinarily hazardous emotional position. Consider what happens to the elderly lady you have been collecting remedies from when she hails you from the front steps saying, "Where have you been? I've remembered a whole lot of cures I forgot to tell you before!" and you answer, "Sorry, lady, I'm not into that anymore." The ramifications are twofold and need to be considered seriously by anyone intending to do fieldwork in folklore or anthropology: (1) the very visits of the folklorist will jog a tradition-bearer's memory so that more items will come to mind (along with a flood of nostalgia, especially in older people or people far from their home territory); (2) a friendship between the collector and the informant will have begun, related directly to these traditions (and the informant will try hard to please the friendly visitor by remembering all possibly related materials). Betraying this relationship can have not only severe cultural implications, but it may have a devastating effect on the informant and on the tradition itself, to say nothing of placing a barrier in the way of all subsequent researchers who may want to study the tradition further. Accepting responsibility for the delicacy of relationship and trust with tradition-bearers must be the basic ethic for fieldworkers.

Just as important, the responsibility is passed on automatically to anyone who controls archival materials and to anyone who uses the materials in scholarship. For these reasons, beginning folklorists would do well to concentrate first of all on people in their own family or traditional group—people, in other words, with whom they maintain close enough contact to know what is appropriate and what is not, what represents honest expression and what represents intrusion or exploitation. One does not need to find an illiterate farmer in a remote valley in order to do folklore research; start at home. Nonetheless, I would not want to argue that folklorists should limit their interests to the people among whom they live, or else none of us would learn anything about others—and folklore represents one of the richest ways of learning interculturally. So whether we collect customs at home or from people we meet elsewhere, we need to develop the kind of sensitivity, respect, and responsibility we would require if we were working with our closest relatives.

We might benefit greatly by junking the terms *collector* and *informant* altogether in favor of *researcher* and *tradition-bearer,* but the former words are so entrenched that a shift seems unlikely. In any case we need to recognize that the informant is neither the subject nor the object of our research (even when studies seem to concentrate on traditional individuals, like Roger Abrahams's study of Almeda Riddle, Edward Ives's book on Larry Gorman, or Michael Owen Jones's work on Chester Cornett). Rather, bearers of tradition are our knowledgeable colleagues, our living "library" of tradition, our primary resource for the expressions we seek to understand. Without them and their cooperation, most folklorists would be looking for jobs at the five-and-dime.

Indeed, folklorists have found that their relationships with their traditional colleagues have been among their most intense and personally rewarding friendships: one thinks of Roger Abrahams and "Granny" Riddle, John Lomax and "Leadbelly," Richard Dorson and J. D. Suggs, A. L. Kroeber and "Ishi," Joseph Epes Brown and Black Elk, Jorge Preloran and Hermogenes Cayo. Not all of these people related in the same way, of course, but in every case it is clear that the folklorist learned more from the tradition-bearer than vice versa, and that the learning took place under the most intimate circumstances. So close did I come to Yellowman and his family that now, some forty years later, I still maintain family responsibilities with them, and they with me.

The Approach to Fieldwork: Tactics

Since most people do not "do" their folklore at the drop of a hat, especially for strangers who request it, the folklore fieldworker may as well start out recognizing that the most practical approach to recording folklore is to plan on considerable reconnaissance and development of rapport with the tradition-bearers most likely to share their materials. The collector cannot expect to walk up to someone's door, hold out a microphone, and say, "Hi there, I'm from the university and I'm collecting folklore. I wonder if you would tell me a few stories or share some of your superstitions." First of all, as we have observed, the frontal assault is hardly the method, and the front doorstep is hardly the place. Moreover, the person at the door may not have the same understanding of the word *folklore* as the researcher does; it may in fact be taken as an insult that some stranger is suggesting the resident possesses old wives' tales, illiterate nonsense, stupid misinformation, or dangerous irreligious notions. More consciously, the housewife at her door may well ask, "Who are you, and why do you want to know?" And the slamming of the door, possibly preceded by a hard look, may end this hypothetical scene.

Surely some kind of friendly introduction is in order in a case like this, and many folklorists have found it helpful to do initial work in a community by asking around town concerning the whereabouts of old-time singers, yarn-spinners, or quilters, using terms that indicate the nature of the material desired rather than professional jargon. Often it will be a local sheriff, minister, or social worker who knows from personal experience who the tradition-bearers are. A doctor may be aware of some old man down the road who specializes in herbal cures, or he may know the midwives in the vicinity. The owner of a local lumber mill may be aware that some of his workers share hilarious stories over their lunch. A policeman may be full of leads about fruit vendors or sidewalk characters along his beat. If the folklorist comes to someone's door, or visits someone's place of employment at the appropriate time, forearmed with the name of a friend, acquaintance, or relative, the chances are far more likely that it will be possible to engage a tradition-bearer in enough of a conversation to ascertain his or her inclination to share folklore. Richard Dorson, trying to collect African American folktales in a small, mostly Black town in Michigan, found it necessary to hang around town for a week while the local people silently checked out his assertion that he was a college professor looking for folklore. When they finally concluded that the leather patches on his elbows identified him as a professor, not an undercover policeman, they cheerfully referred him to J. D. Suggs, who turned out to be an apparently inexhaustible resource for folktales.

When we are invited into another person's home, it is at the discretion of and on the terms of the person doing the inviting. It is not up to the folklorist to be pushy, aggressive, or dazzling. Rather, the researcher should try to blend in as cheerfully as possible with that aspect of the context that seems most likely to help induce and support a traditional performance. If you intend to do folklore research among the members of a Mormon farm family, it will not advance the cause to arrive tipsy. If you wish to study traditional fishing procedures with a group of conservative riverboat guides, it will not be appropriate to show up wild-haired, noisy, and passing marijuana around.

If you wish to record an elderly woman singing ballads, it will probably scare her to death if you arrive with four friends who haul out their banjos and mandolins to give her a taste of what you are looking for. While it is sometimes possible to coax some folklore from a willing person by singing the first line of a song, it is also possible to overdo it so that the traditional singer denigrates his or her own ability to satisfy you. On one occasion, with hearty references from his friends, I visited an old man in Roosevelt, Utah, and proceeded to sing several songs I thought he might know. Although he was described as "the guy who knows all the songs around here," one who sang them at great length at every gathering, I found he was totally intimidated by my singing. Concluding that his songs would not be interesting to someone who sang as well as I, he refused to sing a single note for an entire day. Some of the examples of inappropriate tactics I have suggested here are outrageous enough to be visible to anyone; but they bring up the consideration that must be made, subtly or otherwise, by all fieldworkers: What is the tradition I seek to record, and how can I put the tradition-bearer in such a frame of mind and personal context to encourage the performance of the things I want to study?

Does this mean the folklore fieldworker must be a hypocrite? I suppose it all depends on your definition of hypocrisy. It seems pretty evident that there are ways of inducing a normal context and ways of inhibiting one. For example, very few midwives of my acquaintance will discuss the details of midwifery with me. No matter what references I may have from friends and neighbors, most women simply feel awkward discussing these matters with a man. Similarly, if one tries to collect logger songs in all their obscene glory from a retired logger, the performances will simply not come about if his wife remains in the room or if the collector is a woman. Noting and responding to certain basic inclinations of the tradition-bearers does not require hypocrisy as much as a recognition of those factors that are indeed cultural and psychological parts of the tradition itself. If the fieldworker is not willing to deal with these necessary components of a tradition, it hardly does any good to try to study performances from that tradition.

In my own fieldwork, I usually try to visit a prospective resource person a number of times before I ever bring a tape recorder. I try to get some kind of personal reference to use at the first meeting, if possible a direct introduction by a close friend of the tradition-bearer. Or I may observe someone performing in some tradition, say, at a county fair or a family picnic, and approach the person on the spot and ask if it might be possible to drop around sometime to hear some more stories or to trade some songs. The initial contact made, the next task is to develop the kind of informal footing with the tradition-bearer that will allow him or her to recognize that traditions may be shared with a researcher. I must admit that in many cases only one visit is necessary to establish a friendly rapport, often because the tradition-bearers, especially older people, are pleasantly surprised that anyone would be interested in the old ways they value so highly. Indeed, they will sometimes share their songs and stories with the most idiotic of researchers. Often it is because of an essentially conservative nature that they are already slightly embittered that many of the old ways have passed. In many cases resource people whose folklore stems from their ethnic backgrounds have been seeking ways in which they might remain American and yet still maintain their ethnic traditions. It is often, thus, with a sense of relief that the tradition-bearer hears a folklorist say these expressions are well worth saving and studying. The tradition-bearer often then sees that he or she can play an important role in sharing these valuable expressions with someone who cares about them.

During these first visits, after a rapport is established, I try to see if it is possible to elicit the kind of performance I want to study. This means, for example, that if I were visiting a Navajo family in order to collect Coyote stories, even with the finest rapport I would not be able to hear any performances unless it were winter. In the case of some other kind of performance, say the kinds of songs or dances done at a Greek wedding reception, I would try to show up at a wedding where I might see the performances done in their usual setting. Once I can establish that the tradition-bearer does in fact perform in such a way that warrants further study, I begin to inquire if the person might be willing to share some of the stories, songs, or traditions with me at a later date. If possible, we try to set a date when the context can be reestablished as close to normal as possible: the next wedding for example. In other cases, such as in collecting songs and ballads from old-timers, the best approach may be simply to drop by the person's house for some singing in private.

Once the resource person has shared some traditions with the folklorist, it is usually possible to ask permission to bring a tape recorder or a camera on the next visit. In the meanwhile, the fieldworker can size up the room in which the singing or storytelling takes place, the shop in which the wood is carved, and so forth. The appropriate equipment to bring can therefore be chosen, and a certain amount of practicing can be accomplished at home where, for example, the tape recorder can be used in a similar-sized room. By the time the researcher returns, a minimum of playing around with volume controls and placing of the microphone will be necessary. The more quickly and simply the machinery can be operated, the less likely it is to intimidate the tradition-bearer, who may be far more accustomed to live audiences than to electronics. It is only fair to note that many fieldworkers show up from the very start festooned with 35mm camera, tape recorder, and video camera, so that the informant always associates those machines with the collector—whether the machines are turned on or not. Edward D. Ives, in his widely used book *The Tape Recorded Interview*, provides many wise and practical suggestions about fieldwork tactics.

By the time the fieldworker is actually ready to start recording, he or she will have become familiar enough with the tradition-bearer and with the immediate surroundings and contexts for performance that other particular tactics will have become obvious. Whenever I go to talk to a logger at his home, I try to take a woman folklorist along so that, first, the man's wife will not feel left out of a conversation in her own home (because it is very often the wife whose role it is to be hospitable and conversational when guests are present), and second, to try to detour the wife into another context—perhaps one in which she herself will express some traditions—so that her presence will not inhibit the logger from talking about those subjects that cannot be mentioned in front of women. Sometimes under these circumstances I have found later that my accomplice succeeded in recording more folklore from the wife at her quilting frame or in the kitchen making bread than I could garner from the husband. In any case where these tactics do not seem appropriate, where splitting up a husband and wife for conversation strikes the tradition-bearers themselves as so odd that it constitutes a strain on their sense of propriety, I simply do not put the plan into action.

To a certain extent, one can feel free to manipulate the situation when doing so will allow a tradition-bearer to operate honestly and comfortably. Manipulation of the event becomes manipulation of human beings if the researcher pushes people around in their own home just so folklore may be collected. Some kind of tactics will always be necessary, however, but the researcher must keep in mind that they do not represent an unfair pressure on the tradition-bearer unless they are misused. Rather, they are the same kind of considerations one normally thinks of in any congenial conversation with friends, especially when trying to avoid argument. Certain topics may be dropped and others played up, people may be brought back around to the main subject if they wander too far from home base, examples may be given (such as when the researcher wants to do work with jokes and knows that most people do not tell jokes without being reminded of one by a previously told joke). Obviously "priming the pump" is a necessary, not an unfair, tactic.

Machinery

Some folklorists collect with pencil and notebook, others with sketch pads, others with their memories. It is safe to say that many kinds of folklore items may be handily written in a small notebook; proverbs, cures, figures of speech, regional dialect, local terminology, and the like do not always need to be put on tape. It is probably fair to say, however, that most researchers today try to use sound recorders and some kind of film equipment in their attempt to capture fully the whole performance. This means, basically, work with a tape recorder and a camera. Videotape is more widespread now that the quality of cassette-based, highly portable equipment has been improved. Movies, especially with synchronized sound, are still too expensive for most folklorists to afford on a regular basis, although with recent developments in technology, some Super-8 work is being done (Super 8mm is available with a magnetic strip attached to the film on which sound recordings may be made simultaneously with filming).

Tape Recorders

The whole point of tape recording a folk performance is to capture all the stylistic and intonational sounds that would be difficult or impossible to note by hand; there is also the advantage of being able to capture a performance while it is actually taking place rather than asking the performer to go over it line by line while someone takes notes. Tape recording is valuable to the folklorist, for in it the actual stylistic details of a performance may be captured and studied, thus carrying the researcher far beyond an attention to the mere content of a text or performance (which, as we have noted previously, may not be the central feature). If the tape recorder cannot produce these nuances of intonation, or if the operator of the machine cannot use the machine's capacity fully, then there is almost no point in making a recording.

In most tape recorders, the fidelity of sound is in direct proportion to the width of the tape and the speed with which the tape passes the recording head: the faster the speed and the wider the tape, the more likely it is that the tape recorder will pick up the greatest range of sound with the most careful regulation of quality tone. The slower the speed and the narrower the tape, the less fidelity can be captured. For this reason, studio tape recorders usually use the entire width of recording tape and are operated commonly at 15 inches per second. Until recently, fieldworkers have preferred reel-to-reel tape recorders operated at 7 1/2 inches per second (this is top speed in most portable reel-to-reel tape recorders) and in either full-width (single-track) or half-width (two-track). Since all the sound is recorded on the same surface of the tape, the more tracks provided (such as in stereo or quad recorders), the less tape width there is available for the electrical message to be caught and stored. Many cassette recorders have a very high sound quality today, and fieldworkers have been using the better ones to excellent advantage. But it is well to remember that the thinner the tape is, the more likely it is to stretch (and thus to distort sound), to break, or to "print through" (the electrical impressions on one layer of the tape may eventually seep to the next layer, causing an echo effect). Since cassette tape is thinner than standard reel-to-reel recording tape, it is subject to these problems as well as to the occasional frustration of tape breaks and snarls.

Students should be encouraged to use the best machine available, and to operate it where possible on house current rather than on batteries (which can fade and change the tape speed without the operator's knowledge). If the cassette tape is no thinner than the 60-minute variety, if the machine is well made and in good operating condition, and if the person operating it uses a good-quality microphone in the proper proximity to the speaker or singer, the cassette may indeed be more than valuable. Even so, most folklorists take their materials to archives as soon as possible and transfer them to standard reel-to-reel storage tapes so that the fidelity that has been captured will not be lost. Some folklorists prefer to use high-quality cassette machines to record spoken materials, especially where intonation and style are not primary features, and to use reel-to-reel machines for recording folksongs and ballads, folktales, or any other performances where style and texture are as important as content, or where musical sound is so central that the material would be less valuable for study if it were not recorded in the best possible way. Recently there have been startling advancements in the construction of tape recorders, and those who can afford them use the Nagra or the Nakamichi; these are outside the financial range of the typical researcher, so I am assuming that we are talking about a more modest line of equipment, such as the Sony Pro Walkman. Many folklorists have found that 90-minute cassettes made by Maxell, Sony, or TDK will deliver high quality sound, but I still prefer the 60-minute variety.

Cameras

As with recorders, so with cameras or any other equipment: the researcher should use a good-quality camera and film with a fine enough grain so that it will stand easy enlargement to 8" x 10". Some folklorists prefer to take primarily color slides, which can be projected for scrutiny of detail as well as for use before large audiences. Others prefer black and white so that prints can be produced that will be more readily stored in archives and more available to researchers without damaging the original negative. When taking photographs of folklore performances or folk artifacts, remember that the photograph serves visually the same kind of service as the tape; that is, it should be able to show those surface features of style and texture that allow the researcher to study the particularities of performance of the item or process under scrutiny. Photographs should be taken from as many angles as will reveal these details.

The photographer should operate on the assumption that it may not be possible to photograph the same event or the same artifact again; thus, taking more pictures than absolutely necessary is preferable to not taking enough and coming away with only a partial record. Very often the item being photographed will be only one of a great number of similar kinds of items, and thus the researcher will want to gather photographic evidence of as many parallel examples as possible. Even though most good cameras today have built-in light meters, it is well to take several shots from different angles in order to obtain optimum light quality. As well, if you are using a camera that allows independent adjustment of shutter speed and aperture, you should take several exposures, "bracketing" your shots by admitting slightly more and slightly less light than what the meter directs. You will obtain a spread of color and light values that will give you a greater selection of documentary photos, and you will then have a number of duplicates which will not be so regularly exposed to light. This makes the work of the folklore photographer a bit complicated and certainly brings in a financial consideration that should be dealt with before research commences.

Videotaping is becoming a more readily available and reliably used medium of documentation, and many folklore archives have their own equipment, which can be loaned out to research teams. The bulkier cameras, along with tripod and battery packs, can make a traumatic impression on some folk performers, and field researchers thus tend toward smaller, less obtrusive units. Since these items appear regularly with fetching innovations, it is easy to get caught up in an expensive buying sequence. The field researcher will want to remember that tapes are of varying thickness and quality (so inquiries should constantly be made among people who are actually using video technology often enough to find out what the current best products are); and anyone who wants archived material to be available to others will want to use a camera style and tape size compatible with most players. Currently the VCR is the most common cassette style, but such verities are apt to change drastically (try to find a needle for a stereo hi-fi longplay record player and you will discover how fast dinosaurs are made).

The tape recorder and video or still camera to be used in any research project should be practiced with ahead of time so that mechanical features will not have to be puzzled out in front of people in the midst of a project. The less obtrusive the machinery, the more likely it is that the tradition-bearers will not find their use objectionable. Incessant adjustment of tape recorders and playing back of tapes may rattle a resource person, and certainly the use of flash attachment or spotlight close at hand is not likely to be conducive to the ease of a performer. Thus, adjusting levels properly, using film that can capture available light, being at ease with one's equipment (and therefore with one's resource people), all can lead toward a more successful research venture. One last precaution is an obligatory one: always carry extra film, tape, and batteries. An interview I made with ballad singer Clarice Judkins ended abruptly (just as she was singing a verse I had never heard) only because I neglected to bring sufficient tape for the occasion. There is no way of recapturing traditions lost at such moments; the next time I visited her, she had forgotten the verse; the next time I dropped by after that, she had passed away.

Preparatory Work

Familiarizing yourself with the machinery and the technology of fieldwork is only part of preparing for a successful folklore research project. If the project is not to be a waste of time, you must also prepare yourself for the general topic by doing a considerable amount of background reading. If you are looking for a particular genre, say folksongs, then extensive reading in that area is obligatory. What kinds of songs are commonly found in tradition? In particular, what kinds of songs, or what particular songs, are found in the traditions of the geographical area you are going to study? What kinds of ethnic groups make up the area? When did they arrive? Are some more likely to be participants in a song tradition than others? Have earlier researchers indicated a local song style or preference for certain topics? Do you know some of the songs you might encounter in this area or from a particular singer?

Following up on such questions is not simply a theoretical scholarly exercise; rather, it prepares you to ask appropriate questions, to make remarks that might jog a singer's memory, to be able to mention a line or a title that may trigger an entire performance. In addition, it enables you to have some general notion of how the singer you are documenting relates to the tradition as it is already known, first as a genre recognized by scholars, and second as a local tradition. Then, if you hear the singer performing songs that have never been collected in that area before, or performing texts of words or music unlike those appearing in other collections, there is some way of judging or analyzing other aspects of the tradition and the singer's position in it. Certain tune families may suggest an influence by one ethnic or national group upon another in the transmission of songs. Certain texts may indicate that in this geographical area one ballad has commonly borrowed stanzas from another because they are recognizable as images of local import. Without knowing what to ask, without knowing which sorts of performances to encourage, without some feel for what else has been done in the field, you may have a high old time listening to a traditional singer but may find yourself frustrated as to what it all means.

Another kind of preparation reflects the fact that there are at least two kinds of folklore research: the general survey and the theoretical project. In the survey, you will be satisfied if the ballad singer you have been referred to is actually a singer of ballads, if the barn builders you have arranged to photograph actually show up and build a barn, if the old yarn-spinner you have made an appointment with shows up and is willing to tell yarns, if your roommate actually sits down and lets you record her jokes. The survey, in other words, is an attempt to gauge the breadth and depth of different folk traditions, and performances within those traditions, without trying to solve particular theoretical problems.

The theoretical project, on the other hand, usually begins with the formation of a hypothesis: you want to test a particular idea by subjecting it to the data generated in fieldwork. In this case, the preparation not only entails familiarizing yourself with the genre, the geographical area, the potential tradition-bearers, and so on, but it calls for an analytical focus on some particular topic for which further discussion will provide new perspectives in folklore theory, however small they may be. Hypotheses can vary in focus. A very broad one might be phrased, "No folksongs have ever been collected in this valley; however, most of the settlers are from English-Irish-Scottish families among whom one finds in other geographical areas a considerable song tradition: there must be folksongs here that have never been documented before." Such a hypothesis may be tested simply by mounting an intensive search for folksongs in that particular valley, with the hypothesis being either confirmed or denied by the results.

Somewhat more specific than this might be the following: "The dairy barns along this river all seem distinctive; perhaps the barn designs give some clue to the difference in ethnic backgrounds of the farmers in this area." In this instance, you might go from farm to farm simply interviewing the farmers about their barns, the designs and architectural particulars that are considered traditional, local, ethnic, and so on. During the research, you may indeed find out that from the farmers' point of view the barns are very much alike, varying only in superficial matters such as color and trim. Thus, while the initial hypothesis may simply be unconfirmed or denied, another hypothesis can be constructed in midproject, which says, "While there are many superficial differences in the designs of the dairy barns in this valley, the traditional structural aspects are very much alike; an ethnic similarity may account for these similarities in design." Further research along the same river may indicate that the ethnic similarities are not as close as might originally have been supposed, and that a *local* sense of barn-ness has actually been the deciding factor. No matter how such a project comes out, you will have been able to narrow the problem and come closer to some workable conclusions for it by testing out various hypotheses with the data provided by field research among the tradition-bearers. Obviously, such a project could not be carried out very thoroughly unless you had previously done a lot of reading into the construction of barns in general and aspects of traditional barnmaking in particular.

Similarly, if you are collecting and studying oral expressions—jokes, for example—you will want to read up on what folklorists have been doing with jokes, including their suggestions about how jokes function. For example, just about every joke cycle is based on very current social or emotional issues shared and expressed by great numbers of people (see the discussion of the elephant jokes elsewhere in this book). Logically, we can assume—at least as a proposition to base our research on—that if there is a sudden joke cycle going around, it probably represents the expressive end of a complex cultural response. The folklorist collects as many examples as possible, then looks for themes being dramatized by the joke performances, then analyzes their possible meanings in the light of the cultural context out of which they come. Obviously, to do a collection of contemporary jokes without being aware of the contemporary scene and its shared anxieties, and without considering some of the well-known functions of jokes, would be a waste of time.

For some research projects, both surveys and theoretical researches, it may be necessary for the fieldworker to spend as much as a year in preparation. This means that folklore fieldwork must be undertaken with more planning, preparation, and thoughtfulness than we are accustomed to giving a picnic or a fishing trip. Unfortunately, due to time constraints and sometimes to a lack of seriousness, some folklorists have indeed carried out field research in their spare time with the zeal and efficiency of Sunday fishermen. While it is possible to record folklore without massive preparation or development of expertise, that is no argument that this is how it ought to be done. Rather, it is sobering to reflect on the amount of traditional materials, styles, and textures that have remained unrecorded and therefore not well understood because of the hasty and unplanned efforts of folklore fieldworkers, both amateur and professional.

Aftermath: Transcription and Notes

I suppose that every scholarly enterprise has hidden in it somewhere an element of tedium. For many folklorists it is the transcription of field-recorded tapes and the editing of field videotapes. Tapes of any traditional performance worth studying should be themselves preserved, of course, so that we have as far as possible an accurate sound recording of the event with all its textural minutiae. At the same time, it is necessary to have the words for songs, stories, anecdotes, oral history, proverbs, and so on, transcribed from the tapes verbatim. This is not a job to be foisted off on an archivist; it is the final obligatory aspect of the job done by the researcher, for only the person who made the recording can be relied upon to interpret indistinct phrases, jargon, or regional dialect, and only the researcher can provide the contextual notes on such matters as gesture or name of speaker or time of day that make the tape a fully functioning document. The further value of a transcription is that anyone looking for a particular text can locate it in the transcription and determine whether it is indeed the item desired; one can determine by its setting in the transcription where it may be found on the tape (while tape recorder manufacturers almost always provide a measuring device for elapsed footage, the systems are not totally reliable).

The one proviso that most folklorists use in transcription is that the material must be taken off the tape word for word as it is in the original, including pauses, false starts, ungrammatical constructions, and so on. Most transcribers find it difficult to reflect with any accuracy a regional dialect, so most researchers spell phonetically those words that are distinctly unique variations from standard pronunciation. Some transcribers supply punctuation or other markers of phrasing as well, even though many people do not in practice speak in full sentences. Thus, every transcriber has to come to terms with the peculiarities of the tradition-bearer and must then try to represent those peculiarities as fairly as possible in an exact transcription. In order to carry this out, however, most people find that it takes between eight and ten hours of transcribing to bring off every hour of recorded material. Some archives plan on fifteen hours per hour, including other related paperwork.

Alongside the transcription, marginally or perhaps in footnotes, the fieldworker normally provides notes on elements not recorded but central to the performance: the time of day, number of people present, time of year, gestures, definitions of terms used, special meanings if not apparent in the oral performance—in short, any data from observation that help to make the performance understandable or that are necessary for the performance to have meaning for anyone else. Transcribing and providing notes are not complicated matters; however, they often constitute the difference between a useful recording of a dynamic tradition and a batch of interesting folk stuff.

The tape recordings, videotapes, notes, and photographs are the primary documents of folklore fieldwork. The transcription is an accurate but not fully reliable account of that document. The serious scholar will always go to the primary document for full detail, for it is only there that the nuances of performance, the particularities of style, and the total natural context of meaning are fairly represented for the traditional performer. Respect for our resource people requires that we collect, archive, and study their traditions in the most accurate way possible.

FOLKLORE ARCHIVES

Storage

The word *archives* refers basically to any repository of public records, but in earliest times usually to those documents relating to the official business of a town or community. It is important to recognize that the spirit of that term remains a part of the concept of folklore archives, for the whole point of maintaining such a facility is not simply to afford bulk space to store collected items, but also to provide reasonable access to the materials important to our culture. However, it should be immediately apparent, because of the nature of folklore itself, that the materials have to be dealt with in a variety of ways so that they may be safely stored, so that those who shared their traditions with the folklorist will not be embarrassed by what they did or by how their materials are later viewed or used, and so that the materials will represent folklore fairly.

Because the archives must provide both storage space, filing systems, and facilities for playing back tape recordings (at the very least), most individual folklorists cannot afford one in their homes. Most archives are funded by, or at least take refuge in, public institutions of some sort: universities, historical societies, anthropological museums, and so forth. Folklore archives range in size from a filing cabinet or two to entire buildings. The folklore archives at the University of Oregon are housed in one rather large room of the office building in which the English Department resides. The Randall V. Mills Memorial Archives of Northwest Folklore (named after a professor of English who initiated the scholarly study of the subject at the university in the 1950s and was kept at an instructor's salary because of it by a disapproving department head)—the Northwest Folklore Archives, as it is called for convenience—has a simple physical appearance: An expanding number of metal filing cabinets contain separate field collections submitted by staff and students in addition to critical papers on folklore, dissertations and theses on folklore—all produced at the university—and miscellaneous collections of folklore taken from newspapers, locally published books, student journals, and letters. There are books on folklore and related subjects, an atlas of Oregon, a set of file cards, and a few small artifacts (limited in number because the archives have no safe facility for storing and protecting such items). The furniture consists of a few desks provided for archivists, student assistants, and researchers using the archives. There is also a locked metal cabinet that contains unused tapes and the various tape recorders and cameras allocated to the archives by the English Department and the University Audio-Visual Services.

Archives of this nature are probably fairly typical of a medium-sized university in the United States that has no extensive folklore program. Far larger and more complex archives exist at Indiana University, where undergraduate and graduate programs are offered and where several thousand students study the subject each year. Extensive archives also exist at UCLA, Wayne State

University, the University of Maine, Memorial University in Newfoundland, the University of Pennsylvania, the University of Texas, and Utah State University, where students and staff have, through their own fieldwork efforts, amassed sizable collections of folklore.

The Fife Folklore Archives at Utah State University was established in the 1970s when folklorists Austin and Alta Fife donated their massive library and field collections to the Merrill Library as the foundation of a folklore repository. Since that time, the university and several individuals have added to the book collection with substantial gifts such as the Hector Lee Record Collection, the Skaggs Foundation Cowboy Poetry Library, the Don Yoder Folklife Book Collection, the Wayland D. Hand Memorial Book Collection, the John I. White Collection (over 200 books and pamphlets on western and cowboy song), the Grouse Creek Cultural Survey records (from an intensive field project carried out by the American Folklife Center), the American Folklore Society Historical Records Collection (historical records, papers, books, and correspondence covering the more than 100-year history of the national professional folklorists' association). The most active and rapidly growing part of the Fife Folklore Archives is, of course, the library of student collections, which are turned in as assignments in folklore classes; these collections provide thousands of expressive examples from regional, occupational, religious, ethnic, and family groups in the Intermountain West. Along with these collections and papers, the slides, videotapes and descriptive studies done by members of the folklore faculty, are in constant use by scholars from around the world who seek vernacular examples of American culture.

Many folklorists have worked in a solitary fashion and their own collections may be stored in such a way as to inhibit their use by other scholars. For years, a small folklore collection existed in Salt Lake City, Utah, stored away in a cardboard box or two under the desk of a retired professor. For a while its existence could not even be corroborated. Other partial collections have been hidden from public view because of the whims of their collectors. For example, when Robert Winslow Gordon, the original archivist of folksongs at the Library of Congress, left the Library, he took a number of his most special collected songs with him and stored them under his bed for years thereafter. Long after his death, when his collection of folksongs had been given to the University of Oregon by his daughter, we found that a number of texts actually should have been in the Library of Congress. There are probably hundreds of examples of such small or partial collections that, because of personal taste, fear for the contents, or simple lack of money, have been stored in such a way that the physical materials have deteriorated or have been thrown away or lost by those who had no idea about their contents.

On the other hand, in Europe it is common to find extensive and well-financed facilities for the storage of folklore, especially in the countries which have emerged or re-emerged since the Second World War. In Romania, there is a complex of several buildings in which nearly a hundred government-paid specialists operate a folklore archives and research facility. They have a modern recording studio, the best recording equipment, room after room of books, journals, collections, card files, photographs, movie films, and so on. In many countries the collection and study of folklore has been a direct counterpart to the development (sometimes the re-establishment) of a sense of national, cultural, ethnic identity. Those countries that lived under the yoke of foreign domination for years are especially anxious to encourage their own ethnic roots to come forth again after long years underground. In these countries, folklore becomes almost a part of political reality as a nation seeks to demonstrate to itself and to others the fact of its own separate existence. In such a case, folklore and ongoing vital traditions can be much more functional means of cultural cohesion than the economic or political symbols normally represented by official boundary lines or political party. Folklore can also serve more sinister agendas as well, as William A. Wilson, James Dow, and Hannjost Lixfeld have shown (see Chapter 10).

A similar consideration is now gaining increasing attention from Native American tribes, for in their case as well the existence of ongoing dynamic traditions is a much more accurate marker of ethnic existence than the so-called blood quantum introduced by the government some years ago. In most cases, with encouragement from the government, tribes voted that a person must be at least one-quarter "blood" of that particular tribe in order to be enrolled and to be thus eligible to vote, to participate in tribal programs, or to derive any benefits that might arise from sale of land or resources. This decision was made even though many tribes already had a long history of intermarriage with other tribes. Thus when these regulations came into existence, many members of the tribes were already at the minimal level of membership, for although they were entirely or almost entirely Indian, their grandparents were from different tribes; therefore in the next generation children were born who were less than 25 percent of one tribe and who were no longer qualified to be on tribal rolls. If we project this into the near future, considering the recent heavier intermarriage with Whites and other ethnic groups, many of the Pacific Northwest tribes will, in technical terms, cease to exist before the year 2000—although they will still be there in even greater physical numbers than they are today.

In other words, the Indian culture is still being passed along in each of these tribes, but members of these cultural groups are represented by such a mixture of tribes and peoples that in technical terms they will not qualify to vote or do business in their own tribes. The Colville Confederated Tribes in central Washington, for example, estimate that by the year 2000 there may be no new enrollments, that is, young people born into the tribe will not have enough "tribal blood" to qualify for official membership. This in no way means that tribal traditions are fading. To the contrary; among the Colvilles as in many other tribes in the United States today there is an increased awareness and in fact a resurgence of vitality of those traditions that had been nearly obliterated. For many of these tribes, then, the only hope for establishing a sense of ethnic identity, the only hope for "proving they continue to exist," will be the availability of data to document the ongoing vitality of a distinctive tribal folk heritage. For these reasons, many tribes are becoming increasingly concerned with documenting and preserving their folklore in archival facilities.

We must then realize that folklore archives represent far more than storage space. Folklore collections are more than merely the playground for scholars, for in folklore archives (whether hidden under the bed or spread through several buildings) rests the most telling evidence of the vitality of cultural tradition in our country as well as elsewhere. Thus the care and preservation of materials in folklore archives must be approached in as delicate and reliable a way as possible. Obviously, none of these concerns can be well exercised unless there is room to store our materials, unless we can protect them from deterioration, and unless they can be found again after we have packed them away in a file drawer.

Protection: Physical

The considerations for the protection of physical materials within archives are staggering in their proportions, and I will not pretend to take up their technical detail here. Rather, I would like to suggest some of the important concerns that every archivist (and therefore every folklorist) must keep in mind to assure that materials garnered at so high a cost in time and sensitivity in the field will not be lost to the ravages of decay. A clean, well-lighted room—even on an antiseptic campus—will not be adequate protection for our materials.

Filing

A good filing system will prevent items from going astray. Things can be lost by being dropped on the floor, by being handled by people unfamiliar with archives or their operation, or may be misplaced even by well-intentioned folks who would like to put things back where they think they found them. The basic operation of archives involves some kind of restricted access to the materials, so that a very few individuals are allowed to find an item, take it from the file, and return it when finished. If access is unrestricted, things will be lost, misplaced, and stolen, which is what happens in nearly any library or public facility. Recognizing this should suggest some basic and not very complicated operational rules.

Maintenance

The machines used in and by the archives can malfunction and will eventually wear out. Videotape equipment, for example, can be put out of kilter simply by being carried up and down flights of stairs too often. Not only should access to these sensitive machines be limited to those experienced with them, but they should be stored and handled with extreme caution and care. Moreover, every piece of equipment requires a regular maintenance program: shutter speeds on cameras sometimes need adjustment; battery-powered light meters and tape recorders can be affected by fading (or worse, leaking) batteries. Electric "bugs" can show up in the magnetic heads of recording equipment if they are not regularly cleaned. In general, people will operate a tape recorder without realizing how their lack of experience may affect their success. The same brashness disappears when it comes to repairing equipment, however, and when faced with the prospect of tinkering around inside a tape recorder, most people grow pale and faint. It is well to admit a lack of expertise in these matters and leave the repairs and technical maintenance to trained technicians. At the same time, there are simple, efficient, and inexpensive ways of keeping recording heads clean, lenses dusted off, batteries checked, and so on. People who are not willing to take responsibility in these matters should not be allowed to use the equipment. Since that would perhaps place a severe restriction on fieldwork, the folklore archivist must realize that proper maintenance of equipment is a central obligation for all archives themselves.

Film

If unexposed film is stored in the archives, note the expiration dates. The emulsions of color film continue to change, and they will change more rapidly at higher temperatures. Film bought in bulk may be frozen and thus be preserved almost indefinitely. At least the temperature of the archives must be controlled enough so that any unexposed film does not become outdated ahead of its factory expiration date.

If archives contain color slides, the slides must be protected from being scratched and mishandled. This can be accomplished fairly simply by putting them in slide holders or keeping them stored in carousel trays. There are of course various storage mechanisms, such as sheets of plastic jackets in which the slides can be held in front of a lighted viewing panel. Black and white photographs and their negatives need to be protected not only from each other (since small particles of dust or grime can cause scratches on the surface of pictures), but also from direct sunlight, extreme heat or dampness, or any other situation that can curl, corrode, or alter the materials themselves or the image. Light is a more deadly enemy with older pictures, of course, which can fade very rapidly. If the collections contain pictures, the archivist must have a reliable book on maintaining and preserving photographs. Remember that even fluorescent lights have a deleterious effect on paper and dyes; their erosive qualities should be mitigated by the use of ultraviolet filter sleeves.

Tapes

Tape recordings probably require a lot more consideration than we normally give them. As I suggested earlier, it is possible for sounds on one layer of tape to print through to another layer, thus causing an echo. It is also possible for tape to become brittle, especially under unusual conditions of temperature and humidity change. Most professional archivists therefore find it practical to run each reel of tape through a tape recorder at least once a year to check for brittleness or breakage as well as to redistribute the stress on the entire tape that might have built up by partial use or by inactivity. Some people who work exclusively with sound recordings suggest, beyond this, that each tape be electronically redubbed to a fresh tape every so often, perhaps every four or five years, to cut down on the deterioration of the tape itself and to inhibit printing through.

Paper

One of the deadliest enemies in archives is the presence of acid in paper. Nearly all paper deteriorates because of its own acid residue, which is in turn a part of the process by which paper is produced. Not only is there deterioration of the typing paper on which data are stored, the same problem exists with manila folders and envelopes, cardboard or paper mats and jackets for photographs, and the like. Some kinds of paper have more acid than others, and of course now that archivists are aware of this problem, they can use available "acid-free" papers and folders and boxes. Also available are chemical strips that can be inserted into boxes or folders that will reduce the acid pH of the materials stored. With some papers and cardboards, as the material begins to deteriorate more acid is formed, so the process is hastened, in some cases almost exponentially.

While it is hardly likely that paper will deteriorate before our very eyes under controlled conditions in the archives, it is nonetheless a distinct possibility that within a hundred years entire archives might have to be copied or they are at risk of being lost. If we try to imagine the massive and expensive chore this would be for any archival collection, we can see the necessity of trying to ward off these deteriorating processes before they get well started. It is unfortunate in this regard that most folklore archivists are trained more in folklore than in the physical aspects of document protection; nonetheless, basic first aid may be learned without intellectual pain and with considerable benefit for the archives. Now that low-acid and acid-free papers are available, many archives require their use for any texts being accessioned.

Environment

The total physical environment within a building that houses archives must remain under careful control. The best of all worlds is to have a facility with a separately controlled heating and air-conditioning apparatus as well as humidity control. This is usually available only through larger libraries, so for many folklore collections it is unrealistic. Failing that, however, anyone working with folklore materials must develop a workable plan for providing as much protection as possible from such ironically destructive forces as sunlight and air. Those who live in cities with considerable pollution will find that the air has a greater propensity to attack all conceivable objects, even paper hidden in drawers. Those who live in relatively pollution-free environments need not feel much more cheerful, however, because direct sunlight and the varying humidity of fresh air flowing through an open window can be just as dangerous in other ways.

For one melancholy example, consider the following: A researcher came to the Mills Archives one afternoon and asked to see some black and white photographs of tombstone epitaphs in a pioneer cemetery. These photographs were part of a student collection, and, to protect the photographs themselves, the student had placed each one in a clear plastic folder in which had been inserted a dark piece of cardboard matting as a background. The pictures were brought out and left on a desk in the center of the room for refiling with the collection. Before the archivist had a chance to put the pictures away, however, a beam of sunlight had rested on the photographs for perhaps no more than two hours. When the photographs were to be put away, the archivist found a hole had melted in the clear plastic. A specialist in the university library suggested that the acid in the photographs, combined with the acid in the clear plastic folder, enhanced by the acid in the dark cardboard matting—all brought into more rapid action by the direct sunlight—had conspired to burn a hole in the plastic. If such a thing can happen so quickly, consider the destructive processes quietly at work in the darkness of file drawers, in the various levels of light around the archives, and especially under a direct source of sunlight or fluorescent bulbs. Considering that paper and photographic materials are likely to become increasingly more expensive, the physical problems of preservation within archives are enough to cause genuine concern. While nothing can be done about the forces of decay, at least common sense and good advice can help us inhibit those processes that could eventually rob us of the rich examples of folk heritage we have spent so much time obtaining.

Protection: Ethical

As if the physical problems were not staggering enough, the archivist (and thus the contributing folklorist) must also consider the fact that archives are a repository of other people's most cherished inheritances. Thus the archives must be handled with more human sensitivity than the First National Bank, for these materials are not to be cashed in and out without regard to the feelings of the contributors who made them possible. For one thing, when people are talking among friends and telling jokes, recalling celebrative events like shivarees, or giving oral histories of the union movement, they may say things and recall events that they might not share with total strangers. If a researcher publishes these things without regard to the feelings of the person in the field, there is the possibility of everything from hurt feelings to insult to lawsuit.

Protection of Decorum

Every folklorist has favorite examples of such disastrous outcomes, and I will mention a few more. Among the collections in the Northwest Folklore Archives is one of logger songs, most of them generally considered obscene. The retired logger who sang them did not mind sharing them, principally because the collectors were accompanied by loggers and one of the collectors had been himself a logger. Thus the context in which the collection was made was an easy one to deal with, and the materials shared would normally have been shared by such men under similar conditions. Moreover, the old logger was delighted with the prospect that the songs he had preserved in his own repertoire were actually considered important cultural items by someone else. In addition, he took a humorously devilish delight in realizing that bookish scholars were now finally trying to deal with what he considered the real world of male experience in a hazardous profession.

When the tapes had been made and played back to him, however, he suddenly realized that if anyone else heard him singing these songs he would be embarrassed. He allowed the archive to keep the songs, but insisted on the stipulation that they not be played for any woman under twenty-one. He was concerned, for example, that his granddaughter might possibly come to the university, take a folklore course, find herself in the archives and see that there was a collection of songs from her own grandfather, and might thus expose herself to songs that her grandfather had spent his entire life protecting the women of his family from. The logger admitted that perhaps the granddaughter would not be embarrassed, since young people today have a wider vocabulary than they had when he was brought up, and he was well aware that women, especially from logging communities, are not ignorant of the subjects or the terminologies used by the loggers. However, his own moral ethics were such that he could not abide the thought that as a grandfather *he* should ever sing these songs to his granddaughter.

But of course the case is more complicated than that. Suppose we wait until his granddaughter is, say, thirty, and then we publish his songs in a national journal, identifying the singer and his locality. Is it not possible that a leading patriarch of a community might feel libeled by an article that featured him as the articulate and talented singer of "dirty songs"? This is an ethical dilemma for the folklorist-scholar, of course, and it is confronted nearly every day by professionals who seek to publish the results of their research without embarrassing their resources. But it also becomes an ethical consideration for the archivist, who needs to know the nature of the researcher, the nature of the research, and the intended result before making a judgment on the dissemination of some materials. This question can be resolved more efficiently if such matters are taken up with the field resource people themselves and written into whatever contract may represent the donation of the materials to the archives.

✳ Protection of Occupation

Another example of a similar concern relates to a particular boat style in the state of Oregon. Several rivers in Oregon have local styles of boats used by local fishermen. One very distinctive such boat is the McKenzie River Boat, and one of the most talented craftsmen at producing this type of boat, Keith Steele, makes his living doing so as well as by being a river guide for fishermen. The Northwest Archives wanted to have photographs and detailed drawings of Keith Steele's McKenzie River Boat, but they found that the boatmaker himself was extremely reluctant to let measurements be taken and drawn for fear that others might then have access to his plans and thus, perhaps with the best intentions, put him out of business. He was assured, of course, that the archives would never let anyone make copies or detailed notes of his drawings—and in fact only partial drawings for two views of the boat were displayed on the walls of the archives—precisely so that the full information would not be available to parties who might be able to memorize enough of it to carry it away. Clearly the archives act in a precarious role here: if we provide the fullest view of Keith Steele's boat, we might become the medium through which Keith Steele can no longer make a living building his own version of the McKenzie River Boat. Rather than celebrating his talents, we might put him out of business, which of course would run directly contrary to the whole point of having archived his skill.

✳ Protection of Ritual Secrecy

Other more complicated considerations come into play when ritual material is collected. For example, a number of Native American tradition-bearers have been willing to be recorded singing songs or telling stories and then have placed restrictions on access or usage. Some do not want the Coyote stories to be available to anyone except during the winter, their usual time of use. Sometimes archives may become the repository of traditional information from tribes who feel that they do not have the facilities for safe storage on their own reservations and would like to take advantage of somebody else's, but they do not want their materials shared with anyone except members of their own tribe. If such archives then were to disclose those secret rituals to a well-meaning anthropologist doing research on that tribe, they might advance the cause of knowledge, but they would also completely obliterate any sense of trust that tribe would have in these archives, and might in the long run encourage them never to share or preserve or document their central traditions again.

Some kinds of traditions are meant to be secret among those who share them, even though they do not necessarily represent any religious or ritual secrets that, divulged, might ruin the structure or the stability of any close group. An example might be information such as that shared by fly fishermen along the North Umpqua River in south-central Oregon. The North Umpqua fly fishermen, most of whom go after steelhead, are a very tight-knit group of people as fishermen, even though they come from an amazing variety of professions and backgrounds in everyday life.

While they are on the river, they learn the ways of the stream and of the fish from one another, and this information is placed in a larger framework of esoteric data that includes the names of fishing spots and holes along the portion of the river that is open to fly fishing only. The names of the holes, the order in which they may be followed downstream, the ways in which they must be fished depending on different water conditions and weather, the kinds of tackle used in each case are closely guarded secrets. They exist in the oral tradition of all who share that experience, but they are not divulged to outsiders, least of all to bait fishermen, "worm drowners," who are looked upon with great contempt.

If their secret information, stored in the archives, were revealed inadvertently by a scholar publishing a study of fishermen's language and lore, it would not cause a religious outrage or the dislocation of anyone's cultural bearings. Nonetheless, it is easy to imagine that fieldworkers might ever after have considerable difficulty conducting research among fishermen in this area, for they would have felt betrayed by anyone who placed scholarly interests over concerns more central to the existence of a close group. While this is not an earth-shaking ethical dilemma, it is a secular variety of the problem inherent in storing religious folklore that should remain secret.

To what extent does the scholar or researcher have the right over the proprietary concerns of any group's internal beliefs, customs, and attitudes? If one relies merely on the Freedom of Information Act or the copyright laws, all of the advantages are with the scholar; after all, this is a free country. We can publish what we please, can't we? If one is on the side of human sensitivity, which I have argued must be a basic ingredient of folklore field research, then the answer is not so easy. If we adhere to cultural rules, we will not be publishing Tlingit stories without having been given permission by their separate owners; we will not be publishing most Native American Coyote stories without considering the season of the year; we will not be publishing anything on Hopi language or lore without negotiating written permission from the tribal cultural affairs representative. Clear enough; but what about culturally sensitive materials from groups which have no "cultural affairs officer"? Direct involvement by people from the community provides one way of ensuring that embarrassments and outrages are less likely to occur.

Protection from Libel

A prominent university in the Midwest once started to accession a wonderful collection of tapes that had been made of the oral history and traditions of a particular labor movement. As part of the process of obtaining the tapes, they requested that some lawyers listen to them to see if any legal restrictions should be placed upon them for access and use. The lawyers' advice was that about 90 percent of the tapes should be destroyed immediately, for they contained random observations by people who could be brought to court for libel by a number of parties. For example, someone recalled that the person who founded a certain union local "was a Commie in those days." Now, calling someone a

Communist and identifying the person in a public place has already been ruled by a number of courts to be grounds for a libel suit, whether the allegation is true or false, because it may materially affect the person's welfare, status, and employment. Since archives are, at least in most cases, potentially the repository of publicly available information, it can be construed as published, even when the materials may not necessarily appear in printed form.

This is a legal area that is far from solidly defined at this point; at the same time, it does bring up the possibility that our archives may contain comments and statements that, if not properly handled, might be damaging to the people who said them or about whom they are said. Probably folklore archives, if limited to that orientation, are less likely to contain such potentially complicated materials, but since many archives also contain a large number of anecdotal oral histories, it is a question to which any archivist needs to pay attention.

Protection from the Law

Still other problems may arise if the archives contain any information dealing with folk expressions connected to illegal activities. Students in the past have found a rich store of folk speech, custom, and gesture in close groups whose definition is based on actions or attitudes that might be considered illegal. Such items as "hash" pipes, criminals' speech, marijuana legends; the customs and language of smugglers, prostitutes, and pimps; stories and legends of "crossing the wire" by and about illegal immigrants from Mexico, and the like are contained in a number of archives. Since investigators can easily gain admittance to stored records in order to glean evidence or clues about criminal activity, the collectors and informants of such collections may be placed in a vulnerable position simply by having their names on record. Some archives handle this problem by obliterating names or by substituting fictitious names in all documents entailing problematic legal issues. In this way, the materials are still usable for folklore research, but the archives are not a potential threat to the safety of those who have shared sensitive information or who have revealed their identities. Other archives, feeling that the lack of verifiable names and addresses reduces the scholarly worth of such a collection, simply do not accession such materials, thus avoiding entirely any threat to the people involved as well as cutting down on the number of collections within the archives whose value might be compromised by lack of information.

Sometimes these matters are hard to deal with in advance. During the Vietnam War a student of mine, a conscientious objector in solid legal standing, decided that it would be interesting to collect the many legends, anecdotes, and jokes concerning draft-dodgers. There were hundreds of them in circulation, usually featuring some unique or clever way in which a candidate for the draft had avoided military service (by eating bits of aluminum foil, consuming great quantities of sugar just before a urine analysis, or by trying to make homosexual advances to the military doctor). The stories were in circulation among many who were not themselves draft resisters, and in many cases names were used that might or might not have been the real names of people trying to avoid the draft. Nonetheless, such activity if carried out in reality was considered tantamount to illegal by the government. Since the student was himself legally exempted from the draft, and since he did not ascertain in his two field collections that the tellers of his stories were in any illegal situation, it seemed to me that the presence of those collections in our archives would not represent a threat either to the government or to any individual named therein.

Nonetheless, during a period of intense student antidraft and antiwar activity, when we were aware that law officers were on campus in great numbers conducting undercover surveillance, the two fine collections suddenly disappeared from our archives only to reappear again in their usual places three weeks later. How these collections were taken from the archives and returned is entirely unclear. Did some well-meaning and thorough police officer gain access to the archives after hours to look for clues? We have no way of knowing. If such an occurrence did happen, however, even under the most discriminating of police officers, the names and addresses generated by such collections would by no means have been a fair set of clues as to the identities of those in the university community who were in fact most actively campaigning against the war. Moreover, while such activity was then considered illegal, it was later considered justifiable, thus indicating that information available in archives might be sensitive at one moment and not at another.

In some cases, the issue may be registered on a very personal or practical level. A group of students touring a university's archives were told by the archivist that some collections were not open to the public because of their sensitive nature. One of the students, a journalism major, took issue with this view, noting that university-supported archives were in effect publicly owned repositories of vernacular (i.e., public domain) materials, and thus the interests of the public should outweigh the concerns of individuals. Pressing his case, he insisted on gaining access to a collection he had heard about: a series of ghost stories told about a house a few miles from the university. The collector of the stories had been asked by the informants—who lived in the "haunted house"—not to divulge their identities or their address, for fear of community ridicule, and because they also did not want to impede the sale of their house, then on the market. The journalism student wrote an interesting piece about the house and its putative ghosts, quoting the informants from their narratives in the collection; in addition, the article was accompanied by a large picture of the house, along with directions on how to find it. The owner of the house, who was suddenly besieged by people wanting to interview him and by curiosity seekers prowling around his yard at all hours of the night, promptly notified the university that he would sue for damages (personal reputation as well as loss of money in the ruined house sale). Universities are believed by the public to have immense amounts of money, and this kind of suit can cover nearly anyone possibly connected with the injury: in this case, the student folklore collector, the archivist, the professor of the folklore class in which the project was submitted, the head of the English department in which the professor was employed, the dean of the college in which the English department operated, the vice president for Academic Affairs, the provost, and the university president. Fortunately for everyone concerned, the house became more famous than infamous, fetched a fine price, and the injury was thus hard to prove—but this close call should stand as a precautionary example for anyone who thinks folklore is "kids' stuff" or believes that folklore does not trip off deeply emotional responses in the real world we live in—regardless of whether we believe in ghosts.

Suppose, for example, that certain archives contain several collections of traditional processes for making homemade beer. Then suppose that five years from now a law is passed against private beer production (as has happened in some states already). Would it be fair for authorities to use the archives as a source for a list of people on whom police would like to call to determine if now-illegal activity is still occurring? I think most archivists would consider this an unfair use of folklore archives, yet most law enforcement officers would consider it legal and justified. Since we cannot foretell when something is likely to be sensitive, we may simply need to be aware that it can happen and try to develop some archival rules or responses to such situations.

Filing and Retrieval

As we move more inexorably into the computer age, some larger archives are developing storage and retrieval systems that are partially or entirely computerized. Eventually these archives may become the terminals of larger interlocking systems that will give researchers across the country and around the world access to data that would otherwise require considerable travel and tedious reading. Nonetheless, for most of us in the coming years, the realities of archival work will remain pretty much as they are today: we will need to visit a particular archival collection and see if we can find the materials we need, and then we will need to find some way of getting them out of the file drawer and onto the table for scrutiny before determining what further use can be made of them. One reason for this is the fact that electronic inputting—even with the help of a scanner—can be more expensive in terms of time and computer equipment than most archives can afford. In addition, since access to some collections will always need to be controlled (for ethical reasons mentioned previously, or just simply to protect treasures like family recipes from exploitation by unknown knaves), electronic retrieval will always entail problematic considerations. In spite of the growing attitude that access to information is the central concern today, it will always be the case (I hope) that wisdom, perspective, respect, and responsibility will guide the way in which the information is handled.

In some archives—for example, in the Oral History Collections at the University of Alaska—data which are indeed designed to be made generally available are stored in a system known as the "juke box," presumably because its stack of compact discs resembles the commercial record player of the 1950s. This complex set-up of tape recorders, computers, and discs allows the researcher to bring up a printed transcript of an oral history interview, along with the recorded voice of the informant, along with pictures of people and places, maps, diagrams, etc.—thus making several dimensions of history available to the user at one time. At this writing, few archives can afford the machinery, but its utility has been strikingly demonstrated by Professor William Snyder at the University of Alaska and by Alan Lomax, who uses a similar system to store and study music and dance traditions around the world. In any case, all archives must develop a cataloguing system that will assure that however materials are accessioned into the larger collection they may be readily retrieved and used.

Some archival systems are cross-referenced exhaustively, and the researcher can look up a particular motif or theme or type in an extensive card file or computer system. Other archives are arranged on an intentionally simple model, designed so that the basic larger questions of finding materials can be answered, leaving further comparative and analytical work to the researcher. The Northwest Folklore Archives has a card file that answers the four most common questions asked by researchers: What items do you have of this particular genre or kind of folklore? What do you have from this particular folk group? What do you have from this particular geographical region? What do you have from this particular informant? There is therefore a file of 5" x 8" cards classified as *genre,* a category construed very broadly so that it can include particular recognizable structure-based genres such as ballad, legend, proverb, and so on, as well as larger distinctive kinds of folklore like magic and custom, or groupings such as family folklore. Each person who deposits a collection in the archives is obliged to fill out standard cards in which as many genre cards are completed as seem to indicate the range of folklore in the collection fairly.

There is a file designated as *folk group* as well, again a category broadly construed so as to name or define that particular grouping of people that seems most distinctively related to the kind of folklore in the collection. Under this heading there are loggers, well-drillers, residents of the Rogue River valley, Native Americans (always including a tribal designation), women, teenagers, and so on. There is no suggestion that the folk group necessarily functions as an isolated or rural grouping; rather, the attempt is to find the common denominator that defines that close group in which the folklore under consideration is normally performed.

Another file is designated as *geographical region,* which ranges from the names of particular towns and settlements to definable geographic-cultural areas (insofar as they may be ascertained with any accuracy). There is a distinct Willamette Valley culture in Oregon as there is a distinct John Day Country, and a Central Oregon, and a Coast Range, and a Coastal Area. In other states, some counties, as Sanpete and San Juan counties in Utah, may have distinct traditional characteristics. In some places a whole region may be distinctive, like the northern peninsula of Michigan or the Ozarks of Missouri and Arkansas. In some cases, the folklore in the collection may be distinctive of one of these recognizable regions, and this designation may be an index to some further observations on shared traditions on a regional basis. On the other hand, it may be only by coincidence that a number of people have been interviewed in Seattle, Washington, and before researchers go there to do more fieldwork they may simply wish to know what kinds of things have been collected there and from which particular people so that they will not duplicate the work on the one hand and so that sensible recollecting may take place on the other, if that is called for by the research. Another file is organized as an index of *informants.* I have already expressed some dislike for this word, but in a filing system it seems at present our simplest and most direct term for those individuals who shared their folklore with the field researcher.

In the first three categories here, the file itself is broken down into obvious subheadings: Under *folk group,* tabs mark such subdivisions as *occupational, ethnic, religious,* and the like. Under *geographical region,* separate tabs indicate those cards arranged by city, county, state, by particular regions within a state and among states. Thus, in all cases, if someone comes to the archives to do research and says, "Do you have any stories told by Old Man Jones in Coquille?" an archivist can go to three different files to see if, first, anyone has collected anything from somebody named "Old Man Jones," whether it is actually Old Man Jones from Coquille, and, last, whether the collection consists of stories (perhaps a previous collector found out that he knew some songs but was unaware of a story repertoire or did not have time to collect them). Similarly, someone can ask if there is any folklore from Aurora, Oregon, and can be told quickly, "Yes, there are seven such collections, four of which are available for researchers to use."

On each of these file cards is the title of the collection, the collector's name, and the date of accession. Once it is ascertained that there is something in the area the researcher is interested in, an archivist then consults another card file designated *release.* This is a standard form—and perhaps it is too brief—signed by the collector, which indicates that the collection is being donated to the archives and lists any stipulations and restrictions requested by the collector or the informant. For each collection there is also a master card, actually a table of contents typed out on a standard sheet of paper. The researcher can find if there are folksongs from Aurora, say, and can discover, without taking the collection out of its place in the file, what is in it and whether it may be used for study or publication. If anyone must be contacted for permission, that information is at hand and the researcher can then make any approaches necessary to obtain the proper clearance by contacting the collector or the resource person directly. This system restricts wear and tear on archival materials and focuses the initial steps of research on the filing system and descriptive catalog of the archives. At the same time, such a system certainly burdens the researcher with most of the preliminary labor to prepare for research and analysis. If someone asks whether the archives contain any stories with a certain motif, there will not be a precise answer, but by looking at the master card for each collection, the researcher can find out whether there are stories that seem to be related to the motif under scrutiny.

All archives have some such system that is basic to the process of cataloguing accessioned materials. Larger archives, which may be able to employ archival assistants, will have developed more fully articulated filing systems than others. Even so, an extremely complicated filing system is not necessarily the best tool for research, for the more designations made in a system, the more decisions have to be made by the archivist rather than by the researcher; probably all folklorists have had the experience of finding items by surprise or luck while they were looking for something else. For this reason, if for no other, there is a strong argument for maintaining a fairly simple cataloguing system so that broad areas can be defined and retrieved; then the researcher can make the analytical judgments necessary to the proper pursuit of a given project, unencumbered by others' decisions. And, of course, if the truth were known, there are probably many folklorists who would much rather go through innumerable printed materials in their search for useful information than punch up a lighted or printed display on an electronic marvel.

Paper Work and Ownership

Filing systems such as those described above are how we try to ensure that we do not lose even the smallest item in our large collections. In order for this basic interest to be carried forward, a certain amount of paperwork in the development of the filing system is an obvious necessity. Beyond that, however, there is another kind of paperwork necessary to the proper maintenance and operation of all archives. What, for example, if someone drops in who placed a collection of folksongs in your archives last year and now wants it back? If there has not been some legal agreement that the collection was indeed given to the archives, there is no way this demand can be denied. Or suppose the old man whose dowsing was photographed by a student comes by the archives, having decided that he does not want his picture hanging around in a storage facility? Does the archivist have any means of arguing that the pictures are so helpful that they ought to remain where they are? Again, if there is no formal arrangement by which the ownership of the collection and its photographs was handed over to the archives, it is not difficult to see that the person concerned might have a clear and legal right to retrieve his likeness. So, no matter how seldom these situations might occur in practice, most archives assume that it is a basic necessity to have standard forms that indicate who owns what, what kinds of restrictions are placed on use or dissemination, who should be called on any question about the use or intended publication of the materials, and so on. At the least, the thoroughgoing archives will have the following specific items on paper:

1. A letter, or notes on a telephone conversation, or notes on a private conversation, about the initial contact between the researcher and the field resource person. When was the person first contacted? Was there a reply? Does there need to be any advance work done before the first visit takes place? These and other considerations can be charted by having some recorded information about the initial contact if it was initiated by or at the request of the archives. This particular item may be missing in many collections initiated by students or other people who suddenly find themselves in contact with a grandfather or a neighbor who is willing to tell stories or whittle for the camera or sing songs at a wedding.

2. There should be an official form noting what kinds of equipment have been checked out from the archives for the project, giving such details as serial numbers or identifying marks, any related equipment (microphones, additional tapes, film), and the name, address, and telephone number of the researcher. On another part of the same form, or perhaps if necessary on a second form, there should be an equally detailed way of checking the equipment back in, for the protection of both the archives and the researcher.

3. While most archives use a single release form, most commonly signed by the collector, in all fairness there should really be two release forms. The first is an acknowledgment by the person whose material was collected (the "informant") that the collection will be deposited in an archival collection with his or her knowledge and permission.

4. The second release form should be an acknowledgment by the collector that the fruits of his or her fieldwork are being deposited in the archives for standard archival storage and use. In both releases, there should be a clear provision for any restrictions that the collector or resource person feels are necessary for the proper handling of the material. Among these stipulations, we may expect that some ethnic groups will want to note that the materials are owned in a larger sense by the tribe, say, and that the use of certain items must be cleared in advance with tribal authorities. Some researchers and archivists do not like this consideration; nevertheless, cases have been decided in court on behalf of ethnic proprietorship of certain materials. The standard restrictions and stipulations listed on the two kinds of release forms are, typically, directions on whether the material may be published or not, whether the material may be published only by permission of the collector or the informant, or whether the material must be withheld from public use until a certain date. Other restrictions are possible, of course, and any such release form should allow space for any other

conditions under which the material may be most appropriately deposited in the archives.

5. An accession document of some sort should identify the tape or the photograph or the text or the transcription by the names of the collector and the resource person, by accession date, and it should list other kinds of vital information that identify the work, the date and place it was undertaken, and whether all other paperwork has been carried out in full.

6. Although the idea seems initially too formal to some folklorists, there is a good argument for the use of a request form by which a person who wishes to do research applies for permission to have access to certain materials. Such a form accomplishes several extremely valuable ends. First of all, perhaps in a fiscally political way, it serves as a ready reference to the amount of traffic through the archives during any period of time, thus enabling archivists to demonstrate to administrators the extent to which the archives is used.

Beyond this, it forces the petitioner to be serious and specific in requesting access, which tends to cut down on what might be called academic tourists simply looking for an afternoon of congenial reading. In the case of small archives, which cannot accommodate serious scholars and curious onlookers at the same time, such a form can help the archivist regulate the use of space or intercept at least temporarily those who are not quite sure what they need to consult. Further, such a form, read and signed by the researcher, creates a formal arrangement with the archives that requires the researcher to acknowledge the archives' rules (which may define ownership, usage of materials, matters of publication, format for acknowledgment, and the question of who pays for copies), so there will be no misunderstandings.

Although it may not happen often, the existence of a properly executed request form may also give a later clue to the whereabouts of missing materials. Mainly, however, the request form helps to establish a professional attitude toward the use of the archives. It does not require that one be among the leading folklorists of the world to use the facilities, of course; it simply protects the professional interests of folklorists in general, protects the materials shared by people in the field, and encourages the development of a seriousness of purpose in those who might otherwise approach the archives as if they were a treasure chest of quaint toys or a cheap resource for children's books.

The Fife Folklore Archives uses the following forms for its permissions file; informants may place any restrictions they want on the use of their materials, but very few ever do. I think that the opportunity to do so, the assurance that the informants, not the academics, have control is enough to convince most people that we are dealing openly with them and would respect their concerns. Those who do make restrictions usually stipulate that anyone seeking to use a given item in published form contact the informant first: this allows the tradition-bearer to decide, for example, that a children's book or a church cook book is or is not the appropriate place for this tribal story or that family recipe. (See examples on following pages.)

The best of modern folklore scholarship is an interdisciplinary combination of scholarly fields, sensitive and thorough fieldwork, careful archiving and research, and an acquaintance with those journals, books, and professional meetings that keep the folklorist up to date in the subject. Because of the central roles of field research and archiving in the development of folklore theory, however, some folklorists have come to believe that fieldwork is as obligatory for the interviewees as for the interviewers; that is, the field resource persons are sometimes approached as if they were a natural resource like coal, which has the obligation of being dug up and burned at the discretion of those who need the heat. Similarly, some have dealt with archives as if they were the grave of folklore and not a protective resting place for delicate materials.

However, not all collected folklore gets into archives, and perhaps I ought to admit that not all folklore belongs in archives. And it may be that some singers and storytellers do not care to be researched. Not everyone likes to be observed, preserved, or encouraged to perform, and the very presence of a folklorist with camera or tape recorder may actually keep a traditional process from taking place. Comments like "No, we don't allow that to be photographed" or "You can't have that recipe—it's only given out to family members" or "Hell, I'm not going to sing with *that* thing turned on" are sometimes heard and must be respected.

One small tribe of Indian people on the Oregon coast decided that while they did want to retain their winter stories, recording them might not really lead to preservation, for it would relieve the people of the custom of continual retelling with at least two other tribal members present, and might thus bring about the ironic situation where the texts would be saved but the live contexts neglected. Their refusal to tape their stories might be thought of as a loss by some folklorists, but in their reasoning lies an important lesson, perhaps the most important of all for any folklorist: the people's integrity and the dynamics of their folklore are realities central to our profession. Our main job is not to pin up a large butterfly collection at any cost but to understand live butterflies more fully and help to keep them in their natural circumstances. My Indian friends on the Oregon coast decided it would be more to the point to insist that all tribal meetings begin with the telling of Coyote stories during the winter months so that all present members could hear the stories and participate in their telling. Any fair-minded folklorist would certainly recognize this as an insistence upon keeping the material alive and functional, and we might even argue that in so doing this small tribe was maintaining its own live archives. Under those circumstances, one can hardly lament that the stories are not in fossilized form in a file drawer or on a shelf of tapes. Although the folklorist

Informant Release Form

_____

I,_____, hereby
                        (Informant - please print name)

contribute my interview with _____,
                                    (Collector - please print)

conducted on _____, to the Utah State University
                      (Date)

Fife Folklore Archives.

Signature_____Date_____

It is understood that the interview becomes the property of the Fife
Folklore Archives, where it will be indexed and preserved. The collector
and the informant retain the right to free access to the collection through
normal procedures of the Archives and its personnel.

The Fife Folklore Archives is used by students and scholars, who may duplicate
archived material and may quote it in published form with the permission of the
Archives. Scholars using archived material in their studies, research, and publications
must agree to give proper credit to collector, informant, and the Archives. Further
stipulations and restrictions may be noted below.

( ) No further restrictions.

( ) See below for further restrictions.

Collector Release Form

I,_____, hereby release
(Collector - please print name)

my folklore Collection _____,
(Title of Collection)

to the Utah State University Fife Folklore Archives.

It is understood that the interview becomes the property of the Fife Folklore Archives, where it will be indexed and preserved. The collector and the informant(s) retain the right of free access to the collection through normal procedures of the Archives and its personnel.

Signature_____Date_____

Permanent Address through which you could be reached:

_____

_____

_____

_____

The Fife Folklore Archives is used by students and scholars, who may duplicate archived material and may quote it in published form with the permission of the Archives. Scholars using archived material in their studies, research, and publications must agree to give proper credit to collector, informant, and the Archives or to protect the anonymity of both collector and informant.

may be a master of the discipline, it is the larger process of tradition that should always be dominant.

BIBLIOGRAPHICAL NOTES

Not everyone approaches fieldwork the same way. While I tend to be sparing with equipment, others carry a tape recorder over their shoulder everywhere they go in order to establish an image of "that person with the machine"—as if it were another arm that spectators simply must get used to. Either gambit will produce results if sensitively employed. The present chapter, then, is not a prescription for fieldwork technique but a plea for awareness of the human element in fieldwork, archiving, and research. The following works suggest the range of practical and technical advice available to the folklorist who wishes to see that the people and their lore are not insulted, cheated, or wasted in the collection and study of traditional events.

Approaches to Field Research: Richard M. Dorson, "Standards for Collecting and Publishing American Folktales," *Journal of American Folklore* 70 (1957): 53-56; Kenneth S. Goldstein, "The Induced Natural Context: An Ethnographic Field Technique," in *Essays in the Verbal and Visual Arts,* ed. June Helm (Seattle: University of Washington Press, 1967), 1-6; Michael Owen Jones, "Alternatives to Local (Re-) Surveys of Incidental Depth Projects," *Western Folklore* 35 (1976): 217-26; MacEdward Leach, "Problems of Collecting Oral Literature," *PMLA* 77 (1962): 335-40. All the foregoing deal with context, consideration for the informant, means of eliciting traditional expressions, and so on. Leach in particular discusses the importance of cultural matrix and provides some interesting remarks on folk vs. sophisticated aesthetics. Richard M. Dorson's standard work, *Folklore and Folklife: An Introduction,* has been mentioned previously; toward the end of the book are several sections of particular importance in this discussion: George List, "Fieldwork: Recording Traditional Music," 445-54; Donald A. MacDonald, "Fieldwork: Collecting Oral Literature," 407-30; Warren E. Roberts, "Fieldwork: Recording Material Culture," 431–44. Each of these gives basic observations on the areas mentioned, and each provides a good beginning bibliography.

Rosalie H. Wax, *Doing Fieldwork: Warnings and Advice* (Chicago: University of Chicago Press, 1971), is a personable autobiographical account of several fieldwork projects undertaken by the author and her husband, also an anthropologist. Part 1 (3-55) offers some very penetrating comments on fieldwork based on personal experiences, some of which can only be called fortuitous accidents and unintentional blunders; Wax generously shares the dilemmas she encountered as the bases for observations on knotty problems that some fieldworkers fail to take into consideration until they have occurred in mid-project. Albert B. Lord, *The Singer of Tales* (Cambridge, Mass.: Harvard University Press, 1960) is a classic work that shows how hypothesis about the oral composition of epic poetry led to field research in Yugoslavia that in turn led to rich and sometimes startling discoveries about the nature of oral poetry.

Apparatus and Technique, Especially in Film: One of the handiest books on the use of film in fieldwork is John Collier, Jr., *Visual Anthropology: Photography as a Research Method* (New York: Holt, Rinehart, and Winston, 1967). In addition to dealing with photography itself, Collier's work considers the critical questions behind photographing in terms of what is to be gained and how certain problems may be approached; clearly, the book is as much a suggestion for visualizing a research method as it is a handbook on photos. Karl G. Heider, *Ethnographic Film* (Austin: University of Texas Press, 1976), discusses the ways in which ethnography differs in conception from standard filmmaking. The book lists representative ethnographic films and discusses the techniques and research methods of prominent ethnographic filmmakers. Lenny Lipton, *Independent Filmmaking* (San Francisco: Straight Arrow, 1972), gives a practical description of basic equipment and how-to processes in filming, editing, and visualizing. While it does not deal with ethnographic or folkloristic filmmaking as such, its technical offerings are well worth having for anyone who wishes to pursue any kind of filmmaking independently (as many folklorists are forced to do). In a similar way, Edward Pincus, *Guide to Filmmaking* (New York: New American Library, 1969), gives a useful discussion of hardware and technique. Ivan Polunin, "Visual and Sound Recording Apparatus in Ethnographic Fieldwork," *Current Anthropology* 11 (1970): 3–22, is a basic and sensible view of the machinery most needed and encountered in fieldwork and provides a rather full bibliography. A fascinating account of a fieldwork project that moved neatly from hypothesis to fieldwork, through further research and analysis, to a rich conclusion is provided by Sol Worth and John Adair, *Through Navajo Eyes: An Exploration in Film Communication and Anthropology* (Bloomington: Indiana University Press, 1972), already referred to several times. Their conclusions are too numerous and complex to summarize here, but it is important to note that they discovered the kind of truth that has dawned on many a folklorist: when research includes the subjects themselves as participants (instead of as mere objects of scrutiny), the conclusions are astronomically richer and often far different from what the researcher might have hypothesized alone. Brief but indispensable essays on media documentation are provided in Richard M. Dorson, ed., *Handbook of American Folklore* (Bloomington: Indiana University Press, 1983), Part 3, especially "Collecting Musical Folklore and Folksong," by D. K. Wilgus (369–75); "Sound Recording and Still Photography in the Field," by Carl Fleischhauer (384–90); "Using Video in the Field," by Richard Blaustein (397–401); "Studying American Folkloric Films," by Sharon Sherman (441–46).

Manuals for Fieldwork: Although it is very brief and focuses on a particular geographical and political entity, Jan Harold Brunvand, *A Guide for Collectors of Folklore in Utah* (Salt Lake City: University of Utah Press, 1971) demonstrates how folklore theory can be applied to the study of traditions in a well-defined culture area without unnecessary jargon or overproduction of hypotheses. Kenneth S. Goldstein, *A Guide for Fieldworkers in Folklore* (Hatboro, Pa.: Folklore Associates, 1964) is much more extensive and theoretical than Brunvand, but does not restrict its focus to a particular area. Much of the information and advice on mechanical equipment (cameras and tapes) is now of course outdated by the rapid development of transistorized equipment. Nonetheless, the tenor of the advice is still valid, and many of the other comments on fieldwork in general are as timely as they were when the book was written. There is a good deal of basic advice for researchers working away from their own turf. One of the most practical and overtly helpful guides is Edward D. Ives's *The Tape Recorded Interview: A Manual for Fieldworkers in Folklore and Oral History* (Knoxville: University of Tennessee Press, 1980); it is especially useful in addressing the technical and theoretical problems encountered by archives that include the wide variety of materials falling under the rubrics of folklore, anthropology, and oral history. A more focused view is provided in Maud Karpeles, ed., *The Collecting of Folk Music and Other Ethnomusicological Material: A Manual for Fieldworkers* (London: International Folk Music Council and the Royal

Anthropological Institution of Great Britain and Ireland, 1958). The practical observations on equipment are dated, but overall the manual is very usable.

Another small regional booklet for an area that, unlike Utah, is not so heavily characterized by a single group, is MacEdward Leach and Henry Glassie, *A Guide for Collectors of Oral Traditions and Folk Cultural Material in Pennsylvania* (Harrisburg: Pennsylvania Historical and Museum Commission, 1968), a combined effort to list a few of the most common traditions in various categories and to suggest how those traditions may be sought, found, collected, and preserved. Quite the most exhaustive manual of this sort, no doubt the real ancestor of the regional manuals in America, is Sean O'Sullivan (Sean O Suilleabhain), *A Handbook of Irish Folklore* (1942; reprinted, Detroit: Singing Tree Press, 1970). By giving innumerable examples of the rich and varied traditions of Ireland in the form of questions to be asked potential informants, O'Sullivan's book provides enough leads to keep the fieldworker engaged in conversation for several years. For the American scholar, O'Sullivan's book is primarily useful in suggesting the *kinds* of questions, topics, and approaches that may be most useful in eliciting traditional information in the field.

In addition to Ives's fieldwork book, prospective fieldworkers in folklore and oral history should view his video, *An Oral Historian's Work* (1987; distributed by Weiss Productions). Robert A. Georges and Michael Owen Jones propose a human-centered (rather than information-based) approach to fieldwork in their *People Studying People: The Human Element in Fieldwork* (Berkeley: University of California Press, 1980). Bruce Jackson's *Fieldwork* (Urbana: University of Illinois Press, 1987) enlarges on the human-centered approach and supplies very useful considerations and advice on other dimensions of the fieldwork enterprise, including mechanical and media issues as well as ethics.

Archiving Considerations: First, for some discussion of how archives operate, where they are, and how material may be catalogued, the reader might begin with George List, "Archiving," in *Folklore and Folklife: An Introduction*, ed. Dorson, 455-63. *The Folklore and Folk Music Archivist*, vols. 1-10, published at Indiana University from 1958 to 1968 under the editorship of George List, provides brief but illuminating articles on archives and their contents internationally; Robert Georges, Beth Blumenreich, and Kathie O'Reilly, in "Two Mechanical Indexing Systems for Folklore Archives: A Preliminary Report," *Journal of American Folklore* 87 (1974): 39-52, propose one plan for coding an archival system so that material being accessioned can be categorized according to a multitude of scholarly interests and later retrieved for research. The careful reader of this article will notice that it is as much a theoretical discussion of how folklore may be subdivided as it is a mechanical plan for finding materials in a storage center. Dov Noy, "Archiving and Presenting Folk Literature in an Ethnological Museum," *Journal of American Folklore* 75 (1962): 23–38, presents still another aspect of how folklore materials relate to particular kinds of storage facilities. *Folklore Forum,* Bibliographical and Special Series, no. 1 (November 1968) presented *Folklore Archives of the World: A Preliminary Guide,* compiled by Peter Aceves and Magnus Einarsson-Mullarky, providing a finding list of archives along with current addresses. A great deal of archiving, retrieval, and discussion is now done by computer in ways that were only theoretical a few years ago. Those interested in this arena of archiving should watch for articles by Barbara Kirshenblatt-Gimblett, and should get in contact with the "Bytelore" column in the *American Folklore Society News.* As of this writing, this regular column is presented by Mark Glazer (mglazer@panam.edu), who features regular reports on the development of computer databases, discussion groups, and other issues related to the use of folklore in the virtual world of electronics. The address for the folklore Discussion Group is listserv@tamvml on BITNET and listserv@tamvml.tamu.edu on the Internet.

Preservation of Materials: All serious archives should be equipped with proper advice about the nature of paper, films, tapes, and other materials that constitute the basic physical media of folklore storage. While the following list is not exhaustive, these books allow archives to confront the most pressing dilemmas in conservation and preservation in an efficient way: George D. M. Cunha and Dorothy G. Cunha, *Conservation of Library Materials,* 2nd ed. (Metuchen, N.J.: Scarecrow Press, 1972), offers an extensive two-volume treatment of basic conservation and restoration problems and procedures, threats to different types of media, and principles of archival preservation. Volume 1 contains discussions, helpful appendices, subject and author indexes, and references to other literature; Volume 2 contains probably the most extensive bibliography on the topic and a comprehensive guide to the literature of library and archival conservation. See also Cunha and Cunha, *Library and Archives Conservation: 1980's and Beyond* (Metuchen, N.J.: Scarecrow Press, 1983). Kenneth W. Duckett, *Modern Manuscripts* (Nashville: American Association for State and Local History, 1975) is a basic text on sound archival practices relating to manuscripts. Two chapters are of special interest to folklore archivists: Chapter 5, "Physical Care and Conservation," and Chapter 7, "Non-Manuscript Material," which gives helpful suggestions about films, tapes, slides, and other items. The book includes a long bibliography, a good directory of supplies and tools, and suggestions on where to get special jobs done. Robert A. Weinstein and Larry Booth, *Collection, Use and Care of Historical Photographs* (Nashville: American Association for State and Local History, 1977) is one of the most practical guides to the technical aspects of old photographs. The book brings up philosophical questions, details on restoration, ideas about interpretation, and preservation. A good bibliography is included. Howard W. Winger and Richard B. Smith, eds., *Deterioration and Preservation of Library Materials* (Chicago: University of Chicago Press, 1970), is a highly informative survey of basic preservation problems relating to the nature and deterioration of paper, environmental problems, and other topics, all of which grew out of an earlier library conference. Each article features an extensive bibliography.

One of several standard archival supply companies, Light Impressions (439 Monroe Avenue, Rochester, NY 14603-0940; ph.: 1-800-828-6216) issues a regular catalog which indicates the range of materials, lights, books, and protective devices available to the modern (and responsible) archives. Up-to-date books and manuals on the care and protection of photos and papers, on collection documentation, and of physical treatment of archived items are designed for the use of active, professional museums, and should be consulted for archival necessities before storage and preservation problems arise. Many people, for example, are unaware that the ultraviolet light from fluorescent bulbs (used in most public buildings) bleaches out the color in book bindings, photos, and artwork. Protective sleeves called Filter-Ray UV Shields can be put over each fluorescent bulb to cut out as much as 98% of the ultraviolet rays. Beginning in 1975, the Library of Congress began to issue a series called *Preservation Leaflets.* These contain bibliographical references and descriptions of monographs and articles relating to the problems suggested in the titles and the contents of the previously mentioned books. These pamphlets are available without charge from the Library of Congress, Washington, D.C. 20540. The Library of Congress includes two divisions directly related to folklore: the Archive of Folk Culture and the American Folklife Center. These offices are both willing to help fieldworkers with technical and theoretical problems, and they can offer the use of equipment to scholars doing extensive fieldwork. Anyone interested should contact the center directly for information on recent programs and directions.

Research and Application: It goes without saying that nearly every work cited in this book is an example of some kind of folklore or ethnographic research carried through to an analytical conclusion. I will mention here, then, only a few works whose topics suggest areas of research not covered previously. One of the most helpful general research guides for anyone reading in folklore is Jan Harold Brunvand's *Folklore: A Study and Research Guide* (New York: St. Martin's Press, 1976). Chapter 2, "Reference Guide," is particularly handy because its references are solidly representative of the field; they appear in full notation, including Library of Congress call numbers. The book includes suggestions for paper topics and format (Chapter 3) and is an all-around indispensable research help for the beginner. Richard M. Dorson, "The Use of Printed Sources," in his *Folklore and Folklife: An Introduction*, 465-77, suggests how folklore may be gleaned from and studied in newspapers, popular books, and in other print media that might at first not seem rewarding sources for folklore materials. E. Estyn Evans, "The Cultural Geographer and Folklife Research," in *Folklore and Folklife: An Introduction*, 517-32, applies the resources of folklife and material folklore research to the problems and perspectives of cultural geography. It seems clear from this study that the cultural geographer and the folklorist often deal with identical kinds of information, even though until recently, at least in the United States, there has been relatively little interchange between the two fields on a theoretical level. Louis Gottschalk, Clyde Kluckhohn, and Robert Angell, in *The Use of Personal Documents in History, Anthropology, and Sociology* (New York: Social Science Research Council, 1945), include a chapter on field methods by Kluckhohn as part of a whole section of great interest to fieldworkers in folklore. Personal reminiscences and oral history are as yet underutilized by students of folklore. L. L. Langness, *The Life History in Anthropological Science* (New York: Holt, Rinehart, and Winston, 1965), while not oriented to expressive aspects of culture, stresses the individual's concept of his or her own traditional place in the culture, clearly another particular aspect of oral tradition that bears further study. Bruce A. Rosenberg and John B. Smith, "The Computer and the Finnish Historical-Geographical Method," *Journal of American Folklore* 87 (1974): 149-54, put forward a rather simple means by which a computer can be used to provide a rapid comparison of texts and variations in the same kinds of scholarly study that once took years of careful reading and handwritten notation. Whether such a system will ever be in wide usage may be irrelevant compared to the observation made by the authors that computer work need not dehumanize or change in any essential way the normal operations of folklore research except insofar as years of effort may be saved and analytical problems solved rapidly enough so that scholars in a given generation may join in the conversation.

Robert Wildhaber, in "Folk Atlas Mapping," in *Folklore and Folklife: An Introduction*, 479–96, describes an analytical procedure that has been carried forward for some years now in Europe but has only recently begun to gain extensive support in the United States. Many European countries have folk atlases that show variations in dance steps, costumes, haystacking traditions, and traditional tools in tremendous geographical detail. It remains to be seen whether the United States will ever develop enough interest in our traditions on the official level to warrant the long-range expenditure of money necessary for such a vast project; in the meantime, many folklorists in America are developing among themselves the basis for a folk atlas with the help and leadership of Professor W. H. F. Nicolaisen. Of interest to all scholars using, storing, and quoting oral materials is an undated pamphlet by Joseph B. Romney, *A Guide to Oral History and the Law,* available from the Utah State Historical Society, 300 Rio Grande, Salt Lake City, Utah 84101.

Temari (lit. "hand-balls") were once made to save or recycle colored threads taken from Japanese kimonos, which are totally dismantled for cleaning. Today they have become an ethnically meaningful folk art made from recycled plastic (styrofoam flakes stuffed into a plastic bag), leftover yarn, and embroidery thread. Here, Chiyoe Kubota winds string around a bag of styrofoam bits.

Using a marked tape, Mrs. Kubota insures that the distance is equal in all directions (indicating that her ball is as round as possible) and begins marking out the coordinate points she will use in applying the colored threads.

Temari are given away as gifts, decorations, toys for children (sometimes with a bell built into the center), or—in contemporary America—ornaments for Christmas trees.

Chapter 10

APPLICATIONS OF FOLKLORE

"Applied folklore" is seen by some academics as too pedestrian. Especially for those who believe academic scholarship and research ought to be untainted by practical considerations, the concept has had the same ring that "applied art" or "applied literature" might have. It seems to smack of job rather than profession, of problem solving rather than theoretical speculation, of the immediate live world rather than the library. It stresses doing more than thinking and talking, and the academy has always been uneasy about such subordination of its central role.

I like to encourage students to pose of everything they study the hypothetical question, "So what?" That is, what is it good for? What does it tell us that we needed to know? What does it open up for us? How does it help us to understand something? "So what?" is not meant to be belligerent or cynical, but to serve as a kind of field test to see if a mental exercise has paid off. As a student, I once listened to a long, detailed lecture about the real persons on whom Chaucer might have based the figure of the Knight in *The Canterbury Tales*. At the end, I could not come up with an answer to "So what?" beyond the simple observation (which the professor could have made in one sentence) that Chaucer may have had a live person in mind. But why did students need to know that or think about it? It did not seem to expand our appreciation of Chaucer's art, or our understanding of *The Canterbury Tales,* or our command of medieval literature. Now, it may have been my fault or the professor's that there was no adequate answer for my question, but it remains unanswered to this day—for me, anyhow.

On the other hand, if we read Jan Harold Brunvand's study of Shakespeare's use of a folktale type in *The Taming of the Shrew* and then ask "So what?" there is an answer: we now can see that since Shakespeare used folklore as well as his own genius, we need to deal with both before we can make either broad or specific pronouncements about Shakespeare's art. Which parts are his and which parts are the people's? How, and how appropriately, did he use the folklore, and with what presumable effects on the audience (since they, no doubt, recognized the material)? In how many plays did he do it? These questions should lead us to some important perceptions about Shakespeare's art and its meaning. And we can go back over the work of earlier critics who did not think to look at the folklore deeply enough. What do we know now—what can we say now—that improves our abilities to respond to Shakespeare's dramatic art? These are real payoffs, not mere mechanical tinkerings, yet they are derived from an application of folklore study and theory to an existing field of study, in this case literature.

This is not to say that folklore is an automatic antidote for dull classes, but that in any area, the perspectives of another field may be applied to particular problems with more than respectable results. The lecture "Who Was Chaucer's Knight Really?" was not pointless just because it did not deal with folklore, but because it did not apply any real perspective to a real problem: it did not lead to a richer view of the work. Rather, it added yet more painstaking and detailed information to the already heavy pack of data being lugged around in the minds of young scholars. One might as well have a dissertation on the identity of the original travelling salesman, or of Kilroy; if the treatise helps us avoid dealing with what is funny in the jokes, or with how the message "Kilroy was here" spread all over the world in a few years, it cannot stand up to the question "So what?" It is indeed strange that the amassing of facts often passes for real scholarship, while applying the facts' perspective to a problem is often thought of as a cheap shot.

Additionally, I think we may suspect that there is sometimes a class issue lurking behind academic hesitation to try a practical application of scholarly perspective. It is as if by gearing down their large professional views to the interests of people outside their disciplines, scholars feel they demean themselves— as if they pictured themselves as classical concert musicians being asked to fiddle "Yankee Doodle" on a street corner. How can the *hoi polloi* be trusted to understand or deal with an area of expertise without distorting it? This defensive feeling can be intensified when we suggest that the stories of oral tradition may have some bearing on formal literature; or that the recollections of ordinary people might help understand the processes of history.

Such suspicion of practical application is not as prominent in other professional fields. A medical doctor is someone who applies the scientific and theoretical knowledge of his or her field to problems among live people. While some doctors are lecturers and researchers, no one, I believe, looks down upon the practicing physician as providing a substandard function in the field of medicine. If doctors stopped dealing with patients just because the common person lacks formal understanding, we would accuse them of a dangerous and unrealistic elitism. Similarly, it would surely be ironic if a discipline like folklore, whose entire existence is based on expressions of the everyday person, ever became one in which the information were shared only among the elite, in which the theories became more important than the people.

The ways of applying folklore fall into a few rather well-defined categories: There are intellectual applications, as when folklore is used as an approach or instrument for literary criticism, historical scrutiny, or cultural psychology; there are applications that involve some kind of action being taken, as in the workplace, intercultural relations, urban settlement, ethnic arbitration, and education. Other applications are in the nature of employment, such as when the Smithsonian Institution or a state arts agency employs professional folklorists to organize a festival, to produce cultural exhibits, films, and publications, or to develop culturally rich school curricula.

FOLKLORE AND LITERARY CRITICISM

Suppose we wish to examine the ways in which an author uses folklore—not merely to catalog its motifs but to see its relation to the writer's style, vision, and literary art. How can we apply the resources of folklore to the artistic output of an individual author? What terms do we need to invent or use in order to label the phenomena we see, or which terms may we develop in trying to make our study more clear to those with whom we wish to communicate? Finally, and most importantly, what do we gain by applying folklore to the writings of a particular individual? After all, a novel, short story, or poem written and copyrighted is certainly not in itself folklore. What is the "so what?" of folklore in literature?

First of all, we know that many writers have found folklore and myth to be powerfully evocative of cultural responses in the reading audience. We need to take a close look at any author's use of folklore, then, and see if indeed the ideas, connotations, and responses evoked by folk ideas are appropriate to and integrated into what is happening in the work. In other words, in a large sense, the questions asked about the use of folklore in literature are almost exactly the same ones asked about imagery or symbol: What is the relation between what is said and how it is said? Are the images and symbols related to the content? In the case of folklore, has the author used the materials to deepen and extend the meaning or only for window dressing, for local color? These are the same questions we ask in any close examination of literary style and meaning, but of course they cannot be asked and answered well unless we are willing to develop some expertise in the field.

Earlier we discussed the relationship of the Wife of Bath's red stockings both to folklore and to Chaucer's possible intent. Of course, we need to remember that since authors cannot be brought back to life to testify, we cannot be overconfident about exactly what they meant, but this does not prevent us from speculating on the appropriateness of image to content. We h talked about the connotative power of words like *pig* and *cherry* and we recognized that even entire stories may have rich traditional associations that carry meaning far beyond the manifest content of the words. We may suspect, because of the considerable cultural power of folklore and the depth with which many people register their recognition of their own traditions, that a sensitive writer will not use folklore materials lightly, but will be motivated by the conviction that the use of certain images, phrases, and structures will serve as a powerful emotional link between the shared cultural responses of the audience and the emotional and moral issues in the literature. And, thanks to the work of postmodernist critics, we are now aware of the extent to which cultural convention shapes any work of literature, as we are now more cognizant of the fact that a great amount of literary "meaning" depends on what we bring to the experience.

Some Approaches

The main business of literary criticism is to approach the problem of thinking about and talking about works of literature in such a way as to expand the areas of sensitivity between writer and reader. That is, the literary critic does not see the task as telling what a work "means;" for that, the reader interacts carefully with the work itself. Historical criticism tries to present a clear picture of the historical context of a work; biographical criticism provides data on personal backgrounds that might have been factors in an author's development or in the development of a particular work. Deconstructionists and postmodernists have argued for multiple readings of a text based on cultural "maps" and on information and attitudes brought to the experience by different readers, as well as on "intertextuality"—the effect different texts and utterances may be said to have had on each other. At their best, these and other approaches try to foreground and clarify the various areas of an author's background and intellectual/historical/cultural milieu that led to the production of a particular work of literature, along with assumptions, attitudes, and preconceptions brought into the field of reference by the reading audience. The critic, in recreating these arenas for study, is simply preparing a number of lines along which the field of references between author and reader can be more fully appreciated. Such avenues are not ways of telling what a work means; rather, they operate as points of access, as ways of thinking more fully about, and thus responding more fully and more reliably to, the work.

Some approaches use folklore as an indication of an author's acquaintance with folksy materials or the ability to use tradition as local color, or as a reference that throws light on a difficult passage. These are not dishonest approaches, especially if they are warranted by an author's superficial use of folklore, but they fail to help us understand the extent to which folklore can the spirit and direction of a given work. A few critics, like Daniel Hoff- *rm and Fable in American Fiction,* do deal directly with literary works a body of traditional materials used centrally within them. But the resulting critical approaches have been very general, dealing with rather broad matters like cultural views of the authors or beliefs reflected by their characters. What is needed is a more specific and accurate way to talk about, and to organize, our recognition of traditional materials used by authors, and a way to approach more coherently the question of how traditional themes and forms are used artistically and how they may strike their audience. Other, more recent critics have focused on traditional stylistic factors such as metaphorical nuance, implications of dialect, and rhetorical intimacy between the persona and the reader as indices of the extent to which active folklore permeates and drives more subtle matters than plot.

The Literary Use of Folklore

Many works of literature can serve as models for the kind of study suggested here. For convenience I have chosen a well-known novel because it has striking examples of what I am talking about, and they so saturate the work that without a doubt they are connected to the whole fabric of plot, character, presentation, and theme: Thomas Hardy's *The Return of the Native*.

In the first chapter, "The Three Women," we are presented with a great array of traditional items: There are the November Samhain fires—and, indeed, at this point and throughout the novel Hardy overlooks no chance to make it clear that all important junctures of human involvement coincide with ceremonies connected with the seasonal cycle (the autumn fires, Christmas festivities, Maypole dancing). The early action takes place not only around one of these fires but on a barrow built in ancient times situated on a hill shaped like a human breast. An old man sings a few verses from the ballad "Queen Eleanor's Confession" (Child #156), and a lengthy discussion develops on the ambiguity of Christian Cantle's gender, centered on the proverbially phrased birth superstition, "no moon, no man."

As the novel proceeds, we encounter dreams as omens and brief references to particularly appropriate folksongs (for example, the small boy who has been tending a fire for Eustacia Vye goes home singing "in an old voice a little song about a sailor-boy and a fair one, and bright gold in store," which is no doubt a reference to "James Harris, or the Demon Lover," Child #243, the theme of which is quite appropriate to this novel). There are references to ritual braiding of hair; throwing a shoe after the bride; witchcraft, including sticking pins in dolls and in people; omens such as a sparrow flying through the house on the morning of an ill-fated wedding; and folk medicine, in the attempted cure for Mrs. Yeobright's adder bite (frying adders and applying their rendered fat to a wound). One central character is continually described in terms of that haunting figure Robert Graves has since called "the White Goddess." Hardy says of her, "Eustacia Vye was the raw material of divinity," and he calls Egdon Heath her Hades. He describes her as a beautiful black mare on one occasion and as a delicate, pale, potentially cruel being on another.

Still another character, Diggory Venn, is seen throughout in the role of trickster, whose function is entirely that of a catalyst. Nothing of structural importance in the novel happens without his aid or scrutiny. He is called Mephistophelian, and he is entirely red from the sheep dye he uses, which "spreads its lively hues over everything it lights on, and stamps unmistakably, as with the mark of Cain, any person who has handled it half an hour." In another place we are told, "Among all these squatters and folks of the road the reddle-man continually found himself; yet he was not of them." And yet we notice that he is connected with everything that happens in the novel, and he would have disappeared entirely (and properly) at the novel's end but for the insistence of the serial publisher that he be brought back in, washed up, and married to the heroine, a transgression of his traditional role that strikes us as akin to unmask-ing the Lone Ranger and then marrying him off to the local Sunday school teacher.

One thinks of other traditional aspects of the novel: an eclipse of the moon at a point where human entanglements have assumed ominous importance; the continual stress on the reciprocity between Egdon Heath, its weather, and its simple inhabitants; the mummers' play, complete with masks, during which main characters are masked and unmasked. One also thinks of the particularly vivid scene in which Mrs. Yeobright, having been refused entrance to her daughter-in-law's home, sits down exhausted on a bank of sweet thyme, watches a heron fly overhead toward the west, and thinks a last thought described as "marked by a streak in the air, like the path of a meteor." As she sleeps (and we remember she has just returned from a garden with a central apple tree), she is stung by an adder. Since thyme was a funerary herb, the bird often a carrier of the soul (and "going west" at that), a falling star a death omen, it would have come as no surprise to a rural British audience that she soon dies. It should not surprise the folklorist, either. But it may surprise an otherwise well informed person, who might resist "reading something into" the scene. The real question is, of course, "What can we read *out* of it?"

These and many other traditional references occur in a novel oriented to the mythic year, the whole action taking place between Celtic New Year (Samhain) of one November and that of the next, exactly one year and a day. Hardy's refer-ences to folklore (and they abound in his other novels as well) were catalogued by Ruth Firor some time ago, and her book serves as a handy listing. Much more to the purpose of our present inquiry, however, is not the existence of folklore in Hardy, but the question "So what?" What shall we make of all this: That *The Return of the Native* is a folk novel? That Eustacia Vye is really the lunar White Goddess in her waning aspect? That Diggory Venn the reddleman is the devil? That the novel is really a myth for modern times? No to all of these, because they all make of the work something it quite obviously is not designed to be. Is it possible to conclude conversely that these folk references either are coincidental or are the surface representations of psychological processes too deep for our scrutiny of conscious art? No again, because the correspondences are too neat, the references too many and consistently appropriate to their context for us to dismiss them from consideration as units of conscious art.

Modes and Metaphors

If we approach these references critically, we find they are of varying focuses and applications. Some, like the orientation of the whole novel to a mythic year of seasonal rituals, seem to be concerned with ordering the story's action in terms of forces beyond the observable world, perhaps in terms of cosmic rhythms. Some of the references, however, seem to be more localized in the story; they describe people and events in traditionally evocative ways, and their contexts are limited to the passages in which they occur. The larger organizational assumptions might be termed *modes,* somewhat after Northrop Frye's term. A *traditional mode* would be a conventionalized ordering of literary design according not to the demands of verisimilitude but to the expectations of tradition; or, to make it simple and specific, a traditional mode is a manner of creating an artistic expression according to Olrik's "Epic Laws." There is no assumption that a particular genre, theme, or content will be present. It is simply an observation on the organizational and conceptual assumptions of the author, but with a distinct critical advantage: since we are dealing with tradition, we can treat the features themselves as recurrent enough to be conventional, and we can assume that they will be familiar to anyone who shares the tradition. By extension, we may say that the critic, who may or may not share in the tradition as an insider, can in any case enter the tradition well enough through study to create reliable connotative relationships.

The smaller, more localized units of description and action might be called *traditional metaphors.* In this view, the traditional metaphor is the suggestive, highly charged vocabulary in which the traditional mode reaches expression. The traditional metaphor also comes out of traditional cultural concepts, but its use is not in the ordering of the whole work. The metaphor itself differs from the usual concept of metaphor in that there is no specific simple analogy but rather traditional actions, colors, images, symbols, and so on, that have culture-based connotations. The bank of thyme, the heron, and the meteor image, which combine to foreshadow Mrs. Yeobright's death, are not used to mean simply a bunch of plants, a bird, and an astronomical phenomenon; they appear as a recognizably figurative constellation which suggests death by evoking folk beliefs familiar to the audience (and within our reach through research). One would hesitate to call them symbols, and they appear too closely related to the direction of the plot to be thought of as anything but conscious art. They are effective artistic units that call upon our ability to respond to familiar beliefs and to apply them as translations of image to import.

Applying the concepts of traditional mode and metaphor to *The Return of the Native* and to other works of literature that come to mind, however, we notice some further distinctions. We may say, for example, that when Chaucer takes two traditional stories like the Flood story and the so-called misplaced kiss tale and puts them together in the Miller's Tale, which is itself organized very much along the lines of traditional narrative in spite of its sophisticated poetic embellishments, what we have is an entire work of art conceptualized along traditional modal expectations.

We have the same kind of organization in, say, *Beowulf*, as in *The Return of the Native;* moreover, in these works the mode seems much more infused with a sense of religious urgency, of commitment to processes in which the main characters are models of deeper or more universal human possibilities, conceived of in a mythic way. Thus we might need to subdivide the terms *traditional mode* and *traditional metaphor* and use the term *mythic mode* for the organizational principles that seem to reach toward the ineffable, the Beyond, and the term *folkloric mode* for the organizational assumptions that produce traditional patterns in secular fictive expressions from everyday life. Of course the distinction is an arbitrary one, usable only in discussion. In reality, many kinds of folklore references might go as easily into one category as another. Superstitions and customs of everyday life (folkloric), if they concern death and burial traditions, may actually be concerned with the universal (mythic). In most cases, though, the dichotomy seems to be a fair one to play with.

The same distinction could be made between mythic metaphor and folkloric metaphor. In the mythic metaphor there is the feeling that the image is pregnant with the aura of universal power. The barrows in *Return,* for example, are described as the poles and axes of a mysterious heathery world; the November fires and the mummers carry associations that reach far beyond their immediate plot context, even though their employment in the novel is quite limited. On the other hand, the references to customs (braiding hair and throwing shoes and gathering holly), while evocative, bring up associations concerning local customs, popular beliefs, and observances that simply have to do with participation in a local traditional culture. These folkloric metaphors are not the less useful to the author, however. Take the singing of "Queen Eleanor's Confession" at the beginning of *Return* as a single example. The whole ballad is not sung, but certainly most people in Hardy's day would have recognized it, and they would have been able to sense, we assume, that the novel's narrative was about to concern itself with such matters as disguise, treachery, adultery, and surprise.

The traditional character appears most at home in the traditional mode, of course. The author is able to develop a sense of inexorable movement that, though it is set in motion by the artist, gains its greatest power from the responses of an audience to a customary, not a realistic, concept of cause and effect. Beowulf understandably fights three battles and dies in the third; King Lear quite plausibly asks three daughters a ticklish question and gets from the third the answer that precipitates the rest of the action; we know from the thyme, heron, and meteor that Mrs. Yeobright will die, and from the sparrow in the house that the wedding will fail and that at least one partner will die. And while the omen does not cause the outcome, the occurrence does happen in a way much more clearly related to traditional expectations, to what Olrik called traditional logic, than to our rational observation of real life. This way of ordering and approaching a work of art is what is here called the traditional mode, and it is of course an artistic phenomenon to be found throughout all of English and American letters.

Tradition versus Psychology

We have been discussing the artist's craft (as opposed to the artist's subconscious or biography) in relation to the use of materials from a particular culture, which in turn is depicted in the work as the context of human action. We cannot always determine which of an author's references are borrowed and which are original, perhaps coincidentally drawn from a less than conscious awareness of tradition. But we can at least identify common motifs and references from folklore as existing independently of the author, and we can also study authors' familiarity with folklore, their understanding of it, and therefore their method of using it. Moreover, when we know how a certain folk reference or method is traditionally construed (say, a series of three actions building toward an important climax on the third) and we can see an author using it repeatedly in a way appropriate to the context, we can deal with it a bit more certainly than with a discrete symbol. And since the items we are discussing come from the group rather than the individual, we can speculate more reliably on the audience's reaction to mythic and folkloric stimuli without depending entirely on our knowledge of the author's intent.

According to Jung and Freud and their followers, the images in folklore and mythology can apparently be transmitted by other means than oral tradition; some have even argued that they may be part of the inherited genetic characteristics of entire groups of people or of humanity in general. Regardless of the extent to which this may or may not be so, these images are also capable of conscious transmission and reception. It is to this level primarily (though not to the exclusion of effects incident to the deeper level) that our present discussion addresses itself. I would like to use myth and folklore criticism not as an approach chiefly to the author's mind but to the author's art, and our responses to that art, in as nonclinical a manner as possible. One cannot rule out the deeper psychological levels of human meaning and response, but these are very ticklish to discuss because they so urgently require information from the mind of the author. Thus, psychological approaches very often lie outside the area of folklore while they rest heavily on data inside the mind of an individual or a psychological analyst. If a folkloristic approach is to have any merit, it should be able to distinguish its own aims and approaches from others, and in any case it should be able to refer to materials and ideas that are available for everyone's scrutiny and discussion.

Folklore has an advantage in that it is based on freely available fieldwork and scholarship. In other words, without interviewing the writer (which may, after all, be impossible), we can study the lore of the society depicted and speculate on its appearance in the work and the presumable effects of it back on the society. The data of folklore, and the theories based on them, are subject to continual clarification and study by other scholars. Since meaning and connotation of folk ideas can be determined by fieldwork and by comparison with other research, we can watch for the significant and coherent application of folklore in an author's work, and we may speak fairly of the author's use of folk material as well as speculate plausibly on its impact on certain audiences that share the references brought forward.

The traditional mode, divided here into mythic and folkloristic modes, can be seen as a manner of looking at things that are communally based and culture-specific, that therefore include the audience as participant, communicant. When the traditional mode is used in literary expression it causes readers to be cultural participants, whether they recognize the specific features of the myth or not, for they respond to a manner of seeing and feeling that they share with the members of their culture and that refuses to let them only be spectators. This involvement is based on the readers' relationship to the traditions of their culture, not on personal feelings and opinions, and therefore it does not resemble more than superficially the involvement and response we normally refer to as empathy. In short, we are not simply trying to find out whether a given author thinks that red stockings would make a fashionable, chic dressing for a woman character, nor are we asking an author or reader if there is something about red stockings that particularly represents tension (or eroticism), but we are observing that in an entire culture the color red has for so many generations had a heavy connotation of sensuousness, passion, and even sexuality that an individual author can never be totally free to determine what it means or how it is to be applied if the audience is to understand. If you believe we are totally free from the responsibilities of tradition, suggest to a woman that she wear a red dress at her wedding, or to a matador that pink and lavender would make a much prettier cape to use in the bullfight ring, or to a writer that the term "mauve light district" is a nicer way to refer to the toughest part of town.

The terms *mythic metaphor, folkloric metaphor, mythic mode,* and *folkloric mode* have been used here to label some differences in scope or focus. Do they really aid our understanding? Are they likely to be adopted by folklorists or literary critics in general? I hope the answer to the first question is yes, because in using and supporting the terms, I think I have been able to point out some distinctly observable traits in Hardy's writing that might not have been easily seen otherwise. The answer to the second question, however, is entirely irrelevant to my purpose here, for insight into folklore and an author's use of it is a far more important issue than the acceptance of terminology by a profession or the general public.

The effects of traditional mode are many. It can broaden and deepen our experiential responses to literature. The critic can approach some works of literature armed with information that, far from being out of sight and uncheckable (as is usually the case with psychological approaches), is continually redefined and informed by reference to its own traditional texts. We need not accept the assertion of I. A. Richards that stock responses based on the reader's own experience and tradition are necessarily wrong or irrelevant, for although the response is personal and "external" to the work, it is occasioned by an author working from the same tradition that molds the reader's responses. As conventionalized as these responses may be, they are of the deepest sort because of their antiquity and cultural consistency and are thus quite appropriate to the mode. For the critic or careful reader who does not already share the tradition of the work, the establishment of the field of reference through study of the relevant materials is obligatory; such study will not tell us *what* the work means, but *how* it means, and will represent an extremely important way we can extend and expand the range of our own emotional and critical awareness of possibilities in the literary art of a given culture, including our own. As well, it is likely that folklore provides one of the very best ways (in some cases, indeed, the only way) to approach the connotative possibilities in the literature of cultures other than our own.

For example, one of the finest novels ever to be written in the United States, *Ceremony*, by Leslie Silko, is phrased in modes and metaphors drawn from Laguna pueblo tradition, from generalized intertribal southwestern witchcraft lore, from anecdotal and conversational patterns common to pueblo cultures, and from contemporary assumptions among Native Americans about the power of mestizo cultures. Thus, while it is important for the reader to recognize that the protagonist, Tayo, has been in the South Pacific during World War II and lost his half-brother during the Bataan Death March, it is equally important for the reader to register that the story is told as if it were a recitation of Laguna myth as well as an anecdotally rich recounting of a veteran's recovery from the belief that he has brought a drought upon his people by having cursed the rain during the war. Most pueblo ceremonies are about producing rain. Other Southwest ceremonies deal with protection from "witches," people who take the form or the attitudes of canine animals in order to wound or destroy people around them. The interlocked ceremonies to which the title refers address themselves to the sacred rain, to the recovery of a traumatized veteran, to the blunting and turning back of witchcraft—itself a process so destructive that it is easily associated with atomic power. The reader who is not willing to become acquainted with the cultural dimensions of these issues will not only miss much of the novel's rich meaning, but will also overlook the author's convictions on the complicity of other cultures in the problem and the resolution of current dilemmas facing Natives and non-Natives in the world today. That is, without its cultural context, *Ceremony* is a puzzling story about sick Indians; with its context it is a genuine classic.

The same can be said of other culturally situated works of art. Reading Rudolfo Anaya's *Bless Me, Ultima* without any knowledge of the traditions in curanderismo, reading Maxine Hong Kingston's *The Woman Warrior: Memoirs of a Childhood among Ghosts* without knowing the role of Chinese warrior tales and cyclic time in the expression of cultural values, reading Japanese novels and watching Japanese films without recognizing the complex function of ghosts in the dramatization of Japanese cultural values, viewing Shakespeare's *Taming of the Shrew* without knowing the antiquity and nuances of the joke it is based on, are all dry exercises of intellect which cannot lead to full literary or cultural experience.

FOLKLORE AND HISTORY

For those who believe that folklore is characterized by unreliability of factual data, it must seem absurd to suggest a profitable connection between folklore and the study of history. Historians themselves have been comfortable with the material aspects of folklore, for very often dates and settlement patterns can be inferred and studied in buildings and other artifacts. But with the possible exception of oral history, the more abstract and essentially nonfactual aspects of oral tradition have been more of a puzzle for historians. Yet we can assume that since much of history as we know it was formed by and among members of close groups, folklore must have been on the scene. Is it not possible that the expressions passed along in these close groups might have reflected and even directed the course of events that we now call history?

Oral History

Oral history gives us some very distinctive kinds of expression, some personal and some culture-based. One of the valuable lessons we can learn is that the people themselves have passed on in oral tradition a very perceptive—if local and particularized—set of observations about important events and the relationship of those occurrences to their group. We may not always find what we are looking for in oral history, of course, just as when we read diaries of a certain era we may find one commentator giving copious descriptions of what we now feel may have been major occurrences in the world while another ignores them. The diaries of my great-grandfather, Edwin T. Kimball, were written during the Civil War, yet there is not one reference to that traumatic event; instead, there is a daily record of labor provided to neighboring farmers, cords of wood cut, terse statements like "went a-huckleberrying one pail," and equally parsimonious announcements of family childbirths. I suspect if we had been able to interview him, the same information would have come forth: anecdotes and recollections about the family, about New England farm life, about labor and the scarcity of money in rural Massachusetts, and about occasional pastimes. At first sight we may wonder whether these observations, in diaries or in oral reminiscences, can really tell us very much about the historical events we seek to study. On the other hand, what better record have we of the tastes and concerns of the everyday person upon whose back and with whose labor those grand events in history were achieved and experienced?

Oral history represents the feelings and values of the people accurately: what events are worth remembering and retelling? Historians trying to reach the absolute facts about events under scrutiny will of course be forced to deal primarily with those figures about whom there is an abundance of reliable material in print, on stone, or in storage. But most historians know that history as seen only through the lives of great personages gives us only a partial view of the real course of time. Until very recently, after all, there were always more farmers than generals.

What does oral history have to do with folklore? A good deal, only part of which I will take up here. We notice that even when people are telling stories based on their own adventures, they frame the stories in culture-specific styles. For example, the catching of large sportfish is often described in terms of three attempts. This kind of structural device, in addition to a number of motifs, proverbial expressions, attitudes and beliefs, and general notions about what constitutes a good story (and what parts must be left out or stressed) all derive from the storyteller's command of the folklore and folk styles of his or her own group. Oral history is usually made up of anecdotes and narratives that give the individual's own view or recollection of a familiar life and times. That is, unless the person is a liar, the perceptions and recollections we get are accurate personal accounts, eyewitness reports played through the sensibilities and sensitivities of a particular individual. The content, thus, is expected to be factual, but the style, structure, and metaphor may be distinctly traditional. This is not to say that the latter considerations are in any way nonfactual, but they relate to expressive codes within the society more than to verifiable data. Just as a historical novel may be factual in its details and still be more interesting to us because of the emotional human elements developed by the author within the historical framework, so oral history strikes us as a mix of fact and expression. We need to realize that the nature of the expression in oral history is as important to our concept of the culture's view of itself as is the fact. The *way* something is said is a part of what is being said.

Jeannie Thomas, interviewing an elderly Utah farm woman about the placement of buildings on the farm where she grew up, discovered that her informant could not answer any factual question without first telling a story in which the data were couched. The question "Where was the well located?" resulted in Mrs. Wyatt's blurting out, "Oh, that reminds me of the time our little brother fell into the well while he was leaning over the edge trying to pull up the butter we kept cool there!" Then she asked Thomas to turn off the tape recorder while she joked about how delighted her siblings had been to hear that their bothersome little brother had fallen into the well. Then she allowed the tape recorder to record how concerned they all had been about their little brother's condition. And only then could she actually place where the well was in relation to the house. Examples like this are eloquent testimony to the fact that for everyday people, personal history is not so much a matter of names and dates but of persons and events (and the human responses which make these elements remain important in the mind or in the family tradition).

Family recollections of how they migrated to America, or went into farming, or converted to Mormonism and crossed the plains, or changed their name (or the spelling of their name) are often far more vivid in the dramatization of *why* and *how* than in the accuracy of *who* and *when*. Yet the seeming absence of verifiable "fact" is more than offset by the presence of attitudes, cultural assumptions, social values, and personal opinions which come closer to helping us to account for why things happened as they did: why people married, settled, fought, succeeded, failed, survived as they did.

For this reason, social historians have seized upon the vernacular record as evocative of historical perspectives not available anywhere else. Robert Darnton has used folktales and even the apparently senseless and bizarre customs of urban apprentices in pre-Revolutionary France as indexes of widespread attitudes and philosophical movements which reached conscious articulation in pamphlets and political rhetoric much later, as the Revolution itself was being acted out. Leonard Rosenband has shown how the occupational customs of papermakers and other European trades actually served to dramatize complex political, occupational, and economic issues which have undergirded the realities of occupational life and economics of Europe until the present day. David Hackett Fischer has eloquently demonstrated that the four principal English culture areas in the United States (Massachusetts, Virginia, Delaware, and "The Back Country") derive part and parcel from folkways in four distinct areas of England; indeed, all U.S. presidents but two have come from families out of these areas. Fischer argues that the quality and nature of cultural life in each of these places can be traced directly back to folk traditions and even dialect usages in the four distinct origin regions (East Anglia, the South of England, the North Midlands, and the Borderlands). Attitudes about social rank, about the environment, about other peoples (like the Indians), about politics, about religion, about language and its proper usage—in other words, assumptions governing virtually all dynamic aspects of human history in these formative areas of the United States—are found most readily in a study of regional folklore. If I may paraphrase the currently popular truism "all knowledge is socially constructed," I would suggest that "all history is culturally constructed," and not just conveniently by historians, but on the ground, as it were, by the people themselves. Viewing our study from the perspective of the "Annales" school of social history, we may conclude that without a close knowledge of folklore, we will never know much about the innards of history.

Reliable Lies

If we shift our attention to more recognizable genres of folklore, however, we notice that expression takes on a still larger role, and data reliability in many cases seems to disappear altogether. For example, in every region of the United States there are lies and tall tales about the attributes and characteristics of the locale. On one level, these stories are quite easily identified as nonreliable information; certainly they represent the kind of data a historian would not normally go to for verifiable details of life in a given period. Yet, each local tall tale normally has some germ of truth in it, usually by capturing some key feature of the region in hyperbolic description. For example, one farmer on the Olympic peninsula in northwestern Washington (where rainfall is among the heaviest in the United States) took me to see a huge wooden rain barrel at the corner of his barn; it had overflowed so violently in a heavy rainstorm that the water had undercut the earth below the outer edge of the barrel, tipping it over. "You may not believe this," he said, "but it was raining so hard that the rain was pouring into the bunghole faster than the water could flow out the open end. The water got built up in that barrel so much that it was flowing for three days after the rain stopped." Anyone who has spent time on the Olympic peninsula in the rainy season will realize immediately that it is difficult to tell if this anecdote constitutes a clear lie. It is unlikely the water actually built up so heavily inside the barrel; this part of the story we can recognize as hyperbole. At the same time, the story accurately represents a real feature of the region, and, more important than that, it expresses the attitudes of people native to the area.

Along the Rogue River in Oregon some years ago lived Hathaway Jones, a local character and raconteur who was skilled at telling lies about the locale to outsiders and local folk alike. One of his favorite stories was how he and his father had tried to raise watermelons and squash on the rich farmland in the Rogue Valley. "Problem was that we never got to eat any of the watermelons; that land was fertile, all right, but it was so fertile that the vines grew so fast they just wore them watermelons out draggin' 'em across the ground. We tried building sleds for 'em, and that would work for a while, but when the sun would come up in the morning the vines would move so fast they would just jerk the watermelons right off the sleds and they'd break. Finally we built little carts with wooden wheels, and one of our favorite pastimes was sitting on the back porch watching our watermelon crop drive around the yard. Only problem was, the wheels got to squeaking so badly that we had to spend a good part of the day greasing the axles."

In another anecdote, Hathaway told how he had seen a whole flock of geese lining up at the bank of a nearby stream, but when he took careful aim with Ol' Betsy, his sights were just slightly off, and when he fired the flock flew away, leaving him only "a bucketful of bills." Hathaway and his father were famous for building fireplaces, and several of the stories told by Hathaway, passed on today by others in the area, describe how a typical Jones fireplace drew so well that one had only to open the front door of the cabin and the fireplace would suck firewood in from the pile fifty feet away. Disaster often came about through the efficiency of these fireplaces, however; on one occasion a whole litter of pups was dragged forth to its doom from an expectant hunting dog, and in another case a roaring fire sucked the entire cabin up the chimney. These and other Hathaway Jones stories refer primarily to the local weather, the fertility of the land, the ferocity of life in the rough mountainous countryside along the Rogue and adjacent rivers, hunting escapades, brushes with state authority, interactions with animals, and the like. In other words, taken one by one, the stories do not provide much historical data, while taken together they provide a rich kaleidoscope of human, often humorous, response to actual conditions that must have flavored the history of the times and perhaps even influenced the direction of it.

Reub Long of central Oregon was another teller of tall tales, but his specialty was to celebrate the dryness of the land. He claimed he had never seen a rainstorm until he was eighteen years old, and when he ran out of the house to see what the terrible drumming sound was on his roof, he was knocked flat by a big desert raindrop and "they had to throw six buckets of sand in my face to bring me around." He bragged about how when he was a boy the sagebrush grew so large that there was a substantial sagebrush logging industry, but since the climate had dried out, the sagebrush trees had shrunk. When I asked if the climate was dry on his ranch, he answered me indignantly that a sample of their rainwater had been sent off to the state university and the report had come back that it was 32 percent moisture. He did admit that the percentage was low, but he said it was because it had taken thirty-five years to collect the sample and probably some of it had evaporated in the meantime. When the weather got really dry in his area, people around Prineville and Fort Rock noticed that the sagebrush began to follow the dogs around town.

Benjamin Franklin ("Huckleberry") Finn, formerly a resident on the McKenzie River in Oregon, was fond of telling hunting and fishing stories. Here is one retold later by his grandson Arthur Belknap:

> Grandad was quite a one to fish, too, you know. He'd fish for Dolly Varden [trout]. They're pretty big. One day Grandad was fishing and he hooked something and his line broke. So he got a stouter line and then he hooked something and his hook broke. So he got a bigger hook and then his line broke again, so he got a half-inch rope and went down to the blacksmith's and built him a big hook. And he used some kind of big bait. Well, he tied one end to an alder tree and went away. When he come back that old alder tree was just a-whippin' the water. He pulled on it and finally pulled the fish out. It was three and

a half foot between the eyes [pause for laughter]. Well, his trouble wasn't over then. Booth Kelly [a local logging company] was havin' a log drive and when Grandad pulled that fish out of the water, why the level went down and beached all their logs and he had a lawsuit on his hands.

Finn also loved to hang around the local store and brag to strangers about his prodigious hunting exploits. Once, after telling of several bucks, moose, elk, birds, and fish he had taken that week, two visitors said, "Do you know who we are?" "By golly, no." "Well, we're state game wardens." "Well, do you know who I am?" "No." "Well, I'm the biggest liar on the McKenzie!"

Len Henry, a local Munchausen in Lapwai, Idaho, had similar stories which featured his contempt for governmental authority:

Well, Len came into Heckner and Carlson's store in Lapwai and said, "I want two 30-30 shells." Old Heckner, was kinda slow on the think, said he should buy a *box* of 'em. Then old Len says, "I only need two; your damned game laws only allow me one deer and one elk."

These characters were all real people, and it is important to note that it is their stories, passed on by others, and not the composed Paul Bunyan stories, that have become prominent features in narrative lore. Why is this so? Why should a nationwide network of local liars actually represent more clearly and consistently the traditional views of the people? If this country is as dedicated to fact and practicality as its officials often claim, why do local lies somehow represent our region for us better than the local chambers of commerce? The answer is quite germane to the question of the application of folklore study to history, for in these anecdotes we have a running record of people's *responses* to historical occurrences, government, regional characteristics, the vicissitudes of life on the frontier, and so on. We miss the point totally if we see them only as humorous inaccuracies. When the Nebraska farmer tells us with a straight face that this is such a bad year that he had to run two or three bales through to prime his baling machine, we need not hasten to believe he's lying or crazy; we can make the sensible assumption that he is using humorous irony to comment on the drought or the poor hay crop.

In these tall tales we see a reflection of historical reality as it is played through human responses and a sense of humor that prefers to express regional pride in a complicated way: On the surface, people seem to be complaining about the excessive rain in their region or lamenting how dry it gets, how hard the work is, and how hard the wind blows. But underneath it all lies a strong sense of regional pride. The hyperbole in these stories is laced with a sense of modesty, as if to say, "No, you couldn't stand it around here; it rains too much. Why, I remember the time...." The historical reality represented in traditions of this sort, especially as it reflects regional settlement and local process, should not be overlooked by the historian who seeks to uncover the true attitudes and directions of the people in a particular time and place.

Beyond this, folk expressions often reveal unofficial opinions which run directly counter to the conclusions of formal scholars. Consider the sentiments of the many "Beulah Land" parodies found throughout the West. Echoing the original hymn's praise of heaven in terms of agricultural plenty and flowing waters, the regional ironists sang as follows:

> I've reached the land of dying wheat
> Where nothing grows for man to eat,
> Where the wind it blows the fiery heat
> Across the plains so hard to beat.
>
> Dakota Land, South Dakota Land,
> As on thy burning soil I stand:
> I look away across the plains
> And wonder why it never rains,
> Til Gabriel blows his trumpet's sound
> And says the rain's just gone around.
>
> Our neighbors are the rattlesnakes,
> They crawl up from the badland's breaks;
> We do no live, we only stay;
> We are too poor to get away.

Compare this bleak view with the idealistic praise of westering yeoman farmers expressed by Henry Nash Smith and other scholarly commentators on the frontier experience: the song reveals what Oregon's T. J. Easterwood called "the soft but real underbelly of human history." Which view is the "right" one? Perhaps it is impossible (and unnecessary) to answer that; rather, I would suggest that neither one is much good without the other.

Cultural History in Folksongs

The same kinds of observations can be made from other folksongs as well. An interesting example is one of the earliest American folksongs:

> On Springfield Mountain there did dwell
> A handsome youth I knew him well.
> Lieutenant Merrick's only son,
> A likely youth, 'most twenty-one.
>
> One day this handsome youth did go
> Down to the meadow for to mow.
> He had not mowed quite round the field
> When a poison rattler bit his heel.

He took the scythe with which he mowed
And laid that pesky rattler low.
Then he shouted loud for all to hear,
To take him home to Molly dear.

Now Molly had two ruby lips
With which the poison she did sip.
She also had one rotten tooth,
And so that rattler killed them both.

You can visit the grave of Timothy Merrick in Wilbraham, Massachusetts, and can ascertain the historicity of the event. On the other hand, as students of this song have found, the story in the ballad does not match the events of history. For one thing, Merrick's fiancée was not named Molly, and whether or not she applied the folk medical treatment of sucking the poison from the wound, Sarah Lamb did not die but three years later married Captain Justus Dwight of nearby Belchertown; she had eight children and lived to 95. In this case we can see how pedestrian (though acceptable) real life is when compared to an artistic achievement based on cultural symbolism. We have almost the same kind of development of a good story from an actual occurrence that we find in a good historical novel. The songmaker and subsequent singers have been apparently more motivated by passing on a story that has its own beginning and resolution than by recording and reporting life as it actually occurred.

In addition to this preference for a good story over real life, we need to note some other important details about the song itself before we can see its application to our study of history. The earlier versions of the song do not mention the woman, but follow the style and content "rules" for a New England funeral elegy: a focus on young Merrick, his lineage, the misfortune, the effect of his death on his survivors. As a song, however, it apparently caught on in Wilbraham, and for years it was sung by the people at reunions and picnics. Newspaper accounts and local pamphlets describe the elderly people singing it with gusto. Later it became a stage comedy song, and by that time young ladies named Molly, Susan, Betsy, Polly, Nancy, and Mary Ann had begun to appear as characters replacing the boy's father. While music hall audiences responded to the humor of a sometimes lengthy exchange between Molly and the dying Timothy, I think New Englanders hearing the song in oral tradition continued to relate it to the familiar tombstone verse in local cemeteries, much of which is humorous.

But the song makes the story more complete, for the ending is a direct outgrowth of the drama: using a standard and easily recognizable folk treatment, a young girl brings about her own death and the couple is united—a motif that seems quite similar to other English ballads. Our knowledge that this song was made up in Puritan times (the 1700s) in New England allows us to speculate on whether the death of this young couple through the aggressions of a snake might not have been seen as a subtle parallel to the Garden of Eden story.

Indeed, this may very well be why the death of the young woman is as important as the death of the young man. If we add to this our knowledge that in earlier times the song was often sung to the tune of "Old Hundred," otherwise known as the Doxology ("Praise God from Whom All Blessings Flow"), we can suspect that at least for some singers of this ballad there was the additional level of Providence, an idea central to early Puritan thought, which held that all occurrences come from God as part of His Providence to humanity, whether those events were traumatic or heartening to human witnesses.

It seems to me that we can claim that such a ballad is a complex and revealing item for the historian, for again, instead of concentrating on date and fact and an identifiable personage, the song has expressed a complex of ideas held in common by an important group of people (historically speaking), whose real impact on the events in America is as much to be measured by their attitude as by factual detail. This is not to say, however, that facts about the Puritans are unimportant; rather, folklore may be used to enrich the record by providing that extremely important undercurrent of human thought, feeling, and expression without which the dates remain tombstones.

Widely sung in the American West at the turn of the century was the following song; very likely from music hall tradition, it moved quickly into oral circulation and can still be heard in the repertoires of older singers. Two of my students collected it from a retired logger, Henry Tams, in Moscow, Idaho. I have since heard it sung in Florence, Idaho, and other old-timers have indicated to me that it was heard in most parts of Oregon as well, especially in areas where gold mining took place.

> Old John Martin Duffy was judge of the court
> In a small mining town in the West;
> Although he knew nothin' about rules of the law,
> At judgin' he was one of the best.
>
> One night in the winter a murder occurred,
> And our blacksmith was accused of the crime.
> We caught him red-handed and gave him three trials,
> But the verdict was guilty each time.
>
> Now he was the only good blacksmith we had,
> And we wanted to spare him his life,
> So Duffy stood up in the court like a lord,
> And with these words he settled the strife:
>
> I move we dismiss him, he's needed in town,
> Then he spoke out these words which have gained him
>   renown:
> We've got two Chinese laundrymen, everyone knows,
> Why not save poor blacksmith and hang one of those?

Students of the American West will recognize immediately that the situation described here is not far-fetched: We know, for example that Chinese laborers were numerous in gold mining towns, sometimes making up the bulk of the population. While in some areas they became leading citizens and put down deep roots, in other places they were not allowed even the most basic freedoms or dignities and were denigrated, pursued, and murdered. Old-timers in the mining country around Baker, Oregon, have told me that it was common to hire a gang of Chinese to work in the mines and then not to pay them. When the Chinese began to complain about their pay, a convenient mine explosion was arranged in order to remove the problem. Such heartless treatment of minorities has characterized many dimensions of American settlement, and traditions among these ethnic minorities recall those frightful times, through song, story, and anecdote. In this song, however, the perspective is that of the majority group, which proclaims humorously that Chinese are expendable; that it is much more sensible to retain the services of an important and useful (though untrained) citizen than to have an over-supply of Chinese laundrymen. Historically, then, the ballad is ethnically accurate, even if it may not describe an actual event, as its singers usually claim it does. I have been told that the incident actually occurred in Florence, Idaho, in Jacksonville, Oregon, and not far from Nespelem, Washington. The people who sang me the song, or fragments of it, presented it as about something that had happened "right around here" some years before.

Just as it is clear that such an incident could not have happened precisely in identical ways in those three areas, so it is obvious that the kind of situation described by the song represents a genuine widespread attitude about the Chinese among other settlers and miners, who by this time in history considered themselves owners and proprietors of the land. The song voices tensions about minority groups that are often felt when those groups can provide labor so inexpensively as to threaten the economic and political power of others in the system. And, as we noted earlier, when these psychologically tense subjects are expressed in tradition, they very often take the form of humor or attempted humor, indicating that some of the situations that make us the most nervous and that cause the greatest ethnic anxiety can be dealt with by laughing them off so that we may feel momentarily superior to their effects upon us.

Folklore and Historical Meaning

How does this affect the study of history? Again, I would point out the importance of knowing the attitudes—whether they are made up of tensions or joys—of the people who were engaged in those very processes that are so often displayed to us only through the interpretation of dates and places and prestigious people. The mood of the country, the spirit of an area, the sense of a people, reach the most eloquent articulation in their folk traditions, as social historians and folklorists have amply demonstrated. If we do not apply these traditions and the wealth of perspectives they provide to the story of history, we run the risk of stressing fact over substance. George Armstrong Custer carried out a campaign against the Indians and became famous for his last stand. But his actions and his meaning cannot be understood apart from the context of the tradition and attitude concerning Indians and westward expansion and gold that saturated American culture at that time. Custer did not invent Indian wars; rather, his exploits, and his continued existence to this day as a folk hero in proportions far beyond the merits of his actions, testify to the power with which a culture views its own history from its own distinctively ethnic vantage point. Custer is as much a construct of folklore as an item of history; without the perspectives of both fields his position would be impossible to understand.

Up until recently, the Almo Massacre was believed to have been the last and largest massacre of White emigrants by American Indians. According to the story, a wagon train of about 300 people travelling the California Trail by the "City of Rocks" formation in southern Idaho were attacked by Shoshoni raiders and were wiped out (all except five people who managed to creep through the Indian perimeter at night). Reported as having happened in 1859, or 1860, or 1861, the event has been chronicled in local histories and textbooks, and there is a memorial to the victims in the tiny community of Almo to this day. However, the descendants of the escaped five have never been found; articles reporting the event never appeared in nearby newspapers; the bones, wagon tires, rifles and other solid artifacts of many wagons and 300 people have never been found, and now the historians are beginning to doubt the massacre ever happened. This news is, of course, a bit late in coming, especially since the rumors of the attack were among the winds that fanned flames of White resentment and led to the infamous dawn slaughter of 400 sleepy Shoshoni by militia volunteers at the Bear River Massacre shortly afterward (1863).

The interesting feature of the story is the tenacity with which people in the Almo area cling to it and explain the absence of scholarly and archeological "proofs." What this means is that—whether the massacre or anything like it ever happened or not—the oral traditions, legends, family anecdotes, local values, and assumptions are all we've got. But we do have them, and they can hardly have survived so tenaciously if they had no meaning at all for their narrators and believers. So what is their meaning? At the very least, they vehemently articulate the fears, assumptions, and opinions of those who saw the Shoshoni as bloodthirsty adversaries, and thus they provide us with a vivid cultural-psychological portrait of frontier emotions—out of which came frontier history.

Nestled in the hills of central Massachusetts between Amherst and Worcester lies an 18-mile-long reservoir named Quabbin (a local Indian name meaning "Many Waters"). Up until 1938, it was the location of several small towns and villages, among them Enfield, Greenwich, Dana, North Dana, Prescott, and Smith's Village; at that point the houses were cleared out, trees were cut, cemeteries were relocated, and—after the building of a dam and a dike—water was allowed to fill the valley. It now provides most of Boston's drinking water, but it also generates local stories of houses and lights being seen far underwater, of ghosts wandering the shorelines, and of accidental drownings. Survivors of the valley and their descendants gather near the shore for picnics and nostalgic conversation, and photos from early times there are saved like holy relics.

One of the edifices once central to this valley was the old Congregational church, and local legend has it that it is this Enfield church, not the one in distant Enfield, Connecticut, where Jonathan Edwards preached his famous sermon, "Sinners in the Hands of an Angry God," in 1741, a fact corroborated by the entry on that sermon in *The Oxford Companion to American Literature*, even though an early history of Connecticut claims it as theirs (and even though nearby Suffield, Connecticut, is actually mentioned in the sermon). I have been treated to this story since my earliest years, for this was the valley where I was born, and that was the church in which I was baptized. We of Quabbin heritage note that Edwards was after all the pastor in the Northampton Congregational Church at the time, just over the hill, practically, and it would have been more likely for him to have preached in our valley than to have gone all the way to Connecticut.

When the Enfield church burned down (in an act of arson shortly before its scheduled demolition), everyone took some metal part of the church for a souvenir, and my father took the back door handle. It stands proudly today on my mantel as a token of my (rather intimidating) connection with Jonathan Edwards and early New England, and I show it to you as proof. But whether Edwards really scared my ancestors in Quabbin valley, or someone else's in Connecticut (or both), the only cultural meaning that can be said to inhere in my old hand-wrought iron door handle derives from the stories that are told about it. If it ever ends up in an antique store in the future it will be just one more meaningless old door handle; as long as it remains contextualized within its stories in my family, it is a priceless historical relic.

These applications of folklore to such fields as literature and history are only brief and rather superficial examples for the sake of discussion to indicate that applied folklore is, basically, made up of an easily understandable and perfectly sensible attitude: one may fruitfully apply the materials and approaches of one field to those of another. Our examples are what we must call intellectual or scholarly applications, for they normally take place as part of the ongoing scholarly concern with the development of further knowledge and perspective in academic fields. This is not to say that these perspectives cannot be used in everyday life, however; it simply recognizes that most people who talk about these matters at any length are academicians or writers.

Folklore, indeed, may be applied to practically every other field of human study. Many of our laws were first developed as common law, thus folk tradition and cultural values lie behind their logic and application. Many of our

A hand-wrought iron doorhandle taken from the back door of Enfield Congregational Church (where Jonathan Edwards preached "Sinners in the Hands of an Angry God") and a "Nebraska logging chain" made by an ironic retired blacksmith are among the many artifacts that are virtually meaningless without the stories that their owners attach to them.

medicines (over 250 in fact) have been learned by modern scientists from the folk medical traditions of Native Americans; many other medical discoveries have been carried along in our own oral and customary traditions until some scientist decided to take a closer look. To finish out our discussion of possibilities for folklore application, let me explore again very briefly the arena of folklore and psychology.

FOLKLORE AND PSYCHOLOGY

Various fields of psychology have tried to use folklore as a window on personal and cultural psychology, and indeed the writings of Sigmund Freud on jokes, as well as the theories of Carl Jung about mythic archetypes, are well known. Folktales like "Jack and the Beanstalk" have been used as catalogs of unconscious sexual imagery or as indicators of socially repressed actions, or as dramatizations of childhood fears and concerns. Therapists have used folktales as paradigms of psychological insight—in much the same way that biblical parables were used to illustrate and extend spiritual concepts. Despite the rich possibilities in this area, however, few psychologists and psychiatrists have taken the trouble to get acquainted with the dynamism and variation in folklore, so they have tended to use single versions of a tale (and at that, something found in print in a standard collection of children's stories) rather than study the whole range of articulation found in all extant versions of a tale type. In their attempt to create a single, reasonable text, they often combine parts of totally disparate versions without regard to the cultural context in which each text developed. Thus, in *Women Who Run with the Wolves*, we see a single text of the Bluebeard story described as an "English-Slovak version," a highly unlikely occurrence in folklore. Or, at the other extreme, one single motif or tale type is taken to represent a cluster of universal meaning.

Joseph Campbell's "monomyth" theories come to mind as another example: he presents a myth story as if the narrative dramatizes a single universal meaning, or else all stories of a particular sort (like those about heroes) are regarded as fragments of a single puzzle. Joseph Campbell's *The Hero with a Thousand Faces* (New York: Bollingen Foundation, 1949) is probably his best-known opus on the subject of universality in mythic narrative. Based on early Jungian theories on the nature of "archetypes," Campbell's works tried to demonstrate that many recurrent themes and plots were part of the human psychological inheritance and were therefore susceptible to cross-cultural interpretation. The problem is, of course, that irrespective of the universality of archetypal *images*, different cultures organize and interpret (and thus understand) the symbols quite differently. Campbell could construct a monomyth of the hero only by citing those stories which fit his preconceived mold, and leaving out equally valid stories (such as the "Sun's Myth" discussed previously) which did not fit the pattern.

This monocular notion is used by Robert Bly, in his study of Grimm #136, *Iron Jack* (Eisenhans), the less-common title of a tale usually known as *Goldener* (The Golden One) in German. In the Aarne-Thompson index it appears as Type 314, *The Youth Transformed to a Horse*, and is one of the most widespread of all stories in northern, eastern and southern Europe.

There are three subtypes of this story, each of which seems to flourish in a particular region. Subtype 1, found mainly in the European countries, tells of a youth who—having been promised to a demon, wild man, or magician—is forced to put in a term of service caring for animals. His master interdicts entry into a room, or touching an object, or coming in contact with a spring of water; following standard folktale logic, the youth breaks the interdiction, obtains the use of a magic horse, and sometimes gets himself totally or partially gilded. The youth and his magical horse flee the magician, and the young man hides himself by working as gardener for a king. He is noticed by the princess; in disguise he fights for the king but is eventually discovered and is forced, persuaded, or allowed to marry the princess. In some cases, his liaison with the princess is initially rejected by the king, who makes the couple live in a pigsty. Eventually the horse is disenchanted (often by decapitation) and turns into a handsome prince. This story is found fragmentally in North and South America, but *only* in the motif of the friendly and helpful horse.

Subtype 2, considered by scholars to consist of the oldest, most coherent versions, is found in southern Siberia, Iran, the Arabian countries, the Mediterranean area (including Sicily), Hungary, and Poland. It tells of the young son of a local ruler. The boy befriends a horse because they were both conceived through the gift of a magical fruit and both are born on the same day. The mother (who is involved in a love affair) wants to kill the boy and the horse in order to obtain a magical medicine (or to keep them from exposing her affair). The horse warns the boy, who asks his mother if he might take one last ride; once he is on the horse, both fly away. The boy hides as a servant (often gardener) of a neighboring king and visits his horse daily. The princess sees his golden hair; he fights for the king in wars (in disguise), gets magical medicine for the king, saves the princess from a dragon, is eventually discovered (often by employment of golden apples), and the young couple marry. The horse is beheaded and changes into a prince or princess.

Subtype 3, found in Greece, Turkey, the Caucasus, Uzbekistan, and northeast India, describes the youth as the product of miraculous conception (the magical fruit); a magician tries to kill him, but instead he kills the magician, finds rooms full of corpses (by breaking the interdiction against entering), obtains a magical golden hair, then flees and hides as a gardener whose story develops along the lines of subtype 1.

The German version of this complex story—the one on which Robert Bly bases his discussion of male psychological development—fits into subtype 1, thus it is not particularly typical of the issues developed by the full range of versions. It is also a version *not* found in England or the United States, which makes for a real stretch indeed if one wants to claim that it dramatizes an archetypal sequence of psychological passages which American men universally go through.

"Eisenhans" does indeed dramatize a number of important themes which come up elsewhere in German literature, folklore, and psychology: the boy manages to escape the delicate situation of a mother who is having a sexual affair (the Grimms cleaned up their published version a good deal); he is able to escape his father's elite domination and replace it with the powerful influences of the wild man (society vs. nature). Although he is "golden," his success is mainly due to the powers of *Iron* Jack (iron was considered a powerful antidote against witches, supernaturals, sorcery, and bad luck).

Whether human psychology is culturally constructed—and thus susceptible to study by way of culturally mediated expressions like folktales and myths—is open to debate, but it would seem to be an exceedingly rewarding area of research and speculation. When the leaders in this field become more fully conversant with the study of variants and types, this discussion should really catch fire. Meanwhile, we can say that both dreams and the recurrent images of folktale and myth have been culturally constructed and interpreted enough to have already provided insight into long-standing puzzles in the study of human psychological experience.

One of the best known examples is the so-called "Hag dream," in which a person awakes and is unable to move, feeling totally pinned down on the bed and crushed or pummeled in the chest area. In medieval times in Europe, the experience was attributed to the *incubus* (male) or *succubus* (female) evil spirit who would ride on a sleeping victim, trying to achieve sexual intercourse. More recent victims have interpreted it as a satanic attack, or as a kind of witch's invasion. Many deep-sea fishermen interpret it as a reliable sign that they would be accident prone if they went out to sea the next day, so they stay home, reporting that they have "had a Hag," or have been "Hag-ridden" (from whose widespread usage comes our word "haggard").

Until about 75 years ago, this is the dream people called the "nightmare" in English, for the Anglo-Saxon word *mar* means "crushing monster," and is not a reference to a horse as many believe. The crushing monster that comes by night is known in all world civilizations, and each one has its own interpretation, both of the event and of its importance to the victim. Not until folklorist David Hufford published his book on the phenomenon in 1982, however, did we have available to us a systematic, serious examination of the Hag stories and what they might mean. Since that time, the experience has been recognized by sleep specialists as a kind of sleep paralysis in which one's consciousness comes up from REM (rapid eye movement) sleep, but for some reason one's muscle tone does not (usually both systems come up together, so we can stretch, turn over, answer a call of nature, or find our pillow). When the brain comes up and the muscles do not, we not only feel paralyzed, but may actually have the experience that someone or something is actually holding us down by force. When Hufford wrote *The Terror That Comes in the Night*, most of the available data (remember this was 1982) came from folklore archives, for there was virtually no scientific writing on the subject; today, it forms one of the standard considerations (sleep paralysis) in sleep research. The role of folklore expressions in the early investigations into this topic cannot be underestimated, but take note: Hufford used hundreds of "Hag" accounts, not just one. And he formed his hypotheses from the categories provided for him in the myriad versions: he did not first decide what the phenomenon was, then illustrate it only with examples which fit the preconceived set.

APPLIED FOLKLORE AS A BASIS FOR ACTION

Especially since people do not like to change their minds about matters so close to home as the shared values expressed in folklore, cultural liberals and conservatives alike are inclined to get testy when someone tries to instruct them about how they might get along better with other people, how they might help their government approach problems less chaotically, how they themselves might see their own potentially destructive role in intercultural relationships. Edward T. Hall, in *The Silent Language*, acknowledges that he was originally asked as an anthropologist to develop some perspectives that could be used by political, economic, and agricultural advisers going to other cultures. In many respects, we can see his books as a form of applied folklore, for they advocate that anyone dealing with other cultures must know the gestures and customs of those cultures in order to avoid the possibility of unintentional cultural disaster.

Yet some people argue that human beings are alike the world over, under their skin, and that if we all simply could learn the same language or adopt the same religion or believe in the same political system, everything would be rosy. Until such a millennium occurs, however, it seems apparent to most folklorists and anthropologists that people are culturally not alike the world over, and there is no use ignoring it. We simply do need to know each other's folklore before we can get along very easily. As noted earlier, an American needs to know that an Arab man will probably stand much closer to another man while talking to him than the American is accustomed to. If the American interprets this as an aggressive gesture, or if the Arab interprets the American's physical distance as a reluctance to converse, it suggests that any delicate conversations between these two people will not come off very well. One aspect of applied folklore, then, is to discover the traditional codes that characterize certain cultural systems and then to instruct others so that insults can be avoided and harmony promoted.

Folklore and Life in Multicultural Settings

Other applications require that we notice what sorts of medical or psychological or social traditions constitute normality in any group of people so that we may consider those processes in our dealings with those people. For example, one aspect of applied folklore on the Navajo reservation in recent years has been the practice of medical doctors working for the Public Health Service to study and become familiar with Navajo concepts of medicine and to invite Navajo medicine men ("singers") into the hospital to help in the treatment of ailing Navajos. This is not charitably superficial or symbolic; rather, the doctors have noticed that Navajo customs concerning health stress the psychological dimension more strongly than the physical. Thus, Navajo patients are likely to be severely troubled about the psychological aspect of their treatment even though the physical symptoms may be well addressed by the hospital. Doctors tell of burn patients whose wounds were treated and were in the process of healing, yet they died. What doctors have been trying to do more recently is to learn how tribal traditions may be used fruitfully in scientific attempts to provide adequate medical treatment for the Navajos. If the psychological or psychosomatic aspect of medicine is stronger for the Navajos, then it is certain that from a Navajo perspective hospitals do not normally provide proper treatment. By incorporating the medicine man into the system, the doctors are ensuring that Navajo traditions are upheld; the patient is more at ease and more willing to believe that an actual treatment is taking place, and, if verbal reports are any indication, such efforts have met with considerable success.

A case was reported to me in which an elderly Tohono O'odham (Papago) man had complained to a social worker in Tucson that his Anglo doctor was trying to kill him. It turned out that the doctor had told him quite frankly, "If you don't take your medicine, you're going to die!" But the doctor was unaware that the Tohono O'odham—like many southwest tribes—believe that language creates reality and that, therefore, his patient had interpreted those words as a prediction of his own death. The doctor asked, with some defensiveness, "What do you want me to do, lie to him? It's simply true: if he doesn't take that medicine, he's going to die. Now, my job as a doctor is to treat his illness, not to flatter him because he's a fragile Native elder." I suggested that it might be possible to convey the same information using more positive terms, like "If you take your medicine, you'll get better." "Never thought of that," said the doctor.

And of course, that's the point: very often we just never think that there are reasonable, functional alternatives for the way we do and phrase things. Living in an increasingly multicultural society as we do, it becomes increasingly counterproductive, not to say dangerous and probably stupid, for us not to think of it, and not to make use of the many cultural alternatives now available to us in everyday life not as threats to our integrity but as ways of increasing our ability to live in our society more fully.

Race Relations

Another possibility for applied folklore of this sort is in race relations. Many Whites are unaware of the tone and volume variations that are standard in African

American speech events. Moreover, many are put off by the essentially antiphonal, heavily interactive mode of speaking, especially on issues of excitement among Blacks. For this reason, if a racial crisis occurs in an area populated chiefly by Whites and Blacks, there are very few ways open for negotiation, for in using its own traditions, each side will assume that the other side is trying to gain an unfair advantage in one way or another. That is, the suspicions on each side can be deepened since under crisis situations each group will be "normal" according to its own traditions. Folklorists have sometimes been able to help by giving in-service training to teachers, race relations workers, city officials, and the like, demonstrating the traditional basis of different kinds of communicative and interactive modes. Once people are aware that the actions of another group are normal expressions of the same kinds of tradition their own responses stem from, the explosiveness of racial friction can be considerably lessened.

Education

Education is a particularly important place for the application of folklore to potentially troublesome dilemmas. Not only does each close group develop certain traditional codes for expression, but as we observed earlier, these codes are very often the basis for how people learn, what they learn, how they go about learning it, and what seems logical or sensible or normal to them. For this reason, especially in a multicultural country like the United States, it is possible that in every classroom there are people from traditional backgrounds whose ability to learn is impeded not so much by personal weaknesses (or by what some have labeled cultural deprivation) but by the mismatching of traditional codes: a discrepancy between the codes they bring with them and those used by the teacher.

Let me suggest the complexity of this area by mentioning only a few traditional dilemmas that have been shared with me by friends from various Native American cultures. One of the most commonly mentioned problems relates to eye contact. Many American Indian young people are given to understand that to stare in the eyes of an older person while receiving instruction is a sign of mistrust, disrespect, and disinclination to learn. You will probably recognize immediately that this tradition is almost exactly opposite the one employed by most European Americans, in which eye contact is seen as a sign of being interested, involved, paying attention, being honest. We ask our children to look us straight in the eye when they tell us something, and we expect audiences—including student audiences—to look continually at the speaker during a lecture. Lack of eye contact for most Whites is a sign of disinterest, distrust, or disinclination to learn.

Thus a White teacher, conscientiously trying to make sure that the class is paying attention, may require Indian children to do something that is essentially considered an insult or a breach of etiquette. Suppose, for example, that White children were confronted by a teacher who insisted, "Pick your noses while I'm talking to you!" It might be that some students would be willing to swallow their pride and traditional training and spend the year picking their noses, but most of the students would probably hesitate to do such a thing. Yet, eye contact, for many American Indians, is more embarrassing than picking one's nose.

In many Indian tribes, children are brought up not to speak of themselves as fully developed individuals until they are old, until they have "become someone." Many tribes do not believe in talking about death. A good many tribes avoid talking about the future, for in the view of some the future is an impractical and unknowable subject, for others a totally imaginary situation that does not make sense. Most tribal systems the world over rigorously suppress competition unless it is ritually expressed. Thus, while many tribes use sports as a means of competition, in the classroom or in daily life it is discouraged. Now look at several of these factors together. Suppose the teacher assigns the students a theme in which they must write a biographical description; suppose the teacher asks for a paper on "What I want to do when I grow up;" suppose the teacher requires the students to study epitaphs or to write their own epitaphs; suppose the teacher tries to praise one student in class for having done a good job or tries to call on another because that student probably has the answer: all of these instances, quite common as they may be in the classrooms of Whites, will provide one or another sort of cultural panic for many Native Americans.

In some Indian classrooms, students who try to put themselves forward by answering a question will simply be drowned out by the noise of other students ("shaming them out," some Sioux youngsters call it). Even more likely, the student so singled out will give the wrong answer on purpose so as not to appear competitive. Basketball coaches at Indian schools have told me in exasperation how their team will go out on the floor and play a spectacular game during the first half until they are well ahead, then throw the game in the second half so that they will not win. Usually a coach feels that this is a kind of betrayal, a loss of interest in the reputation of the school, or a lack of pride, when in fact it usually boils down to a wish on the part of the team to show that they play well together and then to illustrate that they are not better than someone else.

Most Indian children are brought up to be quiet; indeed, in some tribes, anyone who talks all the time is simply dismissed as someone with nothing to say. Silence in conversation is thought of as wise, sensible, and normal. Thus, Indian students who are called upon to talk or to converse at length with the teacher, may be reluctant to speak, and the teacher may take this as a sign of disinterest or petulance. Such a confrontation can of course be extremely painful and embarrassing to an Indian student as well, and the typical situation is for the two people to part company more frustrated than at the start. One puzzled high school teacher confided to me that a certain young Indian boy would come to his office every noon and just sit there without talking; when I pointed out that being together with someone in silence was considered a kind of conversation, the teacher was much relieved. Yet that kind of information was easy to find out locally; the answer had been close at hand all the time. The teacher had simply not thought to ask into it but assumed that there was something aberrational about the actions of the student, as judged from the cultural perspective of the teacher.

Indians in many tribes believe that if you laugh or smile at a stranger, it means you are making fun; thus it is common among Indians not to smile when first meeting someone or to show any overt emotion when strangers are present. This is a point of great delicacy in most tribes, and yet it earns Indian people the reputation for being stoic, unfriendly, inscrutable. At the same time, Indian people have told me that they never can tell what White people are thinking "because they smile and laugh at you all the time."

If all of these matters were simply interesting facts for the intellectual tourist, it would not be worth bringing them up in a discussion of applied folklore. But in fact very often education does not take place in our schools precisely because the traditional norms of the teacher do not intersect with the traditional norms of the students. Very often the teacher takes the position that if the students are to get on in the world they need to give up all these old beliefs anyhow and learn to act "normally." Nothing can be further from the truth. Educational specialists continually find that children do not learn well if they are put off balance and made to feel afraid or embarrassed in the learning situation. All one does by ignoring or denigrating the student's traditions is to make it even more certain that the student will have problems in school. By the time the student reaches high school or college age and has intellectualized the culture differences, the topic can become explosive, personally hurtful, and politically sensitive. Learning simply does not take place very efficiently if the learners—or the teachers—are angry, embarrassed, or frightened.

A former student of mine, trying to teach a class in writing to a group of adult Navajos, found that for the first third of the course almost no one had handed in any papers. Finally, one of the older students took her aside and pointed out what the problems were. She had assigned them a paper in which they were to write their own epitaphs; she had read some papers in class noting how well some were written; she had forcefully confronted individuals in the class who had not turned papers in, and to show how earnest she was, she had maintained eye contact with each person she talked to. The woman who took her aside for cultural instruction gently told her, "After all, you know, we don't like to talk about death, and we don't like to compete with each other." My friend now sums up her experience by saying, "I had to learn not to mention death, not to cause competition, not to use eye contact, not to give direct orders, not to put someone on the spot. After that, they wrote some very beautiful themes."

This situation has been duplicated all over the country: once people are put at ease by being able to operate within their own traditional expectations, they do *better* in an educational situation on the intellectual level. Just as an American does not have to apologize about being American or give up religion and language just to learn the German language and culture, so an Indian, a Black, a Chicano, a farm boy, or a South Carolinian need not give up home traditions in order to be properly educated. Folklore can be applied in these circumstances precisely because it is one of the ways in which we can discuss exactly those traditions through which people normally learn.

Folklore and Cultural Relations

The application of these ideas can be made on a number of levels: teachers, doctors, lawyers, public officials, who know these traditions can use them in their professional work. In addition, folklorists can be employed for in-service training, for developing community seminars, for studying traditional health practices of immigrant groups that can then be passed on to doctors, and so on. The doctors on the Texas border whose clinic folded because they inadvertently caused the evil eye clearly needed to learn folklore along the way if they expected to apply their technical expertise to a cultural situation. Lawyers and judges who work in areas of Mexican American or Hispanic American population must know about the in-group, often in-family, justice system that operates among Hispanic Americans. And why should urban planners, architects, and city fathers continue to deprive themselves of the traditional knowledge developed by many African Americans for living in a crowded urban environment? Although the living experiences among African Americans have not always been pleasant, urban Blacks in America have developed extensive means of surviving in the city, not the least of which is an extended street family of brothers and sisters bound together by oral tradition and custom. May we not assume that these traditions and customs reflect and express the emotions of those who live in the cities and may suggest patterns that could be emulated by others as we try to keep cities alive?

Folklorists study the traditions of each particular culture or group or region without considering which one is right or best. It is instructive for us to know, for example, that American Indians have passed along an impressive body of medical and scientific knowledge in the form of oral traditions that we call folktales and legends. Not only are certain herbs recognized and their usage codified in such stories, but the relationships between people and nature are epitomized. When Jacques Cartier was icebound in the St. Lawrence River in 1535, all his men were dying of scurvy. Local Indians came and cured them by the application of what we have come to recognize as vitamin C. Surely we can see in this incident, and there are many of them, that neither the Europeans nor the Indians can be judged as being primitive or advanced. Cartier had sailing ships; the Indians had medicine.

Knowing the validity of each of these areas of cultural concern, how could we ever say that one culture is superior to another? We should remember that

Grinding *chiilchin* (desert sumac) berries on a traditional grindstone, Helen Yellowman prepares the bitter mush which serves many Navajos as a source for vitamin C. The branches of the same bush are split and used to make Navajo wedding baskets.

Pueblo Bonito had eight hundred rooms in it, and was built from about 919 to 1130; it contained some twelve hundred persons and was abandoned in about 1300. It was the largest apartment house anywhere in the world until a bigger one was finally built in 1882. Africa had kingdoms while Europeans were still roaming in small bands bashing each other on the head. Before the Europeans came to Central and South America, the Incas and the Aztecs reigned over vast domains where people were not permitted to go hungry or unclothed.

We need to get rid of the notion of cultural deficit, because cultures the world over come and go, and at any moment *any* culture may have developed ideas, customs, traditions, and institutions that were not developed by others. It is impossible to measure the merit of any of these cultures in relation to any other. Rather, we need to recognize that each culture has its own valid way, and much of that way has been passed on through the oral traditions of its people. Studying the validity of the folklore of each group can lead us away from stereotypes. We will notice sometimes that the same action will be highly prized by one society and abhorred by another. For example, one often hears Whites complain that Indians misspend their money: "If you give an Indian a thousand dollars, he'll go right out and waste it on groceries and liquor for his family and friends." One hears almost exactly the same complaint from Indians about White people misusing their money: "White people waste money; if you give a White man a thousand dollars, he'll go right out and put it in the bank where his family and friends can't share it."

The following story is widespread in Indian reservations across the United States. An old Indian man was sitting in the shade in front of a Bureau of Indian Affairs office one noontime when he was joined by a White administrator who had come outside to eat his sack lunch. Just as the White man began to unwrap his sandwich, the Indian man blew his nose the old-fashioned way, snorting down on the ground, wiping his nose off on his finger, and flicking the excess off by a rapid flip of the wrist. The White man was repulsed and sickened, and threw his sandwich back into his lunchbag, saying, "You Indians are just crude! You haven't learned any manners at all since we've been here. You don't even know how to blow your noses properly. This is just like everything else that's happening around here; we come around and try to give you all the education we can, but you all still insist on doing things the wrong way. That's just sickening. Why don't you people ever wise up and do things right?" According to the story, the old Indian man declined to reply, but sat watching the horizon. Later, when the sun came around the tree a little farther and shone into the White man's eyes, he sneezed, pulled out his handkerchief, blew his nose on it, and returned it to his pocket. The Indian turned and said, "My God, you White people save everything, don't you?"

The very fact that Indian people have circulated this joke is a strong indication that what the anecdote represents is really something that may cause Indian people concern. It is also true that in a number of Indian tribes selfishness and the storing up of items is seen as a symptom of witchcraft. Many Indians, still living in an essentially tribal orientation, bring up their children to value interaction, cooperation, reciprocation, and the sharing of all items, especially food. Thus it is easy for Indians to see and represent the attitudes of Whites as essentially defective and selfish. Whites do seem to collect lots of items and store them prominently on shelves.

Similarly, it is not rare for Whites to look at Indians as reckless with their money, incapable of managing their own affairs, and as poor planners. In White society these are considered negative attributes and are often used to rationalize the continued White jurisdiction over Indian affairs of all sorts. We can see how easily actions turn into stereotypes, for it is quite true that many Indians will indeed share their money and their food at all times with friends and relatives rather than putting them away for their own use. It is also true that it is highly valued among European Americans to save, plan ahead, and manage their fiscal lives well. In fact, in both instances a person's real economic situation may be held in secret: the Indian perhaps has some money or goods stored away and the White may be nearly ruined by overextended credit.

What a folklorist would suggest by a thorough study of both cultures, however, is that the *expression* of each position is perfectly valid in terms of the cultural bearings it represents. Therefore one cannot easily level a finger at one group or the other and suggest that the attribute mentioned is right or wrong or backward or advanced. In other words, the kind of knowledge generated by folklore study, which seeks to relate traditions as they are performed to the worldview of the group in which they are performed, causes us to focus on internal validities and internal logic rather than measuring things against some presumable objective truth (which usually turns out to be an oversimplification of one's own worldview anyhow).

Folklore and Politics

Many of the emerging countries, especially in central Europe, after suffering years of domination by outsiders, have tried to express and retain their own sense of ethnic unity by purposely collecting, archiving, and disseminating to their own people certain key aspects of their own folklore. In this venture, some expressions are considered less than important while others are given a focus beyond what would have originally been theirs under normal traditional circumstances. Here, even though the folklore presented may accurately depict the costumes, say, of a particular region or the dances and songs of another, there is a choreography that has strong nationalistic and political overtones. There is always the chance under these conditions that the real traditions in folklore will finally be subordinated to political ends, and that has sometimes happened, lamentably.

Probably in recent world history Hitler represents the most sinister use of nationalistic folklore for baldly political ends. In his pursuit and extermination of the Jews, he counted upon a fund of active anti-Semitic folklore among the people for support. In addition, Nazi folklorists fashioned a lot of folkloric-sounding legend and political myth to provide an antique and grand cultural context into which these local stereotypes and prejudices could fit. The result was a partly traditional and partly manufactured cultural set in which subsequent barbaric actions struck most of the participants as perfectly "normal." Heinrich Himmler, formerly Munich's chief of police and later inventor of the death camps, was leader of his own folklore society; propagandist Joseph Goebbels was intensely interested in Teutonic folklore and mythology; entire school systems were founded on the idea of reviving ancient Germanic principles in agriculture, daily life, and human deportment. Gigantic outdoor harvest festivals, complete with ancient Teutonic symbols, were staged in a combination of ethnocentric celebration and religious awe; these gatherings later developed into the famous outdoor spectacles which featured uniforms, flags, torches, and thousands of voices raised in song. University professors of folklore who tried to expose this flagrant misuse of tradition simply lost their positions (and many disappeared into the camps). Hitler's regime provides us a macabre example of how selected folk traditions, channeled carefully by propagandists, can provide a mental stage for "normal" actions that might otherwise be considered inhuman and inhumane. There is no overlooking the deep power of folklore to galvanize human feelings and actions, even when the end results are not as disturbing as the German case. Many countries have used a heavy-handed manipulation of folklore to help establish a common sense of culture, especially when emerging from the domination of another country or when proclaiming the integrity of a country which was not there previously. It will come as no surprise that folklore has had a strong role in the development of Soviet Russia, many of the central European nations, and Finland (where nationalists enlisted narratives like the *Kalevala* to demonstrate the ancient continuity of nationhood). Clearly, folklore is not only entertaining: it can serve as a political force.

Folklore in the Public Sector Today

Various government agencies, private foundations, companies, and community groups have found folklore increasingly relevant to their needs and directions. For some years the Smithsonian Institution has sponsored the Festival of American Folklife on the Mall in Washington, D.C., as a way of providing the nation with a living counterpart to the exhibits in the Smithsonian's museums. The Folk Arts Program of the National Endowment for the Arts was the developer of the National Heritage Awards, which are given to ten or twelve people each year who are the finest exponents and practitioners of their traditional arts: basketmakers, beadworkers, wrought iron workers, instrument makers, traditional musicians, ethnic dancers, singers, vernacular poets. The United States Forest Service and the Park Service have found folklore to be helpful in some of their programs. For example, the Forest Service has jurisdiction over thousands of acres of land that contain certain locations sacred to American Indian tribes. With the help of anthropologists and folklorists, impact statements are developed, special sites are defined and protected, and names and signification are clarified. The American Folklife Center in the Library of Congress is another government agency employing folklorists in the job of canvassing, collecting, preserving, and disseminating the folklore of the country.

Virtually every state has an office of folklife programs or a folk arts coordinator (often working within the state arts agency). These professional folklorists help to document and nurture the folk arts of their areas, often producing radio and television shows, tape and CD recordings, and live presentations which showcase the active traditions of local communities. They often create festivals which bring all the groups together in an exciting celebration of their varied cultural expressions: for example, the Living Traditions Festival, held annually in Salt Lake City, Utah, presents more than 80 ethnic groups who share their foods, stories, dances, songs, and customs with other interested citizens. Other state festivals center on a single local ethnic group, or an occupation (like fishing or logging). The public sector folklorists do not cause the folklore to happen, but rather encourage its retention and call attention to its role in the rich fabric of local society.

Folklore is used as an introduction to literature in the schools, especially where ballads and folksongs can provide a vivid example of poetic and musical talents of people in general that can offset the notion that poetry is composed—and understood—only by rare geniuses. One of the most widespread and exciting uses of folklore today requires folklorists and teachers to collaborate in bringing folk artists and craftspersons into public school classrooms in order to show how deeply the vernacular arts intersect with arts generally, as well as with history, language, society, and science. The Arts-in-Education programs of many state arts councils now routinely employ professional folklorists to bring about this meeting of traditional performers with learners of all ages. Folklore is sometimes used in retirement homes where people can maintain mental exercise and a sense of cultural stability by sharing jokes, anecdotes, songs, and historical reminiscences that express the validity of their own lives.

All the activities described in this chapter fall under the category of applied folklore because their functions rest on the assumption that one must go beyond the simple intellectual discussion of folklore to gain certain ends. Whether those ends are served by massive government programs on the one extreme or by individual folklorists acting as consultants to schools, companies, and other groups who need cultural perspectives, applied folklore exists as a very broad field of cultural knowledge in action. As a set of possibilities that show the continued importance of folklore study in the modern world, applied folklore allows for a great number of meaty answers to that important analytical question, "So what?"

BIBLIOGRAPHICAL NOTES

Every teacher of folklore has favorite examples of good and bad books, of pointless and inspiring assignments, of boring and exciting mentors. John Matthews Manly, "A Knight Ther Was," *Transactions and Proceedings of the American Philological Association* 38 (1907): 89-107, while not dull and boring, is nonetheless a detailed study that ends only with the timid suggestion that Chaucer had Sir William Scrope in mind as he wrote his famous description of the Knight. Jan Harold Brunvand's *The Taming of the Shrew: A Comparative Study of Oral and Literary Versions* (New York: Garland, 1991), on the other hand, is a clear example of what careful folkloric analysis can offer for a fuller understanding of a text whose author can no longer offer elucidations of his own.

One of the very best essays on folklore and literary criticism is Roger D. Abrahams, "Folklore and Literature as Performance," *Journal of the Folklore Institute* 9 (1972): 75-94. In it he encourages the reader not simply to look for traditions and customs within written literature but to consider how the traditional materials convey a cultural environment imbued with vitality. Among the hundreds of articles and books written on literary relations of folklore, the following are among the most useful; the more recent ones are likely to be more concerned with interpretation, while the older ones are mostly addressed to matters of identification and terminology. Russell K. Alspach, "The Use by Yeats and Other Irish Writers of the Folklore of Patrick Kennedy," *Journal of American Folklore* 59 (1946): 404-12; Tristram P. Coffin, "Real Use and Real Abuse of Folklore in the Writer's Subconscious: F. Scott Fitzgerald," in *New Voices in American Studies,* ed. Ray B. Browne, Donald M. Winkelman, and Allen Hayman (West Lafayette, Ind.: Purdue University, 1966), 102-22; Carvel Collins, "Folklore and Literary Criticism," *Journal of American Folklore* 70 (1957): 9-10; Robert C. Cosbey, "The Mak Story and Its Folklore Analogues," *Speculum* 20 (1945): 310-17; R. M. Dawkins, "Presidential Address: Folklore and Literature," *Folklore* 40 (1929): 14-36; Alan Dundes, "The Study of Folklore in Literature and Culture: Identification and Interpretation," *Journal of American Folklore* 78 (1966): 136-41; Dundes, "'To Love My Father All': A Psychoanalytic Study of the Folktale Source of *King Lear,*" *Southern Folklore Quarterly* 40 (1976): 353-66; Richard M. Dorson, "The Identification of Folklore in American Literature," *Journal of American Folklore* 70 (1957): 1-8; William R. Ferris Jr., "Folklore and the African Novelist: Achebe and Tutuola," *Journal of American Folklore* 86 (1973): 25-36; John T. Flanagan and Arthur Palmer Hudson, eds., *Folklore in American Literature* (Evanston, Ill.: Row, Peterson, 1958); Daniel G. Hoffman, *Form and Fable in American Fiction* (New York: Oxford University Press, 1961); MacEdward Leach, "Folklore in American Regional Literature," *Journal of the Folklore Institute* 3 (1966): 376-97; Max Lüthi, "Parallel Themes in Folk Narrative and in Art Literature," *Journal of the Folklore Institute* 4 (1967): 3-16; Bruce A. Rosenberg, "Folklore Methodology and Medieval Literature," *Journal of the Folklore Institute* 13 (1976): 311-25.

The critical school I have termed *architectural* is represented by Northrop Frye, *Anatomy of Criticism: Four Essays* (Princeton, N.J.: Princeton University Press, 1957), in which "modes" and "archetypal meaning" are used to describe organizational assumptions and dynamic structural aspects of literature. The area of study I have termed *psychological* is represented in literary criticism by such books as Norman Norwood Holland, *The Dynamics of Literary Response* (New York: Oxford University Press, 1968), which deals less with elements of structure and mode in the work and more with the receptivity and responses of the reader. Robert Graves, *The White Goddess: A Historical Grammar of Poetic Myth* (New York: Vintage, 1958) is both exciting and frustrating. Since Graves does not support any of his thousands of matter-of-fact assertions, folklore and myth scholars have been justifiably suspicious of his theories. Nonetheless, his insights are penetrating and brilliant and are well worth reading for the perspectives they provide. His passion for the subject supplies an exciting element missing from more reliable, objective studies in myth and folklore.

Ruth A. Firor's *Folkways in Thomas Hardy* (Philadelphia: University of Pennsylvania Press, 1931) is one of those exercises D. K. Wilgus called "zebra counting"; Firor locates and names several hundred traditional references in the works of Thomas Hardy (missing quite a few along the way) and then provides almost no commentary on why the knowledge is worthwhile. More modern scholars, foremost among them Donald Davidson, have been working much more seriously with Thomas Hardy's folklore; the rather superficial treatment of Hardy presented in this chapter is not meant in any way to reflect a summary of their complex and rewarding work. Axel Olrik originally published his famous essay as "Epische Gesetze der Volksdichtung" in *Zeitschrift für Deutsches Altertum* 51 (1909): 1-12; it is reprinted in English as "Epic Laws of Folk Narrative," in *The Study of Folklore*, ed. Alan Dundes (Englewood Cliffs, N.J.: Prentice-Hall, 1965), 129-41.

All in all, literary applications of folklore have constituted one of the most solid ongoing arenas of discussion in the discipline. The following are only a few of the most interesting and useful: John D. Niles, "Understanding *Beowulf:* Oral Poetry Acts," *Journal of American Folklore* 106 (1993): 131–55; Jay Mechling, "The Failure of Folklore in Richard Wright's *Black Boy,*" *Journal of American Folklore* 104 (1991): 275–94; Steven Swann Jones, "The Enchanted Hunters: Nabokov's Use of Folk Characterization in *Lolita,*" *Western Folklore* 39 (1980): 269–83; Anne Wilson, *Traditional Romance and Tale: How Stories Mean* (Ipswich, UK: D. S. Brewer, 1976); Sandra Dolby Stahl, *Literary Folkloristics and the Personal Narrative* (Bloomington: Indiana University Press, 1989); Marilynn Callander, *Willa Cather and the Fairy Tale* (Ann Arbor: UMI Research Press, 1988). In her dissertation, *"Every Word Counted for Twenty": Storytelling and Intimacy in Willa Cather's Fiction* (University of Nebraska, 1994), Evelyn Funda argues that Cather used the styles and modes of oral narrative in order to achieve particular effects—to "play across the footlights," in Cather's words. Utilizing different stances of oral narrative performance, Cather was able to suggest more or less intimacy between the personae and the reader; since folk art is predicated on a shared set of contexts, her narrators are shown interacting with each other and with us in systems of reference based on our cultural intimacy. Much of modern literary criticism now assumes we must consider the cultural "codes" and "maps" supplied by the vernacular traditions of the culture in which the literary work is contexted and from whose worldview premises it is constructed.

Probably all good literature can be called "ethnic," insofar as the cultural assumptions and values of any authors or audiences are centrally engaged in plot, metaphor, and characterization. Since the late 1800s in America, ethnic minorities have been developing their distinctive literary voices, often in a dialectic (to put it politely) with the mainstream (i.e., Euro-American) canon. In such works, cultural elements are foregrounded because of their emotional charge for the members of ethnic groups, and because cultural features are among the most powerful ways to register and articulate the real and imagined frictions between majority and minority. See Leslie Silko, *Ceremony* (New York: Viking, 1977); Rudolfo O. Anaya, *Bless Me, Ultima* (Berkeley: Quinto Sol Publications, 1972); Maxine Hong Kingston, *The Woman Warrior: Memoirs of a Childhood among Ghosts* (New York: Vintage, 1976); and expect this kind of literature to continue expanding our concepts of what American literature is and can be.

My brief excursion into traditional aspects of history does not pretend even to scratch the surface of the broad and complicated field now called oral history. Folklorists and historians have tended to approach the subject from different directions anyway, the folklorists paying more attention to the expressive element of reminiscence and the historians fastening upon details, date, and information. From a folkloristic point of view, the following are illuminating and helpful studies: Richard M. Dorson, "Oral Tradition and Written History: The Case for the United States," *Journal of the Folklore Institute* 1 (1964): 220-34; Ronald Grele, ed., *Envelopes of Sound* (Chicago: Precedent, 1975), a symposium of specialists discussing method, theory, and practice in oral history; Edward D. Ives, "Common-Man Biography: Some Notes by the Way," in *Folklore Today: A Festschrift for Richard M. Dorson*, ed. Linda Dégh, Henry Glassie, and Felix J. Oinas (Bloomington: Indiana University Press, 1976), 251-64; W. Lynwood Montell, *The Saga of Coe Ridge: A Study in Oral History* (Knoxville: University of Tennessee Press, 1970); Montell, *Don't Go up Kettle Creek: Verbal Legacy of the Upper Cumberland* (Knoxville: University of Tennessee Press, 1983); and especially Montell's *Killings: Folk Justice in the Upper South* (Lexington: University Press of Kentucky, 1986), which illustrates not only the function of oral history and vernacular lore in the construction of historical reality, but also shows how oral traditions can help "make sense" of regional logic on the subject (and practice) of justice. Robert Darnton's work in social history includes *The Great Cat Massacre and Other Episodes in French Cultural History* (New York: Vintage, 1985); some of Leonard Rosenband's uses of vernacular history can be found in "Hiring and Firing at the Montgolfier Paper Mill," in *The Workplace before the Factory: Artisans and Proletarians, 1500–1800*, ed. Thomas Max Safley and Leonard Rosenband (Ithaca: Cornell University Press, 1993), 225–40; see also Carlo Ginzburg, *The Night Battles: Witchcraft and Agrarian Cults in the Sixteenth and Seventeenth Centuries*, trans. John Tedeschi and Anne Tedeschi (Baltimore: Johns Hopkins University Press, 1983).

In Richard Bauman's "Performance and Honor in 13th-Century Iceland," *Journal of American Folklore* 99 (1986): 131–50, we see folklore used as a way of decoding literary phrases as well as providing insights into cultural history. Karen Becker's "Picturing Our Past: An Archive Constructs a National Culture," *Journal of American Folklore* 105 (1992): 3–18, shows how photos brought together in an archive not only document and record history, but may be used to construct it. Jack Santino, writing in the same issue of *Journal of American Folklore* (19–33), demonstrates how a historical view of an emergent custom helps to understand the contemporary employment of decorative symbolism, in "Yellow Ribbons and Seasonal Flags: The Folk Assemblage of War." The essays in Barbara Allen and Thomas J. Schlereth, *Sense of Place: American Regional Cultures* (Lexington: University Press of Kentucky, 1990), although they are ostensibly focused on regional expressions, also function to articulate the historical accumulation of shared culture, and thus present us with considerations about the way local ideas are carried forward through time as regional constructions of cultural and social reality. Similarly, although the essays in Thomas J. Schlereth's *Material Culture: A Research*

Guide (Lawrence: University Press of Kansas, 1985) deal with the material expressions which carry cultural "freight," their vernacular perspectives in social history cannot be underestimated.

The tall tales discussed in this chapter are quoted from the works mentioned under that designation in Chapter 3 above. The T. J. Easterwood Papers in the Special Collections Division of the University of Oregon Library (Eugene), carefully compiled and annotated by Martin Schmitt, former curator, are (or at least were) a stunning repository of Northwest folklore, regional dialect, folksong, vernacular drama, and local history; the last time I visited the university to work with these papers, however, the entire collection had disappeared. Jeannie Banks Thomas's M.A. thesis, "Honoring the Farm: Identity and Meaning in Personal Narratives" (Logan: Utah State University, 1987; 402 pages) is on deposit in the Fife Folklore Archives in the Utah State University library. The Almo and Bear River Massacres are discussed in Brigham Madsen, *The Shoshoni Frontier and the Bear River Massacre* (Salt Lake City: University of Utah Press, 1985).

Typical versions of the ballad "Springfield Mountain" are provided by Albert B. Friedman, ed., *The Viking Book of Folk Ballads of the English-Speaking World* (New York: Viking, 1956), 302-7. The version of "Springfield Mountain" printed here is my recollection of the way it was sung in my maternal grandmother's family, the Kimballs of Pelham, Massachusetts. The *proper* historical view of "Sinners in the Hands of an Angry God" is provided under that heading in James David Hart, ed., *The Oxford Companion to American Literature*, 6th ed. (New York: Oxford University Press, 1995). Because of the humor on some of New England's oldest tombstones, however, I do not accept the argument that the comic element entered the song only after the stage comedians of the 1830s and 1840s began using it as a parody of New England rusticity. "Judge Duffy" was collected by two of my students, Marion Cupp and Cliff Michel, near Pullman, Washington, in August 1959. Bruce A. Rosenberg discusses Custer traditions in a number of places, among them "Custer and the Epic of Defeat," *Journal of American Folklore* 88 (1975): 165-77.

William H. Desmonde's "short but wild Freudian interpretation" of Tale Type 328, "Jack and the Beanstalk," along with Alan Dundes's cogent commentary on its narrow perspective, are as instructive to read now as thirty years ago: it appears in Dundes's *The Study of Folklore*, cited previously, 107–9, and is followed by a more eclectic commentary by psychologist Martha Wolfenstein, "Jack and the Beanstalk: An American Version," 110–13 (originally published in *Childhood in Contemporary Cultures*, ed. Margaret Mead and Martha Wolfenstein [Chicago: University of Chicago Press, 1955]). A currently very popular book, Clarissa Pinkola Estes's *Women Who Run with the Wolves: Myths and Stories of the Wild Woman Archetype* (New York: Ballantine, 1992) often makes the assumption that *archetype* = *symbol,* and omits the kinds of comparative, culture-centered considerations that folklorists and anthropologists would consider essential to the fullest treatment of such an important theme. Similarly, Robert Bly's concentration on a single (and rare) version of "Eisenhans" in his *Iron John* (New York: Vintage, 1992) results in a delightful discussion but spurious conclusions.

I am indebted to Thomas Duncan, M.D., for sharing with me his insights on the current treatment of Navajos in Public Health Service hospitals on the Navajo reservation; Dr. Duncan served for three years at the Tuba City hospital on the western Navajo reservation. A revealing study of how the materials of folklore may be applied to the predicaments encountered by southern mountain people when they move to a large city is Ellen J. Stekert's excellent essay "Focus for Conflict: Southern Mountain Medical Beliefs in Detroit," *Journal of American Folklore* 83 (1970): 116-55; reprinted in *The Urban Experience and Folk Tradition*, ed. Américo Paredes and Ellen J. Stekert (Austin: University of Texas Press, 1971), 95-136, including discussion from the floor. For an international view, see Margaret Mead, "The Application of Anthropological Techniques to Cross-National Communication, *Transactions of the New York Academy of Sciences*, series 2, no. 9 (1947), 133-52; reprinted in Dundes, *Every Man His Way*, 518-36.

A fascinating account of the European "discovery" of vitamin C from Native Americans who had known of it for generations is given in Virgil Vogel, *American Indian Medicine* (Norman: University of Oklahoma Press, 1970), 84–86. David Hufford's *The Terror That Comes in the Night: An Experience-Centered Study of Supernatural Assault Traditions* (Philadelphia: University of Pennsylvania Press, 1982) is not only an impressive study of a psychological phenomenon in and of itself, but remarkable because it opened up the discussion of an experience shared by about 20 percent of the world's population which had been largely ignored by scientists even though the world was full of vernacular accounts. A similar case is provided by the work of Shelley R. Adler, whose work on sudden nocturnal death among Hmong immigrants to the United States is contexted within the narratives and the protective customs used by the Hmongs themselves to understand and ward off the experience. More recently, scientific investigators have coined the term Sudden Unexpected Nocturnal Death Syndrome (SUNDS) in their attempt to start dealing with the phenomenon. See Adler, "Sudden Unexpected Nocturnal Death Syndrome among Hmong Immigrants: Examining the Role of the 'Nightmare,'" *Journal of American Folklore* 104 (1991): 54–71; Adler, "The Role of Nightmare in Hmong Sudden Unexpected Nocturnal Death Syndrome: A Folkloristic Study of Belief and Health" (Ph.D. diss., University of California, Los Angeles, 1991); and Adler, "Terror in Transition: Hmong Folk Belief in America," in *Out of the Ordinary: Folklore and the Supernatural*, ed. Barbara Walker (Logan: Utah State University Press, 1995), 180–202. In *Healing Traditions: Alternative Medicine and the Health Professions* (Philadelphia: University of Pennsylvania Press, 1995), Bonnie O'Connor shows how important our understanding of traditional healing practices can be in treating ailments (like the unexpected Hmong deaths, cancer, and AIDS) which have no reliable "formal" cures to expect from standard medical practices. The fact that the practice of traditional methods seems to produce a feeling of well-being and may indeed promote recovery to some extent should point to this arena as still another wherein scientific investigators might find some rich leads in the substantial accumulation of human experience and cultural interpretation.

Hitler's use of folklore is discussed by Christa Kamenetsky, "Folklore as a Political Tool in Nazi Germany," *Journal of American Folklore* 85 (1972): 221-35. The political employment of folklore has ranged from idealistic nation-building to social destruction and holocaust. Some scholars are convinced that the early folkloristic reports of missionaries to Africa allowed the colonial powers to manipulate cultural customs and beliefs to their advantage, and in later years, virtually every emerging nation in Europe employed, invented, and reinvented "ancient" traditions on which their own self concept could be founded. See Eric Hobsbawm, *The Invention of Tradition* (Cambridge and New York: Cambridge University Press, 1983); William A. Wilson, *Folklore and Nationalism in Modern Finland* (Bloomington: Indiana University Press, 1994); James

R. Dow and Hannjost Lixfeld, eds., *The Nazification of an Academic Discipline: Folklore in the Third Reich* (Bloomington: Indiana University Press, 1994); Hannjost Lixfeld, *Folklore and Fascism: The Reich Institute for German Volkskunde*, ed. James R. Dow (Bloomington: Indiana University Press, 1994).

At the present time, we estimate that somewhere between a third and a half of all active professional folklorists are employed in the public sector, working for cities, states, museums, arts councils, and the like. An unknown number of folklorists work in the private sector, mostly as advisors and consultants to health delivery networks, multi-ethnic corporations, and businesses with overseas or intercultural connections. Work in the public sector seems to have been the most rapidly and dramatically expanding arena for the employment of folklorists. For some eloquent examples and discussions of public sector folklore, see David E. Whisnant, *All That Is Native and Fine: The Politics of Culture in an American Region* (Chapel Hill: University of North Carolina Press, 1983); Whisnant, *Modernizing the Mountaineer: People, Power, and Planning in Appalachia*, rev. ed. (Knoxville: University of Tennessee Press, 1994); Bert Feintuch, ed., *The Conservation of Culture: Folklorists and the Public Sector* (Lexington: University Press of Kentucky, 1988); Richard Price and Sally Price, *On the Mall: Presenting Maroon Tradition-Bearers at the 1992 Festival of American Folklife* (Bloomington: Indiana University Press, 1995); and Robert Baron and Nicolas R. Spitzer, eds., *Public Folklore* (Washington, D.C.: Smithsonian Institution Press, 1992).

For a spectacular display of what public sector folklorists have accomplished on the national level, see Steve Siporin's *American Folk Masters: The National Heritage Fellows* (New York: Harry N. Abrams, 1992); this work chronicles the efforts of public sector folklorists to find, nurture, and promote the best practitioners of folk art in America by nominating the exceptional ones for national recognition—on the order of Japan's Living National Treasures Program. Their words (quoted briefly in a previous chapter) and the photographs of their artistic expressions provide a stunning testimony to the role of vernacular expression in America, and to the services of public sector folklorists who bring them to our attention.

It is clear that applied folklore has become the ground-level activity which matches and grows out of the theoretical work of academics; indeed, the thinking and the doing go best when they are viewed as a partnership. Not all folklorists agree that a balance has been reached; for example, see the critique leveled at the Smithsonian Festival of American Folklife by Robert Cantwell, in "Conjuring Culture: Ideology and Magic in the Festival of American Folklife," *Journal of American Folklore* 104 (1991): 148–63. But see also the articulate and well-argued reply of A. H. Walle, in "Theoretic vs. Applied Folklore: Apples vs. Oranges," *Western Folklore* 53 (1994): 171–78. As Michael Owen Jones and others have eloquently demonstrated in *Putting Folklore to Use* (Lexington: University Press of Kentucky, 1994), the perspectives of folklore research and study are already being employed in education, in museums, in aiding the homeless, in environmental planning, in medicine, in art therapy, in organizational research, in tourism, in work with the aging, and in economic development. Is it any surprise that a network so integral to the functioning of a culture—as folklore is—is so widely usable in the expressions, problems, and structures of that culture? No. Folklore is central to what and who we are as a culture, and that constitutes the first answer to the question, "So what?"

Index